TREATISE ON MONEY

Joseph A. Schumpeter

TREATISE
on
MONEY

Edited by Fritz Karl Mann

Translated by Ruben Alvarado

WordBridge
PUBLISHING
εν αρχη ην ο λογος
AALTEN, THE NETHERLANDS

WORDBRIDGE PUBLISHING
Aalten, the Netherlands
www.wordbridge.net

English translation by permission of Vandenhoeck & Ruprecht
Copyright © 2014 Ruben Alvarado

German original © Vandenhoeck & Ruprecht GmbH & Co. KG,
Joseph A. Schumpeter, Original title: *Das Wesen des Geldes,* Neuauflage, Göttingen, 2008

The cover photograph is of a check from the Bullion and Exchange Bank of Car-
son City, Nevada, drawn on the Anglo-Californian Bank of San Francisco, dated
1895. Schumpeter viewed the bank check as the primary means by which the
monetary system displaced the bullion- and coinage-based money method (see
e.g. pp. 235 ff.).

ISBN 978-90-76660-36-3

Table of Contents

Orientation
by Fritz Karl Mann

The following volume gives the light of day to a work discovered among the papers left by Joseph Schumpeter at his death. For those who interpret and continue the line of Schumpeter's thought, it is an indispensable resource. Although provisionally and – especially in the later chapters – only fragmentarily conducted, it revised and supplemented, and melded in systematic manner, the thoughts regarding the theory of money contained in earlier writings.

I will later give an account of the genesis of this work. At this point I only make mention that the approaches taken in it go a ways back. A concise draft and research agenda are already contained in the doctrine of economic statics presented at the age of 25.[1] *The Theory of Economic Development*,[2] appearing four years later, formed the second leg of this research, and traced the phenomenon of money in the stream of the capitalist process. Shortly thereafter, the start of a systematic construction became briefly visible in "Das Sozialprodukt und die Rechenpfennige" [The Social Product and Money of Account], published during the First World War and which, despite its obfuscating subtitle, was considered to be a declaration of war on the reigning school of thought.[3] Among the other building blocks pertain two writings on the theory of credit published in the 1920s.[4]

---

[1]Joseph A. Schumpeter, *Das Wesen und der Hauptinhalt der theoretischen Nationalökonomie* [The Essence and Chief Content of Theoretical Economics], Leipzig 1908, S. 276-297 (Ch. 4: Foundations of the Theory of Money).

[2]Schumpeter, *Theorie der wirtschaftlichen Entwicklung* [Theory of Economic Development], Leipzig 1912, 2nd ed. München-Leipzig 1926, pp. 70 ff., pp. 201 ff.

[3]Schumpeter, "Das Sozialprodukt und die Rechenpfennige. Glossen und Beiträge zur Geldtheorie" [The Social Product and Money of Account: Annotations and Contributions to the Theory of Money], in: *Archiv für Sozialwissenschaft*, vol. 44 (1917), pp. 627-715.

[4]Schumpeter, "Kreditkontrolle" [Control of Credit] in: *Archiv für Sozialwissenschaft* [Archive for Social Science], vol. 54 (1925), pp. 289-328; "Die goldene Bremse an der Kreditmaschine" [The Golden Brakes on the Credit Machine], in: *Die Kreditwirtschaft* [The Credit Economy], vol. 1, 1927, pp. 80-106.

The process of ripening appears to have ended at this time. Indeed, the publication of the present book was announced by Verlag Julius Springer in 1929, at the height of Schumpeter's teaching activity at the University of Bonn, bearing the title - infelicitous but customary in academic lectures - *Geld und Währung* [Money and Currency]. This book was to be published as volume 36 of the *Enzyklopädie der Rechts- und Staatswissenschaft* [Encyclopedia of the Science of Law and State], in the department overseen by Arthur Spiethoff and Edgar Salin. Apparently Schumpeter had another goal beyond that, because in various statements in the manuscript he spoke of a second expected volume.[5] I will have something to say about the vicissitudes of this plan and its ultimate failure at the conclusion of my introduction.

We will initially concentrate on the foundational character of the work, primarily the epistemological goal and the method of investigation, then the theoretical and political perspectives provided by that investigation, and, last but not least, its relation to the social-scientific system that Schumpeter envisioned.

Epistemological and methodological goals

a) In similar fashion to his studies in other areas of research, Schumpeter's investigation of the phenomenon of money runs in diverse channels: on the one hand, he makes use of the tools of "pure" theory, concentrates thereby on quantitative relations and leaves numerous empirical facts to one side; on the other hand, he exceeds the limits customarily set by economic theory and treats the phenomenon of money in a broad historical, political, institutional, and sociological framework. Though the justification for such a methodological dichotomy might be called into question from many angles, this will not occupy us any further at this point.

I will pay just as little attention to Schumpeter's numerous pleas for the right of existence of mathematical economic doctrine [mathematische Volkswirtschaftslehre].[6] When he began his teaching activity at Harvard - at the height

---

[5]Cf. below, p. 220. He similarly referred to the limits of "this" volume (cf. below, p. 252).

[6]I discuss this in more detail in my essay, "Bemerkungen über Schumpeters Einfluß auf die amerikanische Wirtschaftstheorie" [Remarks regarding Schumpeter's influence on American economic theory], in: *Weltwirtschaftliches Archiv* [World Economic Archive], vol. 81 (1958), pp. 149-175.

of his fame – he was considered a banner carrier of "pure" theory, even the econometric investigation unfolding at that time. Back in his youth he had already confessed that the thought-forms of higher mathematics were simply forcing themselves upon economists.[7] And he belonged among the founders of the American Econometric Society, serving as its president for four years, 1937-1941.

Despite this, he by no means neglected the far-reaching social-scientific view. I only mention here an ambitious work concluded in America at the same time: his two-volume *Business Cycles,* the subtitle of which already ruled out that analytical restriction.[8] In Schumpeter's view, a plethora of grounds spoke to this goal: for instance, the argument dear to the German Historical School that the doctrine of economics is only a province of the social sciences, for which reason its competence must also be based upon extra-economic connections. Although this agreement with the Schmoller school did not stand in the way of his preference for mathematical analysis and econometrics, it nevertheless by all accounts was resented in broad academic circles – predominantly in America – as being out of bounds or inconsistent. Even specific social-scientific themes were treated so often by him that an enumeration here is prohibitive. I only mention his *Vergangenheit und Zukunft der Sozialwissenschaft*[9] [The Past and Future of Social Science] and two oft-mentioned sociological treatments: *Zur Soziologie des Imperialismus* [The Sociology of Imperialisms][10] and *Die sozialen Klassen im ethnisch-homogenen Milieu* [Social Classes in An Ethnically Homogeneous Environment].[11] Another two examples may be mentioned here. As part of his farewell to Bonn, he presented to a closed group of colleagues the hitherto-unpublished lecture, "Zur Soziologie der Außenpolitik" [Concerning the Sociology of Foreign Policy] (1932); and, at the start of the 1940s, the largely

---

[7]Thus already in *Das Wesen und der Hauptinhalt der theoretischen Nationalökonomie* [The Essence and Chief Content of Theoretical Economics], p. xxi.

[8]Joseph A. Schumpeter, *Business Cycles: A Theoretical, Historical, and Statistical Analysis of the Capitalist Process*, 2 volumes, New York-London 1939.

[9]Munich-Leipzig, 1915.

[10]*Archiv für Sozialwissenschaft*, vol. 46, pp. 1-39, 275-310.

[11]*Archiv für Sozialwissenschaft*, vol. 57, pp. 1-67. [Translations of both are contained in *Imperialism and Social Classes* (Cleveland and New York: Meridian Books, 1955)].

socio-political book, *Capitalism, Socialism, and Democracy,* in terms of sales his most successful.[12]

It therefore hardly surprises us that Schumpeter initially treated the phenomenon of money discussed in this book from the perspective of social science. As he puts it, "Money, like any other economic institution, is an element of the overall social process and as such a matter for economic theory, for sociology, and finally for historical, ethnological, and statistical 'fact research.'"[13] But the historical and social-scientific aspects were not, as with previous writers, relegated to secondary status.

"Everything that a people desires, does, suffers, *is* – is reflected," Schumpeter assures us, in a people's monetary system. In his view, the ultimate data of social and political occurrences are also the deepest motivating grounds of monetary policy and the history of money: "the geographical and political situation of a people, the objective and subjective opportunities provided by its economy, its social structure and political organization, its attitude toward economic matters and the future, its morale and energy, everything that is covered by the words 'national spirit' and 'national character.'" "Nothing demonstrates so clearly what a people is made of than how it conducts its monetary policy."[14] The second chapter, pretentiously entitled "Regarding the Sociology of Money," is devoted to some of these connections. In this manner we can understand why the Harvard faculty dedicated its volume in Schumpeter's memory, published after his death, to "Schumpeter the social scientist."[15]

Even so, we dare not underestimate the inspiration he gained from Leon Walras' general equilibrium analysis – not even in the design of the work of monetary theory here published. But the statistical analyses derived from Walras could be coordinated with the method of historical development, as Schumpeter explicitly declared.[16]

---

[12]New York 1943. Numerous translations into other languages (German: 2nd edition, Bern 1950).

[13]See below, p. 13.

[14]See below, pp. 1 f.

[15]*Schumpeter, Social Scientist,* ed. by Seymour E. Harris (Cambridge, MA: Harvard University Press, 1951).

[16]In 1908, the young Schumpeter wrote to Walras, indicating that his book *Das Wesen und der Hauptinhalt der theoretischen Nationalökonomie* [The Essence and Chief Content of Theoretical Economics] was "the book of a follower [eines Schülers]"; "I will always seek to work upon the bases indicated by you, to continue your work" [moi je m'efforcerai toujours de travailler sur les basas indiquées par vous, de continuer votre œuvre]. Letter dated October 9th, 1908, printed in *Correspondence of Léon Walras and*

b) Schumpeter justified his methodological broad-mindedness, so foreign to school-bound economists, upon other grounds as well. Because these have partly been overlooked and partly misconstrued in previous writing, they will also occupy us. Some already confront us in the wide-ranging foreword of Schumpeter's maiden work.

"The winged words 'to know all is to forgive all' contain good sense," began the youthful author. "But even more incisively one might say 'to know all is to know that there is nothing to forgive.' And this holds true in the sphere of knowledge as well." No method of investigation can be absolutized, he warns the reader. In this context he referred to the argument, admittedly specious, current in American pragmatic philosophy: every method of investigation is good that in its sphere of application yields "useful" information. From this, Schumpeter concluded that in the choice of method all a prioris must be avoided – at any rate, with the proviso that one must always proceed reasonably. And even though he described himself in terms of the correlation of being a follower of both Leon Walras and Friedrich von Wieser, he rejected absolutely any methodological monomania. From a pragmatic standpoint, he criticized pure theoreticians as working too much with the concepts "correct" [Richtig] and "wrong" instead of with the concepts "efficient" and "inefficient;" for although it is every thinker's good right to get his hypotheses in order such that they in his view reflect the processes of reality, they remain "creations of our caprice" [Willkür].[17] After all, neither these nor similar later defenses of the "pragmatic method" are to be understood as a confession of methodological agnosticism, nor even – as Fritz Machlup surmised – as a denial of the problem of method, for, as Machlup explained, Schumpeter only demanded "methodological tolerance," in the sense that he was "only intolerant of the lack of education [Unbildung] and lack of tolerance."[18] Such interpretations miss the mark. Beyond

---

Related Papers, ed. by William Jaffé, vol. III: 1898-1909, Amsterdam 1965, p. 378, letter nr. 1709. In the preface to the Japanese edition of the *Theory of Economic Development,* he stated that he owed more to Walras than to any other thinker, but added that his conception of economic development as a unique process engendered by the economic system was identical to that of Karl Marx (Preface to Japanese Edition of *Theorie der wirtschaftlichen Entwicklung* [1937]. Reprinted from the translation. by I. Nakayama and S. Tobata, in: *Essays of J. A. Schumpeter,* ed. by R. V. Clemence, Mass. 1951, p. 159 f.).

[17]*Das Wesen und der Hauptinhalt der theoretischen Nationalökonomie* [The Essence and Chief Content of Theoretical Economics], foreword.

[18]Fritz Machlup, "Schumpeter's Economic Methodology," in *Schumpeter, Social Scientist,* p. 95.

that, they neglect the fact that Schumpeter kept posing the question as to what from the theoretical viewpoint is efficient or "useful," for which reason he often – as in the present book – switched between analytical tools.

Be that as it may, Schumpeter's methodological lack of prejudice goes without question. It also explains other inclinations, such as his often effusive praise for the achievements of other scientists of the most diverse orientations together with self-criticism bordering on self-denial. Despite the worldwide echoes, already initiated during his lifetime by some his pupils, he wished to be considered neither a pioneer nor the head of any school. As he put it in one of his farewell speeches, to the student body of the University of Bonn, he was fundamentally far removed from any dogmatic bond. As he confessed, his scientific labor only pursued provisional knowledge, "because I don't wish to say the last word." Or in a metaphor often cited since then by followers and critics, "if I have a function, it is not to close doors but to open them." Never – he added – did he strive "to bring about anything like a Schumpeter school. Such a thing does not exist and will not exist."[19]

c) Along with the breadth of his conceptions and his theoretical and methodological tolerance, came a third, often criticized characteristic: Schumpeter's adaptation to contemporary political and world-view-oriented currents. Even to our ears, accustomed as they are to the party strife, ideological struggle, and opportunism of our time, it once in a while becomes difficult to understand how Schumpeter seemed to warm to both democratic and aristocratic forms of government and society, declaring now socialistic, now capitalistic, now authoritarian ideals. These swings understandably are explained as inconsistency and fickleness. Similar to his contemporary rival John Maynard Keynes, he was not spared from being claimed by many pressure groups, ideological orientations, and parties. Even in scientific circles, he is put down partly as an advocate of monopoly capitalism, partly as a "convinced socialist."[20] Such rash characterizations do not fit well with the picture of his personality. Lest we forget, the young Schumpeter – like most young German economists at the turn of the century – had fallen under the spell of Max Weber. Social science and politics – as he also asserted – had nothing to do with each other. "I distance myself from practical

---

[19]Schumpeter, "Das Woher und Wohin unserer Wissenschaft" [The Wherefrom and Whereto of Our Science], farewell speech (June 20th, 1932), in *Aufsätze zur ökonomischen Theorie*, [Essays in Economic Theory], Tübingen 1952, p. 600.

[20]In the introduction to the German edition of Schumpeter's *Capitalism, Socialism, and Democracy* (Bonn, 1946), Edgar Salin remarked that "Schumpeter is a socialist – a convinced socialist" (pp. 8 ff.).

politics and have no other goal than knowledge."[21] For the purity of science, objective knowledge, must never be muddled. For this reason, he even rejected any scientific research oriented to the practical needs of an incidental historical situation. He combatted just as forcefully the tendency to decide the problems of science in terms of political preference. This explains his zeal against the "Ricardian vice," as well as his severe criticism of John Maynard Keynes' much-admired *General Theory of Employment, Interest, and Money.* "Economics will never have nor merit any authority until that unholy alliance is dissolved."[22]

d) Finally, Schumpeter's treatment of the problem of money is based upon an epistemological presupposition that is overlooked by many commentators, to wit, that empirical analysis, despite its indispensability for political economy, is only capable of comprehending the surface of events [Vorgänge], or the reflection of transcendent reality in the world of sense, while "the essence of things" or "the meaning of phenomena" can only be grasped by the intuition, or, as Schumpeter usually terms it, "vision." With this Aristotelian concentration upon the general and generally valid, he was not the teachable follower of Leon Walras but rather Carl Menger.[23]

Indeed, we confront the traces of this in countless statements, as in the systematic work of his youth, already oft-mentioned, that besides the "chief content" also presents "the essence" of theoretical economics. This pursuit of the general and generally valid likewise pervades his theory of money. He rejected an historicist meaning, for example the development of a variety of theories of money valid for every stage of culture or every "economic style" (Spiethoff); for, although the cultural world of each epoch establishes its own conditions, sometimes even in such a unique way as not to be understood by later cultures, it is the goal of the theory of money to understand the "essence," the "meaning," or the "function" of money in the economic life process.[24] In that we will be encountering characteristic expressions of this at every step in the work before us, I will restrict myself to a few samples from the earlier systematic treatment "Das

---

[21]Schumpeter, *Das Wesen und der Hauptinhalt der theoretischen Nationalökonomie* [The Essence and Chief Content of Theoretical Economics], p. vii.

[22]See Schumpeter's discussion of Keynes' work in *The Journal of the American Statistical Association,* Dec. 1936, p. 792. Regarding the "Ricardian vice," see Schumpeter, *History of Economic Analysis,* New York 1954, p. 473.

[23]Concerning Menger's ontologism, see Emil Kauder, *A History of Marginal Utility Theory,* Princeton 1965, pp. 97-98.

[24]See below, p. 14 f.

Sozialprodukt und die Rechenpfennige" [The Social Product and Money of Account].

I refer firstly to the programmatic statement that the theory of money is not to discover "the surface of the matter" but "the essence of money"[25] and to the turns easily flowing from his pen during the course of the presentation: "the essence of the matter," "the essence and meaning of the process," "the essence of the process," "the essence of the phenomenon" or "contemplation of the essence" [Wesenschau]. He preferred it also in stricter money-theoretical analysis. He referred to "the essence of the money circular flow," "the essence of monetary devaluation," "the essence of modern credit," "the essence and economic meaning of repayment" and "the essence of the money function."[26] To appease his epistemological scruple, he did not even shy from stylistic prolixities: for example, in speaking not of the "economic role of the bank note," as is customary, but of "the economic essence of the role of the bank note."[27]

The work before us is also constructed in terms of this viewpoint. From the "Sociology of Money" (chapter II) and the "Outline of the Development of the Doctrine of Money" (chapter III) it turns to an analysis of the money function, initially indeed in the socialistic community [Gemeinwesen], later in the capitalistic economic process. The analysis attains its high point in chapter IX, entitled "The Essence of Money" and which, Schumpeter explains, is "to explain to us the essence of the social institution of money."[28] Because Schumpeter's manuscript which I have before me did not carry a title and because he considered various alternatives for earlier drafts, I viewed the title of the ninth chapter as the most appropriate title for the book.[29]

The Money Circular Flow and the Economic Settlement Process

---

[25]Schumpeter, "Das Sozialprodukt und die Rechenpfennige" [The Social Product and Money of Account], pp. 635-636.

[26]Schumpeter, "Das Sozialprodukt und die Rechenpfennige" [The Social Product and Money of Account], pp. 673, 640, 647, 634, 652, 707, 662.

[27]Schumpeter, "Das Sozialprodukt und die Rechenpfennige" [The Social Product and Money of Account], p. 658.

[28]See below, p. 215.

[29]As previously mentioned, the first version of the book was advertised with the title *Money and Currency*. Apparently, Schumpeter rejected this designation later on. In the book *Business Cycles* published in the United States a decade later, he referred to the imminent appearance of the *Treatise on Money* (*Business Cycles*, vol. I, p. 109, n1), a caption that however can only be construed as an anti-Keynesian gesture.

In Schumpeter's view, the theory of money had no business being sepa-rated from general economic theory, because "monetary processes" are only the reflexes of processes in the goods world. From this viewpoint, he likewise re-jected the customary historical constructions, especially the assumption that the use of money only became established at a higher economic level and therefore – as put forward by Bruno Hildebrand through his separation of natural econ-omy and money economy – effectuated a break in economic history. Every the-ory of money, argued Schumpeter, should start with the recognition that "mon-etary quantities and monetary processes in the economy receive their meaning from goods quantities and processes in the world of goods, to which they cor-respond, for which reason the understanding of monetary operations requires understanding of what happens in the world of goods and cannot be taught independently thereof."[30]

Schumpeter did not take credit for this insight but rather attributed it to an Austrian teacher of the greatest importance to him. "The novelty of Von Wieser's teaching is that it emanates from these economic contexts, from the theory of the economic process itself, and comprehends monetary phenomena *from out of* that process. This is what the comprehensive statement of Wieser's means, that the value of money is determined by the relationship between money income and real income."[31] This puts Wieser's sponsorship of Schum-peter's theory of money beyond doubt. As he explained already in his book about the essence and chief content of theoretical economics, "in terms of our construct, the theory of money forms an integrating component of the system of pure economics in general, in the sense that one cannot separate it from the other parts of that system."[32]

From this thesis, Schumpeter drew a further conclusion, namely, that the theory of money must be valid for all economic organizations, since without money the "economic settlement process" necessary to the essence of the eco-nomic circular flow would be impossible. In other words, the use of money is not only presupposed by him with the capitalistic economic system but just as well with the socialistic communal economy, that operates independently of the motive of acquisition, is without private ownership of the means of production, and is centrally guided. From the analytical standpoint, he even reversed the

---

[30]See below, p. 124.

[31]See below, p 82.

[32]Schumpeter, *Das Wesen und der Hauptinhalt der theoretischen Nationalökono-mie* [The Essence and Chief Content of Theoretical Economics], p. 270.

customary order: the socialistic model, he declared, is to be preferred in that "the meaning of economic action" [der Sinn des Wirtschaftens] and "the social economic plan" comes more clearly and transparently to the fore than in the capitalistic form of economic action; for in the latter, "the results of the inter-action of individual income interests" must be "arduously pieced together."[33] After all, he did not wish to overdraw the contradistinctions arising from a comparison, for in each economic system there are two mutually-conditioning exchange markets: the market of consumption goods and the market for the means of production.

Every model of the economic circular flow therefore presupposes two groups of transactions, wherein on the one hand, the means of production (or "factors of production") are transformed into consumption goods, and on the other, consumption goods are transformed into means of production ("factors of production"). Beyond this, the circular flow taking place also in the socialistic community can only be rationalized – or, in other words, the economic result, the social product, or the popular welfare can only be "maximized" – when the socialistic central office continuously settles accounts. To do this, it requires a "relevant datum" [Bedeutungsziffer] for every kind of good and for every quantity of that kind of good, that is to say, a unit of account [Recheneinheit] (for which Schumpeter makes use of the simpler concept "money of account" [Rechenpfennigs]), hence a magnitude the choice of which, as he explicitly demonstrates, is more or less arbitrary. It would be best, he speculates, to choose a "meaningless" unit of account or to leave off of naming it altogether, because any name could only evoke a misleading association.[34]

These considerations at the same time compel the conclusion that both the technical shape given to the unit of account and the organizational principles set up for its utilization are not to be taken as all that important. Even the suggestion developed by theoreticians and politicians, to create physical "labor notes" to be given back by worker-citizens at the warehouses of consumption goods, which then return to the economic circular flow by being exchanged by the socialistic central office against new means of production, does not change anything about the state of affairs, that the economic circular flow is only possible with continuous settlement of accounts. The decisive factor, concludes Schumpeter, is the "procedure of *clearing* operands," which, as the further analysis indicates, was not first discovered by capitalism. This method is based upon

---

[33]See below, p. 91.
[34]See below, p. 109.

a system of "mathematical equivalences" that "numerically reflect the entire economic life of the community, each element of which would correspond to an element of the economic circular flow."[35]

Therefore money appears to us to be only a market-technical institution. This character of money confronts us with particular clarity in the socialistic communal economy.[36] Independently of its physical shape, money serves as "certificate," "claim," or "unit of entitlement," as Schumpeter alternately calls it. Only with its help can the economic process continue in an enduring and rational fashion.

At the same time we note that a part of this thesis was already formulated in Schumpeter's older works, principally in the disquisition *The Social Product and the Unit of Account.* "Monetary calculation [Die Geldrechnung]" does as little to change the economic process, he elaborated then already, "as the use of tokens does to the essence of a game." Yet despite this exclusively market-technical import, monetary calculation is by no means irrelevant: "it rends the great heartbeat of economic life ... into two great groups of exchange acts." The economy now falls into two markets: the market for means of production and the market for consumption goods. Furthermore, an insight decisive to the problem of the value of money follows from this: in the condition of stationary equilibrium, the sum of the prices of all consumption goods must equal the sum of the price sums of all production goods, and both likewise identical to the sum all of money incomes. The insight, continued Schumpeter, corresponds to the fundamental equality between sums of income and social product, already formulated by Friedrich von Wieser; likewise also the equating of money with a "claim for goods," once put forward by John Stuart Mill, lately by Friedrich Bendixen, as well as the characterization of money as "warrants of productive performances, joined to the estimate thereof."[37] I will return to these consequences later.[38]

The preparation of a complete dogmatic-historical pedigree is not the point here. I only refer to the dependence on Leon Walras already strongly emphasized by Schumpeter. Not only the priority of publication of the new doctrine of money, but also the fame of its most complete version, is owed him.[39]

---

[35]See below, p. 108.

[36]See below, p. 109.

[37]Schumpeter, "Das Sozialprodukt und die Rechenpfennige" [The Social Product and Money of Account], pp. 634-636.

[38]Cf. below, pp. xxiii f.

[39]Similarly already in the article "Das Sozialprodukt und die Rechenpfennige" [The Social Product and Money of Account]: "It was Walras who first dug deeper; only

Walras already incorporated the settlement mechanism into the general equilibrium system, that contains as many determining equations as variables and with the help of mathematical presentation eliminates qualitative differences. Schumpeter's dependence upon Walras extends also, as is known, to a core item of the theory of distribution: the elimination of entrepreneurial profit arising from the economic process, thus the assumption of an "entrepreneur making neither profit nor loss," as well as the "*principle of cash-holding (encaissé désirée)*," which, as Schumpeter emphasized, was equivalent to the principle formulated by Friedrich von Wieser regarding the relation between money incomes and real incomes.[40]

At any rate, with these considerations we remain at the analytical approaches of Schumpeter's theory of money. In the investigations that now follow, the socialistic circular flow model – according to Wieser's method of diminishing abstraction – becomes increasingly permeated with profit-economy or capitalistic institutions and furnished with the monetary-policy equipment produced in modern times. To the same degree, the accounting process loses its previous uniformity. Nor is the economy led any longer by an all-powerful socialistic central office, representing "the social whole," but by a blend of autonomous or semi-autonomous organs that cooperate according to a principle of order that changes in space and time. However, despite the absence of a central office it is now expected that payments and income coalesce into the "*organic whole of a social economic account.*" A social economic calculation continually consummated in this manner is – as Schumpeter highlights – "not any the less real because it is not elaborated in a physically existing central bookkeeping."[41] According to Schumpeter, two chief groups function as vehicles of this complex accounting process realized in the market economy, households and firms (with the concept of the firm broadly conceived). In particular, banks and the central bank belong among the firms, although they clear credits and debts not only by transferring coins and other physical money tokens but mainly according to the rules of the current account contract. In so doing, the repertoire of possible clearing transactions is increased, the more so that these are expanded by the variations of "bank-mediated money creation" used in the market-economic system.

---

after his appearance did monetary theory begin to form part of the general theory of the economic process" (p. 631).

[40]See below, pp. 83 f.

[41]See below, p. 131.

With the stepwise approach toward "reality," numerous other connections also become recognizable, as when the hypothesis of stationary equilibrium is dropped and historical and dynamic factors as well as short-term cyclical wave movements of various sorts, economic development and economic growth, and the heterogeneous complex of "external disturbances" are considered in the analysis.

The Dialectic of Money

With this easing of assumptions, a further question arises: whether the insights gained through the dynamic-institutional investigation model can be reconciled with those from static circular flow analysis and the monetary-policy principles derived therefrom. Indeed, we confront a number of contradictions that are difficult to reconcile. Here I will firstly elucidate Schumpeter's sublimation of the original concept of money.

Like his static circular flow analysis demonstrated, money played only a passive role economically: it was a "token" or a "unit of account," an economically neutral technical instrument. It lacked the capacity to propel itself and to give shape to the economic process.[42] Under these presuppositions, money – to use one of Schumpeter's metaphors – only functions as a "satellite of commodities." Monetary processes were only, he supposed, reflexes of processes in the goods world.

Arthur W. Marget already referred to this: "Money ... has no organs of locomotion in itself. It flows (or ceases to flow) in response to decisions, made by economic units" ("The Monetary Aspects of the Schumpeterian System," in *Schumpeter, Social Scientist*, p. 63).

Schumpeter zealously busied himself to make this *capitis diminutio* plausible by means of other comparisons. Occasionally he described money as the "epidermis of economic life," as the "shell of the goods world" or "the shell of the economic body" and, to top it off, assured us that "the truly relevant" takes place in the world of goods. Or he spoke of the "shadow existence of monetary symbols" and the "servant role of money." Often, however, his comparisons went beyond such unexceptionable formulations; in particular, then, when they were to characterize the economic functions of money. Originally, as earlier

---

[42]Arthur W. Marget already made reference to this: "Money ... has no organs of locomotion in itself. It flows (or ceases to flow) in response to decisions, made by economic units" ("The Monetary Aspects of the Schumpeterian System," in *Schumpeter, Social Scientist*, p. 63).

mentioned, he agreed with older writers that money had to be conceived as a "claim." Later he criticized this definition, because it suggests "a misleading association with the legal concept of a claim" and expressed a preference for the then-fashionable expression "sign theory."[43]

He rejected the variations of "legal theory" or "conventional theory" far more decisively. He mocked them as a *barren sandbank*.[44] He restricted himself to the thesis that money is subjected to the influence of law and custom, which is no more than self-evident. As he argued in greater detail elsewhere, Knapp's "state theory of money" could not explain the essence of money. In the most favorable case, it is only a theory of the "essence" of money recognized as a legally valid means of payment, hence is just as true or false as the statement that the institution of marriage is a creature of law.[45] Beyond this, theorists of law and convention involved themselves in an insoluble contradiction: on the one hand, they rejected the application to money of the law of value which holds in the sphere of commodities, and on the other they resorted to exchange operations to explain the phenomenon of money.[46] He added that Knapp's proposed term "nominalism" was "very unfortunate."[47]

Yet referring to his analysis of the economic settlement process, he also characterized money as a "warrant" or as "a ticket to the goods reservoir"[48] or even as a "theater ticket,"[49] therefore also approximating the concept of "voucher" and "claim." Be that as it may, it is not my intention to spend time in

---

[43]See below, p. 43, n4.

[44]See below, p. 50.

[45]Cf. Schumpeter, *History of Economic Analysis*, p. 1090.

[46]See below, p. 43, n4.

[47]See below, p. 43, n4.

[48]In the article "Das Sozialprodukt und die Rechenpfennige" [The Social Product and Money of Account], Schumpeter already combined this comparison with the notion of economic machines: "every economic subject puts his contribution into the great economic machine and receives, through the play of the mechanism, a quantity of goods in return, which, together with the quantities of goods owing to the remaining economic subjects by virtue of the market value of their contributions, precisely exhausts the social product" (p. 633).

[49]With the latter comparisons Schumpeter relinquished any claim to originality. The images of e.g. "ticket" and "entry pass" were, he noted, already used by John Stuart Mill, and as far he knew were first used by a pre-Physiocrat economist, the witty English bishop George Berkeley in his *Querist* (1735-1737; see below, p. 78).

the difficulties of reconciling Schumpeter's luxuriously multiplying comparisons.

In any case, they led Schumpeter to the further conclusion that only a "reflected value" is attributable to money and that, in consequence, money – against the reigning viewpoint – need not comprise valuable material or be "backed" by valuable material.

This train of thought, expressed in the present book, originated from an earlier time: the value estimates of market players for money – which is how Schumpeter explained it in *The Social Product and Money of Account* – were "simply reflected," because they already presupposed specific ratios between money and commodities, so also the purchasing power that they were supposed to explain, which is, and can only be, nothing other than the reciprocal value of money prices of a few commodities. Money therefore not only had no use value but also no exchange value in the same sense as commodities. Or in connection with the comparison to theater tickets: money only has exchange value in the sense of the exchange of a theater ticket in connection with the seat to which it refers. Or conceived in yet another fashion: its exchange value corresponds to the space available to the theater-goer in the standing room.[50]

The historical fact that money often possesses a commodity value, usually a precious metal value, may therefore from the standpoint of logic – which for Schumpeter means from the standpoint of the theoretician of money – be neglected.[51] Quite as theoretically irrelevant is the possibility that it acquire other economic tasks, as for example the hoarding function.[52] On the other hand, a negative quality is logically significant: money is not a good in the customary sense. It embodies – as Schumpeter previously already formulated it– a method to dispose of goods.[53]

After all, the novelty at the time of this way of thinking should not be overestimated. Partly it was anticipated by earlier research. Schumpeter's achievement restricted itself chiefly to the derivation, the conception, finally also the arrangement in a coordinated system of thought. The remaining theoretical debit account may be adjusted by future historians of dogma. We linger

---

[50]Schumpeter, "Das Sozialprodukt und die Rechenpfennige" [The Social Product and Money of Account], pp. 646-647.

[51]Similarly already in the lecture, "Die goldene Bremse an der Kreditmaschine" [The Golden Brakes on the Credit Machine], p. 159.

[52]See below, p. 233.

[53]Schumpeter, "Die goldene Bremse an der Kreditmaschine" [The Golden Brakes on the Credit Machine], pp. 159, 163 n4.

here only for a single function that illuminates Schumpeter's close relation to the individualistic heritage. John Stuart Mill had already expounded that both of the functions of money according to classical economics, the means of exchange and the measure of value, are incapable of changing the essence of goods exchanges ("makes no difference in the essential character of transaction"), for money, as Mill had explained, was only a technical auxiliary, "a machine" providing for the speed and convenience of goods traffic. At the most, he adds mockingly, money is influential when the machine gets out of order. Still other notions that merged into Schumpeter's theory of money flare up here. I mention in this regard only Mill's thesis contradicting everyday experience that money is the most indifferent thing in the economy.[54] As mentioned, Schumpeter also actively emphasized that what is "truly relevant" for the economic process takes place only in the world of goods.

That, however, signals an end to Schumpeter's agreement with the technical-instrumental concept of his predecessors, "pulling back the money veil." In the subsequent chapters devoted to the static circular flow analysis, the assumption of the passivity of money increasingly loses importance. Schumpeter seeks rather to demonstrate that money is not a magnitude dependent upon the economic process but helps to determine the extent and direction of the economic process and – he adds – has an "economic autonomy" [ökonomische Eigengesetzlichkeit]. A glance at his weightiest arguments will suffice here.

The cornerstone is the detailed demonstration that "the economic process of itself can only determine the ratios of prices to one another, not absolute prices." To accomplish this, it requires a "factor,"[55] an "arbitrary number regarding the value of the money quantity of the area of investigation," characterized by Schumpeter as "the *critical number* of the system."[56] This number "subjects all monetary economic variables, initially prices, to a new condition, itself foreign to the logic of the economic process," to which Schumpeter likewise attaches a new characteristic name: the *"money tie."* The money tie follows its own

---

[54]"There cannot, in short, be intrinsically a more insignificant thing in the economy of society, than money; except in the character of a contrivance for sparing time and labour. It is a machine for doing quickly and commodiously, what would be done, though less quickly and commodiously, without it; and like other kinds of machinery, it only exerts a distinct and independent influence of its own when it gets out of order" (John Stuart Mill, *Principles of Political Economy*, ed. by W. S. Ashley, London 1926, p. 488 [Book III, Chapter VII, § 3]).

[55]See below, p. 267.

[56]See below, p. 227.

law and forces the implementation thereof: it causes all prices to adjust to it through actual or potential changes.[57] In this manner, with the help of the "critical number" and the "money tie," absolute prices arise.[58] Or put another way, besides the relationship of prices to each other established through the economic process itself, the "price system" characterized by relative prices, there henceforth arises another factual situation, absolute prices, therefore the "price level" of an economy as conceptualized in connection with François Divisia. Accordingly, Schumpeter arrives at the conclusion that *"this indirect and essentially nonsensical method makes up the essence of the social institution that we call money."* It is behind all historical methods of social accounting. But this does not yet mean that commodity currencies, which contradict the essence of money, in particular the showpiece thereof, the classical gold currency, lack economic advantages. Despite its logical imperfections, the main source, in Schumpeter's opinion, of all purely monetary problems, "our admiration for this ingenious trick of cultural history cannot be great enough."[59]

In what consists this autonomy of money as hypostatized in this connection? Initially it derives from the practical impossibility of continuously adjusting the critical number so as to keep the economic process from having to undergo adjustments founded merely in the logic of its system of computation. In this manner, an autonomy arises that does not take changes in the body of commodities into account, that in fact from the standpoint of the body of commodities is "senseless."[60] In consequence, holding the critical number constant is already considered a symptom of autonomy. And still other adjustment processes come up, forced by the critical number. This point of view brings Schumpeter to a further conclusion: *"the money method is that method of social account-settlement, according to which the critical number of the economic system changes autonomously."* Any such method, he adds, creates units of account that as such - physically or on the books - exist, and that subject the economic quantities to a new condition, to which they must adjust.[61]

To this is added [p. 236 below] a second factual situation that determines the functioning of money: economic life defends itself against the money tie, or, as Schumpeter pictures the process, against "the bridle that the autonomous critical number straps onto its settling-up and settling-through process, and it is

---

[57]See below, p. 267.

[58]See below, p. 267.

[59]See below, p. 233.

[60]See below, p. 233.

[61]See below, p. 233.

actually able to evade it to some extent." One such revolt, as exemplified repeatedly by Schumpeter, follows particularly in the case of a "damaged currency."

Might we not object that these cases contradict the previously coined concept of money? Do they not revive the assumption that money is only a servant of the world of goods? Or, to resume with Schumpeter's own comparison: does not money, the servant of the world of goods, henceforth recollect its own powers and usurp the role of master? At any rate, the analysis forces Schumpeter to conclude that a harmonious automatism is lacking. The assumption that economic life "creates the purchasing power" that it "requires" is so misleading that it can better be avoided.[62]

Furthermore, all money existing physically or on the books can change the course of the economic process in another manner. Experience teaches that the total number of applications of money, thus initially the "changing hands" of coined money and paper money, can exceed the total number of transactions conducted on the goods market, the exchange of commodities for money and money for goods. According to the usual analytical premises, the acceleration of the velocity of circulation has the effect of an increase in the quantity of money. Nevertheless, Schumpeter believed he had to forego this customary index. For, as he complained, what is the use of the most excellent indices if one does not know what one intends to measure with it? In place of the velocity of circulation, he therefore drew upon a purified concept referring to the turnover of the social product between firms and households, and the turnover of productive performances between firms and households, which he wished to characterize as the "*efficiency of coins* or of the deposit unit." This efficiency is measured "by the number of times in which a coin unit or deposit unit is spent by households for consumer goods during the observation period – that it renders a service *vis-a-vis the social product.*"[63] In terms of the conceptual specification of the index, Schumpeter further – as will here only be touched upon – distinguished between the "frequency" and the "disposition" of the coins. Hereby, two factual conditions that often encounter each other in the course of the economic process are separated from each other: "the elements of efficiency that are objectively given from the standpoint of individual firms and households, and those that are immediately amenable to the caprice of subjects of the payment process."[64]

---

[62]See below, p. 236.
[63]See below, p. 251.
[64]See below, p. 253.

Broader spheres of influence open up - and in increasing degree over the course of history - if money frees itself from the bonds of a material substrate, and not only through the replacement of coins with state-issued paper money or banknotes, but also through the use of bills of exchange, and beyond that through the contractual figure of the current account and network of bank transfers. Because experience teaches that the largest transactions are conducted with the help of book entries, the need for physical means of payments diminishes. In this manner, the essence of money also changes: it has to be seen in the credit or the order or the claim. Because of this, though, the received concept of money has to be modified again.

Money's leverage increases under these conditions, for "the scope of the operands of the economy" can be steadily increased through the fresh creation of deposits, thus credit creation.[65] Schumpeter had already earlier impressively demonstrated the significance of this for capitalistic development. When, for example, at the end of a slowdown the "innovations" contrived by a business pioneer are employed and hopes of a revival of the economy are awakened, the banks vouchsafe the "additional credit" needed for investment until the economic boom has started. By the way, using Schumpeter's terminology this is another case in which economic life frees itself from the bridle of money.

In this analysis of historical development dating from his earlier work, Schumpeter had already recognized a twofold heresy: for the increase in investment and the stimulation of commerce was made possible first by money in the customary sense and secondly by other means of payment. In consequence, to the latter were also attributed "an essential role," for the processes in the sphere of means of payment were "not mere reflexes of processes in the world of goods ... in which everything essential originated."[66]

But in the finished presentation now published, he softened this conclusion, defending himself against the conclusion that money and credit dominated the economic process; he even refused the obvious assumption in the financing of innovations, that money and credit exercise an economic initiative. Rather,

---

[65]See below, p. 238.

[66]Schumpeter, *Theorie der wirtschaftlichen Entwicklung* [Theory of Economic Development], p. 140. The English translation puts it thusly: "For every form of economy in which the leader has no direct power of disposal over these services, this again leads us to two heresies: first to the heresy that money, and then to the second heresy that also other means of payment, perform an essential function, hence that processes in terms of means of payment are not merely reflexes of processes in terms of goods" (p. 95).

he sought now – and in contrast to his own static circular flow analysis – to place accents more cautiously. I quote here the formulation that mitigates the contradiction: "Money and credit do not play a merely subservient role therein, in the sense that they register only what would happen independently of them, although neither are they a first cause [primum movens] that would produce a wave motion – an alternation of positive and negative phases of the economic process, that without them would not exist." With the help of the account-settling system, money and credit are able to draw existing means of production away from their previous uses and apply them to new uses. They therefore have the ability "temporarily to commandeer transactions in existing goods." The account-settling system allied with money and credit is indeed "the midwife of the new, but not more than that. It does not create the new, nor does it initiate it."[67]

After all, the conceptual opposition is not solved with this comparison. It seems to me that it can be characterized as Schumpeter's "dialectic of money." In addition to the technical function of money initially analyzed by him, in the course of his investigation there increasingly appear limiting regulatory economic functions exercised by money and determining its essence. Or logically comprehended: through the negation of the original, merely market-technical concept of money, the technical and regulatory functions of a comprehensive, richer concept of money is obtained in the course of the investigation.

About the Provenance of the Manuscript

Prior to interrupting his teaching activity at the University of Bonn in the summer of 1930, in order to appear as visiting professor at Harvard and, subsequently, to embark on a world voyage, Schumpeter deposited the draft of this book with his colleague at Bonn and presumptive editor, Arthur Spiethoff. Indeed, as Spiethoff stated to me, he provided alternate instructions. In case he should return safely to Bonn in the following year, the manuscript should be returned to him; but if something were to happen to him during the trip, the manuscript should be published unchanged in its provisional version. When Schumpeter returned the following year and received the manuscript back, Spiethoff asked him the question obvious to the editor: when would the work already announced in the *Encyclopedia of the Science of Law and State* appear? According to Spiethoff's report, Schumpeter responded "Never." Whether the interview took such a dramatic turn cannot be ascertained today. That it ended with Schumpeter's rejection, however, is likely beyond doubt, for the

---

[67]See below, p. 306.

publication of the treatise has been postponed until now. The correctness of the assumption is supported by the fact that a former colleague of Schumpeter's, Professor Gustav Clausing at Erlangen, remembers that shortly after his return to Bonn Schumpeter deposited his "money book" in a room of the political science seminar. He thereby noted that it dealt with a specific volume in the Encyclopedia but that it probably would not be published in its present form.

At any rate, he later regretted this renunciation. In looking through the manuscript it can be seen that he soon resumed the work, as early as his first years in America. And a plan of publication – now in English – was soon developed. Schumpeter referred to this in the first volume of his *Business Cycles,* published in 1939.[68] At the same time an advertisement appeared in the *American Economic Review* announcing that Schumpeter's book about money would soon be published by Harvard University Press. This implies that a formal commitment must have been made by Schumpeter at this time. After this second (English) plan, the release was further delayed and eventually fell through. Perhaps Schumpeter hesitated with the publication for a similar reason as with another equally unfinished life's work, his *History of Economic Analysis,* the possible conclusion of which he discussed with me only a few days before his death: the scientific resistance that awaited him appeared too great to make one last effort worthwhile.

At his death, the German-language version of the manuscript was found among Schumpeter's posthumous papers, and was soon entrusted by Mrs. Schumpeter to Professor Arthur Marget, now also deceased, for translation into English. In subsequent years Marget, at the time director of the Division of International Finance at the Board of Governors of the Federal Reserve System in Washington D.C., worked on the translation with several assistants, and, because he knew of my interest in Schumpeter's work, passed to me a copy of the German text of the manuscript. I have based the following edition upon this copy. According to information gleaned from many involved persons, the remaining copies – also used by Marget – at this time are no longer available.

---

[68]In a footnote to the chapter, "The Role of Money and Banking in the Process of Evolution," he noted that "the theoretical background of the analysis of credit to be presented in this section will be developed in the writer's treatise on money." Schumpeter, *Business Cycles,* vol. 1, p. 109 n1.

The characterization "treatise on money" was certainly not intended as final; it might also be a reference to Keynes' work of the same name. See p. xviii above, n29.

In publication, obvious writing mistakes are corrected and, here and there, omitted words are included in brackets. Since Chapter XII lacked a title, a prospective replacement has been added in brackets. On the other hand, bracketed ejaculations such as "Why?" or "In what manner?" often encountered in the manuscript have been suppressed, as they apparently were directed by the writer only to himself.

I owe special thanks to my colleagues at the University of Cologne; for consultation regarding mathematical questions, Prof. Dr. Johann Pflanzagl; for bibliographic suggestions, Dr. Arnold Price of the Library of Congress in Washington D.C.; for additions to the bibliography, graduate economists Hans Joachim Frye and Manfred Burkart, both of the University of Cologne; and for the preparation of the indices of persons and subjects, graduate economist Karl Weinhard of Ingolstadt.

Introduction to the English edition

It is now 75 years since the English-language version of Joseph Schumpeter's prospective treatise on money was first announced, and 86 years since the first plans were announced for a German edition. It has been a tortured journey for the English edition, one which now finally finds fulfilment. It joins the German edition, originally published back in 1970 (of which this is the translation), as well as Italian[1] and French[2] editions.

There has been a great deal of speculation as to why Schumpeter never "pulled the trigger" and went ahead with publishing his book on money.[3] The usual explanation invokes the supposed daunting achievement of John Maynard Keynes, which is to have had the effect of discouraging Schumpeter from coming out in print with his own version of monetary matters. Keynes' *Treatise on Money*, published in 1930 – right about the time Schumpeter was preparing his own manuscript for publication – is said to have had this effect. Smithies in 1950 put forward the (now discredited) thesis that Schumpeter decided to destroy his own work after Keynes published his. Swedberg, following Kulla, argued that Schumpeter felt upstaged by Keynes, repeating the story put forward by Salin to the effect that Schumpeter burnt the manuscript. Allen, for his part, argued that Schumpeter postponed the publication of his treatise in order to digest "the more mature level of analysis" contained in Keynes's work. Messori takes Allen's approach and builds on it. In his view, although the two works diverge, Schumpeter still suffered by comparison. This is supposedly evidenced by notes sent by Schumpeter to Keynes, congratulating him on his achievement. Messori would have Schumpeter evincing "a sincere appreciation tempered by envy." And as recently as 2013, Medearis still furthers the claim that Schumpeter "felt

---

[1]*L'essenza della moneta,* translated by Elvio Dal Bosco (Turin: Banca CRT, 1990).

[2]*Théorie de la monnaie et de la banque,* 2 volumes, translated by Claude Jaeger and Odile Lakomski-Laguerre (Paris: L'Harmattan, 2005). This edition includes three additional chapters, not included in the Mann version here translated. For further information about these chapters, see Messori, n3 below.

[3]I follow here the useful summary given by Marcello Messori, "The Trials and Misadventures of Schumpeter's Treatise on Money," *History of Political Economy,* Winter 1997 29 (4), pp. 639-673; the summary begins on p. 645.

he had been upstaged by John Maynard Keynes's publication of *A Treatise of* [sic] *Money* in 1930" (Medearis 2013, pp. 33-34).

Yet the actual notes breath not envy but empathy. Schumpeter wrote, "I have been, and shall be again, suffering enough from the weight of the labours of composing anything like a 'treatise' on money to be able to form an idea of how you must feel relieved."[4] The true sentiment here is Schumpeter's suffering similar labor pains in composing his own treatise, pains from which he never experienced the relief he imagined must be Keynes', because he never could get the manuscript into the shape he desired.

With the hindsight of 75-plus years, it is easier now to hazard a guess as to why Schumpeter could not get the manuscript into a form that he found satisfactory. The key is provided by Mann (see p. xxxi above): "Perhaps Schumpeter hesitated with the publication for a similar reason as with another equally unfinished life's work, his *History of Economic Analysis,* the possible conclusion of which he discussed with me only a few days before his death: the scientific resistance that awaited him appeared too great to make one last effort worthwhile."

Ah yes, the scientific resistance. The grain of truth in the thesis that Keynes's work discouraged Schumpeter is this: it showed him which way the wind was blowing. Keynes's method as represented in the *General Theory of Employment, Interest and Money*[5] caught on, not only in terms of intellectual consensus, but in terms of policy. And this was no accident; the one explains the other. Keynes's approach was tailor-made to a policy prescription that resonated in countries going through the throes of economic depression. But for Schumpeter, this was the one evil that needed to be avoided: for him, "the purity of science, objective knowledge, must never be muddled," noted Mann. "For this reason, he even rejected any scientific research oriented to the practical needs of an incidental historical situation" (p. xvii above). To do this is to commit something so egregious that Schumpeter coined a famous phrase for it – the "Ricardian vice."

What needs to be understood is that Schumpeter's treatise represents what might be considered the high-water mark of interwar monetary theory, the development of which was interrupted by the advent of the Great Depression. That series of events constituted such an earth-shaking phenomenon that it caused even the work of Keynes to be lifted out of its previous bed and shunted

---

[4]*The Collected Writings of John Maynard Keynes,* vol. XIII (Cambridge: Cambridge University Press, 1973), p. 176.

[5]*The Collected Writings of John Maynard Keynes,* vol. VII.

on to the alternative course as represented in the *General Theory*; for Keynes's *Treatise*, for all its differences with Schumpeter's work, could be considered a part of this interwar theoretical body, while the *General Theory* took an entirely different approach.[6] It was this alternative approach, represented initially by Keynes and later by both monetarists and Austrian economists, that became dominant. Its overarching characteristic is that it simplifies the monetary system and restricts it to the workings of central banks (monetary policy) and government (fiscal policy), with everything else entirely derivative and secondary.

The approach represented by Schumpeter is diametrically opposed to this. Instead of focusing on central banks and government policy, it focuses on the banking system as a whole, to what Schumpeter referred to as the "social central bookkeeping in the capitalist economy" the main characteristic of which is the current account relation (pp. 132 ff. below). This yields an account-settling and clearing functionality which exhibits the true essence of money.

Schumpeter thus here provides a detailed version of the "credit theory of money" that he contrasts with the "monetary theory of credit" which, as he explained in *The History of Economic Analysis*, has been the predominant understanding. "It may be more useful to start from [credit transactions] in the first place, to look upon capitalist finance as a clearing system that cancels claims and debts and carries forward the differences—so that 'money' payments come in only as a special case without any particularly fundamental importance" (p. 717). To do this, of course, is to turn matters on their head, but in Schumpeter's view it is only to reestablish the proper relationship, which otherwise is "inverted" (see pp. 233 ff. below).

At the heart of this account-settling and clearing system is the creation and extinction of credit and debt. That this takes place throughout the banking system is something only vaguely understood and even less given its proper place in theory. The interwar theory constituted a valiant attempt to do so, but was stopped in its tracks. Schumpeter bemoaned this situation at length:

> It proved extraordinarily difficult for economists to recognize that bank loans and bank investments do create deposits. In fact, throughout the

---

[6]By way of indication, this from the *Treatise:* "We must now embark on a very long argument as to the manner in which the creation of deposits by the banking system is related to the price level" (*The Collected Writings of John Maynard Keynes,* vol. V, p. 43). This evidences the interwar approach, no trace of which can be found in the *General Theory*. See also Colin Rogers and T. K. Rymes, "The Disappearance of Keynes's Nascent Theory of Banking Between the *Treatise* and the *General Theory*," in *What Is Money?,* ed. John Smithin (London: Routledge, 2000), pp. 257-269.

period under survey [from 1870 to 1914 and later] they refused with practical unanimity to do so. And even in 1930, when the large majority had
been converted and accepted that doctrine as a matter of course, Keynes
rightly felt it to be necessary to reexpound and to defend the doctrine at
length, and some of its most important aspects cannot be said to be fully
understood even now. This is a most interesting illustration of the inhibitions with which analytic advance has to contend and in particular of
the fact that people may be perfectly familiar with a phenomenon for
ages and even discuss it frequently without realizing its true significance
and without admitting it into their general scheme of thought (*History
of Economic Analysis*, pp. 1114-1115).

The collapse of "new era" 1920s finance and the extended misery of the
Great Depression found its scapegoat precisely in the doctrine of credit creation.
The Austrian theory of the business cycle put credit creation at the core of its
analysis of booms and busts, blaming it for those swings. Hahn, whose theoretical achievement in analyzing the phenomenon of credit creation was highlighted by Schumpeter, ended up renouncing the phenomenon as "Keynesian,"
even though Keynesianism proper had nothing to do with it. The result was the
dissolution of a coherent body of monetary thought.

By 1948, academics like Albert Gailord Hart were writing, if not in
lamentation, at least with a sense of disguised apprehension about the changed
state of play.

> Only a few years ago, money was the prize course in many economics
> departments – the surest to command spontaneous interest among stu-
> dents, and the one in which the teacher had the strongest sense of show-
> ing how useful economics could be. Today, the subject of money looks
> much more drab. Courses in the 'fiscal policy' aspects of public finance,
> in business cycles, in international trade, and in 'pure theory' now eclipse
> courses in money. They are so stimulating largely because so much of
> their subject matter has been appropriated from 'money and banking'
> courses.[7]

Monetary theory was now being parceled out among cognate disciplines;
it no longer received its wonted attention. The theory now was little more than
that money was a passive blob in the hands of technocratic central bankers and
fiscal policy practitioners in government, pumped to wherever, and injected into
whatever, it was (in their eyes) needed.

---

[7] A. G. H., 'Preface,' in *Money, Debt and Economic Activity*, by Albert Gailord
Hart (New York: Prentice-Hall, 1948), p. v.

Schumpeter saw all of this happening and knew his analysis, diametrically opposed as it was to this, now-reigning approach, did not have a prayer of a decent reception. His *Business Cycles*, the best thing on the subject available, was dismissed as tendentious and inconclusive, at least in part because the central role of credit creation in business cycles made it too foreign to the reigning dogma.[8] His *Theory of Economic Development* was dumbed down to a mere explanation of economic development in terms of the entrepreneur *in vacuo*, oblivious of the essential role of credit creation precisely in enabling the entrepreneur: "among the types of economic agents that the analysis of reality brings out, the entrepreneur is the typical debtor."[9] Credit creation is the means by which the entrepreneur is made capable of intervening in the economic process at all.

In other words, Schumpeter had managed to avoid the Ricardian vice. He remained true to his theory because of its faithfulness to reality, regardless of its utility, or lack thereof, for policy and consensus-building. And he paid the price for it: oblivion, to the degree that such was possible to someone as brilliant as himself.[10]

His own critique of Keynesianism sums up his position vis-à-vis the consensus:

> It is ... highly significant that, as late as June 1927, there was room for the article of F.W. Crick, 'The Genesis of Bank Deposits' (*Economica*), which explains how bank loans create deposits and repayment to banks annihilates them—in a manner that should have been indeed, but evidently was not even then, 'time-honored theory.' There is, however, a sequel to Lord Keynes's treatment of the subject of credit creation in the *Treatise* of 1930 of which it is necessary to take notice in passing. The deposit-creating bank loan and its role in the financing of investment *without any previous saving up of the sums thus lent* have practically disappeared in the analytic schema of the *General Theory*, where it is again the saving public that holds the scene. Orthodox Keynesianism has in fact reverted

---

[8]In a review (*New Republic,* July 12th 2007) of Thomas H. McCraw's *Prophet of Innovation: Joseph Schumpeter and Creative Destruction* (Cambridge: Belknap Press, 2007), renowned economist Robert Solow dismisses *Business Cycles* as "essentially unreadable." In fact it is quite readable, but perhaps only after first digesting the present volume.

[9]This fragment is translated from the German original (p. 148). The English translation has "he is the typical debtor in capitalist society" (p. 102).

[10]Although he is enjoying something of a comeback. See e.g. the review cited in n8 above.

to the old view according to which the central facts about the money market are analytically rendered by means of the public's propensity to save coupled with its liquidity preference. I cannot do more than advert to this fact. Whether this spells progress or retrogression, every economist must decide for himself (*History of Economic Analysis*, pp. 1114-1115, n5).

So then, what this book presents is the outworking, in the field of money, of the system Schumpeter initially put forward in *The Theory of Economic Development* and later elaborated in historical and theoretical minuteness in *Business Cycles*. As such, it constitutes a key element of the Schumpeterian method, and indeed provides the missing key to a comprehensive understanding of the elements contained in these other works. This makes it eminently worthwhile and even essential reading for anyone who wishes to come to grips with the true Schumpeter.

Notes on the Translation

The text is the direct translation of *Das Wesen des Geldes*, published by Vandenhoeck & Ruprecht GmbH, Göttingen, in 1970, and reprinted in 2008. The title has however been changed. Rather than retain Mann's *The Essence of Money,* it has been decided to use the title made reference to by Schumpeter in his own published work, viz., *Business Cycles,* where the book is referred to as the "treatise on money" in various places throughout the two volumes. Furthermore, the suggestion made by Messori (see the article referenced in n3 on p. xxxiii above) to use "the theory of money and banking" would seem to miss the connection noted by Mann on p. xviii above, to the effect that Schumpeter saw his book in connection with Keynes's. Indeed, it pursues the same goal and covers the same ground; it is a product of that era, and breathes that era. The title makes that connection more clear.

The usual translation conventions are followed, but with a twist. Square brackets [like this] are used either to show the original text in cases where the translation is not straightforward or unambiguous, or where the original text is unique in some way (to show, e.g., Schumpeter's use of Greek or Latin terms), or to show English translations of foreign-language titles. Colored text is used to show interpolations by either the original editor of the manuscript, Fritz Karl Mann, or the translator. Text in blue, like this, is Mann's, while text in red-orange, like this, has been added by the translator.

TRANSLATOR'S ACKNOWLEDGEMENT

I wish to thank Susannah Black for a brilliant job fishing out textual and translational errors. Without her help, this book would have been strewn with more than a few of each. The remaining are, of course, my own.

TRANSLATOR'S DEDICATION

To Robert Christopher Alvarado (1956-2013), who was my biggest fan, and I think still is.

Chapter I
Introduction

Monetary Policy in Context

1. *Monetary policy* [Währungspolitik] means more than forms, influences,[1] rules for a separate sphere of technical matters relating to the market economy. The often passionate, always great interest in the practical questions of money [Geldwesens] and its value is explained by the fact that everything that a people desires, does, suffers, *is* - is reflected in money, and at the same time, that a people's monetary system [Geldwesen] exercises a fundamental influence on its economic activity and its destiny in general. The condition of a people's monetary system is a symptom of all its conditions: a government budget deficit, the manner and spirit of financial policy even without a deficit, *every* measure of trade and commercial policy at all that promotes or discourages economic activity, finally the revival or decay of economic life, must exercise a fundamental influence on currency even when they are not immediately visible in every case. This we understand up front, regardless of the difficulties of diagnosing a concrete situation, even before our discussion has gotten under way.

But then it follows that all the aspects and all the social and political happenings that explain the deficits, the financial, economic, social policies, recovery or decay, must be reflected in the state of the currency: victorious wars and defeats, war preparations, revolutions, foreign policy successes and failures, domestic political constellations, the strength or weakness of governments - and the more so, when in the *historical* course of events all of these things had an effect in terms of monetary policy not only when they led to corresponding measures or changes in the economic process, but when they, as they sometimes do, exercise a direct influence. This includes general despondency that alters

---

[1]The decisive thing thereby is the *fact* of influence and not the *intention*. A prince who debased the coin did not necessarily intend to change the value of money. A spendthrift Parliament usually did not think about the effect of its action on the currency. But both drove monetary policy in the sense of the definition implied above. See §. 3.

people's monetary dispositions before anything else is done directly to affect interest rates or exchange rates. *Any* kind of policy can then become monetary policy, any kind of event a monetary event. And finally, it follows that the ultimate data of social and political events are also the deepest determinants of monetary policy and monetary history: the geographical and political situation of a people, the objective and subjective opportunities provided by its economy, its social structure and political organization, its attitude toward economic matters and the future, its morale and energy, everything that is covered by the words "national spirit" and "national character." Nothing demonstrates so clearly what a people is made of than how it conducts its monetary policy.

Of course, this aspect of the matter can also be overestimated, to the detriment of practice and knowledge. Understanding these broader relationships does not attain to grasping monetary processes in their nature and in the influence that they in turn exert. He who, e.g., explains inflation by national calamities (Germany) or in other cases by the economic possibilities of the massive discharge of national will (Japan), has *not* explained this inflation as a monetary phenomenon. He who contents himself with a reference to overall social processes, with inflation occurring as an element thereof, has skipped over the specific monetary-policy problem. And a characteristic class of monetary-policy and monetary-scientific shortcomings, the nature and scope of which will gradually become clear to us, is a consequence of the belief that ascertainment of complex social causes of a monetary phenomenon coincides with ascertainment of this phenomenon itself. This would only be so if the complex social cause uniquely determined the monetary phenomenon. But it is immediately clear to the unprejudiced that, to stick with the example, a political and social situation of a type that renders inflationary monetary policy practically understandable, does not with equally automatic necessity determine the actual emergence, and even less with equal clarity the extent, of inflation, in the manner that an abundant harvest determines the fall in prices of agrarian products. The one who says, for example, that the collapse of the German currency was due to the invasion of the Ruhr has said *nothing* as far as monetary policy is concerned.

As little as it is surprising when we say that the condition of the skin of an animal's body depends on the condition of all its organs, but also that the condition of the skin is an essential element of the condition of all the other organs, just as little should it seem strange to us when we reciprocally say that monetary policy and the condition of the currency exercises a constant major influence on everything that a nation desires or does, and on all elements of its social and economic being. This is true both in the sense that monetary policy and the condition of the currency materially mutually determine any other policy and any other type of condition, and in the sense that the consideration of monetary policy and the condition of the currency help to determine the relation between seemingly remote fields, and help to explain conditions that seemingly have nothing to do with the currency.

The generation that lived through the World War and the postwar period need not have explained to them that monetary difficulties are the central problem of fiscal policy and can dominate it; nor that generally every social policy and economic policy can be dependent upon the currency and the consideration thereof; nor even that exchange rates sometimes determine the economic loss or success of individuals, and boom or depression in the economy, and bring about economic and social regroupings the quantitative overall significance of which is far greater than the effects of any revolutions that have taken place in the same historical period. During this time we have seen the internal and external policies of states with debauched monetary systems dependent upon the condition of the currencies of those states. And we have all experienced the disorganizing effect of currency breakdown on national character, morality, and all branches of cultural life. However, the events of the war and the postwar period afforded as little that was new in term of economics or sociology as in other areas, but only provided well-known phenomena on an enlarged scale; all of this might be shown just as well, for example, in the events of the Napoleonic era or in the social and spiritual tensions and releases of the 16th century – the latter case in particular purity, because the price revolution, which roused the people and created the atmosphere of unrest, by which traditions and customs lost their authority and the social organism pulsated feverishly, was mainly monetary, brought about by the accident of precious metal supplies from America and internal damage to the currency. *Qualitatively*, things are quite the same in quiet times. The direct observation of practice shows us how every weakness of the currency weakens the internal and external political position of a people; how, through the link of central bank policy, the impulse of any variation in the condition of the national currency spreads over the entire economy and makes itself felt in all the symptoms of economic being – employment, wage and income level, export and consumption figures, etc.

But even this aspect of the matter may be overestimated to the detriment of practice and knowledge, both in terms of its importance, particularly the causal role of monetary conditions, and in terms of what monetary *policy* can accomplish for the currency itself and for the economy. As an example, the obviously absurd attempt that is made to explain the demise of the ancient Roman Empire by the depletion of the supply of precious metals. Of more practical importance is the widespread, almost mystical attitude among laymen to the effect that the opaque monetary system is a source of dark influences in the weal and woe of the people, and of almost all social ills. A sharply-defined type of social reform monomaniac sees money, its reform or abolition, as a social panacea: his existence has always formed one of the biggest troubles to the profession of monetary policymaker and money investigator. But even without degenerating into the pathological, overestimations of the power of monetary policy or the value of certain monetary systems are frequent and disruptive enough.[2] One finds even among otherwise reasonable, upstanding people, especially in the business world, a fanatical monetary policy creed, accessible to no argument and the root of which is often difficult to determine. Many a man who is otherwise unprejudiced and accommodating even on sensitive issues, cannot keep himself from regarding dissenters in this area as rogues. Our purpose here is only to warn against two opposite, equally false, basic orientations.

The Limits of Monetary Policy

2. *Monetary* policy is *policy*. For this reason, scientific analysis can be produced, effects and tendencies of money systems and currency conditions can be made comprehensible - they can "explain the facts" - and thus also indicate the monetary-policy *means* that can be applied in order to achieve *given goals*, but they cannot provide any "final" goals to political action, i.e., no goals that are not in turn subordinate to other given goals. Leaving out of consideration the case in which the motivation behind setting a specific goal is in error regarding factual interrelations [Zusammenhänge] - in which case, of course, the scientific clarification of the interrelations determines the fate of the goal - the means of an empirical scientific discipline such as social economics, while they can explain why certain goals appear under certain conditions among certain people, cannot indicate whether the goal itself is "correct" or "wrong."

This principle was already formulated in classic conciseness by Senior and, later, Sidgwick. The interested reader is referred to the statements of Von Gottl, Sombart, and Max Weber at the Vienna meeting of the Association for

---

[2]No example shows how amenable the public is to such an overestimation as clearly as the huge instantaneous success of [William Jennings] Bryan's speech containing the - after their kind - immortal words: "You shall not crucify mankind upon a cross of gold." This was one of the candidate's speeches in one of his battles for the presidency of the United States. He was not elected. The audience was gripped at heart, and yet the statement lacks any common sense.

Social Policy in 1909.[3] Using an example from our area: until the mid-1890s, American farmers were for silver currency; then they became supporters of the gold standard. These monetary-policy objectives are understandable to us, if we note that up to that time the farmers were mainly quite a debtor class, while from then on they increasingly acquired active bank accounts, and at times other investments as well. They therefore were first interested in easing their debt burden; then this motivation dropped and indeed a weaker albeit contrary one took its place. Silver currency was an appropriate means of debt relief because, under the circumstances of the time, silver currency meant declining monetary value. Gold was then a suitable means to maintain intact the purchasing power of assets, because with the circumstances of the turn of the century, the purchasing power of gold was relatively stable. Therefore, these monetary policy objectives that we have recognized as dependent upon "final" targets given by us, thus factually recognized as a "means," we recognize as "correct" from the standpoint of the given "final" objective – just as we would have had to characterize them as "wrong" if the silver currency had been intended as a means of lowering the rate of interest – without being untrue to the viewpoint of science, or mingling our own will with our knowledge, or, finally, judgmentally and politically taking sides.

The "final" goal itself we can see and understand. But from the standpoint of science we cannot make that judgment. Of course, we can show the participants aspects that they otherwise might overlook. So in this case, the farmers can be shown that a long-lasting reduction in the value of money is likely to worsen credit terms or the prices of industrial supplies that farmers need to buy, or finally cause disturbances in the economic or social process, the circumstances of which could be expected to rob the farmers of part, all, or more than all of the advantage. If it were not farmers but a socially leading stratum of large landowners, we would also be able to argue that the objective economic advantage to them should be sought at least in part in the interest of social and political acceptability [Geltung] and that monetary policy set in the pursuit of immediate gain would be harmful to the political standing [Geltung] of this stratum. The economic interests of immediate advantage and that of *enduring* advantage must always indeed be distinguished, within a broader sphere of still very "practical" interests between the *economic* and *social* interests of a

---

[3]Friedrich von Gottl-Ottlilienfeld, Werner Sombart, Max Weber in *Verhandlungen des Vereins für Socialpolitik* [Proceedings of the Association for Social Policy] in Vienna, 1909, *Schriften des Vereins für Socialpolitik*, Leipzig 1909.

group. But while in this manner we push ever in the direction of more comprehensive final goals, and we gain ever more ground within which scientific knowledge can be "intermediate goal-setting," at bottom the particular final goal must remain out of reach.

Let us refrain from the epistemological gap between what "is" - or "counts" - and what "ought" - or "should count" - and ask ourselves purely practically about the impossibility of "scientific politics" in the true meaning of the words. It lies firstly in the fact that social groups gear their monetary-political will, like every political will, to their own interest, and a decision between various monetary policies is only possible by taking sides in a judgmental manner. But that's not all. Even if no group sought to realize its interest but only to realize the "common good" no matter how conceived, we have gained little. For each of the standpoints from which individuals and groups in the social world view things, and in which they are instructed by surroundings or spiritual inheritance, sees this common good differently. No analysis, no matter how conscientious, can, for example, put the importance of keeping intact the rights of creditors in the same light to the socialist, who rejects the existence of such rights generally, and the conservative, who considers it an essential element of the social order. Everyone's entire social world, what everyone loves and hates as light or dark and good or bad, penetrates here into judgment. No mere clash of interests is ever as sharp as the contrast between those who neither want the interests of individual groups represented nor actually represent them, but rather put their focus on different ideals regarding the national or social future.

But this result requires a limitation which, although not fundamental, is of so much more practical significance. As the doctor may give his advice without having to add every time, "*if* you want to be healthy," just as the criteria of the condition which we refer to as health are shared by the vast majority of people, and the majority harbor this same wish to be healthy in terms of these criteria, just so can the economist speak of right and wrong measures, of good and bad currency conditions, without having to add the caveat, if the monetary-policy objectives of the people were *factually* sufficiently similar. Without the fundamental divide between the realms of knowledge and volition thereby disappearing, the importance thereof to the work of science and practice would disappear if everyone wanted the same thing. In the realm of final opinions, currently especially in the realm of the contrast between the socialist and the private-economic ideal, such parallel wills cannot but be impossible. But in many other such realms this is not the case.

And we even see under the moving surface of the political struggle, the opposition of goals becoming milder at important points; "matters of principle" tend to recede to the background. Nowhere is this more the case today than in the field of monetary policy. Here the recovery from the turmoil of the war and postwar period, still in everyone's consciousness, has had the consequence, not of producing the same desire in everyone regarding monetary policy, but nevertheless a very similar desire regarding monetary policy among such a majority as in practice to leave divergent objectives virtually out of consideration, such that, at present, divergent goals are taken into consideration as little as divergent ideals regarding health and hygienic "final" goals are taken into account by the vast majority. Therefore, in our area we can make use of the judgmental categories of "right and wrong," "good and bad" with greater freedom than would otherwise be permitted, although we can never forget that such epithets, if they are to have scientific meaning, always imply *either* that a group interest is given among us the standpoint of which we express, *or* that, under the circumstances of the case, a commonality of goal for all or substantially all groups can be presumed.

The Three Currency Ideals

It is easy to formulate the "ultimate" monetary-policy ideal that in our time is so widely accepted - even by people who would directly benefit from a differently-oriented monetary policy - that we can refer to it as the general one. To this end, we have to make clear a trivial fact, which really needs no further mention: apparently, monetary policy and currency conditions are attributed such great importance only because an element of economic welfare depends on them. But monetary policy only gains relevance to economic welfare or to economic events in general because and insofar that they influence the prices of consumer goods, or as we say using a common expression, *the purchasing power of money*, or the "value of money." If they did not do that, it would be a technical triviality that would interest no one and would never have entered into the circle of great national questions. Interest in monetary policy and currency conditions therefore is interest in the *value of money*. Monetary policy at the end of the day is money-value policy (von Mises). This simplifies our question regarding the current currency ideal - there can then only be three currency ideals, the ideal of increasing, decreasing, and constant purchasing power of money. We will see later that these terms are by no means as simple, and as easy to find fault with in various aspects, as laymen think them to be. We now use the terms in their popular sense, known to everyone, richly imprecise though they are.

Deflation

a) The goal of the gradually increasing value of money, because it corresponds directly to the *creditor interest*, has never been popular or is scarcely explicitly represented. The identical target of lower prices often is, although the idea of fundamentally lowering *all* prices is often mixed with the notion of the *relative* cheapness of large masses of consumer goods, which has nothing to do with it. The depression-oriented symptoms that as a rule have accompanied general price reductions have made this goal totally unpopular. But it should be mentioned here that it cannot be rejected for the reason by which alone science can discard an ideal, namely, because its motivation implies objective errors. Not only is nothing like this on offer, but it can even be shown that the reluctance to deal with this goal itself partially implies errors, such as an overestimation of the damage to the production process brought about by a *slow and predictable* decline in prices. We just need to place ourselves within a foreign mentality to understand that with a correspondingly high estimate of creditor interest – whereby *fixed income* is also concerned – the savings premium involved in increasing monetary value may appear very plausible for the "common good," and even more the idea that the fruits of economic development "should" accrue to all parties in the form of rising purchasing power of the income unit rather than in the form of increasing the nominal amount of income. By the way, we will see that the capitalist economy, left to itself, to a certain extent has the tendency to realize this ideal; in other words, in the absence of "other" disorders would show declining prices over the *long term*.

Inflation

b) The goal of the slowly declining value of money is to be distinguished from the question of whether, in a particular case, lowering the value of money is not an appropriate means to cure depression symptoms or some other temporary evil. What is on view here is declining monetary value as a normal, enduring phenomenon. This would only make sense from the standpoint that no attainment "should" be linked to a fundamental perpetual claim on the national economy, and therefore the gradual dispossession of respective beneficiaries of monetary claims is desirable[4] – a viewpoint hostile to capital, but not socialistic. It is discredited to some degree by the fact that it often appears associated with monetary policy utopias and charlatanism, but objectively is as little absurd as its opposite number. None other than Knut Wicksell has represented this view-

---

[4]Here "depreciative money" [Schwundgeld] would comprise what has been variously proposed.

point. Incidentally, it has also found supporters as a means of promoting production and relief of the most active element of the economy, the entrepreneur – with a kernel of truth, albeit mixed with a multitude of factual errors. Our time is still so much under the influence of the radical despoliation of the creditor and the effects of the type of production stimulus that it has seen, that it has little appetite for this monetary ideal.

Stability

c) The goal of "stable" or "constant" purchasing power dominates the hour. In it, the will of the politician and businessman, expressed or – even more importantly – considered to be above discussion, converges with the opinion of the best authorities of the subject. This volition and this opinion are not new. An analysis of the actual monetary behavior of men and institutions that formed the practical tradition of the 19th century shows the goal of stable purchasing power to be its objective meaning, regardless of the pronouncements that were expressed and however inadequate the means that were employed. The best central bank directors, the best representatives of both *bimetallism* and a pure gold currency, *actually* sought nothing more than this. Even older is the realization by monetary researchers that at least a good deal of the fluctuations in the value of money are not functional, in the sense that they indiscriminately scatter profits and losses throughout the economy, which do not, as do other gains and losses, play a definite role in the economic process – they are technical flaws and nothing more, although regarding the question as to whether this affects all fluctuations in the value of money and, if not, for which cases it might be true, there are very different views. To this the desire attached itself, both for the purpose of science and practice, to make sums of money comparable across different times and places, and thereby in turn the quest numerically to determine actual monetary fluctuations, so that even the person who does not make the ideal, wholly or partly, his own, must recognize that much of the best work was done with reference to it. And this led to a whole series of monetary reform proposals – the serious reform proposals are intended to serve this purpose almost exclusively – many of which are linked to some of the best names of our science (Walras, Marshall, Irving Fisher, Keynes).

The experiences of the war and the postwar period have only blown fresh wind in these sails and put the goal of *stable monetary value* on the agenda of practical discussion. Here, a new horizon opened: monetary policy for the first time came into view as *therapy for the economy*, as a means of economic policy formation of the industrial body, to a large circle. For the time being, however, the stability of the monetary value as such stands in the foreground – even where nothing further is pursued than a "sound" currency and a safeguarded exchange rate. We will usually argue from the standpoint of this objective, without however identifying with it.

We maintain that *sound currency* today practically means a currency which is suitable to preserve the purchasing power of money from fluctuations. In America the term spilled over into the arsenal of political weapons (*"sound money"*), first during the time of the paper money economy and later during the struggle surrounding silver. Originally it meant money consisting of gold or redeemable in gold, without much emphasis being placed on the fluctuations of gold itself. But from the moral connotation gained by the expression, we know that it was only a precursor of further knowledge and a crude expression of the desire for stable money. The "sound money man" was the man who disapproved of monetary fluctuations and profits flowing from speculative activity as morally and professionally "unreliable," who above all thought of "sound" money as *honest* money – but that, interpreted according what has been said, leads back to the ideal of stable money, although at the time an inadequate means for its realization, gold, had to suffice.[5]

Let us take note of yet another strand of such connections, which has now atrophied. The programs of the strict liberal parties[6] were always attached to the *gold standard*. First, from the point of view just mentioned, and because they conformed to the *liberal economic ethic* of the market-oriented *do ut des*, although, as I said, not entirely. But then came the added connotation that today has lost its political power. For liberalism, gold-money became sound money because it was money removed from, or at least less amenable to, *political manipulation*, and left domestic price formation and the foreign exchange rate to the vagaries of gold production and the mechanism of gold movements. From this as well came one of the *psychological* sources of the modern intellectual's dislike of gold as a metallic currency, savoring as it does of the autonomy of the private sector, and causing difficulties for both socialistic and neomercantilistic intervention.

---

[5]But *because* this medium was enough for those times, for which gold guaranteed stability, an association between "honest" money and gold money emerged that has still preserved an ethical note – which on the one hand is very important in terms of monetary policy, and on the other forms a good example of the *associative thinking* of the policy.

[6]The American Democratic Party was not one of these.

Of course, the ideal of stable money does not necessarily mean that one has to advocate the perpetuation of the value of money dominant at *any* particular time. Given, for example, a damaged [havarierte] currency, this objective requires the transition to a "sound," i.e. stable, currency. At what rate that happens, whether the currency unit should be worth more, less, or the same, as the damaged currency at that moment, is another matter. This objective in itself also stipulates only that the purchasing power of the monetary unit undergo no long-term changes. Again, it is another matter whether short-term fluctuations, namely those [corresponding to] changes in the performance of the economy and in the seasons, are to be allowed or even to be promoted. Finally, a warning that is even more necessary with this currency ideal than with the other two: without deeper analysis, it is vague and nebulous, not only in its particular expressions, but in its essence. It would be a good preparatory exercise for the reader to make clear to himself what he and others understand by this ideal, and in this way persuade himself regarding the wealth of issues to be tackled here.

Chapter II
Regarding the Sociology of Money

How to Theorize About Money

1. Before we say something about the development and progress of research into money, we wish in this chapter to touch on a range of topics in a field that might be called the sociology of money. These issues lie beyond our actual task, but they have an effect on it, and the state of scientific debate makes it desirable to go into them briefly. We will use the terms in their everyday meaning, without defining all of them. And we will make use of the opportunity to prepare the ground for future trains of thought.

Money [das Geldwesen], like any other economic institution, is an element of the overall social process and as such a matter for economic theory, for sociology, and finally for historical, ethnological, and statistical "fact research" [Tatsachenforschung]. This is not the place fundamentally to analyze the relation of this latter principle to "theory." Suffice it to say that what "fact research" has to offer us is not only an object of theoretical explanation, not only a means of verification of theoretical propositions, but that constant interaction between "theory" and "fact research" in problems, ways of apprehension, and exploitation of knowledge seems to exist that corresponds with the essence of any empirical discipline. In the sense of our discussion in the first chapter, the requisite factual material even extends far beyond the mere "history of money" or the statistics of money, almost without supposed limit.

We must be aware that only together do the history, statistics, and ethnology of money, credit, and currency, and the theory of money, credit, and currency, represent the science of money, and are so inseparable that it is impossible to bring forward a satisfactory history of the monetary system independently of theory, or to gain a complete theory that in one breath would fundamentally weld *all* the available facts together. So also in the context of our problem, a single monetary-historical fact can only take its place as an example, because its task is to give a pointer in the comprehension and interpretation of monetary phenomena, although it is also desirable that none of the "big" events of the history of money remain unmentioned, i.e., those events, which, whether

instructive *for our knowledge* or not,[1] as historical occurrences, as historical individuals, were of symptomatic or causal significance *for the contemporary
course of events* in business and society. We will further develop the theory of
money and credit transactions in a scheme that is taken from its modern form
and oriented to modern problems. And not just for the sake of didactic convenience, but because it also seems factually more correct than to work from a state
that is as primitive as possible. Because all states of the monetary system hitherto observed, even those only mentally recognized as possible, are done justice
by appropriately adapting our scheme, dropping some features, inserting others,
while the opposite procedure does not, and why this is so, will be seen by the
reader; if he doesn't, it could only be the fault of our presentation. This procedure, which thus objectively juxtaposes problems pertaining to different times
and incommensurable cultural worlds, and in which the historic final shape of
our subject matter becomes the basic theoretical form or the most proximate
"actual" neighbor of the theoretical form, now raises two fundamental questions.

One sounds like this: is there *one* theory of money for all historical periods or *economic styles* (Spiethoff), or must a particular theory be constructed
for each and every one? Even this question entails the rejection of a possible
position, namely the position that the cultural world of every era is *so* unique
that it will be incomprehensible and inaccessible to the categories of the cultural
world of every other epoch. That may be so; only whoever takes this position
cannot accept with an intellectual's naive overconfidence that it is nevertheless
possible precisely for him, with his time-bound eyes, to look different cultures
in the face, but he has to surrender the activity of specific scientific disciplines
as well as simple historiography. If one doesn't go that far, one gains the standpoint to which social science in all fields, e.g., in the history of law and legal
theory, owes much: that one should not judge conditions and processes of other

---

[1]"Generally interesting" or not: of course a historically significant occurrence can
theoretically be so simple that it offers us no theoretical interest, while another occurrence hardly noticed by the historian due to the smallness of its practical effects, or to
the smallness of the country in which it takes place, offers us unique fundamental insights. See *Macauley's Essay on Sir William Temple,* New York, 1878, and Max Weber,
"Roscher und Knies und die logischen Probleme der historischen Nationalökonomie.
1903-1906" [Roscher and Knies and the Logical Problems of Historical Economics. 1903-
1906] in *Gesammelte Aufsätze zur Wissenschaftslehre* [Collected Essays on the Theory
of Science], Tübingen 1922.

cultures foreign in time or place by the narrow horizon of the moral and material interests of one's own culture; we ought not project our - even if logical -
standards onto foreign cultures, as the sociologically uneducated of all ages -
not only the 18th century - are always inclined to do.

But because this view implies that foreign cultures are still accessible
somehow and in some sense to us, the attempt to provide the analytical means
for their interpretation can fail at most in individual cases; it cannot in principle
be pointless. Whether these means are different every time, or are always the
same, is a mere question of fact which only practical work can solve, not philosophizing. Certainly, money is very different in the mind and behavior of people
of different cultures. It may be difficult or impossible to reduce its *cultural meaning* for different times to a common denominator. But this kind of meaning is
not what matters with the science of money. It is rather - if we must speak of
"meaning" - about *that* meaning that lies in the *function* of money in the economic life process. For *this* meaning, the *other* is only relevant as it influences
the actual behavior of people in relation to money, and the question as to
whether it is possible to comprehend the elements of the cultural world that are
essential to explain events in monetary history is a factual one, answerable only
in the individual case.

An example: if the object which fulfills the function of money is a sacred
object at the same time, and disposal of it is subject to ritual requirements, the
money transactions of the relevant community will not only look different culturally than they would otherwise, but also economically. For example, the tendency as far as possible to retain pieces of this object may be unreasonable in
terms of "mere" economics but nevertheless may take on dimensions very important to the course of events. But this also exhausts the relevance of that mentality or culture in this case. As important as further analytic penetration might
otherwise be, *in terms of monetary theory* we have nothing to gain here. And
because our analytical apparatus works in the same way with such a case as with
all others, and for the treatment of such a case one must only take care that, in
addition to the other concrete data which can always be "inserted" in a theoretical train of thought, the actual effect that the sacred character of the money-
good has on the behavior of the people is taken into account - therefore there
arises from such a factual situation no argument for "epoch-bound" theories
against "general" theories.

But the shape of monetary relationships can be so different from epoch
to epoch, that it would be virtually nugatory separately to put forward a "general" theory restricted to meaningless generalities. At first glance, matters really
do so stand - what does bank-transfer payment have in common with Homer's

"cattle accounting"? Furthermore, some manners of apprehension accord with individual historical conditions so much better than others that one might be tempted to call the former "correct" and the latter "wrong." Hence, a theory of money could very well take the form of conceptual processing of "types" of successive historical conditions. This would provide us with a list of monetary theories appropriate to these styles. And that would bring not only the historic qualification of our subject but also the practical problems of each era very clearly and vividly to expression.

It could not then so easily come to pass, as it sometimes does, that one extends the analysis of a peculiar set of circumstances [Verumständungen] to other sets of circumstances that do not present the same features, such as in the discussion of the transfer problem in today's Germany, in which one argues as if international relations in trade and in automatic gold movements exhaust the subject as they did a hundred years ago, and overlooks the movements of short-term capital - to mention just one aspect. If we wished to proceed in this manner, we would find that we actually had to repeat a lot of things each time and, moreover, that we would be repeating precisely the theoretical essence of the matter, the principle of understanding, and the most important lever of analysis.

For example, we could not say that the intrinsic value of the money material in 10th century Germany pertained to the essence of money, and that of 20th century Germany did not; rather, it would turn out that this feature either *always* is part of the essence of money or it *never* is, although it may very well be true that if we knew of no other circumstances than those of 10th century Germany, we would not have come up with the idea that there could be "materially worthless" money.[2] Also note that this has nothing to do with the question of whether intrinsic value of the substance of which money is made was not perhaps practically indispensable. This question might be answered in the affirmative. For the people of that time, another kind of money might have been incomprehensible and unusable in traffic, although this is not to say that this was in fact the case. It does not follow that the theoretical interpretation of the money of that economic world would have to go through the feature of material value. In passing, one should be made aware of the great importance in monetary policy of distinguishing between "virtually unavoidable" and "theoretically essential." The monetary policy of today, for example, as we shall see, for all

---

[2] The insight of the persons actually involved is entirely indifferent altogether. For example, the - not very valuable - income concept is directly applicable to the economy of the German early Middle Ages, despite the fact that, according to Bücher, those then living did not have it.

practical purposes cannot easily forego the connection of each currency with gold. Should the monetary policy of a single country do that, it would undoubtedly open up a source of inconveniences. But that does not mean that it would belong to the essence of money to be made *of* gold or be connected *with* gold.[3] This refutation does not however dispose of the practical point of view unless the latter is based on nothing more than this theoretical conviction - which hardly occurs.

Historical Versus Logical Priority

2. The second question is: must we not, in view of the fact that modern monetary and credit transactions are rather complicated, and the additional fact that they have *developed* from primitive and historically early conditions, go back to the historical, ethnological, prehistoric "origins" of money, as the natural starting point of our analysis? One might call it the question of the relation of historical and logical priority.

Of course we must expand our factual material in space and time as much as we can. But he who investigates the historical and pre-historical "beginnings" of the monetary system in the hope that the nature of the case would there automatically present itself to him in its purest and simplest form, is in danger of going wrong in three different directions. First, in the historical and sociological study of social institutions one tends to supplement the material of prehistory with ethnological material, in the assumption that the conditions of primitive peoples today are similar to relics of our past. This assumption can be made only with special precautions. The primitive or poor culture of today has a past behind it, during which it was pushed farther and farther into ever more necessitous environments; it is run down and may have acquired "primitivisms" that were not previously its own. But apart from that it is a prejudice to believe that the historically antecedent or the culturally more primitive on the face of it is logically simpler and less complicated.

This can best be shown with an example: if one wishes to approach more closely to the essence of the modern entrepreneur by tracing the historical type, one soon lands in a social condition in which the entrepreneur seems to be miss-

---

[3]The name *"metallism"* has become common for this view (Knapp). Thus we see that we have cause to distinguish this, *theoretical* metallism, from that monetary expediency that we wish to call *practical* metallism. *These have nothing in common and can be represented independently.*

ing. In fact, however, the essential function is not missing, but only lacks embodiment in a particular type of economic agent. It becomes an element of a unified social leader-position that combines military, often priestly, judicial, and administrative functions. But in order to understand this factual relation and to recognize the element of entrepreneurship in, e.g., a chieftain in the primitive horde, one must otherwise have gained clarity regarding the theory. And even then, for primitive conditions it is not a simple but a complex factual situation that exists. Only with time does the entrepreneurial function gain sharper contours. But even a hundred years ago, we find this function being combined with the capitalist function with such regularity that the earlier theory almost ubiquitously threw both together, apparently even believing that the latter function was the key. In this case, therefore, the nature of the thing has emerged only in the course of history, and the modern manifestations of it in particular are logically the purest and factually the simplest. Of course, conversely, one should not assume that this is always the case. Rather, logical and historical "development"[4] must always be kept apart in principle. And since it is not obvious from the outset that the historical sequence must show all possible or any significant or interesting features of the object in all its purity, it does not justify the expectation that fundamental understanding must arise as a necessary by-product of historical perspective.

Applied to our case: if one has the *theoretical* view that money in its essence is a commodity which is also used as a medium of exchange, and also has the *cultural-historical* view that money "originally" presents itself as such a commodity, then one states that the "essential" form of money is historically the oldest too. Such a conjunction is sociologically interesting. But from the standpoint of practical analytical work, in itself it is quite *by accident*. Such a theoretical view can have as little regard for the possible cultural and historical fact as can a cultural-historical assumption be based on that theoretical view. No monetary theory may refuted by demonstrating the falsity of any claims by its author regarding the early history of money, nor can any be proven correct by demonstrating the accuracy of such claims by its author.[5] And the historical

---

[4]This word is here intended in an entirely unphilosophical, and above all non-emanatistic, manner. Furthermore, one must always distinguish between the history of factual developments and the contemporary perspective regarding those developments, thereby continually posing the question as to whether the same word indicates the same situation in each case.

[5]The juxtaposition of the genetic and the analytic problem is characteristic of all monetary research, up to and including Menger.

condition that is to be considered the "basic form" – if any – for each researcher results from his theoretical knowledge, not vice versa. The view here held to has already been indicated. In terms of this view, it is precisely the primitive forms of money that appear complicated, veiling the essence of the matter the most thickly. And precisely *that* commerce that uses a commodity to fulfill the functions of money theoretically presents the greatest aberration of reality from the "essence of the matter" that there is.

Yet we must beware of rejecting the thought process of all the authors who have fallen into the error alleged here, merely for that reason. Rather, in each case it is a question of fact as to what is invalidated by this error. But we must also beware of attributing the alleged error to every author whose presentation looks as if it has fallen into it. That would be to misunderstand a manner of presentation that in the past was very common in our science. Just as it would be unfathomably unintelligent to object to the epic form of expression of social utopias or social scientific knowledge, that once was so popular and so attractive, [simply] because the things in question have never taken place "like that," so also, regarding the form of expression of social scientific knowledge that has developed from the epic form and has maintained itself with us for an unduly long period, [is the objection] that one ought not make an assertion about cultural-historical conditions because an assumption is clothed in pseudo-historical forms.[6] Even if an author [mistakenly] *believes* he is expressing a factually tenable assertion, the content can still be useful in the character of an assumption for the purpose of constructing a simple factual situation and for the separation of different logical stages of the presentation.

Exploring the History of Money

3. Through this insight, the problem of the genetic origin of money loses nothing of its sociological, socio-psychological, and cultural-historical significance, but much of its monetary-theoretical significance. The observations that we nonetheless have to make, we insert here. In addition, we refer to the

---

[6]This also applies to constructions such as Rousseau's *Social Contract*. Furthermore, Robinson Crusoe only represented a not entirely flattering concession to the comprehension of the reader.

literature, of which for the purposes of economists the best introduction is still Menger, and among recent authors in particular Burns.[7]

First we need to determine to which phenomena in the economies of primitive ages we want to appeal as historical sources of later money economies. For expediency's sake, we proceed to the four functions of money which the doctrine of the 19th century, especially the British doctrine, distinguished and put at the head of their discussions. Some or all of them are meant by the historian, anthropologist, paleontologist, when discussing the origins of money. These functions are: medium of exchange, standard of value, standard of performance, and store of value.

Medium of Exchange

a) Where exchange transactions take place, although we do not always see it, already in very primitive cases goods are taken and given in exchange, in which the receiving end is not used up or consumed but is used for further exchange. If we ask why this happens, there can be only one answer: because it is apparently so efficient[8] that it continues, under the influence of progressing experience, during the course of millennia, wherever there is regular exchange with

---

[7]Carl Menger, "Geld" [Money], in *Handwörterbuch der Staatswissenschaften* [Concise Dictionary of State Sciences], vol. IV, 3rd ed., Jena 1909, pp. 565 ff.; Arthur Robert Burns, *Money and Monetary Policy in Early Times,* New York, 1927. [For a treatment taking into account the latest research, see Ruben Alvarado, *Follow the Money: The Money Trail Through History* (Aalten: WordBridge, 2013.]

[8]Note that without "indirect" exchange, barter exchange could not lead to the otherwise achievable maximum benefit for all parties involved. As an example, if we have three products, A, B, C, which can only be exchanged directly, and whereby thus only two are ever interchangeable with each other, it creates three "markets" where a ratio between two goods is formed, independent of the ratios on the other two markets. Therefore, it could occur that, if we call the units of goods a, b, and c, on "market" I 3a is traded against 2b; on market II, 3a against 1c; and on market III, 4b against 1c. But then the owner of 4b, who wants to have c, will apparently be better off if, instead of acquiring 1c for his 4b on the market of b for c, he first enters market I, where he initially gives 6a for 4b, which he does not wish to have, but on market II he gets 2c for it - this is the essence of arbitrage. If our man could not do this, he would not only suffer the discomfort mentioned above, but a *loss of utility*. Walras was the first to raise awareness of this. The use of the word "arbitrage" in the discussion of a process in a primitive tribe illustrates the distinction between "function meaning" and "cultural meaning," which to overlook has so often led to irrelevant objections.

more than two goods. Note: When we say that it must be very time consuming, inconvenient, and often impossible to find an exchange partner who has just what you need, and needs just what you have, which is why *indirect exchange* became established and is maintained, whereby one assumes that what one does not need, or not in these quantities, but which one yet may expect to sell against what one really wants to have – we do not attribute to the primitives antecedent knowledge regarding the usefulness of the process, and absolutely no conscious rationality, or even a particular decision-making capacity, just as little as we attribute to a bee colony the knowledge of the geometrical properties of the honeycomb cell. Nor is an "invention" of money in question.

Precisely for this reason we understand *that* this practice became established without yet knowing *how* it became established. This is an entirely different question, a part of the great complex of questions that attaches to the origin of all social institutions. Just as unjustified objections to the answer to the first question on the basis of our – the observers' – understanding of the needs and advantages of the economic situation regarding self-developing barter arise from the fact that the objector only sees this latter question, so do unjustified claims regarding the former question arise from the claimant overlooking the presence of and independent significance of the latter. An example of this situation from a different field: if we ask *why* the domestication and breeding of domestic animals has come about and why this practice has maintained itself, the answer can of course only be that the products and services of domestic animals have crucially enriched the economic process. But with this realization nothing is gained regarding the question of *how* animal husbandry came about. For it is not only not certain but not even likely that prior knowledge of these benefits led to it, if only because the entire extent only afterwards manifested itself and could not have been foreseen. The original motive of domestication must therefore have been different from that which later became decisive for retaining and expanding the custom. Only in the path of a function transformation, based on experience with previously tamed animals, could domestic animals be enlisted in their later economic roles (E. Hahn). And inasmuch as all thinking of primitives is tinged with the sacred, it is very reasonable to assume that the original motive was rooted in religious beliefs and that religious commandments and prohibitions mediated the closer acquaintance with certain species, which constituted the precondition for the discovery and exploitation of serviceableness. Nevertheless, within the bounds of a particular problem the fact of this serviceableness remains a valid and necessary explanation, which no reference to sacred aspects can replace.

In the case of money we further understand that the use of highly *mar-ketable* or *salable* goods, i.e., those that everyone more or less can use or wishes to have, become customary in indirect exchange and that such goods gradually become recognized as a medium of exchange without express agreement or legislative compulsion, even without any consideration for the common interest (Menger, p. 558). We observe as well that, in each case, such goods take their place as media of exchange that are especially popular in the economic situation in question, such as furs – including scalps – ivory, coral, slaves, pets, salt, mats, tools, tea, tobacco, amber, cacao beans, bananas, glass beads, dyes, grain, rice, pieces of metal,[9] or even simple tools such as knives, axes, etc. It is quite beside the point, which circumstances aid the medium of exchange to gain its preferred position: the circumstance, for example, that it is a popular national product or a preferred subject of importation and not domestically produced, or, by contrast, is a staple article of export. In all these cases, which are not restricted to particular areas or specific races, the medium of exchange owes its function to its own economic importance, which undeniably is independent of the medium of exchange function itself.

A doubt in this direction is only possible with jewelry objects.[10] That is to say, while a different type of use or consumption immediately presents its explanation, a jewelry object still raises the question as to why it is considered a piece of jewelry. And here it could happen that by first performing the medium of exchange function, it attains a *distinguished position,* in particular a *distin-*

---

[9]Bronze pieces from about the fourth millennium B.C. onward. The most important cases are from Egypt, China, Babylon. Later, lead, gold, silver, iron, among others, occur; gold sooner than silver; iron mainly in Greece.

[10]In general, objects of socio-psychological note, and cultural objects, or those that imply social distinction. In itself, it should be stressed again that for the economic "why" – as opposed to the cultural and historical "how" – this question is completely irrelevant. It is not even alleged that the medium of exchange function developed using profane goods or commodities serving the satisfaction of "material" needs. *Sacred character* would explain valuation and thus *goods* character as well as, e.g., suitability as food. Also in another sense the "barter exchange" theory of the genesis of money is independent *of,* and compatible *with,* a religious aspect: to wit, one can be of the opinion that money essentially served to facilitate trade exchange and *therefore* arose, and *at the same time* corresponded to a divine command – as can be read in St. Thomas Aquinas.

guished significance. A use function based only on the medium of exchange function would of course not be suitable to explain the latter.[11] Such a case may be with the use of shells, especially cowries, which have been found in Paleolithic remains, and which continues an extraordinarily long life in coin form that simulates the shape of the shell, and in linguistic relics. With modern-day primitives, the jewelry meaning is sometimes entirely lacking – as in the complex system of shell money of Rossel Island[12] – which of course does not prove that it was always lacking in these cases.

Despite this limitation – a very important one; in fact, the only important one – the supporting documentation for this view of the genesis of money is of such overwhelming abundance that we need to understand its life force, especially if we bear in mind that the differences and controversies between the different varieties of this view do not affect their basic ideas. In addition, at least important cases of barter exchange, in which one might be tempted to deny the importance of the commodity meaning of *exchange media* and to speak of a *token form of money,* clearly refer back to earlier commodity meanings. Hence, according to Max Weber, there was *fur money* in Russia, pieces of fur without utility; but the idea that this fur money *without* use value refers back to fur money *with* use value, suggests itself too quickly for it to prove more than that *materially worthless* forms of money do exist, which is not relevant here and which we knew anyway – in the manner that, according to what has been said, Weber's classification[13] (jewelry money – use money – clothes money – fiat money) is of no fundamental importance generally.

The biggest impression is made by the fate of the most important ethnological example of a pure fiat money without any goods-meaning which has yet been put forward by the doctrine of money. The natives of the Portuguese colony of Angola used a value token in their internal transactions, called the *macute* by European observers, which seemed to lack any commodity significance. The writers on money of the 18th century, including Montesquieu and Steuart, put

---

[11]Cf. a similar circular argument *apparently* committed by marginal utility theorists: money has use value, because it has exchange value, and has exchange value because it has precisely *that very* use value.

[12]Cf. W.E. Armstrong, "Rossel Island Money: A Unique Monetary System," in *Economic Journal,* vol. 34, London 1924, pp. 423 ff. Regarding China, cf. Chi Zang Waung, "The Ancient Coins and Currency of China," in *Economic Journal,* vol. 23, London 1913, pp. 524 ff.

[13]Max Weber, *Wirtschaftsgeschichte* [History of Economics], edited by Siegmund Hellmann and Melchior Palyi, Munich-Leipzig, 1924, p. 211.

the greatest emphasis on this, and even Mill held the macute to be an authentic case of a conventional unit of a pure money of account. But it now seems clear[14] that the macute originally was a garment, thus that it represented a typical case of commodity money, and only gradually was reduced to an unusable piece of cotton material or mat, which was eventually incorporated into the Portuguese right of coinage, first simply by affixing a stamp to the material, and then by replacing this material with a coin - so that the historical connection to a commodity money is given here, completely sufficient in *this* context.[15]

So, as things stand, not only must the genesis of money from barter be considered a safe bet, but also (which is a separate issue), so must the development of the medium of exchange function from the respective particular marketable commodity be as well. Perhaps even greater is the success of this view over that regarding the piece of metal prepared for transaction purposes - the coin - which the spirit of language later in many cases considered to be actual money (cf. the Latin *moneta* with its French, Italian, Spanish, Portuguese and English derivatives, the Russian *denjgi*, the Hungarian *penz,* etc.). Not only do coin denominations and coin images often refer to goods meanings - again: *such symbolism* does not contradict, but rather speaks for the emergence of money from the most marketable commodity - and not only did coinage often traceably replace commodity money used in earlier times in the same place, but even the conversion of commodity money into coin is traceable step by step.

Current unit-amounts of the exchange metals is the necessary precondition [Prius]. The next step, which can be traced in Mesopotamia and Egypt, is the appearance of officially standardized weights and their determination by officials. Then the old practice of marking [markieren] contracts by pressing a seal was transferred to the marking [Bezeichnen] of metal pieces. This seal initially was purely private: for example the seal of a merchant company, as with the Semitic *shekel* and the Chinese *tael.* The origin of this practice erroneously used to be put in the seventh century B.C., but recent finds of coins and charters in India, Egypt, and in Assyria and China as well, point back to much earlier times. Roundabout the Aegean sea, in the Greek sphere of influence, although

---

[14]Cf. A. Sommer, "Die Makute, ein Irrtum der Geldlehre" [The Macute, An Error of the Doctrine of Money], in: *Jahrbücher für Nationalökonomie und Statistik* [Annals for Economics and Statistics], vol. 131, Jena 1929/II. The author overestimates the significance of the erroneous conception of fact for the theoretical argument put forward by those writers.

[15]The theoretical problem as to whether such a connection is logically necessary, is certainly not advanced thereby.

not precisely first in Greece itself, the further step then took place: the more perfect treatment of the metal piece, and the monopolization of embossing by public authorities (the *monopoly of coinage* as the exclusive competence to reg-ulate the monetary system, namely to determine *coin weights* and *rates,* and the *prerogative of coinage* as an exclusive right to carry out the embossing). This is all just as one could want it to be from the standpoint of a representative of the view under discussion. But if we believe we thereby have gained something for the essence of money or even of coinage, then a serious derailment is on offer. On the other hand, the reluctance of newer and older researchers of money to *define* coins as stamped pieces of metal, and to see in the *die* only the official *declaration of fineness,* rests on an entirely appropriate feeling. But *historically* coins and dies were initially nothing else.

Objections only touch on side issues, when they are not simply based on misunderstandings or are completely useless, such as the one asserting that the account of the genesis of money provided here is rationalistic and individualistic and therefore is to be rejected from the outset. While all the same it still is not entirely satisfactory, this is because of a circumstance that may be called the original "subsidiary character" of indirect exchange. Despite what we said about the desirability (indeed - from a certain point of view - the necessity) of indirect exchange, it is not only analytically a *further* step, but also historically a *later* one. Real exchange trading may be conducted through long periods without there being an indirect exchange and the formation of an exchange-mediating good. Regarding primitive cases, the so-called "silent trade" comes mainly into consideration, as it occurs, e.g., between agricultural black peoples and hunting dwarf peoples on the Upper Congo today. Although the economic scheme of exchange fits it perfectly, it lacks the exchange agent. The practice of exchanging that which one wants to give directly against what one wants to have is still today entirely traceable and occurs even in Europe, as in the case of southern Portuguese farmers. Finally, international trade was originally only direct ex-change, which is still in service between peoples of very different stage of cul-ture, just as, back in the day, a trading nation like the Phoenicians did not stand out at all in the development of exchange mediators.

This firstly opens the possibility that with many peoples indirect ex-change only could have arisen using an exchange agent, and only long after this did the rest of the features that we are in the habit of connecting with money assert themselves. But apart from that, it should be noted that direct exchange is the more obvious, and indirect exchange may have come about in such a way that direct trade was the object every time and in principle, with the detour of

indirect exchange only taken when the direct way was impassable. And if indirect exchange initially was a makeshift, a *subsidiary means of commerce*, the
viewpoint that the original medium of exchange would have been the most marketable commodity would seem to take a back seat to the viewpoint that the
original medium of exchange would have been a material that one does not
gladly part with and only does so out of necessity. And this latter viewpoint
indicates hoarding and not exchange mediation as the "most original" function
from which the remaining ones may have evolved, although they became more
important, with exchange mediation in particular doubtlessly growing up into
the fundamental aspect.

Measure of Value

b) By "value" here is understood *exchange value* expressed in money.
Thus, its unit price, when we are dealing with the current unit quantity of a
good - a physical good or a service - or, if it has to do with something else than
the unit quantity, the price times amount. If one says that money is acting as a
"measure of value," one usually means in *this* context that the exchange ratios
of the goods with each other are replaced by the ratios between each of them
and money, so that money is a "means of expression of ratios" and the market
valuation given by those relations to that quantity of goods. Of course, the idea
that any quantity of goods contains an "exchange value amount" independent
of the actual acts of exchange, that itself determines the ratios, and that money
measures *this* exchange value, would be completely absurd - just as it actually
goes back to very primitive ideas.[16] But the money prices of market goods can
be referred to as measures of "exchange value" insofar as there are no exchange
values without exchange *acts* and ratios *established by those acts,* and yet those
exchange *ratios* are a real phenomenon, the existence of which is independent
of the intervention of money, and which only finds expression in money prices.
Taking our reasoning in the following chapters into consideration makes it desirable to clarify the concept of *this* "measure of value" and introduce the concept of a measure of value with another meaning.

Above all, then, the "measured" or "expressed" "exchange value" of a
quantity of commodity is *that quantity of a commodity times the price at which*

---

[16]Note, however, that when the market valuation is given of a good compared
with all other goods except one, and only the changes vis-a-vis this one are looked into,
then this manner of expression gains meaning.

it, in the period under review, is actually[17] *sold or could actually be sold* – possibly taking into account the condition that this sale changes the price that previously predominated. This is the only useful significance of the much-abused term "exchange value," which one is better off avoiding, and replacing with "price."

Sometimes, however, it also makes practical sense not to multiply the quantity of the product by the price as just defined, but rather by the actually prevailing market price, *without* regard to the fact that it would be different if this quantity of goods were offered. Thus, for example, for the purposes of calculating a wealth tax on a shareholding, a market price is chosen *without* regard to whether the shareholding could be disposed of at this price. It is not now our concern to inquire into the meaning of this. At any rate, that meaning is not the above-mentioned meaning.

After all, this was also a *real* price. But sometimes we operate with a mere proposed price or a range of proposed prices. Whoever thinks to himself that he would buy a car of a certain sort if it were to be had for 3000 marks, and two cars of this sort if the price were 2000 marks apiece, when in fact the price of the car is 4000 marks, in reality buys none at all. So what is the point of his reflections? Apparently, in practical terms firstly to clarify to himself his disposition in relation to *possible changes* in car prices – which is by no means a purposeless game, either in consumptive or in corporate behavior. But if we look more closely, we see that determining that a car of a certain kind is worth 3000 marks to a particular individual at a specific time, has yet a much broader and deeper meaning: at bottom it has as little to do with possible prices as with the actually prevailing price. It means nothing more than the attempt of the individual to clarify his *estimate of use value* of an automobile, *to quantify that use value.*

So we basically have also *left* the sphere of exchange values, even if furthermore the unit of the *means of quantification* is a means of expressing exchange value, and its significance in the minds of evaluating people is owing to this very fact. And we are *entering* a sphere in which there is a manifestation that does not, in the manner of "exchange value" critiqued above, arise only

---

[17]We will later learn a method by which one can separate such fluctuations from a time series in prices of certain goods. The thus "adjusted" prices are still the same "real" prices but are expressed in an unreal, "ideal" monetary unit. We call them *real prices* as opposed to the actual "listed" *nominal prices* mentioned above. "Nominal" has nothing to do, firstly, with nominalism; secondly, with the meaning of the English word "nominal;" thirdly, with "face value."

through the exchange act, but in principle is independent of the existence of any market transactions at all, and hence its measurement – whatever other difficulties it might have – *to that degree* does not display the same logical absurdity that sometimes is implied when one speaks of measuring "exchange value." *Not every magnitude expressed in money terms* that confronts us *is therefore a price magnitude* or a price multiplied by a quantity of a commodity. And we are now talking of a "measure of value" in an entirely different sense, and allow associations with the idea of a price at best entirely to lapse. "Measure of value" in this sense – for those of us who disapprove of the term "measure of exchange value," it is the real meaning – signifies the practice of *life* and the practice of *science* attaching to life, *ascribing numerical quantities to subjective value feelings or objectively visible manners of behavior* in such a way that the object of value feelings or behavior is compared with a number of units of any other object of value feelings or behavior, and through this comparison is *set in relation to all objects of value feelings or behaviors lying within the field of vision of the observing subject.* The actors that we are observing, and we, the observers, gain by this method *quantitative indices of value and behavior*, that apparently are of the utmost importance to the rationalization of action itself, and to our consideration of that action, on the same level of significance as language and writing.[18]

We have here touched upon a very controversial issue, or actually two. Both are repeatedly hinted at in our thought process. One is: how can we think of "measuring" "value feelings" (= assigning numerical magnitudes to them), which are not "magnitudes," or at least not "extensity magnitudes," but at most

---

[18]Above all, the question of the relationship of the economic measure to other measures suggests one regarding *measuring* and *counting* generally. First, there are interesting parallels: the use of length, volume, tempo, and weight units is preceded by the exercise of raw comparisons, such as the showing of the hollow of one's hand, the phrase "the time it takes to tell two brothers apart" or the phrase "the distance at which one can just distinguish the horns of an ox." The use of *direct* units of measure *follows* the use of derived ("absolute") units with the help of the relation between "immeasurable" processes and "measurable" objects – *dimension.* This teaches much about the sometimes alleged "essential difference" between *comparing* and *measuring.* But of even more importance is the consideration that the occasions that taught primitive measuring and counting must have been primarily economic. And the assumption follows closely, that measurement in general could have penetrated the cultural world of mankind via the economic side rather than vice versa, the economic measure representing a late and dubious transfer of a "physical" way of thinking.

only *intensity magnitudes?* The other: how can we think of making this measurement with the aid of money, this creature of exchange transactions that gains its meaning only through such transactions? Even these questions contain preconceived - and erroneous - opinions both regarding *this* problem of measuring and about the nature of measurement generally, from which one must free oneself if one is to make progress within the ambit of these issues. Here it is enough to say to the unprejudiced reader - as opposed to the expert predetermined by generic counter-arguments - that he holds in his hand that which matters, if he has ever in his life said "I would give 100 marks not to have to go to those boring dinner parties." The currently most important case of a scientific application and refinement of this method in practical life is the concept of *consumer surplus,* which, first envisioned by Dupuit, was rediscovered and introduced into the daily use of economic theory by Marshall.

The price someone pays for a specific quantity of a commodity can, of course, never be greater than the amount of money equaling the satisfaction expected from this quantity by the observed subject, to wit, 3000 marks for the automobile in the above example. This amount of money is equal to the price that the subject would pay for the car in the extreme case, *but itself it is not a price.* If the car can be had for 2500 marks, the difference 3000 - 2500 = 500 marks represents a measured value - if we continue for simplicity's sake to use a psychological expression of not quite indubitable correctness - of the net gain in satisfaction which attaches to this application of 2500 marks as compared with yet other possible uses thereof. This measured value is called *consumer surplus.* We now assume that each considered *potential* outlay relative to the subject's total budget is so small that through them, even if they would be made in full amount - the consumer surplus would then be equal to zero - the importance of the individual mark for the subject is not changed significantly, and that each good is perfectly divisible - in the case of goods such as the car, it means that we break it down into individual services rendered, which one could also purchase individually, e.g., by renting a car for a single journey. Hence we clarify with Marshall[19] - and thus also, as is easily seen, with Gossen's law of the satiation of want - in the following way.

---

[19] Alfred Marshall, *Principles of Economics,* 1st edition, London-New York 1890, ch. VI.

Take, for example, a household that buys tea *in each budget period.*[20] Observation teaches that in the extreme case, the household is willing to buy a pound of tea for 20 marks, but only *one* pound *per budget period.* Obviously the behavior of the household or, psychologically speaking, its valuation of tea in the special place of "first pound per budget period" is thereby characterized, quantified, *or measured.* Observation further teaches that the same household under the same circumstances would rather pay 14 marks for a second pound of tea *per budget period* than go without *that second pound.* This teaches us the same thing about its estimate for the second or for a "behavior" regarding the second pound as does the first observation of its estimate regarding the first pound *per budget period.* But it teaches us nothing more regarding its estimate of the first pound per budget period, as if, say, this estimate would be affected by the consumption of the second pound: under our assumption, the estimate *even* for the first pound remains the same as what *it* [i.e., the subjective estimate] was, and its numeric expression what *it* was.[21]

Although the household would spend 28 marks on tea and no more if the price actually were 14 marks, these 28 marks still are not the measure by which it acts. This follows indeed from the consideration that under our conditions the household would pay 20 marks for a pound, if that was the actual price, and that it would then buy yet another pound at 14 marks should the price drop *unexpectedly* to 14 marks: if, for example, the household had to deal with a monopolist asking 20 marks per pound, who also gave his customers to understand that he would maintain this price, then our household would buy the pound of tea at this price; should the monopolist nevertheless turn around and lower his price to 14 marks, he would indeed be able to pry 34 marks from the household, which is only curious to us because, in the consideration of successive purchases from inadvertently falling prices, we are used to each preceding purchase at higher prices having an effect on the significance the buyer attaches to each individual mark.

Continuing in this manner, we observe for instance that the household would pay at most 10 marks for a third pound of tea per budget period - which practically means that it would buy three pounds and no more at a price of 10

---

[20]The highlighted addition is needed to avert one of the most unintelligent objections raised against this method, namely the objection that the utility of the consumption of cups of tea diminishes equally every day, and not, say, from 1 January to 31 December!

[21]All the same, the *fact* that, for a given total consumption, the scale or curve of value estimates of the subsets is different than it would be for a *different* total consumption, is not therefore denied.

marks per pound – that it would sacrifice six marks for a fourth pound, four marks for a fifth, three marks for a sixth, etc. If, for example, the actual price is 4 marks, the household would buy five pounds for a total of 20 marks and receive something whose welfare significance [Wohlfahrtsbedeutung] is given by the sum 20 + 14 + 10 + 4 + 6 = 54 marks, putting the consumer surplus at 54 - 20 = 34 marks.[22] It is easily seen that this approach indeed uses price magnitudes in the discussed case, but in principle proceeds from something that is not a price, and would make sense in a closed economy, except that the dimension of the sacrifice compared to the measure of the quantity of satisfaction would not coincide with actual prices paid, as it does (misleadingly) in this case.

The reader is asked thoroughly to master this most important tool of analysis by making a careful study of Marshall's presentation.[23] Here reference can be made only to one point. Applying the presented procedure step by step to all consumer goods that enter into the budget of a household, and adding up the results, one comes first to the result ∞. This is quite natural, because to all the income assets taken together, including the possible replacement goods that come into consideration, even the survival of the household, there attaches a value that does not correspond to any finite magnitude. Therefore, we wish[24] to leave the subsistence level out of consideration and restrict our attention to the remainder of income. But apart from that there is the following apparent absurdity: our household receives an income of 10,000 marks per budget period, from which we deduct 2000 marks as subsistence wage. The remaining 8000 marks are used by the household for consumptive purchases of, say, a hundred

---

[22]The 54 marks give the measure of the *total utility value* or total value (*total utility*). The 20 marks are the outlay in the example above. But not merely this: rather, this expression is comparable to the total value expression only in a different meaning, namely the meaning of foregone utility [Nutzentgang] – another welfare quantity calculated in money. The independence of *this* meaning emerges when we assume that this family receives, e.g., 6 pounds per year as a gift. In that case, for them this amount would be equal to 18 marks *regardless* of the actual price of tea, leaving resale possibilities out of consideration. J. Fisher has given the name *utility value* to this magnitude. It is identical to Wieser's total value concept, which, however, we do not adopt.

[23]This representation is an approximation method. Great analytical difficulties stand in the way of advancing beyond it, which, however, do not interest us here, and do not upset the practical usefulness of the method.

[24]We do not *have* to do that. But if we did not, we could not attribute any psychological sense to the sum of consumer surpluses, which is not necessary (and never correct), but fitting in terms of presentation.

different items. We perform for each of these the described treatment, and so calculate one hundred consumer surpluses. Of each of these, the phrase is often used that they constitute an amount that the household would be willing to spend on the particular good in the extreme case beyond which it actually spends for it - hence a "savings," in a non-technical sense of the word, with which it buys other goods.

If one takes this view, it follows that the addition of these savings on all items purchased is wholly meaningless. The household does not put this sum aside but always applies what is "saved" in this sense on *one* article, to actually intended outlays for *other* articles. Hence the belief has arisen that, if not the concept of consumer surplus of each good, yet the notion of a sum of consumer surpluses of *the same household* leads to *absurdity*. For this reason, the question has been raised as to what it means then, if our household actually spends 8000 marks and, what's more, has no more to spend, that it realizes an "income" of, we said, 30,000 marks, and also that, although in reality it can "save" nothing, yet can boast of a "savings" of 22,000 marks. Besides the fact that the word "save" is used here in two different senses, the absurdity disappears immediately when we remember the true meaning of our method. Those consumer surpluses, which add up to zero, are not at all what it is about. In fact it is not about real prices and real money income or expenses as situated in the ties [Ligamen] of markets and money circulation, but only the use of the *value proposition that attaches to the unit of the relevant income,* for the quantification of magnitudes of demand or welfare, or of *indices of behavior.* Any other entity the substrate of which does not fill the other functions of money, would be just as suitable. And, so as to distinguish things that fundamentally differ from each other, we would have carried out such a separation of the unit of account and the unit of circulation, if it had not been a question, precisely for didactic purposes, of separating these things in complex factual situations and in the misleading terminology of practice and science.

If ones realizes this, then there is nothing strange in the phrase that the 8000 marks that our household pays for consumption above its subsistence level produces a welfare magnitude to which - taking the commercial importance of this mark[25] as a unit - the number 30,000 is assigned, although the household

---

[25]This utility or welfare meaning of a mark certainly presumes a given purchasing power and therefore already existing prices. But it is essential in order to understand our argument to realize that the presence of prices is not essential for such measurement, and thus is not a *necessary prerequisite for any quantification of values,* although the established exchange economy, *after the fact* and *accidentally,* seems to produce such a factual

would be in a very different situation if it really had an income that exceeded the subsistence level by 30,000 marks. One should note that this use of each unit of money as a unit of account – in contrast to its use as a calculation unit in the conduct of business – in itself is not dependent on the assumptions we have made above, namely that each considered value magnitude is too small, in case it is paid out, noticeably to change the meaning of the monetary unit for the paying household. Nor is the disposal over actual money in the appropriate amount necessary to perform these estimations, nor does every change in the meaning need to be taken into account, when the meaning of a statement can be put in the following form: "I consider a certain welfare gain to be of equal value to a hundred times the welfare magnitude that the possession of an apple would assure me under the condition that all other apples which otherwise would have entered into my consumption combination, are secured to me any-way." In such a context, as we might also express it, one hundred apples or marks are equal to one hundred times an apple or a mark. They aren't that any longer when it comes to actually giving them away, because, strictly speaking, of the progressively greater importance of the second apple or mark to me, up until the hundredth, which one may sometimes, but not always and not in prin-ciple, disregard.

Finally, two remarks on this important subject. First, although we have now gotten to know a measurement method for economic affairs, it is obvious that this measurement method is extremely imperfect. If it is used, in particular, with a unit that has a commodity meaning, then the metrics that it delivers are entirely beholden to the fluctuations in value of this commodity and therefore cannot be compared over time. In addition, the metrics that it provides for the same location and the same time are incomparable across different households. This, to begin with, for the reason that the tastes of different families are different and because it can never be determined whether the unit used by different evaluative subjects in some sense has "the same" meaning; furthermore, for the reason that the economic situation of different families is different and they therefore evaluate differently – even if their tastes were exactly the same and this state of affairs could be ascertained satisfactorily. Indeed, the long series of objections that are raised against the idea of a utility or welfare measurement divide into objections which deny the *fundamental* possibility of such measure-ment and those which deny the *technical* possibility. But the job of the re-searcher is not to derive the "impossibility" of this or that goal from general

---

situation. For one does not need to choose a unit that first is given meaning by market transactions. The apple values mentioned below are an example of this.

considerations, and to rejoice that the matter is settled, but rather to contend with the difficulties. Similar to what was already noted about converting, in *one* specific sense, quantities that historically are incomparable into quantities that are comparable, so here our purpose is to draw attention to the task of converting the quantities with which we just dealt, and which in yet *another* sense are incomparable, into comparable quantities. At this point we only note that our measurement method only has meaning *within one and the same household* and only *for a given condition;* strictly speaking, that is, *for a single point in time.*

Second, we wish to recall the old controversy, mainly though not exclusively relevant to the measure of the value function of money, namely the controversy over the question of whether there could be a "value-free unit of value." Of course, this does not mean that the unit of our metrics, which enables them to come into existence, must comprise something that *embodies* an economic value. For units of account do not need to be physically present.[26] Rather, it is only a question of whether it is essential for the unit of measurement to be associated with the unit of a good or multiple goods. This in turn is not equivalent to the question as to whether the unit must have a value-meaning: no sensible man can ever deny that. Also it is clear that *historically* a use value unit, while unrelated to an object without *exchange value,* yet not easily unrelated to an object without - independent of the measurement function - meaning in itself (this meaning certainly does not also have to be a use-value significance in the narrowest sense) could come into existence, as could an "exchange value unit" without reference to an object with its own marketability, independent of its role as exchange mediator. Whether it is *logically* impossible that the unit in one of these meanings, or both, *arose,* or *existed,* apart from association with certain goods, will come up later.

The measure of the value function of money in its second and proper sense is thus basically independent of the medium of exchange function.[27] It can manifest itself apart from this and vice versa, and one thing can be a medium of exchange at the same time that another can be a measure of value. Nevertheless,

---

[26]Although it is a common opinion, this is not true for entirely primitive states: the primitive must physically have the items in front of him that he will be counting, although he soon takes that step of abstraction consisting in replacing these objects with his fingers and toes.

[27]If however one only *calls* "money" *that* which acts as a medium of exchange and is convinced of the historical priority of the latter function, then the measure of value function, when met by money in this sense, becomes an accessory function of *this* money. This has only terminological significance. Do not be led astray!

it is equally clear that the exchange act is such an important *occasion* for the quantification of economic deliberation that the use of a customary measure of value may very well historically have developed from the use of an exchange intermediary – as it is also clear that over time the medium of exchange and the measure of value tend to coalesce. Our finding that money does not have a single function, nor a main and a secondary function, but at least two equal functions, does not in itself speak against the concept of a historical priority of exchange mediation. It is only good as a counterargument against this insofar as proponents argue that the priority of exchange mediation was the only possible course, or even fundamentally deny the possibility of any other kind of economic quantification than the pricing principle.

Thinking of the words "measure of value" in their first and usual meaning, it is admittedly extraordinarily suggestive to see this historically and logically as only a derivative of exchange mediation, because the application of *such* a value or price measure or *price indicator* (Menger) presupposes the existence of money prices. But even that is not strictly correct. Rather it only presupposes the existence of exchange ratios, which can be very well expressed by the choice of a good as common denominator even without this changing hands in exchange *mediation.* Also, the individual exchange does not need to use this good, and certainly not a particular individual good. For in that case the money price would only be created by using the "measure of value" in this sense, and cease being its prerequisite.[28]

We have reason to leave open the possibility of the historically independent emergence of money as a measure of value in the sense of "price meter," in which the historically prior origin, while not necessary, is implied as another possibility. If we, the observers, understand that, with regard to the medium of exchange function, a very marketable good is suited to it, then we also understand that, with regard to the measure of value function as well, one and only one good is expedient for it, and indeed only in this way can it effectively correlate all economic variables. Even so, we also understand that, for the consciousness of the actors, it is not necessary either for the measurement of welfare or for the expression of the price that the good which is most marketable, or promises to be so, obtrude itself. The procedure is to be thought of like the process

---

[28]Menger (*loc. cit.*, p. 600) was therefore wrong in his assertion that "the function of money as a 'measure of exchange value' (and price meter) developed of *necessity* from the original function of money as a mediator of the commodity market and therefore everywhere attained its appearance with the emergence of means of exchange"; consequently also in his polemic against Wagner (*ibid.,* p. 601, note).

of acclimatizing a medium of exchange: as gradual and arational. "Measure of value" is that which imposes itself as such. If a medium of exchange already exists and exchange transactions already play a large enough role, then the measure of value could easily enough be the medium of exchange. But only then. Otherwise the notion of a particularly important asset object would appear, even if it is not a medium of exchange.

Now then, this consideration fits very well with one of the most important cases of primitive "money," namely the custom - which we encounter very early, as well as in later documents referring back to early conditions - of expressing services by specifying a number of *cattle*, and by giving an idea of the value of an object by equating it to a number of cattle. Linguistic relics (*pecunia*, the Gothic *faihu*, the Indian *rupya*) and images on coins testify to the extremely wide geographical and historical scope of this exercise. However, proof that cattle went from hand to hand in exchange transactions is lacking. It is not likely. Laum[29] has pointed out that the cow's suitability for this does not readily make sense - although this argument only has full force in those cases in which daily exchange also includes small quantities of goods as part of the normal economic process. In addition, primitives do not voluntarily part with cattle, the most prized possession from the Neolithic era onward, any more than they slaughter cattle. Primitive nomadic herdsmen stole cattle, paid fines and tribute in cattle if they had to, but they conducted a trade in cattle as little as they ate beef. All in all, it would be far from them to make cattle the article of trade par excellence [κατ᾽ ἐξοχὴν]. Thus, if cattle played a role - which is certain - then this could only be as the measure of value in the sense of exchange value, perhaps also in the sense of use value[30] (cf. incidentally point c. below). In this context the primitive custom is not uninteresting, of expressing in exchange ratios units of one good but accepting equivalent values in other goods. The previously mentioned macute is an example, which is not nullified by the likewise mentioned misinterpretation. Should, as has been reported,[31] a slave be sold, the price is initially

---

[29]Bernhard Laum, *Heiliges Geld* [Sacred Money], Tübingen 1924.

[30]In this context, the fact is interesting that it is often attempted - as in the Zend Avesta - to mitigate the shortcomings inherent in *cattle accounting* by clarifying the "unit" in terms of age and quality and bringing it into a fixed relation to other domestic animal units, and that one relates "money" or "other money," such as the Carolingian *solidus*, to cattle units of a certain quality - such as yearlings in autumn - as being of relatively stable value.

[31]*Dictionnaire Universel de Commerce* [Universal Dictionary of Commerce], edited by Jacques Savary, Copenhagen 1759-65; cited in Sommer, *loc. cit.*

set in macutes. Exchanged goods are then delivered, each likewise charged in macutes until the amount is completed. If one allows this report to sink in, one can easily see that it is not meaningless.

Standard of Deferred Payments

c) This immediately understandable expression apparently comprehends the remaining transactions, in addition to exchange mediation, in which money intervenes. Including under this title all payments that are not immediate payments for a commodity, we immediately encounter very important and, in particular, "original" sounding cases among the culturally deficient [Kulturarmen] that pertain here, namely *offerings*, *penance* and *tribute* connected with relations of power. They often consist simply of the kind of things that the dead, the gods, the priests, the chiefs immediately can use and wish to have, such as food and the like. But quite often we encounter here the tendency preferably to use certain types of goods for these purposes. The reason may be that the good in question already is a medium of exchange or measure of value. But this *need* not be so, rather it is quite conceivable that another, especially popular asset is applied as the means of performance [Leistungsmittel] in this sense, one that does not, or has not already, fulfilled those functions. And it could be that it is precisely these benefits that trigger the quantification of economic ideas, that thus become the historical source of the measure of value function, and through this, or directly, the medium of exchange function.

This is similar to the way in which, in various historical periods, the money economy and monetary-economic rationality penetrates in regions and countries not before acquainted with such, as when a state power outside the cultural sphere exacts tax payments in money – for example, in the case of some Balkan provinces of the Byzantine Empire. In such cases, one can certainly speak of an *imposed* [oktroyierten] *means of payment* (Max Weber). But the aspect that resonates in this expression is not essential and does not go deep.[32]

---

[32]Just how shallow this runs is shown by the consideration that *if* it were true, as Max Weber argued, that the function of the "imposed means of payment" is historically the oldest (it would be otherwise if it had to do with an imposed *service*) and appeared first in services of subjects for chiefs, to which performances of chiefs to followers attached themselves only secondarily, yet the question arises as to which chief or follower may have started it. The reference to Carthage or the Persian Empire, in which gold coinage "only arose for the production of military means of payment, not from means of exchange," does not illustrate the matter (*Economic History, loc. cit.,* p. 209), because

The imposed performance must be objectively possible and reasonable. And therein, not in the imposition of means of payment as such, is the essence of the thing economically. Likewise with the religious aspect, that with some of these services emerges naturally: it tells us only the cultural-historical "how." It may be that it is in the genetic base case [Grundfall], or at least in a primitive case, that it initially had to do with substituting human sacrifice with the blood of an animal, that in connection with this the pieces of this animal type were given to the priesthood as gifts, and that from here this animal type became a means of performance generally, subsequently also measure of value and, possibly, a medium of exchange. But here as well, nothing has been said about the economic "why."[33]

We have earlier seen the possibility that cattle may have been used as a "measure of value" without *first* - and, in principle, without *ever* - becoming an exchange mediator. Although its status as the most important asset was completely sufficient to this end, it could have come about through the detour of a prior function as means of performance, thus in a manner such that this function was what particularly singled out cattle in the minds of people. We widely encounter fines and charges of all kinds in this form, such as in Rome, where fines were converted to copper only in the middle of the fifth century B.C., whereas they were previously expressed in cattle and sheep.

Store of Value

d) Stockpiling is also found outside of human economic activity and genetically is the initial expression of economic behavior in general. It is plausible

---

it already presupposes coins that took shape in the market. This criticism is perhaps unfair since the posthumous publication of this text does not have the final sanction of the author, but similar aspects resonate in Weber's broader economic sociology.

On this occasion, Weber coined the term: *exchangeless money,* which may be strange from a yet frequently held standpoint, but nevertheless has common sense.

[33]Like many other historians of social institutions - a famous example is Fustel de Coulanges in his *Cité Antique* (2nd edition, Paris 1866) - Laum, in the book cited, overestimated the explanatory value of such a derivation. But at least he did not overlook the fact that they are not necessarily in contradiction with derivations of the state of affairs comprehended by observers, and showed the existence of that possible link formulated in the following paragraph of our text. The view that the cattle unit could have become established only through transactions of sacrifice with the gods, seems to me to go too far. Burns' polemic (*loc. cit.,* p. 6 note) comes up short in various directions, including by translating "human transactions" [menschlicher Verkehr] as "human trade."

that this is connected above all with that form of stockbuilding that we denote by *hoarding*. It would fully correspond to the positive, completely alogical impulse of the will to possess: in the way that "fighting" and "fighting for the sake of a rational target" are very different social phenomena, and the former precedes the latter – and even today the *impulse* to fight must be divorced from a rational *goal* for which to fight, which is often only an *ex post* rationalization – in the same manner, the *arational desire to possess* is the necessary precondition [Prius] – and later the true driving force – of the rationalized will to possess. The behavior that we thereby make understandable – in this case, from the point of view [ex visu] of the psyche of the participant – certainly usually operates on objects that at the same time give it a rational meaning, especially in the case of food. But a will to possess – although possibly traceable thereto – can also be found to which only a vague, or *no,* idea of rational purposes is connected, a will to possess for the sake of possession or the exclusion of others, the object of which can be an object contrasting with the surroundings, e.g., a specially shaped stone.[34] The impulse to fight can operate regarding any such object, and connected with it a note of *social validity* or *magical* or *religious significance* can emerge which is also both a result of an initial experiment at primitive rationalization and, in the broader nexus of interactions, a motive for the selection of objects on which the will to possess operates.

The considerations that we employ in the socio-psychological phenomenon of fashion already explain this. As they do with the entire spiritual world of primitives, magically- or sacrally-tinted social customs and *interpretations* of such customs by the participants make much more sense in terms of this state of affairs, corresponding as it does with the environment and the associative thinking of primitives (Levy-Bruhl), than in terms of the assumption of a practice of "reserve holding" of especially marketable commodities arising from the needs of commodity trading.

All the same, our *observers' rationality* will lead to this last aspect as the "objective" function of hoarding, and suggest the observation to us that the primitive in possession of a good treasure is in an analogous situation to the

---

[34]This gives a principle of explanation for the *stone money* in the Carolinas, which consists of large, heavy transportable pieces, and probably also for the *Vaygua* of the Trobriand Islanders (north of New Guinea), which includes various types of high-value things like axe blades, and necklaces of certain shells, which hardly ever have any use but are gathered as a symbols of wealth and used for gifts to chiefs and the like (see B. Malinowski, "The Primitive Economics of the Trobriand Islanders," in *Economic Journal,* vol. 31, London 1921, pp. 1 ff.).

modern with a sizeable bank balance. On the other hand, contrary to this is the fact that bank balances give one the disposal over something which for other reasons is "money" and is held in reserve for that very reason. Because something which functions as money in the sense of other functions can be hoarded, so can that which is sought after as a means for hoarding become money in the sense of other functions.[35] The lack of alternative use value forms as little a difficulty as does the valuation of a lapdog that is "good for nothing." The hypothesis that we have here to do with the original function of money is supported by the above-mentioned subsidiary character of indirect exchange and by the coercive nature of most unilateral services – which is consistent with the fact that the primitive does not like to alienate his hoard and usually does so only when other means fail.

But we do not insist on this assumption. In contrast to a theorem that can *only* be correct within its system of preconditions, if at all, different views on the historical genesis of a social phenomenon may be correct for different cases. So it is indeed *potentially* vain to strive for *the* correct "theory" (= doctrine) about the emergence of cities. It is *certainly* wrong to believe that there could only be *one* correct one.

---

[35]The relationship to the "measure of value" in particular suggests itself: the objects of the hoard are more clear in the mind's eye of the primitives, are more carefully guarded and counted than others.

Chapter III
Outline of the Development
of the Doctrine of Money

1. Regarding monetary research, the historical development with which we now wish to acquaint ourselves in rough outline, something similar to monetary policy holds true. Just as the latter, through cause and effect, is connected with almost everything, monetary theory likewise is connected to almost every other theoretical problem - it makes itself felt in every other space of the theoretical structure, so noticeably that mentally one cannot live in it without the help of money-theoretical knowledge, while the theory of money itself only has meaning in relation to the knowledge available in every other area of the theoretical building. Would it at all be possible to characterize the history of a problem area by a single trend, in our case it could be sought in the implementation of this point: monetary theory can be called a specialized discipline only with reservations, although its literature, estimated roughly at 15,000 books and essays, separates itself from the rest of the economic literature with a severity that is not objectively justified.

The relationship between theory and practice, the interaction between knowledge and actual events, is basically the same in the money-theoretical realm as everywhere else. But compared to other economic understanding, money-theoretical understanding has gradually come into a more favorable position, not only from the already mentioned reason, that at least today its "final goals" do not diverge as strongly as final goals otherwise tend to do, but also from the additional reason that business and political practitioners in this field, which at first glance is already recognizably technically complicated, are more trusting of scientific findings and less trusting of their customary practice than generally is their wont. More than in other areas, this science has things to say to the practitioner, that he neither knows nor believes he knows. The strand of this interaction running in the opposite direction is so clear, that one only need warn of its overestimation. Self-evidently, the history of money provides the observational material for the theory of money, and just as self-evidently, the immediate interest in conditions, events, and questions of the present time are far and away the source of most publications and the motive of by far the most workers in this field. But it would be as foolish to overlook the proper motion

of scientific thought and to consider issues and results only as the reflection of
present reality and its concerns, as it would be foolish to see in physics nothing
but successive attempts at solutions to tasks posed by production technology.

Monetary Theory in the Ancient World

We can see this already in the first attempts at analysis about money we
receive from the Greeks. The Greco-Roman economic world never lacked in
striking monetary conditions and processes, and interesting problems of monetary policy. Significant issues arose from the interest of princes and states in
mints and mines, others from the problem of the *content of money debts*, above
all comprehended socio-politically, others from the relative volatility of the
value of the monetary metals silver, copper, and gold, yet others from the great
periods of inflation that occurred and that – as in the Ptolemaic Empire,[1] which
lasted from the third century through the second and first, and provided such a
beautiful example of the way in which social and political disorganization works
into the monetary system, as well as in the Roman Empire in the third century
after Christ, etc. – basically differ in nothing from the inflation of the World
War; and finally one other, from measures which can only derive from deliberate monetary-political will, even though the content of the will is not always
clear, as was the case with the limitation of northern Italian gold production
decreed by Rome in the first century B.C.[2] But all of that has either borne no
scientific fruit or only that which is lost to us. The former is more likely.

Substantially, and apart from entirely insignificant things, such as, e.g.,
Xenophon's proposal for the development of the mines of Laurion, only the
statements of Plato and Aristotle come into consideration. But general remarks
on the nature of money are of much less interest than he who holds our science
to be a conglomerate of philosophy and dogma believes. Regarding science, what

---

[1] Regarding this, cf. Fritz Heichelheim, "Wirtschaftliche Schwankungen der Zeit
von Alexander bis Augustus " [Economic Fluctuations in the Age from Alexander to
Augustus], in Spiethoff's *Beiträgen zur Erforschung der wirtschaftlichen Wechsellagen*
[Contributions to Research in Economic Fluctuations], Jena 1930.

[2] Regarding Roman currency conditions, cf. in particular Theodor Mommsen,
Geschichte des römischen Münzwesens [History of Roman Coinage], Berlin 1860; Harold
M. and Edward A. Sydenham, *The Roman Imperial Coinage* I, London 1923; Tenney
Frank, *An Economic History of Rome to the End of the Republic,* Baltimore 1920; also
Burns, *loc. cit.,* and Michael Rostovtzeff's well-known work, *The Social and Economic
History of the Roman Empire,* Oxford, Clarendon Press, 1926.

matters is what is made of such points of departure. When Plato called *money* a *sign* - even though he related it to the facts of the division of labor and market commerce - we have before us nothing more than a lay opinion that everywhere precedes the systematic reflection on the subject, although it later reappears with a different - specific - meaning.

More important is what Aristotle has to say, because of the uninterrupted line that leads from him to scholasticism and natural law [theory], through to the science of the 18th century. He derives the phenomenon of money, and even the stamp of the coin, entirely according to the sense of the exchange mediation doctrine,[3] thus from the commodity that, due to its inherent use value, is most suited for exchange transactions, which for this reason becomes the generally taken medium of circulation and therefore, in turn, is stamped in a manner certifying sort and quantity - thus purely "declaratory." The subsequent statement of policy, that money subsists νόμῳ [nominally, by law] and not φύσει [physically, by nature] seems to be at odds with this. At any rate, we have seen that neither this nor any other historical claim about the emergence of money prejudices our conception of the essence of money.

In this respect, nothing would prevent us from taking the latter phrase literally and declare Aristotle a representative of the *legal or conventional theory*,[4] but it is probably more accurate not to attribute this distinction to him,

---

[3]*Politics*, I. 3; *Ethics*, V (5), 11-16. It is essential that these statements allow of no other interpretation than similar things said by monetary theorists in the 19th century.

[4]The term is self-explanatory. After what has been said, it would hardly be worth the trouble to respond to the various "basic assumptions" of money more than is done, in passing, in what follows. Mises has divided them into *catallactic* and *acatallactic* (Ludwig von Mises, "Zur Klassifikation der Geldtheorie" [Regarding the Classification of Monetary Theory], in *Archiv für Sozialwissenschaft und Sozialpolitik* [Archives for Social Science and Social Policy], vol. 44, 1917-18, pp. 198 - 213). However, since each money researcher, even if he derives money from "convention" and does not apply the law of commodity value to it, and yet can explain its validity only from market exchange transactions, so there are really no "acatallactic" monetary theories in the literal sense. The relevant contrast seems to be between those views that link the *essence* of money with a monetary substance of value in itself, for which the expression *commodity theory*, used several times above, is suitable - *theoretical metallism* is then merely a special case of it - and those that do not. For the latter, I have used the term "claim theories" [Anweisungstheorien]. But since a misleading association with the legal concept of a claim is intrinsic to this term, another may be more advisable, for example, "sign theory," in which case, of course, it should not be construed as if a theory falling under this category

but rather to consider the first-named version as the actually relevant one and the last-named one only as a formulation of the self-evidentness that money is subject to the action of statute and customary law, and also that it does not serve us through the use-properties of the material of which it is made. Because Aristotle emphasized that money is a good like the rest, and for this reason varies in its value, hardly another interpretation remains to the specialist. This would make him a representative of the *commodity theory*. And besides, because according to his way of thinking, which was received up to the 18th century, the emergence of an institution is always introduced under the form of an invention or conscious agreement, an objectively inconsequential variety of convention doctrine is, with him, incompatible with the commodity theory.

Monetary Theory in the Medieval Period

The earlier and later Middle Ages also were acquainted enough with currency problems, rooted in particular in the technically imperfect nature of the coins, in scarcities cropping up at various times in various places– perceived as a disturbance after having become accustomed to the Roman coinage – and in coin debasements by the prince and fraudulent interventions by private parties. The *Frankish coinage* had an interesting unit of account, first introduced by Pippin for punitive damages – twelve pence to the shilling – which penetrated into Bavaria and beyond. But there Roman gold actually firmly held for a long time, while Western France had to switch to silver earlier, so that in the East, by way of practice [via facti], already prior to the assumption of its own coinage, a particular currency arose primarily by limiting Eastern Roman undervalued gold coins – *mancosi* – which led not only to a different coin distribution of *long shillings,* but also to a different movement of value. The effort to avoid such inconveniences, for which examples could be multiplied, comprises Carolingian

---

must be identified with everything ever said under this heading. The expression *nominalism,* which through Knapp has become customary as a term for the opposite of metallism, is very unfortunate, not only because of its - meaningless - philosophical association, but also because of the emphasis on the incidental aspects of the *nominal value* of money that it seems to imply, and which in themselves have nothing to do with the theory of signs.

Of course, these doctrines about the essence of money are something other than theories about the determinants of the "value of money," especially the so-called *quantity theory,* which therefore should not simply be put on a line with them, as if they taught a particular view of the essence of money.

monetary policy, which therefore often resorted mainly to the standardization of services in other current assets, as for example with the valuation rates of the *Saxon Capitulary* of 797.

The following period until the 15th century came under the influence of the interest on the part of developing princely territories in the capture and exploitation of the *coinage prerogative*. This meant not only the right of coinage according to a monetary standard, which was given over almost entirely to the mercy of the coining authority – and a stamping fee (*strike rate*, "seignorage"), which in the modern era shrank to only the stamping cost-covering fee or disappeared – but also the right of the *coin exchange*: "a penny only has value where it was struck." Besides this, the sovereign could undertake to *devalue the coin* (cry down [Verrufung], renewal [Erneuerung]), i.e., call in the existing coins to be collected and replaced with new ones. All of this became the main source of funding for the growing princely power, that faced the tasks of its progressively widening power with very inadequate means; and is to be judged as a monetary reflection of this all-encompassing social process.[5] Of course, the estates resisted, but in this field as others, only with occasional success. Thus, under pressure from the estates, the territorial lord of Styria, in the privilege of the year 1237, bound the coin exchange to the consent of the estates. In Austria in 1359, Duke Rudolf IV bought their approval of a tax. With the decline of the power of the estates, any remaining restriction was lost, and with the complete victory of princely rule, opening up as it did abundant sources of tax revenue, this practice was restricted to times of political distress.

The thought of scholasticism at first moved entirely on the Aristotelian path. This was especially the case with Thomas Aquinas – only that, added to the profane *nomos* of the Greek age of enlightenment, came the aspect of divine order, which did not change anything in the nature of the case, nor the analytical

---

[5]In the other direction as well, if we could go into the social history of the time, we could find a causal link between the currency turmoil and economic and social disturbances with roots in the broader meaning developed in §. 1. For instance, the second half of the 14th century was the time of the Black Death, to which a fourth of the population of the German Empire fell victim. Along with this came the Hussite Wars and, since the defeat of Nicopolis (1396), the Turkish threat. Such a deeper analysis gives the currency turmoil the appearance of the superficial expression of the people's fortunes. A highlight of the currency deteriorations, only attained again in the Thirty Years' War, occurred in the years 1457-59, when in places in southern Germany it came to a complete currency devaluation. In Vienna, the children are said to have played with the pennies ("Schinderlings") in the street.

nature of his thought process. Therefore, it was neither a new discovery nor a break with tradition when the later achievements of the scholastic thinkers in our field, who so constituted the basic doctrine – and likewise also already in an all too independent role – in their positioning vis-a-vis contemporary conditions brought the material value of money to the fore, as we see in Buridan (first half of the 14th century) and especially in Oresme (1383), whose treatise on the origin, nature, and law of money and coin exchange consummated that independence.[6]

2. A fault line appears to the philosophical historian of dogma who seeks world-view associations in the *valor impositus* [imposed value] and cannot bring himself to reconcile it with the simple meaning of "legal tender" [gesetzlicher Zahlkraft]. Later authors often only wished to define the notion of legal money when they attached importance to the state determination of an object as money, which the radical metallist also could do without giving away something of his basic position: this does not yet indicate a position regarding the question of material value. Of course, the highlighting of material value, as in Buridan and the entirety of subsequent literature, standing under the impact of coinage debasement, signifies one of several possible answers to the great question of the time. Just as well, and also from the standpoint of the existing theoretical tradition – which was too little developed to dictate a clear answer – one could say that coin debasements only led to social ills insofar as they involved new demand for commodities or a new supply of money. But we thereby have the explanation as to why that answer was actually given. Any other explanation is more complicated and assumes a deeper elaboration of monetary relationships.

On the other hand, the material value of coins lies much closer to the naive consciousness. This is where the affliction, the monetary disease [morbus numerarius], takes hold. The frequent attempts to conceal the fact of deteriorated fineness upon exchanging the coinage – a practice with which, incidentally, the Ptolemies were already acquainted – gave the process that character of fraud that caused Dante to direct the dishonest mintmaster into hell. The people feels that it is being scammed, and sees the scam in the stealing away of metal from the coin. For the monetary researcher who wishes to say something of practical relevance, it can be added that any other type of monetary reform than restoration of the previous fineness was hopeless under the circumstances of the time. And so he proclaims that the material value, *valor intrinsicus,* is not irrelevant

---

[6]Rudolf Kaulla, "Der Lehrer des Oresmius" [The Teacher of Oresme], in: *Zeitschrift f. d. gesamte Staatswissenschaft* [Journal for Joint State Science], vol. 60, Tübingen 1904, p. 453; Émile Bridrey, *Nicole Oresme, La théorie de la monnaie au XIVe siècle* [Nicholas Oresme, the Theory of Money in the 14th Century], Paris 1906.

to the *valor impositus*[7] without dwelling on the question as to whether market value, *valor extrinsicus*, could not also be regulated in another way.

But the currency turmoil continued, always giving occasion to emphasize the same point of view; thus within scholasticism with Gabriel Biel (1501), outside scholasticism with Copernicus on the occasion of his report to the Graudenzer Assembly (written 1519), with the author of pamphlets in the controversies in Albertine and Ernestine Saxony, and with a number of writers up until the end of the 18th century; so that a tradition developed wherein money was spoken of as the *universal commodity*. This tradition continued, culminating in the well-known statement of Roscher, that the false definitions of gold were divided into two groups, those that held it to be *more*, and those that held it to be *less* than the more marketable commodity. And according to Menger's definition (*loc. cit.*, p. 561): "commodities that have become general ... customary exchange mediators are characterized in scientific language ... as money (cattle money, shell money, salt money, etc.)."

Practice sought to protect itself in various ways. The easiest way was to use reliable foreign money. Thus we observe that good Venetian coinage penetrated into the internal traffic of the neighboring territories, while in the 13th century Bohemian grotes or gold florins penetrated into the Duchy of Austria. Sometimes *calculation* was done only in "more stable" money, similar to our use of dollars during the Inflation, or even in a *metallically defined money of account* (e.g., "silver mark"). Furthermore, we also very early encounter currency forms of the type of the Babenbergers of Leopold V, which were transferred by the ordinance of the monetary system to a privileged association, the Mint Inmates [Münzer Hausgenossen] – but later only in communities in which the civil interest in "good money" prevailed with the rulers over the interest in the state-financial exploitation of currency, and where we encounter the connection with the trade in bills of exchange and in banking, which we cannot go into here. An example is the Bank of Hamburg, founded in 1619 and which implemented book money, the "mark banco," defined in silver and fully backed by silver and gold deposits, and the Bank of Amsterdam, founded in 1609 on the same principle – violated by its directors – whereby transferable metallic deposits were accepted, for which depositors were credited in guilders "redeemable" at any

---

[7]Here one also realized that undervalued coins quickly pushed full-value coins of the *same type* out of circulation. This is the original content of *Gresham's Law* so-called, which was later generalized in the popular statement that "bad" money drives out "good," which simply means that money, the material value of which allows of a better use than that of being spent in domestic commerce, flows into those better uses.

time by the return of the deposit slip and payment of a percentage charge (⅛%) for professional services rendered, and which understandably commanded a premium. The whole point in both cases was a commitment to metallically defined money, and while this point was achieved by "full backing" by which this bank money *in principle* was not acquirable otherwise than by depositing the full equivalent value in metal, it nevertheless is a misunderstanding to see in it a materially valueless *money of account,* or any money of account at all, or in fact anything else than a convenient method of transferring quantities of metal.

But one still had reason to be dissatisfied with the functioning of the monetary system, even apart from the coinage debasements. To wit, from the 13th to the 14th century a violent overthrow of silver took place across Central Europe, that in places drove gold to twenty times the value of silver. And gold then very quickly fell back to the ratio of 10:1 or 11:1 against silver, there to remain until the end of the 15th century. Against the evils which thereby arose, of course, no full-value coinage could provide protection: this was the harbinger of a new practical problem. But only in the 18th century did it push itself into the foreground, in those countries in which gold and silver coins circulated without a fixed relation, or with only a locally fixed relation.

Monetary Theory in the Early Modern Period

In the 16th century monetary research was carried forward by another circumstance, namely, by the influx of precious metals from America. Every time something like this happens, it is claimed in the scientific discussion that the inevitably and invariably occurring price increase at least *also* has other causes, and very possibly has nothing to do with the production of precious metals. The never-lacking other aspects that tend to be relied upon are certainly not plucked out of thin air. In our case, social shocks and devastating wars certainly had a large share in the price revolution of the 16th century. But that does not interest us now. Rather, it is only important that in the 16th century, the relationship was clearly recognized and decisively set out.

How big the step was that was taken can be seen when one considers how far removed it is from primitive notions and direct observation. The man of that time saw prices rise stormily, and he could have observed the influx of new precious metal. But he did not at first bring them into connection, and having this pointed out to him, initially would just as naively ask: what has the import of precious metals to do with the prices of all other goods? In the same way that so many of our monetary-policy authors asked during the World War, as to what does the note-printing press had to do with goods prices. Bodin,[8] who himself said that thus far no one had mentioned this "main and almost sole" cause - it is a further merit that he leaves room for other factors - and with whose name this achievement tends to be connected historically, took not really one but two steps forward in a single bound. He first recognized that the "abondance" of gold and silver is by far the most important of the four or five causes of inflation. And he clarified and made more general the meaning that the most important cause of inflation, wherever it befell, is the "abondance" of that which "gives estimate and price to goods." So not only the importance of the increase in circulating precious metal generally is recognized, but also that this importance is exhausted in its effect on the quantity of money. This is the birth of the most primitive statement of that which is called the *quantity theory*, but because he does not formulate a monetary theory but only a single connection, it is better termed the *quantity theorem*.

Bodin's merit is not lessened because echoes of this phrase can be found in many older writers, and further investigation would certainly unearth more predecessors[9] - which is the case with any of the more important theorems. Nor does the fact reduce Bodin's merit, that he did not seem to be aware either of the conditions or the limits of the durability of his theorem. He did not even sufficiently refer to the relativity of his "abondance" of money to commodities existing in the same area. And it took the labor of the fourth part of a millennium - during which the statement appears in so many different settings and contexts that one must be careful not to speak of "the" quantity theory - to take, while extending and criticizing, everything out of it that was in it, then perhaps to throw it away as an empty shell.

Now what matters is not the statement itself, nor the merits or shortcomings of Bodin's formulation, but the significance of both for thinking regarding money. And that significance is very great. Leaving entirely to one side the practical insights that he derives, initial approximations of a character that

---

[8]Jean Bodin, *Réponses aux Paradoxes de M. de Malestroit touchants renchérissement de toutes les choses* [Answers to Paradoxes of Mr. Malestroit Touching the Rise of All Things], Paris 1568.

[9]Hale's [actually, William Stafford's] treatment in dialogue form, *A compendious or briefe examination of certayne ordinary complaints of divers of our countrymen in these our dayes*, in that these "complaints" were attributed to the devaluation of money stemming from the import of American gold and silver, although first published in 1581, already appears to have been written in 1579 (cf. Lamond in *English Historical Review*, 1891).

very quickly progress to the untenable, Bodin was primarily a logical bridge to the further development of the theory of money. If one gives oneself over to its meaning without bias, there arises in the mind's eye first the analogy between the effect of an increase in precious metal as far as it penetrates into the circulation, and the effect of coinage debasement and *counterfeiting*. Once one has but understood this analogy, the relationship between the material value and the market value of money – which historically forms the basis of the first real insight of the money-theoretical kind – begins to fade in its fundamental importance; our conception of money begins to detach itself from the material value, and then the views embodied in the words "sign," "trademark," and the like, at once gain relevance to serious money-theoretical work. In other words, *that theorem first made monetary theories possible that emanated neither from material value nor accrued from the barren sandbank of "legal theory,"* and indicated a third possibility, although beyond this the "legal theories" themselves thereby also gained economic content. The yet to be discussed variety of legal theory that reappeared in Germany 25 years ago wrestled not only with the commodity theory, but at the same time with the quantity theory – whatever might be understood thereby – so that today the relationship is obscured. Therefore, it was important to point out that the quantity theorem, precisely because it says nothing about the "essence" of money, although it is compatible with any theory of money, yet just for theories other than the material-value or commodity variety – whether they be legal theories or not – was essential to the first step beyond the "essence-view."

The thought as well as its development in the indicated direction may now be pursued in detail until its degeneration into a poorly defended, groundlessly rejected byword in popular discussion. We have to meet some milestones along its purely scientific road, which we now string together proleptically. The first is one of the most beautiful literary achievements in economics: Davanzati's lecture before the "Umanissimi Accademici Fiorentini"[10] which he later supplemented with notes and an appendix on exchange rates, which however had less to offer than what Lawrence de Rodolfis (*De Usuris*) already had to say about it in 1403.[11] Davanzati represents no convention- and no sign-theory, although he

---

[10]Bernardo Davanzati, *A Discourse upon Coins, being publickly spoken in the Academy there* (Florence), anno 1588. Printed in London 1696.

[11]The discussion over economic and legal questions pertaining to the circulation of bills is of course yet much older. Relatively early memorials to the same are the *Practica Mercatoria* of Pegolotti (14th century) and the *Practica della Mercatura* of Giovanni di Antonio da Ussano (1442). For the subsequent period, see Payons, "Observations

says half-jokingly that the people, to discountenance the nature of the precious metals, that contribute so little to our lives, "i sono accordati" ["are agreed"] to make of them what holds for all other commodities. He even defined money "metallistically." But this aspect of the matter recedes while the juxtaposition of the *quantity of money* and the *quantity of goods* come to the fore. This counterpart of the first, implied by Bodin, is now explicitly manifest: all goods taken together "vagliano" [are worth] as much as the whole coinage of gold, silver, and copper, that circulates simultaneously among them.

A hundred years later, the mathematician and astronomer Montanari (his two works were written in 1680 and 1683-1687) based his work directly on Davanzati.[12] He only improved a point here and there - for example, in the concept of money he includes all goods that perform the role of money, and not just gold, silver, or copper - or he added something here and there, thus discussing, e.g., the approximation of the "levels" (livello) of the *value of money in different countries by international precious metals flows and the prices of individual goods through commerce*, while he treats the discount and many other things in the old way; his explanation of the circulation capacity of token coinage and paper money, while not wrong, is quite awkward. In order to be fair to his achievement, one must know how to read him with the eye of the expert - otherwise one attaches too much importance to comments such as that "the prince" could make money for internal circulation as he would like, and overlooks the caveat, that it just should not be too much.

The next step was taken without visible connection to these achievements. In his *Verbum Sapiente* (1664), which entirely assumes the primitive idea that there is in every case a specific need for money that the actually existing money supply answers to or not, Sir W. Petty[13] speaks of something that he calls

---

d'écrivains du XVIème siècle sur les changes et notamment sur l' influence de la disparité du pouvoir d'achat des monnaies" [Observations of 16th-century Writers on the Exchange and in Particular on the Influence of the Disparity in the Purchasing Power of Currencies], *Rev. econ. intern.*, Brussels 1928.

[12]Geminiano Montanari, *Breve trattato des valore delle monete in tutti gli stati* [Brief Treatise on the Value of Money in Every State], in: *Scrittori classici italiani di economia politica* [Classic Italian Writers in Political Economy], Milano 1804.

[13]Sir William Petty, *Verbum sapienti, or an account of the wealth and expences of England and the method of raising taxes in the equal manner*, 1665, published as an appendix to *The political anatomy of Ireland* 1672, London 1691. Already in his earlier work, *A Treatise of Taxes and Contributions*, London 1662, the expression "frequency

"circles" of the "revolution" of money, that can be translated as *velocity of circulation* and stands in entirely the same connection as the remark of Adam Smith, that the quantity of money in circulation should be much lower than the annual income paid from it. The *term* "quickness of circulation" is then found in the "Considerations of the Consequences of Lowering the Interest and Raising the Value of Money" by [John] Locke (1691) but neither here nor in his changing statements on issues of monetary theory does he betray an awareness of the importance of this velocity for the price level. This should not be surprising. For what also seemed self-evident behind it had yet to be discovered, and the history of all science is full of the latent self-evident.[14] The concept only developed very slowly and made virtually no progress up to the present time. But not only what will be discussed below, the investigation of money, but even the quantity theory owes much to Locke. The juxtaposition of money and goods is, even with the emphasis on the material value of the coin,[15] the crucial point. In particular, he addresses the question of the relationship between the interest rate and the money supply as counterpart to commodities, which is a whole new viewpoint. He also sees that, in the case of money, supply and demand cannot be spoken of in the same sense as with commodities, in which lies, at least in embryo, the ultimate justification for the lifting of money out of the world of commodities, and one of the best refutations of any commodity theory.

The entire 18th century did not cross over that line. In fact, it remained in the area of the quantity theory up until Adam Smith. Regarding velocity, this is true even for Hume, who for the rest, in addition to a perfect formulation of the theorem, extended it to exchange-rate movements within the gold points and so developed the, to that point, only rudimentary theory of the mechanism

---

of commutations" appears. For this reason Marx already referred to this text as the origin of our concept.

[14]More information about the history of the concept is contained in the essay by M.W. Holtrop, "Theories of the Velocity of Circulation of Money in Earlier Economic Literature," in: "Economic History Series," No. 4 of the *Economic Journal,* London, 1929, and for our entire subject, Arthur Eli Monroe, *Monetary Theory before Adam Smith,* Cambridge, 1923; also Friedrich Hoffmann, *Kritische Dogmengeschichte der Geldwerttheorien* [Critical Dogmatic History of Monetary Value Theories], Leipzig, 1907.

[15]To which is attributable the attempts to make Locke out to be a "legal theorist."

of international gold movements.[16] In the 19th century, bank credit and commercial credit in general was drawn into the sphere of the quantity theory, first in two forms, both of which were fruitful more for their defects than their merits.

On the one hand, based on the commercial payment instrument, there for the first time arose a professional opposition to the quantity theory, that prior to this - in contrast to the rejection by practitioners, based initially only on a lack of understanding - only sporadically manifested itself: because the quantity theory *looks* only to metal and paper money, it for practical purposes becomes false because it *overlooks* how the commercial loan creates the circulating medium that it needs, and how it eliminates it when it no longer needs it - a common argument yet today.

On the other hand, a particular variation of the quantity theory was formulated, the so-called currency theory, wherein metallic money and paper money - under which banknotes were included - were equal in their effect on prices, in fundamental contrast to the means of payment of credit transactions: the quantity of, and only of, metal money plus paper money (banknotes) has an initiative effect, an effect that any other type of payment, which is "only" a claim to that "money" and is dependent on the quantity thereof, does not have. This variation, besides those that crudely make the value of money depend upon the production of precious metals, became the main focus of contemporary and subsequent criticism, but it lives on, especially in the refined form that accepts the aggregate volume of circulating medium as being the direct determinant of the general price movement, although this value itself cannot be determined from the pulse of commodity trading but from the reserve proportion of the sum of metallic money plus paper money.

John Stuart Mill was the first one and for a long time the only one who realized that the first aspect could be accounted for without abandoning the quantity theory - that in general there is no contrast between the two - and that also the second aspect is not easily disposed of. This realization is the main merit of his masterly statement of the theorem, which appears from his hand for the

---

[16]Regarding the possible priority of Jacob Vanderlint, whose "Money answers all things" was published in London in 1734, while Hume's essays were published in 1741 (*Political Discourses*, 2nd ed. Edinburgh, 1752), see J.W. Angell, *The Theory of International Prices. History, Criticism and Restatement,* Cambridge, Mass., 1926, p. 26, and the same author on the performance of Harris. Richard Cantillon, *Essai sur la nature du commerce en general* [Essay on the Nature of Commerce in General], completed in 1734, was to my knowledge the first to ask the question as to how a monetary expansion raises prices, and to equate an increase in velocity with an increase in money.

last time by a theorist of the first rank, as signifying a stringent causal relationship.

In fact, its further fate is characterized by the following three points: (1) more and more, the idea loses strength that the quantity of commodities and velocity of circulation are relatively constant magnitudes, or at least variable according to their own laws; that prices are the passive element while the quantity of money - however defined - is the active element in the interconnected magnitudes wrapped in the ligaments of the quantity theory.[17] More and more, the emphasis is placed, in line with the overall understanding of the interaction between all the economic variables, on this relationship itself. As it might also be expressed: the quantity theorem, stripped of all special theses attached to it, is reduced to a simple equation of exchange, with which we will be dealing. (2) This equation of exchange in the hands of researchers with whose names this outline will end, becomes a mere - albeit necessary as such - *conditional equation* of economic equilibrium, behind which deeper grounds of explanation become visible. If in the former regard the fate of the quantity theory is comparable with that of another, even more famous statement of the older political economy, namely the statement regarding the greatest good for the greatest number, which the economy left to itself realizes - which today has largely lost the former content, filled with practical significance, and which in theory mainly plays the role of a mere conditional equation - so in the latter regard its fate is comparable to the old law of costs, which, theoretically newly underpinned, has now won also a changed meaning and has become a transit station to deeper insights. (3) Both enemies and friends of the theorem have tried, using ever more perfect methods and ever better data, to test it against the facts, by which the entire discussion has entered into a new stage. The origins of this trend lie far back, but in our time - the central achievement is linked to the name of Irving Fisher - it has gone so far as to seriously affect the question.

3. We return. The period from the end of the 16th century to the French Revolution is filled with instances of currency turmoil and attempts to get extricated from them, which really and lastingly succeeded only in England - where the problems indeed were never as bad - and everywhere else only temporarily. The worst situations were of course in Germany, not only due to the absence of a powerful central authority, but also because in Germany not only were domestic social struggles fought out - for the most part, those of other

---

[17]See the description by Arthur Spiethoff: "Die Quantitätstheorie insbesondere in ihrer Verwendbarkeit als Haussetheorie" [The Quantity Theory, Especially in its Usefulness as a Boom Theory], in *Festgaben für Adolf Wagner*, Leipzig, 1905.

nations were fought out there as well. The ravages of the Thirty Years' War and its precursors resulted in the first quarter of the 17th century in the great "Münzkalada." That was the real age of *Kipper und Wipper* [seesawing of the scales], the indescribable chaos of which it is not easy to give an idea. The contemporary judgment that put the blame on exchange rates as such, in turn, misses the point insofar as the monetary policy of the princes simply grew out of the plight of the times, and no monetary system, no matter how healthy, could have survived the Thirty Years' War: when blooming landscapes are turned to deserts and cities to rubble, and blood and misery disorganizes and demoralizes the rest of the population, all economic behavior must depart the normal paths, and the monetary system must then also degenerate pathologically, if it were not exposed to a single inflationary intervention. And although things improved already in the 17th century and the reversals in the 18th were usually relatively mild, this entire period is still dominated by the practical problem of undervalued money, which nevertheless was not a new problem for science.

In the main, however, a new method of inflation in the 18th century began to replace the method of coin debasement – the *paper money economy*. It occurs in many places, within the German Empire especially in Austria – note the peculiar *discrepancy*, intertwined with the political system, *between political will and economic capability*, at that time and for a long time thereafter – but nowhere as strong and dramatic as in France under the regency. It is it interesting to note that, while in terms of *motive* and *sequence of events, this* case of the paper money economy was rooted in the state budget deficit, it was not so *in principle;* rather it was one of the first stirrings of the high-capitalist method of movable-property bank credit [Mobilbankkredit]. The idea of the leading spirit, John Law, was at bottom no different from that realized by the brothers Pereire in their Crédit Mobilier some 150 years later with more initial success, and accomplished in much more perfect manner, and which was finally realized with tremendous success in the later development of the banking system, nowhere more than in Germany, there also surviving the not entirely absent failures. This basic idea was initially based on the practical observation, already long since made, that any "unilateral" money creation had the consequence that we today, using a very common expression, label "false prosperity." To be sure, the joy is of short duration. But the economic consequences of the process depend very much upon what happens during this false prosperity. If it serves to finance large enterprises that have lasting success, the economy may be better off as a result of *such* inflation than it otherwise would have been.

The objection that enterprises reckoned to be healthy necessarily have to be economically feasible even without inflation, is true if what is meant is that they *would be* profitable even without price increases and, precisely when they are healthy, *must be*. But it does not hit the mark practically, if it means that any company that promises real success even without inflation would always already be funded with money quantities that are already present in the commerce of those economies. For these pre-existing funds, growing slowly through saving, were as often as not tied to the credit needs of existing businesses, in the hands of those who neither could nor would venture something new – very peculiarly the case in the petit bourgeois relations of the penny-pinching 18th century, and nowhere more than in France. As the French government at that time had expenses flowing from its structure and world situation that could scarcely be covered other than by inflation, the issues of industrial and commercial expansion were probably not easily financed otherwise either. To this is added the consideration which of course neither Law nor anyone else at that time consciously put forward, but which, given the state of contemporary quantity theory, one very well could have – namely, that an increase in money *accompanied* by an increase in the quantity of goods would cause no damage to the currency and no disorganization of business life, if the extra money remained permanently in circulation. And one need only imagine something which is not logically impossible, the colonial enterprises of the bank founded in 1716 as having been as great successes as they actually were failures, to see that the collapse of the so-called Law swindle, as well as any other of the countless failures of this method of raising funds, did not stem from the basic concept but is to be explained simply by the failure of the purposes for which these funds were supplied.

But this knowledge, or at least its theoretical evaluation, had to wait for almost two centuries. If we disregard the not entirely felicitous start made by Macleod[18] in the 19th century, we can say that, in the technical banking literature, these things led an existence restricted to short-term commercial paper credit, while leaving the theory of money, indeed general economic theory, unaffected up until our time.

---

[18]Henry Dunning Macleod, *Lectures on Credit and Banking,* London 1882; *The Theory and Practice of Banking,* 5th edition, London 1892; *The Theory of Credit,* 2nd edition, London und New York, 1893, 1897.

However, the thought of John Law, who incidentally also has other achievements in monetary theory to show for himself,[19] is associated with other elements, which in themselves are foreign to it, but both in the practice and the theory of the matter came to the fore, and were suited to discredit it still further. In particular, the way credit was actually used: in the notes of the Bank, for consumptive purposes for court and the state, which always was the reason for the princely taste for *note-issuing banks* and by itself would have been sufficient in this case to bring about the collapse. These origins must be kept in mind if one wishes to understand the stance of monetary theorists and politicians towards the banknote up to our own time. This can be demonstrated with examples from both countries where note-issuing banks became centers of widely condemned, egregious abuses, as well as examples of countries where there have not, or have only rarely, been such abuses. All note-issuing banks have their root in the financial need of the states, although in the course of a most interesting change in significance, they have become the central organ of commercial traffic, and only in times of extreme distress, which breaks every law, again become what they were originally. In *this* respect Law's bank was the historical forerunner of the Bank of France, as constituted by Napoleon I, and a younger sister of the Bank of England,[20] founded in 1694 after a long debate in connection with a government credit transaction.[21] This debate did not yield a money-theoretical harvest, although an aspect did emerge that we find on a larger scale in Law's plan and which generally had undeserved vitality.

Perhaps it is on the basis of the commodity theory that we may best understand the notion that money, if it does not already consist of a material of intrinsic value, must represent something of intrinsic value, and that this role preeminently suited the most important asset of the time, land. He who denies

---

[19]John Law, *Money and Trade,* Edinburgh 1705, in a French translation in the Daire collection. Daire is among the fighters against the doctrine that money is a creature of the law or by agreement created "artificially."

[20]The reader must here already be made aware that more knowledge of the banking industry and its history is needed for understanding the theory of money than can be conveyed here.

[21]Macaulay in his *History of England* – in all its political and socio-psychological blaze of color – is still the classic presentation. Also, the extensions of their privilege in the subsequent period, namely from 1697, 1709, and 1742, which was the first to give the bank exclusive rights – the right of private bankers to issue notes was only questioned in the 19th century – are causally related to the cash-strapped state. [Thomas Babington Lord Macaulay, *The History of England from the Accession of James II*, 5th ed., London 1849.]

the historical value of the quantity theory ought to consider that thereby the path is also blocked to this insight, mediated as it is from that standpoint. For it is then obvious that money which poses as a claim for land or as a mortgage bill on land or some other asset that is not a part of commodity traffic, constitutes a "unilateral" increase of money as well, and will have the same effect as it would if it were not "secured" in this way. This is only a naive association – or a speculation on this association – with the deep-rooted belief in the popular consciousness of the particular economic security of property. Nonetheless, an agrarian competitor, the Land Bank, came about in 1696,[22] which also extended the government a loan and which was to issue notes on the basis of land ownership valued at one hundred times the yield [Rente], and which at any rate failed already in its very first beginnings. The same idea underlay the assignats[23] and land mandates [Landmandaten] of the French Revolution, and many later projects of the worst kind.

The problem of the relation between gold and silver coins, and sometimes even copper coins, remained alive during this period in large parts of Europe and especially in Italy, although elsewhere, and particularly in England, it was pushed into the background by the transition to actual and statutory *monometallism*. In terms of the history of science, it is of interest that thinkers fundamentally could not cope with the problem and did not clearly recognize either the essence of bimetallism with legal relation nor a *parallel currency* without such a relation. Excellent minds committed malpractice in the treatment of these issues in a way that is difficult to comprehend. Thus, some authors assumed the proposition that the value of monetary gold against the value of monetary silver – if only these two circulate – necessarily behaved in reverse fashion to their physical quantities. For example, none other than Beccaria even provided a proof for this (*Works*, ed. Custodi, vol. II, p. 203),[24] the defectiveness of which is infinitely instructive for anyone who is interested in the path of the inquiring mind.

---

[22]The most interesting propagator of this plan was John Asgill, *Several Assertions Proved*, 1696 (ed. Hollander).

[23]Regarding this, see above all the most recent treatment: Seymour Edwin Harris, *The Assignats*, Cambridge 1930.

[24]Marchese Cesare Bonesana de Beccaria, *Gesamtausgabe*, Milan 1821-22.

Throughout this time the policy of a statutory maximum interest rate is discussed. Of particular importance for monetary theory is the English discussion in the second half of the 17th century. Barbon,[25] Petty, Locke, and an anonymous author[26] are mainly considered. The practical argument comes only to this, that an artificial interest rate cut would be ineffective or harmful and that low interest rates can only be the consequence and not the cause of prosperity. This is of no further interest to us. But in connection with it, the detachment of the interest phenomenon from the money phenomenon is being prepared, the first beginnings of which detachment go far back – at least to Biel. It was only completed in Hume and Smith, the latter dressing down Montesquieu (who otherwise was quite weak in monetary theory) for representing popular opinion that the interest rate depends on the money supply. The main thing concerned here is the negative result that lies in the refutation of this opinion, in other words, the distinction of *price* (value) *of money* in the sense of capital interest and the *value of money* in the sense of purchasing power or market valuation. Although the fine nuances of both only are only suggestively present in the picture of interactions, and from the standpoint of later research even allow some objection to the radical divorce of money and interest which then ruled for over a century, viewed from the perspective of the times [ex tunc] this was a great gain in insight and overview, and the death sentence for many persistent errors.

Mercantilism and Monetary Theory

The remaining achievements of this era are best arranged in terms of the big debate about its economic policy, *mercantilism*, which to contemporaries initially appeared to be the highest wisdom, and eventually appeared the highest folly, although its critics announced themselves early on, while its proponents maintained themselves into the 19th century. In the reign of the Historical School we better learned to understand that policy as that of the nascent nation-state and the consolidated princely territory, their aggression outwards, their will to formation inwards. We correctly recognize the problems of their time and thus the behavior of the long line of statesmen from Peter of Vinea and Jacob of Capua in the Sicilian kingdom of Frederick II until the ministers of enlightened absolutism in the 18th century; namely, we distinguish clearly between the very different factual situations that fall under the word mercantilism, and the very different ideas and insights of its sponsors. Thus, the policy of Colbert, which in the final analysis had free trade as its goal, had very little to do

---

[25]Nicholas Barbon, *A Discourse of Trade,* Baltimore 1690.
[26]*The Interest of Money Mistaken*, 1668.

on the one hand with the primitive beginnings of the distant past and on the other with the bureaucratic degeneration that everywhere finally came to pass, which wiped out all memory in the minds of contemporaries and later critics of the fact that the internal economic policy of mercantilism was originally a rationalization of the chaos of ancient privileges which had become meaningless, of overlapping fiscal rights, etc., and a system of transition measures in favor of a nascent industry. But this only with reservation saves the *arguments* of the serious mercantilist writers [Schriftsteller], those of *popular* mercantilist writers [Tagesschriftsteller] not at all. In addition to much that, as we gain more knowledge, appears in a more favorable light than it did to Hume and Smith – who, incidentally, were very far from completely discarding mercantilist policy – there is much that is *simple* blunder, compared to which the criticism of mercantilism was *entirely* and enduringly progress. Here the modern attempts at rehabilitation, usually made by theoretically untrained practitioners [Fachgenossen], often goes too far.

All this is also true of the monetary policy and the monetary-theoretical views of mercantilism, which certainly cannot be dismissed with the phrase, the mercantilists confused wealth with money, and can only conditionally be characterized with the milder phrase, the mercantilists held *favorable trade balances* to be desirable because the influx of gold and silver that these compelled was their ideal. First, it would not *ipso facto* prove their trade policy to be futile. For both the circumstances of the time, which knew little[27] in the way of international credit transactions and no developed internal money market, as well as the aggressive militarism of the youthful nation-state, that presupposed the disposition over liquid means – even France had to bring important elements of war requirements, e.g., horses, in from abroad, not to mention the fact that at times the majority of European governments were in its pay – give meaning to such a policy, which cannot be seen from the arguments adduced for it. But these also often emphasized the very obvious point that gold, silver, jewels, etc., were the most practical form of international wealth.[28]

For an analytical achievement already lies in the *theory of the favorable balance of trade* – which was not a theory in the scientific sense – even when the just-mentioned political or sociological considerations are left out of consideration. Namely, it marks an important step in the recognition of the determinants

---

[27]Of course, the later Middle Ages already knew international credit transactions. The English crown, for example, borrowed from Florentine bankers just as modern states borrow in England, or borrowed in America during the World War.

[28]Cf. William Petty, *Political Arithmetic,* London 1691.

of national *exchange rates*. The currency troubles produced the weakness and vacillation thereof, which naturally had been regarded as a serious evil since the time that international trade generally gained sufficient importance. And the first "theory" that was held in this regard was that the exchange rate is the work of evil speculators hostile to the country's interest, to which one must put a stop. For example, already in the time of Queen Elizabeth, Sir Thomas Gresham attempted to act on this in an official capacity, in the course of which he produced all the arguments and measures that in our time we had opportunity to become acquainted with regarding the *"foreign exchange centers"* and *"exit points"* of the war and which sometimes were already hinted at in the *foreign exchange policy* of the pre-war period and in the discussions regarding it. The writers representing this view were called *bullionists*.[29] Gerard de Malynes[30] should be mentioned as a later, already purged representative.

On the other hand, it was an achievement to draw attention to the correlation of the exchange rate with the trade balance, even though that correlation does not rest on any deeper truth; to recognize the former as the mere and inevitable consequence of the economic condition; and to struggle through to the recognition of the worthlessness of *money export prohibitions* – an achievement that opened the door to further infiltration. We find this in all of the better writers of the mercantilist period, at the earliest with Antonio Serra (*Breve trattato delle cause che fare possono abbondari li regni d'oro e d'argento, dove non sono miniere* [A short treatise of the causes that can make realms abound in gold and silver, where there are no mines], 1613, Milan 1803), from which one can already discern the later theory of *international gold movements*; then with Mun,[31] the British Merchant, Child etc. in England, then in general in the 18th century, as in the Frenchman Melon (1734), the Spaniard Ustariz (1724) and with those excellent men who so well embodied the spirit and the standard of

---

[29]One therefore does those tendencies and arguments too much honor, when he calls them *neomercantilist*. They were *pre*-mercantilist – bullionist.

[30]Gerard de Malynes, *The Maintenance of Free Trade*, London 1622. He wished the exchange rate to be set by the king and considered every export of money to be a national loss – a by no means forgotten standpoint. Once again one sees the degree to which this "has a place" in the consciousness of the laity. One of the first and best arguments from the mercantilist view to oppose the bullionist was developed by Antonio Serra in his work quoted below against the bullionists, *De Sanctis.*

[31]Thomas Mun, *A Discourse of Trade from England unto East-Indies,* 1621, reproduced from the first edition, New York 1930; *England's Treasure by foraign Trade,* posthumously published, London 1664.

the reign of Maria Theresa and who conceptually and practically helped to rev-
olutionize all areas of state administration: Beccaria,[32] Giovanni Rinaldo Carli
(*Suile monete* [Regarding Money], vol. I, Milan 1754; this book had European
success) and Pietro Verri.[33]

Nor is it true that the difference between the balance of payments and
the balance of trade was overlooked. Precisely such progress as was not quite of
the first rank, but of great practical importance, characterized the literature of
the late mercantilist period. Verri, who besides, protected and promoted by the
witty and wise rescripts of Prince Kaunitz, worked out the first statistical determination of the trade balance of Lombardy - one of the milestones on the way
to "realistic" theory[34] - knew and theoretically considered all the other items of
the balance of payments, even capital flows. And Beccaria's formulation of *ec-
cesso di bisogno* [excess demand] (on foreign assets) and possible deviations from
parity (deviation: exchange sum + transport costs of adverse balance: adverse
balance) fits perfectly with the balance of payments. Carli (1764), with the
Frenchman Dutot (1738) and the Englishman Fleetwood (1707), shares the fame
of first attempting *measurements of the change in the value of money* otherwise
than by investigating price movement of a single - considered to be particularly
important or stable - commodity, the latter method having been proposed by
Locke among others.

However, there is absolutely no monetary theory of mercantilism, which
for the rest is not a scientific unity but only an orientation - not even an entirely

---

[32]Marchese de Beccaria, *Elementi di economia pubblica* [Elements of Public Econ-
omy], posthumously published in *Scrittori classici Italiani di economia politica, Parte
Moderna* [Classical Writers on Political Economy, Modern Part], Part XI and XII, pub-
lished by Custodi, Milan 1804; *Del disordine e de' rimedi delle moneta nello Stato di
Milano 1762* [Of the Disorder and the Remedy of Money in the State of Milan, 1762] in:
Opere [Works] *of Cesare Beccaria,* Milan 1821-22.

[33]Pietro Verri, *Meditazioni sulla Economia politica* [Meditations on Political Eco-
nomy], Genoa 1771.

[34]Desperation regarding the almost insuperable difficulty of the enterprise, in
view of the lack of reliable data - this topic will be discussed again and again - caused
Genovesi to accept the exchange rate itself simply as evidence of the credit or debit of
the trade balance: [to expect] such [a degree of] precision [from] the doctrine of the "determination" of the exchange rate through the trade balance, however, is positively wrong
(Antonio Genovesi, *Lezione di Economia Civile* [Lectures on Civil Economy], 1765, in
Scrittori classici Italiani di economia politica [Italian Classical Writers on Political Econ-
omy], Milan 1803).

clear one – to practical issues, that only owes its role in the history of economics to the improper habit of grouping authors according to their economic beliefs. Commonality of theoretical conception is then lacking even in those points where the commonality of trade policy views would lead us to surmise it. Hence, a positive valuation attached to an export surplus and the inflow of precious metals apparently suggests a commodity theory of money. But such is not always held by those mercantilists who address fundamental questions at all. Beccaria, for example, called gold and silver "real," while Verri called gold the "universal commodity" – the latter even claiming, in stark contradiction to the facts, that the money supply could "never" deviate from the value of the metal in the coin – but Locke is only a "practical," not a "theoretical" metallist, while Sir James Steuart (*An Inquiry into the Principles of Political Economy*, London, 1767) was actually – besides Montesquieu – the representative of a "value-free material" conception of the nature of money who was least encumbered by doubt. Furthermore, almost all authors in the secure possession of the *quantity theorem*, although this might suggest both the impossibility and the worthlessness of a permanent *export surplus*, yet in any case make the mere reference to the desirability of money import into an inadequate reason for it – which illustrates the truth that a scientific argument is never explained merely by reference to the practical goals of its representatives, nor uniquely determined by these. For our purposes, we therefore can entirely drop the distinction between mercantilists and non-mercantilists and assert that they all, united in a higher meaning, contributed to the construction of monetary theory.

Barbon is to my knowledge the first author in whom resonates what today is called the *purchasing power parity theory*.[35] He saw that the balance of trade or payments is not the "final" cause of an outflow or inflow of precious metal, but only occurs when the purchasing power of the precious metal in the trading countries differs, while – as one might well construe – otherwise the import and export of goods condition and balance each other. Sir Dudley North (*Discourses upon Trade*, 1691)[36] finally brought to full clarity that – of course, only with full-value currency – no political intervention is needed to get the "necessary" money in one country, that instead the circulating money supply governs itself. Even so, the step in this direction from the aforementioned prior approaches is not great. For North seems to have less in mind the price mecha-

---

[35]Should one not wish to find it already in De Mercado, *Summa de Tratos y Contratos*, Seville 1571. Cf. also Sayous, *loc. cit.*

[36]Reprinted Edinburgh 1822.

nism that causes this arrangement than a situationally determined money demand, to which minting and money inflow and outflow adjust immediately,
which is not a very felicitous way of viewing the matter. Locke *sees* this pricing
mechanism and the relationship that follows *from this* between prices in
different countries. His powerful formulation of the quantity theorem also leads
him to the highly comprehensive insight that everything that hinders or facilitates trade and industry, affects the value of money. But, strangely enough, the
automatic distribution of precious metal monetary supply to all countries is still
not as clear to him as it was to North; otherwise, he could not have considered
a trade deficit to be as tragic as he did.

Hume therefore must be set considerably higher than his predecessors,
although regarding details he falls short of them and every one of the insights
that can be found in him is detectable before him. He stated, more acutely than
anyone else, that the absolute quantity of money is totally indifferent in a country because prices so adjust to each that any volume of business can be managed
by any amount of money, that only in the course of an increase in money does
this increase temporarily benefit industry, that money is a mere calculation
method, a set of counters, that should a part of the value of money disappear
from a country, the export capacity enhanced by the price decline would bring
it back again, at which point these additional exports would cease, just as any
unilateral money import would only increase prices and imports and so undo
itself, which appears provisionally to verify the automatic distribution of the
quantities of metal between all countries.

Many achievements, especially those of a summarizing and formulating
nature, must still be named, such as that of Genovesi, of Giammaria Ortes
(*Della Economia Nazionale libri sei*, 1774), and perhaps especially the excellent
book by the witty and biting Abbé Fernando Galiani (*Della Moneta*, Naples,
1750). We restrict ourselves to a word on the monetary theory of Adam Smith.
He runs, following the oldest tradition, from the division of labor and exchange
to money; on the one hand, without committing to the commodity theory, on
the other hand without committing to Hume's bold statement regarding "counters." How else could he glide out over the surface, deliberating reasonably and
evading deeper trouble? Certainly in the case where money consists of material
of intrinsic value, the production of which costs money, he put forward a cost
theory of the value of money, indeed applying precisely those aspects of his cost
theory according to which the costs are equal to the applied physical quantity
of labor. This was pure happenstance, as he could just as well have used another.
So here we have the archetype of Marx's conception of monetary value, only
that he was of the view that this theory excludes the quantity theorem, or makes

it unnecessary. Mill then, as mentioned, demonstrated the contrary, but even with Smith there is not such a contrast. Certainly, he did not formulate the quantity theorem explicitly, because he was not a man of exact wording - which many impute to him as merit - but he implied it as well as he did any of the other statements formulated by Hume.[37]

Monetary Theory in the Modern Age

Ricardo's Achievement

4. Discussion stagnated on the plateau attained, until the impetus of the monetary consequences of the Revolutionary and Napoleonic wars made it flow again. The paper money economy had a very different extent in different countries and, stemming not quite from the same cause, correspondingly was not all of the same character. Only in France was there utter collapse. This grew out of social disorganization: the image of the paralyzed social and governmental organism, incapable of adaptation, makes a great impression, of which the living nerves, as soon as they are affected by the revolution, immediately fail in every respect, even in matters of taxation, while the innovators, without desiring it, in fact while initially struggling against it and condemning it, take the path of least political resistance and hurtle into the paper money economy, in which there is no stopping[38] until the moment at which a ruler, to whom all join themselves, restores the social order and the normal habits of economic activity.

---

[37]His theory of the effect of paper money issues is evidence *for* this, not against it.

Similar views are in evidence, in the full completeness of a main topic, with Johannes Georg Büsch, *Abhandlung von dem Geldumlauf* [Treatise on the Circulation of Money], Hamburg-Kiel, 1780.

[38]The cited work by S.E. Harris (*The Assignats*, Cambridge, 1930) is strongly recommended to everyone who wishes to study all phases of an inflationary process in all its social-psychological reflections, and with all its consequences. Not even the aspects that characterized the inflation of the World War, especially the German, are missing. Here we have before us all the pathological degeneration that the economy and the habits of the people undergo in such a case, and no less all the unsuccessful attempts of state power to control the evil and its effects: criminal punishment, trade in government bonds, government commodity exports and imports, price ceilings, rationing, and the like. The vicious circle runs in ideal purity, wherein each situation leads to further inflation, and that further inflation leads to ever more unsustainable situations, from one step to "only the next one," until the final collapse (1796). And the causes and the relative justification

It was not so elsewhere. In Austria, the second great example, it was military spending and only this that ever and again scuppered the balanced budget, contention against which never ceased – this applies not only to the Napoleonic wars themselves but to the entire period from the final years of the reign of Maria Theresa until 1866, even in peacetime. Army expenditures, due to foreign entanglements[39] and, in 1848 and 1849, internal difficulties, each time removed the previously almost attained goal. This was due not simply to army expenses in themselves, but in relation to the financial incapacity of an agrarian economic body. The first aspect also applied to England, there even reinforced by the policy of the subsidies, but not, of course, the second. Despite the economic difficulties, especially during the time of the continental blockade, the financial strength of the City remained essentially unshaken during the entire period and the taxing power grew to cover at least a significant part of the war expenses. Therefore, the process in England was incomparably milder: the note-printing press was used only in relatively modest degree and only in a manner which could still be comprehended in terms of loan transactions taken seriously.

Precisely for this reason, the diagnosis of the English situation could be equivocal for monetary policymakers of academic rank, and a fruitful subject of discussion.[40] The more so because the outflow of gold from the Bank to the

-----

[Recht] of that state of mind we understand, for which it is never the inflation itself that produces that evil, but always some other elements that indeed truly *in each moment* more clearly present themselves than the step on the path of inflation, which is taken at the same moment. It is as with the morphine addict: his sufferings appear caused by other circumstances (take note: *not* entirely without justification), and the increased morphine consumption that follows appears at most a consequence, and even the remedy.

[39]The measure of 1811 – the so-called "national bankruptcy" – probably would have stabilized the currency if the subsequent final struggle against Napoleon had not brought new war spending. The reform of 1816 – the foundation of the national bank – was not initially a success because the goal of transferring the note masses into funded debt and an ordered banknote currency was tackled on too narrow a basis and too quickly, but in the next few years normal conditions approached step by step: only the costs of military intervention in Sardinia and Naples (1821) undid the achievements. In 1830, the government deficit was again almost eliminated, but the European unrest of 1831 in turn swelled the military budget. This was repeated understandably during the period 1846-50 (Revolution, Italian campaign, threat of war with Prussia), 1853-56 (Crimean War, which led to the formation of an army in the east), 1859, 1864-66.

[40]Partly because of material that was not available to contemporaries, a modern discussion of the issue has evolved that has taken on stately proportions. See in particular

Continent, to the internal market, and into hoards, which had been the immediate cause of the suspension (dressed in the form of a prohibition) of the bank's
obligation to convert notes (Bank Restriction 1797-1821), [likewise] preceded by
a year the resumption of convertibility, during which the bank was obliged to
dispense *gold bullion* against their notes first for £ 4-1-0 per ounce, then around
£ 3-19-6 and finally for the coin price of £ 3-17-10½, bullion, and not less than 60
ounces, so as to eliminate demand for small change. It was quite similar to how,
after the Gold Standard Act of 1925, the government did not forego particular
availments of the bank: the bank had already during peacetime violated the pe-
nal provision of the privilege of 1694, which forbade the granting of advances to
the state without the consent of Parliament. Thus, these advances amounted to
an average of about nine million pounds in 1792, and after a temporary rise to
thirteen million they again dropped below that level towards the end of 1796.[41]

---

the presentation of Ralph G. Hawtrey in the 18th chapter of *Currency and Credit* (3rd
ed., London 1928); also A.W. Acworth, *Financial Reconstruction in England 1815-1822*
(London, 1925); Cannan in his introduction to the edition of the likewise to be noted
Bullion Report (*The Paper Pound of 1797-1821*); J.W. Angell, *Theory of International
Prices,* Appendix A, Cambridge, 1926; and, valuable with regard to the referenced mate-
rial but disfigured by an infelicitous manner of interpretation, the studies of Norman
Silberling, "British Prices and Business Cycles, 1778-1850," in the *Review of Econ. Statis-
tics,* 1923, and "Financial and Monetary Policy of Great Britain during the Napoleonic
Wars," in the *Quarterly Journal of Economics,* vol. 38, 1924, p 214.

[41]This was apparently a success of the bank's remonstrances, the position of
which in England was entirely different than continental central banks had, or ever have
had. But it actually only remonstrated for two secondary reasons.

One was because its leadership was uncomfortable with the illegality of its action. The government acted on this argument by introducing a law in 1793 that granted
indemnity for the past, and for the future gave it the right - *without* the restriction demanded by the bank - to make means available to the government without special act of
Parliament. Of course, this measure had to weaken the resistance of the bank. With this,
and in connection with the suspension of convertibility and the ban, not of all gold export, but of the melting-down and exportation of gold coins and coinage gold, we have
before us the main elements of the arsenal of inflationary war financing, which were also
everywhere put to use during the World War. The notes of the Bank did however receive
forced exchange - in the World War, they even *formally* maintained their convertibility
- first in 1812, after signs of refusal to accept payment in notes became manifest, whereas
previously the nation had so stood firmly by the note, as in 1745 during the time of the

Moreover, since the bank vigorously and ruthlessly (even by rationing discount credit) tightened credit to the private sector, and the exchange rate was entirely, or nearly, at par with Hamburg and Lisbon at the end of 1796, it was only political causes, such as the invasion panic and foreign payments by the government, that led to that crumbling of the gold basis of the notes.[42]

Of course, even back then, inflation was not lacking; in particular, the subscriptions for war loans were partly inflationary. But it was kept within the bounds that a healthy currency can withstand, albeit at the cost of a credit crisis in 1796. Then, of course, it was different after the repeal of the convertibility requirement in 1797, and to the eye of the British business world, accustomed to financial correctness, it must have appeared as if government and bank had only been waiting for the political opportunity to get rid of the shackle of convertibility in order to propel inflation: in fact, the floating debt, note circulation, and the price level rose forthwith, and already in 1800, hence before the Peace

---

invasion of the Pretender in Scotland, when no one thought of taking advantage of the discount of the notes or even of hedging against its disadvantage.

The second reason for the bank's continually renewed remonstrances was withdrawals by the government on Treasury bills, which accounted for only a small part of the total advances, but which were particularly disturbing to the dispositions of the bank, unpredictable as they were, especially when demand for gold payments and *subsidies* abroad were concerned. Claims of this form were then kept within a moderate range. But political foreign payments were unpleasant enough even if funds were not requested in this form, and the bank already in 1796 went so far as to declare that another allied loan in England "will in all probability prove fatal to the Bank of England." We are brought to understand how much this aspect was at the forefront of the concerns of bankers and the public, and how hard it had to be for non-theorists to seek the cause of the unfavorable shape of exchange rates elsewhere. The *balance of payments theory* of exchange rates must have drawn nearly insurmountable strength from this.

[42]This was also the view of Ricardo (*Works*, McCulloch ed., London, 1846, p 406). It is true that in the course of 1795, during the collapse of the assignats, French domestic commerce in actuality returned to metallic circulation. This certainly contributed to the outflow of gold from England. Nevertheless, Hawtrey likely overestimated this aspect (*loc. cit.*, pp. 326 ff.). French deposits in England that could have been repatriated were not available on a large scale. Nor could investment of British capital in France – in the midst of martial law – have played an important role. And at that time France could not have exhibited a large increase in exports such as would have forced an influx of gold. If nevertheless "sufficient" metallic money circulated in France in the middle of 1796, it could only have come from hoards and the plunder of the armies.

of Amiens (1802), a premium on gold bullion and exchange rate weakness were in evidence. The peace brought relaxation, but after the resumption of hostilities the whole process began again, with the maximum amount of floating debt (54.2 million pounds) being reached in 1813, the maximum price level (by Silberling's index, the base year being 1790, 198 per cent) in 1814, and the maximum figure for notes of the Bank of England in circulation (28.3 million pounds) in 1817. The most unfavorable exchange rate came in 1811. One would think that would be clear. But one can see that the correspondence of the critical points is not as tight as the layman and the practitioner would require in order to accept a diagnosis unsympathetic to themselves - both rely on "facts" as opposed to "ivory-tower" theory only if the former seem to speak in favor of their current conduct. Also, this inflation did not go so far - such is only to be expected in the last stage of a monetary disturbance - as to overshadow any other events and any other causal connection; rather, we can still clearly perceive the pulse of the economy in the inflation-swollen ciphers, especially, apart from the Continental System, the relatively small extent of the disruption of production and trade; and almost the entire period was a time of vigorous development of the British economy.

In itself alone, this would have been sufficient to mitigate the impact of inflation and its symptoms, making it harder for the "untrained" eye to see. Even less clear and even less understandable to laymen and specialists alike were the phenomena of the subsequent period of deflation, which ended in the crisis of 1825 - which for all that cannot be seen simply, nor even primarily, as a deflation crisis. Finally, the statistical picture of the process is very poor - as was said, contemporaries did not even have all the data available that we have today - to which is to be added that wars in themselves arbitrarily change some numbers, thus the *gold points* move apart as a result of increased transport risk, unusually ample room is given to speculative forecasting, etc.

One has to keep this in mind if one would understand the course of the famous English discussion[43] of the monetary policy of the Napoleonic period

---

[43]This is the only one with significance enough to discuss here. In France, the turmoil at the time was probably to blame that so little was achieved that deserves mention. The best bibliography I know of is in the appendix of the cited book by S.E. Harris. It was not like that elsewhere. In the Austrian memoranda penned by ministerial scribes, there is quite a lot of sound insight. Count Buquoy (regarding whom see E. Thomas, *Georg Graf von Buquoy*, Munich 1929) might also be characterized as a monetary theorist. Germany also had some to mention, regarding which see S.P. Altmann, "Zur Deutschen Geldlehre des 19. Jahrhunderts" [Regarding German Monetary Theory in the 19th Century], in *Die Entwicklung der deutschen Volkswirtschaftslehre im 19. Jahrhundert.*

and estimate the importance of its scientific fruit. There is something else as well: both in these discussions as well as in the "revision negotiation" being conducted today by the court of science regarding the rights and wrongs of the parties, there are two elements that distort its scientific image and cloud its atmosphere. It may be that, as even Minister Perceval officially declared, inflation was inevitable to the successful conclusion of the war and the "enemy" of inflation was wrong insofar as having suggested something that practically would have subjected the nation to disastrous conditions. But that can as little be held against a *theoretical* analysis of the currency condition as can the most indubitable fact that the hasty attempt to return to the gold standard was responsible for the setback in 1817. Furthermore, the anti-inflationists may have made a mistake in showing a tendency to make the bank's management solely responsible for inflation – certainly, not only an injustice lay therein (the bank leadership put the brakes on as best it could, and it only had *that* influence on the *note issue* of the many *country banks* that derived from the latter's developing practice of holding an ever larger share of reserves in notes of the Bank of England) but also much narrowness and superficiality. Even so, that does not affect their merits in terms of monetary theory. For our purposes it is essential to remove this aspect, because in important cases, behind apparently sharply opposed points of view, a fundamental identity of scientific conceptions emerges.

Finally a third point: the practical cause entailed that the struggle against quite primitive errors[44] came to the foreground, such that the principles from

---

Gustav Schmoller zur 70. Wiederkehr seines Geburtstages [The Development of German Economics in the 19th Century. Gustav Schmoller, the 70th Anniversary of His Birth], Leipzig 1908. Regarding the *romantic theory of money* cf. Melchior Palyi in the *Archiv für Sozialwissenschaft* [Archive for Social Science], Vol. 42, 1916-17. The merits or demerits of the views of Adam Müller regarding money depend on what precise content is attached to phrases, such as money being the economic expression of the inner spiritual unity of the many, that corresponds with the nature of man, or that metallic money is the most perfect expression of national power, and the like.

[44]The practitioner saw especially the *discount* of the banknote against gold bullion and the unfavorable state of the exchange rates and was inclined to explain the former by a *"rise in demand"* for gold" (thus Charles Bosanquet in his remarks on the likewise to be mentioned Bullion Report: *Practical Observations on the Report of the Bullion Committee*, London, 1810), and the latter by denying any relationship to the rise of the note amount and to seek the causes of the problems in the trade balance (or *balance of payments*), much like what happened during our World War (thus e.g. the representative

which the best thinkers argued did not fully receive their due, and in fact often were developed with so little care that even today they provide difficult issues of interpretation, and the individual achievements are not so easy to recognize as they would be if they were available in the form of scholarly papers or systematic textbooks. And this is leaving aside the fact that, in the struggle for the assertion of the most important truths, the practical diagnosis often understandably underwent exaggerations and undue simplifications.[45]

The discussion centered in the most famous document of monetary history, the so-called Bullion Report (*Report, together with Minutes of Evidence and Accounts, from the Select Committee appointed to Inquire into the cause of*

---

of the Bank of England before the Bullion Committee, Whitmore, Pearse, and Harman, all of whom were of the opinion that the notes, after all issued only to satisfy a "necessary want" for notes, could not possibly affect the price of bullion gold or foreign exchange rates. The reasons given for these views - to the degree that any justification at all was sought and the practitioner in question did not simply express his "conviction" or appeal to his practical experience - contained palpable error. But even here it should be emphasized that the "practitioner," even when helpless against the opposing argument, yet did not unjustifiably feel that the argument at least did not contain the whole truth and did not exhaust all elements of the concrete situation. Later we will see that, notwithstanding the rights of the theorems either then or now comprehended by the untrained observer, in explanation of the specific circumstances of a historical point in time - in particular, it is short-term symptoms that are dealt with in that case - sometimes other things can be more important than they are, and that this often enough had to do with easily correctable flippancies of expression, when seemingly it was basic truths that were transgressed.

[45]Overlooking these aspects makes some modern writers look unjustly on the scientific achievements of the discussion, and in particular Ricardo. How else can this presentationally most difficult of all economic writers be understood if one does not only collect *all* the scattered fragments of his thoughts, but also interpolate the missing links? If one does this, the apparent contradiction between his advocacy of a return to gold parity and his statement before the Committee of the House of Commons in 1819 that this remedy can sometimes be worse than the disease, is cleared up. The place where the inability to understand Ricardo's nowhere systematically executed basic conception leads, is shown in Silberling's deplorable thesis that Ricardo, having just become a landowner in 1819, represented different interests after this than before. Regarding the utter groundlessness of this thesis, see Jacob Viner, "Angell's Theory of International Prices," in *Journal of Political Economy*, 1926, where other examples of similar misunderstandings are to be found.

the High Price of Gold Bullion and to take into Consideration the state of the
circulating medium, and of the exchanges between Great Britain and Foreign
Parts, 1810, reprinted for the book trade in the same year, reprinted in Cannan,
The Paper Pound from 1797 to 1821, published 1919). Edited by Horner,
Thornton, and Huskisson, it points out that gold's premium (the "high price of
bullion" [in notes]) could be attributed to inflation ("excess of currency," "re-
dundant currency," as Ricardo put it) as well as that the unsatisfactory state of
exchange rates could be solved by contracting the paper circulation. Whatever
one might think of the wisdom of practical advice to conduct a policy of
deflation in the midst of a war, whatever one thinks of the material collected by
the Commission, however grimly one goes to court with individual deficiencies
of argument, one must always respectfully look back on this document of moral
courage, which intends to state the truth to its own people in a situation in
which the spread of comforting illusions is often counted among the duties of
patriotism, and, in opposition to a phalanx of practical authorities on the one
hand and a clearly hostile mood of the political world on the other, sticks to the
– actual or presumed – right thing [sachlich Richtigen]. And momentary defeat
was followed by eventual victory.

But if the authors and instigators of the report and all those who from
1800 on took up for the "inflation" diagnosis also paved the way in important
aspects for scientific truth and captured public opinion – and basically that is all
we can expect from a "practical cause" – they added hardly anything essential to
the existing stock of scientific knowledge. For the time being one did not even
get beyond Hume.[46]

---

[46]The questions surrounding the discount of the banknotes were not new any-
more, even for England. The restoration of the undervalued currency at the end of the
17th century resulted in a deflationary crisis, during the course of which the bank in 1696
already had to instate redemption of its notes, whereupon a discount was instated. The
discussion therefore always returned when this case came up, the uniqueness of which,
however, was by no means clearly recognized. After all, it is to be seen as progress that
the new question of the – unilateral or reciprocal – dependence between note issues of
the Bank of England and note issues of the country bankers was being investigated. This
is the more important because the same question, carried over to the modern form of
bank money, i.e., bank deposits, later on played and still today plays a major role in
monetary theory and monetary policy. Walter Boyd, in his "Letter to the Rt. Hon William Pitt" (1801), took the first step to my knowledge. Moreover, he derives the discount
of notes from their overissue, contrasting the effect of such money increase very nicely
with the effects of an increase in full-value metallic money. Thornton (*Enquiry into the*

Nature and Effects of the Paper Credit of Great Britain, 1802) shares the merit of being first with Boyd, inasmuch as he adds the opposite-running strand to Boyd's analysis of the influence of the issue of the bank on the credit provision of the country bankers. He also boasted a theory of international price formation and currency movement that followed in Hume's footsteps and added essentially nothing more and nothing else to what Hume had to offer. But he did work out a point, or add to it – the brevity of Hume's representation makes it difficult to say which of the two is the case – which was opposed by Ricardo and has remained controversial. Since he was of the opinion that the agio [of gold vis-à-vis banknotes] and [the depreciation of] the exchange rate do not stem from the increase in the note issue, the task was incumbent on him to specify other causes for these, and he pointed, just exactly as did the leading banking practitioners, to poor harvests and political payments abroad, i.e., to the deficit of the balance of payments, which as such seems to be an independent cause of unfavorable exchange rates. He then attempted a theoretical justification of this. Understandably, he had the success that always attends on the theoretical representation of currently-held beliefs: not only was he approvingly reviewed by the incoming chairman of the Bullion Committee, Horner, in the *Edinburgh Review* of 1802 and by Malthus in the same journal in 1811, who protected him against Ricardo's attack, but the majority of the authors also followed him. As an example, the meritorious Torrens may be mentioned (*Essay on Money and Paper Currency*, London, 1812); as an exception – in fact, a precursor [of Ricardo's] – Wheatley (*An Essay on the Theory of Money*, 1807). It is however less understandable that Ricardo not only remained almost alone, but also that John Stuart Mill, John Elliot Cairnes (*Some Leading Principles of Political Economy Newly Expounded*, London, 1874), indeed most later authors in general explicitly or implicitly seem to have held Ricardo to be in the wrong. A recent discussion in the *Quarterly Journal of Economics* (1917-18) between Taussig, Wicksell, and Hollander resumed the controversy, which obviously is of the greatest importance for the theory of the inflationary process, capital movements and German reparations. And here as well, Ricardo fared poorly. See also Jacob Viner, *Canada's Balance of International Indebtedness*, Cambridge, 1924, Chapter IX, and "Die Theorie des auswärtigen Handels" [The Theory of Foreign Commerce], in *Die Wirtschaftstheorie der Gegenwart* [The Economic Theory of the Present], ed. by Hans Mayer, Vol. 4, Vienna 1927-32; Hollander, "The Development of the Theory of Money from Adam Smith to David Ricardo," in *Quarterly Journal of Economics*, vol. 25, 1911, p. 429; Edmund Whitaker, "The Ricardian Theory of Gold Movements" (*ibid.*, 1904). By the "classical" or "Ricardian" theory of gold movements is usually understood the mechanism described by Hume, by which gold is driven to the regions of where price levels are lowest and thereby *tends* to induce an automatic adjustment of those price levels.

But Ricardo's genius, which outshone all allies and enemies, probed further.[47] He knew *everything* we know today, only lacking *theoretically* the concept of the price level – yet today still unsolved – and *practically* the method of index numbers – already existing in his time, but unknown to him. This prevented him from achieving complete success here, similarly to the way the shortcomings of his theory of value – which he felt was an expedient and therefore accepted it only because the way of use value seemed to him impassable – prevented him from that achievement elsewhere. Apart from *that*, the nature of money was very clear to him, and it was *this* which kept him from explicitly saying that material value does not essentially or necessarily appertain to money.

Besides the authors mentioned, still others authors of that time deserve significant credit for shaping public opinion and making more felicitous or more complete formulations. Thus Blake (*Observations on the Principles Which Regulate the Course of Exchange,* 1810); Lord King (*Thoughts on the Restriction of Payments in Specie ...,* 1803); Lord Lauderdale (*The Depreciation of the Paper Currency of Great Britain Proved,* London, 1812); Lord Liverpool (*Treatise on the Coins of the Realm,* London, 1805), all of which are still worth reading, although they often handle the crucial arguments quite awkwardly and face the collateral problems of a monetary system *entirely* divested of gold or capital flows as something almost completely foreign.

[47]He first came on the scene with three articles ("letters") in the *Morning Chronicle* of 1809, which then were published as a pamphlet (*The High Price of Bullion, a Proof of the Depreciation of Bank Notes,* initially London 1810, since 1811 with the important appendix "Observations on the Depreciation of Paper Currency," which contains his monetary policy proposal). Then he defended the Bullion Report in the *Reply to Mr. Bosanquet's Practical Observations on the Report of the Bullion Committee* (London, 1811). The most far-reaching, it seems to me (quite apart from the proposal itself) is his *Proposals for an Economic and Secure Currency,* 1816. Finally, the comments in the *Principles* – and not only in chapters 27 and 28 – come into consideration, as well as his correspondence with Malthus, McCulloch, and Hutches Trower, and his remarks before the Committee of 1819. Even from those *titles*, especially as the representation in the *Principles* is fragmentary, one sees how difficult the interpretation which one must infer from applications and volatile hints of the theoretical background, often poorly formulated in apparent haste. *Letters of David Ricardo to Thomas Robert Malthus, 1810-23,* Oxford, 1887, *Letters of David Ricardo to John Ramsay McCulloch, 1816-23, Publications of the American Economic Association,* vol. 10, nos. 5-6, New York in 1895 and London in 1896. *Letters of David Ricardo to Hutches Trower and Others 1811-23,* Oxford, 1899. Reports from Committees, in *The Parliamentary Debates* (published under the superintendence of TC Hansard), London 1812 ff., vol. 3, in 1819.

The meaning of a gold standard, he states with unsurpassable clarity of expression (Sec. II of the *Proposals*), is "that the only use of a standard is to regulate the quantity and by the quantity the value of the currency." He had nothing to add to the quantity theorem. But he was the first to maintain it with that accuracy, the hallmark of which is - unfounded - doubts as to whether he really advocated it. This, in addition to his ignorance of the price index method, is the reason why he prefers to measure the depreciation of money by the premium on gold - with a proper feeling that price movement alone allows no conclusion on the *monetary* causes of inflation. The theory of *purchasing power parity*, as we have seen, was very old; besides, it was also implied in the antimercantilistic argument, and Ricardo did not take the final step, presupposing the concept of the price level. But if he did not take the final step, he did take the decisive one: he first argued consistently from its standpoint and sought to refute the fallacies that, with its older representatives, were quite compatible with its essential recognition - it is in Ricardo's hand that this analytical tool first shows itself in its true form. Like any major accomplishment, this also had its immediate precursors, but the degree to which it was ahead of its time can be seen in today's discussion of the same question, the standard work for which is still Ricardo's *High Price of Bullion.*

Ricardo's monetary policy proposal - a paper currency only redeemable in gold bullion - will now occupy us. Here we consider the theoretical knowledge from which it arose. First, the knowledge that the stability of purchasing power is the decisive factor in assessing a monetary system; then, the knowledge that made Ricardo into the scientific progenitor of any serious plans of *manipulated* currencies, that "by the judicious *management* (my italics, S.) of the quantity" a paper currency can attain a degree of *stability* ("uniformity") "which is by no other means attainable" (*Works*, McCulloch ed., London, 1846, p. 399); and finally, that statutory reserve requirements for the country banks - he thought about balances of government bonds with a state agency: the system that reigned in the United States for a long time - are a suitable means to secure the credit edifice. Even the knowledge of the essential equality of banknotes and bank deposits, far in advance of the conditions of the time, is found in him.

But the best of Ricardo's achievements remained closed to the times - which understood essentially only his fight for the re-establishment of the English gold currency - and had to be reconquered later and in another connection by Basen among others. The discussion of subsequent decades - again it is the English discussion that leads the way - followed contemporary events, initially without going any deeper. Purely practically, it was first and foremost discovered that by conscious *discount policy* - which to that point had been so far from

the Bank's mind that between 1694 and 1830 it changed the discount rate
scarcely a half-dozen times – the Bank could affect the money market and exchange rates. The complete theoretical comprehension of the connection between interest rates and monetary value, which already began – in particular
with Locke – at the end of the 17ᵗʰ century, initially opposed the theoretical
tradition, which had developed in the fight against primitive errors and – a pretty
example of the fact that views, which had been helpful in one problem situation,
could become restraining in another – tended to deny any connection between
interest rates and the value of money. But in the reciprocal effect between the
developing practice of bank issue and the monetary-policy discussion, the position developed that the discount rate affects the extent of credit provision and
through this, prices, and through these, exports and imports, and so regulates
the state of business, which brought this position to "classical" status and caused
it to pass from banking into money literature.

But something else became the focus of interest after the currency reform
and the resumption of gold redemption of banknotes: the development of the
banking system (and especially all the small banks, which also issued notes)
brought with it the role of scapegoat, upon which public opinion heaped the
blame when the economy went bad, especially in the crises that then progressed
so catastrophically. "The contemporary assumption was that any economic distress was to be blamed not on unalterable conditions and individually committed errors, but only on the note-issuing banks" (Adolf Wagner). The practical
question was whether the note issue[48] could be left to the bankers in the same
way that the production of a commodity is left to the producer, or whether the
circumstance that the "commodity" of the banker was of an entirely unique
kind and not readily subjected to the brake of production cost, required statutory regulation. The end was the Bank Act of the Peel ministry (1844), which

---

[48]Only this was concerned, not bank credit in other forms. We will yet become
acquainted with the sense that this idea of the special nature of notes had. First, the note
was just simply more visible, especially since the time of modern deposit banking had
not yet arrived. The renewal of the bank privilege in 1833, by establishing the legal purchasing power of the notes of the Bank of England, helped the country banks – in case
of crisis, they could more easily find support from it. But even before this, the government took action against note issue by country banks, by banning the issuance of notes
under five pounds. From then on, the basic trend of official bank policy was the suppres-
sion of the issue rights of country banks to the greatest practicable degree, at least in
England itself, and the sharp restriction of the note rights of the central bank, although
Sir Robert Peel, who would implement this tendency, in 1819 declared against it.

radically implemented the last point by *maximizing the absolute amount of unsecured* notes issued by the Bank of England and by gradually drying up the note issue of the other banks. This regulation was shaped by the clause that the note amount must be adjusted such that the sum of metallic money plus banknotes should be related as if it consisted entirely of metal. One could not appeal to Ricardo for this position.

The discussion lacks the luster that only a great personality and the highest skill are able to impart; the voices in the dispute were only knowledgeable practitioners and nothing more. Both positions contained much practical wisdom, and they could unite quite well on a higher level of theoretical insight. To be mentioned are Lord Overstone, at that time victorious, and Fullarton, representing the unsuccessful side. Now the latter fell far short of the former in analytical training, and committed numerous blunders in the argument of which Overstone would have been incapable. Nevertheless, it is not Overstone but Fullarton who deserved to live on, as he was the first to grasp the fundamental difference between lending for productive purposes in its full monetary-theoretical meaning – even if he expressed it imperfectly – and made the process that was later called *"money creation"* a basic fact of the theory of money. It is incorrect to make him the father of a *"banking theory"* of money. This person does not exist, and Fullarton found nothing less interesting than any of the basic questions of theory. Nor did he analyze more deeply the process of the origination of bank money with commodities and its expiration by the reflux of money in the repayment of the loan to the lending banker (Fullarton's Principle). But all the credit that lies in the conquest of a new element of reality for a theoretical discipline, is his.

Among the opponents of the Bank Act of 1844, Thomas Tooke must yet be mentioned, because of all the authors of that time, only he made a vision of money his own that situated it within the overall context of all the economic body's expressions of life, for which reason all of these expressions of life were relevant to him in terms of monetary policy. He not only programmatically proclaimed this vision, but converted it into scientific fact in his *History of Prices*, in which economic and social history were converted into the history of money, and vice versa. In that sense forming a diametrical opposite to Ricardo, nevertheless he was neither Ricardo's nor the Currency School's worthy opponent: he also, like so many economists of his type, sacrificed clarity to overabundance and deprived his life's work of force and acuteness, as he did not know how to separate vagueness from realism.[49]

This period culminated in the summarizing achievement of John Stuart Mill, in which the inventory of facts and the insight of the times formed a whole: the banking and currency viewpoint, theorems of production costs[50] and quantity, theories of material value and of claim [Anweisungstheorie] - Mill speaks of money as a "ticket"[51] - equally come into their own. Both friend and foe went to school, in the strictest sense of the word, on what the *Principles* had to offer; and for decades both monographic and textbook presentations differed only in whether their authors had been good or bad students. And much of what only in our time has gained acceptance, first germinated in its unassuming pages.[52]

The Contemporary State of Affairs

5. The eighty years that have elapsed since the publication of Mill's book have also been rich in monetary events, questions, discussion. First, the policy of Peel's Act in England, which cut down the development of the banknote and repressed the classic business form of current payment and credit transactions - commercial bills discounted via banknotes. *Deposit transactions* and *checking accounts* developed in the freed space, but not merely as a result of that legislation. Elsewhere the legal restrictions on banknote issue were lesser - although they also asserted themselves - but other aspects worked out on the Continent

---

[49]The origin of the work, which in collaboration with Newmarch eventually evolved into a monumental price history of the years 1793-1857, is to be found in *Thoughts and Details on the High and Low Prices of the Last Thirty Years*, which appeared in 1823 in London. Also to be mentioned are his *Considerations on the State of the Currency*, London 1826, and *An Inquiry into the Currency Principle*, London, 2nd ed. 1844.

[50]The production-cost theory of money was received by Ricardo and given a place in his general theory of value. But its full development came through Nassau William Senior: *Three Lectures on the Cost of Obtaining Money*, London, 1830.

[51]To my knowledge the first use of this image was by George Berkeley in his *Querist*, 1735-37.

[52]Mill considerably altered and rounded out the presentation in the various editions. The comparison of them provides an interesting insight into the development of his views. Important, to my knowledge, are the additions of 1865. One must, if one wishes to understand his *monetary* theory, study the *whole* of the third book of the *Principles* and allow it in its unity to have its effect.

as in England. This threw up new questions regarding the technology and security of money transactions, reserve requirements, the adequacy of a central reserve, and so on. Then the bimetallist controversy came and went, which for a time moved the spirits with a vehemence hinting of the religious struggles of the past. Order was finally restored to the monetary systems of many countries, especially Italy, Russia, Austria-Hungary, the North American Union; the acclimatization of the gold and gold core currencies, which passed over into these countries, was a source of transitional phenomena and corresponding issues.

From the turn of the century onward, two groups of phenomena arose that actually contradicted each other. On the one hand, the huge increase in South African gold production asserted itself beginning in 1894. Rightly or wrongly - that does not interest us now - from all sides the price increase of the last prewar decade was attributed to it, so that the issue as to whether the purchasing power of money should be left to the contingencies of gold discoveries or the development of production methods of gold gained new urgency. On the other hand, we observe, although the steady increase in gold production had to strengthen the reserves of central banks and facilitate the stabilizing of exchange rates - of this there can be no doubt - increasingly marked difficulties in the functioning of the gold currencies, and not only in the countries that had just gone over or were about to do so. Under these circumstances, so-called *foreign exchange policy*, which had been previously considered only as an expedient for a period of transition, now appeared as a new alternative of a permanent condition. Quantitatively the most fruitful time, but in terms of actual gain the most penurious, was the war and postwar period, the manifestations of which, as already stated, offered the expert no new problems and the discussions of which were not much more than a renewed resurgence and renewed refutation of old errors emerging as new wisdom.

During this entire period, monetary investigation was connected initially to its problems and attained much of value in the analysis of specific issues and situations. One further busied oneself in systematizing, expanding, defending, sifting the extant. A tradition of monetary theory was formed that passed into the textbooks of the time and also engendered textbooks on monetary theory which have a certain family resemblance - less so in England (Nicholson, 1888) and France (de Foville, 1907), more so in America - here F.A. Walker (1878) and Laughlin (1903) are to be mentioned[53] - and Italy (Martello, Messedaglia, 1883).

---

[53]But we do not wish to forget the achievement of Simon Newcomb in his *Principles of Political Economy* (New York 1886), which, ahead of its time, besides containing

Germany is well-represented in this tradition, the patron saints of which are Hume, Ricardo, Tooke, and Mill. In the first period of his work, Adolf Wagner was primarily a currency expert: molded by the English debate, he labored extensively on works devoted to Peel's Bank Act (1862), the Russian paper currency (1868), the note-issuing bank question (1873), the theoretical yield of which he systematically elaborated in his *Theorie des Geldes* [Theory of Money] (1909).[54] As a leading currency expert he was succeeded by Wilhelm Lexis, whose main achievement in monetary theory – the treatise *Uber gewisse Wertgesamtheiten und ihre Beziehung zum Geldwert* [On Certain Value Entities and Their Relationship to Money Value], 1888[55] – must be mentioned here and whose *Allgemeine Volkswirtschaftslehre* [General Economics] (1st edition, Berlin, 1910), offers an excellent monetary theory of Ricardian brevity and clarity. Carl Knies (1st part in 1873) in his *Geld und Credit* [Money and Credit] [Berlin] created the standard work of German monetary theory. The article by Carl Menger, which appeared in the third edition of the *Handwörterbuchs der Staatswissenschaften* [Handbook of the Sciences of State] and has already been cited several times, should be considered as the high-water mark of this "older theory of money." This group includes the well-known works by Helfferich

---

one of the first formulations of the equation of exchange, also had much that was original.

[54]Adolf Wagner, *Die Geld- und Kredittheorie der Peelschen Bankakte* [The Monetary and Credit Theory of Peel's Bank Act], Vienna 1862 (reprinted Essen 1920); *Die Russische Papierwährung* [Russia's Paper Currency], Riga 1868; *System der Zettelbankpolitik, mit besonderer Rücksicht auf das geltende Recht und auf deutsche Verhältnisse. Ein Handbuch des Zettelbankwesens* [System of Note-issuing Bank Policy, with Special Attention to Standing Law and German Conditions: A Handbook Of Note-issuing Banking], Freiburg on Breslau, 1873; *Theoretische Sozialökonomik oder Allgemeine und theoretische Volkswirtschaftslehre, 3. Bd.: Sozialökonomische Theorie des Geldes und Geldwesens* [Theoretical Social Economics, or General and Theoretical Economics, Volume 3, the Socio-economic Theory of Money and the Monetary System], Leipzig 1909.

[55]In *Zeitschrift für die gesamte Staatswissenschaft* [Journal of the Joint Sciences of State], vol. 44, Tübingen 1888, pp. 221 ff.

(*Das Geld* [Money], first presented in 1903)[56] and Diehl (in the framework of his *Theoretischen Nationalökonomie* [Theoretical Economics].[57]

But the significant development of theoretical research into money during the same time period, the result of which can probably be described as a new theory of money, owes little to those phenomena of that time, much less so than the monetary theory of the Ricardian era owed to the Napoleonic currency turmoil, although its approaches were applied to the issues of their time, which took their first public shape in important cases thereof. Rather, it is the fruit of the work of analysis as such, that, even without the practical problems, would have created the new science. It is one of the effects of that new and purely scientific impulse in the second half of the 19th century that revolutionized all of theoretical economics. At the foundations of that economics lies exclusively the work of researchers who are among the first founders, or successors of the founders, of modern economic theory. However – despite this personal union – the monetary-theoretical arsenal that we have today is not simply a derivative of modern economic theory. At least, not of the marginal utility theory in its original form. Which is not to say that a more intimate relationship with its present form, the theory of equilibrium, does exist. This too is quite natural. In whatever way any individual monetary theorist prefers to think about the nature of money, everyone agrees in this at least, that money differs from goods or, if you will, from *other* goods, by peculiarities which are not indifferent to the formation of its value. Regardless of whether these peculiarities are important or unimportant, of this kind or that, they always form a special feature of the theory of money, the treatment of which requires special tools. Only ignorance of the subject matter may demand that a theory of value produce a theory of money from itself, without a new element being inserted in the explanatory process. We understand, therefore, that a new theory of money was not *ipso facto* given along with the new value, price, and distribution theory, but rather that many researchers who created or further developed marginal utility theory, stayed with older conceptions, although just about all of them have monetary-theoretical achievements to show for themselves.

Of the three founders, Jevons, Menger, and Walras, this holds true for the first two. Monetary research owes Jevons very much. But his achievements

---

[56]Karl Helfferich, "Geld und Banken" [Money and Banks], in *Hand- und Lehrbuch der Staatswissenschaften* [Hand- and Textbook of State Sciences], Part 1, Volume 8, Leipzig 1903.

[57]Karl Diehl, *Theoretische Nationalökonomie* [Theoretical Economics], in three volumes, Jena 1916-1927.

are in the field of some sub-questions, especially index numbers, while he left the foundations unaffected. Menger's achievement lay precisely in a masterful formulation of these foundations. He shows us how far one can progress upon this old foundation, but it is not he who is the creator of something new, but Von Wieser. Its first publication came in 1903 - the Vienna inaugural speech. This was followed by the contributions to the Vienna meeting of the Vereins für Socialpolitik [Association for Social Policy], 1909,[58] and finally the article on "Money" in the fourth edition of the *Handwörterbuchs der Staatswissenschaften* [Reference Dictionary of State Sciences] [vol. IV, p. 681]. Researchers proceeding directly from his suggestions include F.X. Weiss,[59] Ludwig von Mises, *Theorie des Geldes und der Umlaufsmittel* [The Theory of Money and Credit] (Munich 1912) and Friedrich von Hayek (especially *Preise und Produktion* [Prices and Production]).[60]

Of course, when working on any particular problem of monetary theory and monetary policy, one runs into the discussion of all economic relationships generally. The novelty of Von Wieser's teaching is that it emanates from these economic contexts, from the theory of the economic process itself, and comprehends monetary phenomena *from out of* that process. This is what the comprehensive statement of Wieser's means, that the value of money is determined by the relationship between money income and real income. Perhaps an illustration will better reflect the essence of the matter. The new monetary theory differs from the old like the dermatologist who diagnoses and treats a skin disease from organic causes, versus a dermatologist who only sees what can be seen on the skin itself, and diagnoses and treats it "locally." Now this illustration does not indicate the economic and general political aspects, the consideration of which is always obligatory in the analysis of a given currency situation: it rather treats

---

[58]Friedrich Freiherr von Wieser, "Der Geldwert und seine Veränderungen" [Money Value and its Changes], in: *Die Produktivität der Volkswirtschaft* [The Productivity of the Economy], Schriften des Vereins f. Socialpolitik 132, Leipzig 1910; reprinted in F. v. W., *Gesammelte Abhandlungen* [Collected Essays] , edited by F. A. v. Hayek, Tübingen 1929.

[59]Franz Xaver Weiss, "Die moderne Tendenz in der Lehre vom Geldwert" [The modern tendency in the doctrine of money value], in: *Zeitschrift für Volkswirtschaft, Sozialpolitik und Verwaltung* [Journal for Economics, Social Politics, and Administration], Vol. 19, Vienna and Leipzig.

[60]Friedrich August von Hayek, *Preise und Produktion* [Prices and Production] , Vienna 1931.

of the purely theoretical point of view, that the *theory* of money must grow out of the *theory* of the economic process.

This point was comprehended and implemented with unsurpassed clarity and accuracy by Léon Walras, by making the theory of money into a part of the general theory of economic equilibrium. In the first two editions of his *Éléments d'Economie Politique Pure* [Elements of Pure Political Economy] [1874-1877, Lausanne/Paris/Basel 1926], this was not yet achieved in fully satisfactory form. Only his *Théorie de la Monnaie* [Theory of Money] (Paris 1886), the essential content of which passed into the late editions of the *Éléments,* brings the *principle of cash-holding (encaissé désirée)* as the cornerstone of the theory of money, *equivalent to Wieser's principle of the relationship between money income and real income.* As in the field of value, price, and distribution theory, so here Walras already accomplished what in the cases of Jevons and Menger the first successors did, and he deserves not only credit for the priority of the publication of the new theory of money, but also the glory of its most consummate version. But he was not understood at first, especially not by the author who in other areas continued his work: in this area, Vilfredo Pareto failed completely. Only after some time did it find followers, among whom A. Aupetit (*Essai de la Théorie Générale de la Monnaie* [Essay in the General Theory of Money], Paris 1901) and K. Schlesinger (*Theorie der Geld- und Kreditwirtschaft* [Theory of the Money and Credit Economy], Munich 1914) stand out.

The third of the creators of the new monetary economics, Alfred Marshall, first attempted his presentation of the fundamentals when his strength was paralyzed (*Money, Credit and Commerce*, London, 1923), and had previously only expressed himself on individual issues (as in his contributions to the inquiry of the Royal Commission on the Depression of Trade and Industry, 1886, the Gold and Silver Commission, 1887 and 1888, the Indian Currency Committees, 1899, and in his article "Remedies for Fluctuations of General Prices", 1887, the latter in the *Memorials of Alfred Marshall* [ed. A.C. Pigou, London, 1925], the others contained in the volume published by the Royal Economic Society under the title *Official Papers of Alfred Marshall,* recently published in 1926).[61] His fame as a monetary theorist and monetary policymaker originally rested on these individual achievements (see also the biography by

---

[61] Alfred Marshall, "Answers to Questions on the Subject of Currency and Prices, Circulated by the Royal Commission on the Depression of Trade and Industry, 1886," in: *Official papers by A. Marshall, published for the Royal Economic Society,* London 1926; "Memoranda and evidence before the Gold and Silver Commission 1887," *ibid.*

Keynes).[62] But a sympathetic eye can identify the decisive point of view in the work of his old age, and the testimony of his pupils allows us to shift this development in Marshall to the decade 1867-1877. Marshall created a new English tradition, and the U.K.'s leading monetary researchers follow in his wake. So especially Ralph George Hawtrey, who expressed himself most thoroughly about the basic question (*Currency and Credit* [3rd edition, London 1928], first in 1919), John Maynard Keynes, whose great *Treatise on Money* [New York 1930] dominates the debate today (hitherto the main work to come into consideration was *Indian Currency and Finance*, London, 1913, and *A Tract on Monetary Reform*, London, 1923), A.C. Pigou (in particular for basic questions: "The Value of Legal Tender Money," in *Quarterly Journal of Economics*, 1917), and Dennis Holme Robertson (*Banking Policy and the Price Level*, 1926, and *Money*, 2nd edition, London 1928).

Pointing in the same direction, and resting on the same principles, are the achievements of Gustav Cassel, Gustavo del Vecchio, and Knut Wicksell. The name of the first is connected exclusively with the theory of purchasing power parity put forward by him and once again up for discussion, and with his extensive expert activities in the period of currency renovations, so much so that it must be emphasized that even those fundamentals owe him much. Already in *Nature and Necessity of Interest* (London, 1903) one may find the first hints, and the first elaboration in an article in the *Ekonomisk Tidsskrift*, in 1905. His textbook[63] provides a presentation of modern monetary theory, to which one might first be referred for an introduction to that subject. Wicksell started directly from the opposition between Ricardo and Tooke, and in the area of the relationship between monetary and interest rates (*Geldzins und Güterpreise* [Interest of Money and Goods Prices], Jena, 1898) gained entirely original results and significantly advanced the discussion of the monetary role of bank credit. His textbook presentation (the second volume of his *Vorlesungen* [Lectures][64]) must be highlighted. In parallel with the work of these two, and, like them, advancing from the Walrasian basis, the doctrine of the leading Italian monetary theorist

---

[62]J. M. Keynes, "Alfred Marshall 1842-1924," in *Economic Journal*, vol. 34, London 1924, pp. 311 ff.

[63]Gustav Cassel, *Theoretische Sozialökonomie* [Theoretical Social Economics], 4th edition, Erlangen-Leipzig, 1927.

[64]Knut Wicksell, *Vorlesungen über Nationalökonomie auf Grundlage des Marginalprinzips* [Lectures on Economics on the Basis of the Marginal Principle], two volumes, Jena 1922.

Gustavo del Vecchio was developed, whose most important works were published in German summary.[65]

Our survey has shown – what in fact is only natural – that the credit and banking system is so connected with all the monetary issues that credit-theoretical considerations often indistinguishably flow together with monetary-theoretical ones. We saw this, e.g., in the cases of Law's bank, the Peel Acts, etc. The fundamental question: credit and commodity prices, early became a standard chapter in the theory of money, while the textbook representation also showed a marked tendency, proceeding from the heading "Money" to the heading "Money and Credit" or "Money and Banking." Even so, the doctrine of banks fundamentally led a separate existence, which only at certain points spilled over into the theory of money. A key feature of the theory of money today is that it incorporates this area into itself, and just as surely underpins the monetary system with the theory of credit as it underpins the theory of credit with the theory of money. Add to this that it is not the credit theory of yesteryear, but one that is substantially new, that is the subject of this merger and puts the aspect of "purchasing power creation" by credit, an already well-known accessory, at the center of its analysis, which hereby realizes economic and interest-theoretical results. Here Robertson (*Banking Policy and the Price Level,* London, 1926) and L. Albert Hahn (*Volkswirtschaftliche Theorie des Bankkredits* [Economic Theory of Bank Credit], 3rd edition, Tübingen 1930) are to be mentioned.

Nor can the bank-policy literature as such be gone into. The way in which the discussion of bank policy becomes a discussion of economic policy in general, is best seen in Felix Somary's *Bankpolitik* [Bank Policy] (2nd edition, Tübingen, 1930). From the literature concerning the legal problems of money we highlight Martin Wolff (in Ehrenberg's *Handbuch des Handelsrechts* [Manual of Commercial Law] IV, 1, 1917) and Arthur Nussbaum (*Das Geld in Theorie und Praxis des deutschen und ausländischen Rechts* [Money in the Theory

---

[65]Gustavo del Vecchio, *Grundlagen der Geldtheorie* [Foundations of Monetary Theory], Tübingen 1930. Jacques Rueff, *Théorie des Phénomènes Monétaires* [Theory of Monetary Phenomena], Paris, 1927, also may be mentioned in this context, as well as Ernst Wagemann: *Allgemeine Geldlehre* [General Theory of Money], Berlin 1923, whose *balance theory* stands in the wider context of its author's economic research. Robert Liefmann likewise shows an affinity; regarding him, see Alfred Amonn, "Liefmanns neue Geldtheorie" [Liefmann's New Monetary Theory], in *Archiv für Sozialwissenschaft* [Archives of Social Science] 1927-28.

and Practice of German and Foreign Law], Tübingen, 1925), of which the excellent achievements regarding this aspect of the matter are here pointed out once and for all.

Germany and the Influence of Knapp

6. In the German monetary theory of the beginning of the century, it was not the lack of achievements of the first rank that was peculiar so much as the circumstance that the effect of these achievements not only did not reach the public at large, but did not even reach the larger part of the scientific profession, and was restricted to small groups of people. In 1905 a book entered the scene that must here be considered because it has had a broad effect, has been widely taught, and has inhibited progression along a straight line of development for almost two decades – the *Staatliche Theorie des Geldes* [State Theory of Money] by Georg Friedrich Knapp.[66] There would be little point in touching on this smoldering controversy if it were not for the fact that loyalty to the excellent teacher did not still cause many, who followed him at the time or were inspired by him, to refer to him such that, among both beginners and more advanced students, we today not only *in addition* but *above all* encounter his name and doctrine.

Early on, Knapp gained a recognized position as a statistician; late in life, by virtue of his own clarity of vision of economic history, he became one of the great figures of German economic history and historical economics. Only in advanced manhood, but then as completely as it corresponded to his closed personality, a passionate interest in the fundamental problems of the monetary system seized him. He did not approach it from the literature, nor even from the logical train of theoretical thought, but from the contemplation of monetary-policy processes, which went back to early impressions of the paper money economy of Austria and Italy. He gave shape to what he believed he saw, like he gave shape, in his classic work on landownership and goods ownership, to that which he beheld so vividly in the historical material. With this latter subject, [it was as if] a friendly spirit gave him a theme on a researcher's silver platter. For this, original vision regarding concrete life content in all its wealth was no more and no less than everything, while the technical requirements of historical labor receded entirely into the background – although to the degree that they were indispensable, he could not overlook them. But then he took hold of a topic, the successful management of which required a technique of thought foreign to him, the need for which was not readily apparent to the economists who

---

[66]Munich-Leipzig, 1918; first published in 1905.

were products of the schooling of that time; and furthermore, it required an original vision of the inner logic of abstract objects, which is something other than the kind of vision that he possessed.

The probability of failure was therefore given from the outset, and in fact he proclaimed a doctrine that at heart was neither sustainable nor – as fertile mistakes often are – beneficial. Whatever might be built upon happy formulations or correct observations in details, nothing can be adduced for the proposition that money is a *creature of the law,*[67] nor for the point of view that the theory of the monetary system had nothing to do with the price level, unless one denatures both and renders them pitifully self-evident, as for example by advancing, as if it were Knapp's discovery, the statement that the state and the law have much to do with the monetary system.[68] It is only to be established here[69] that Knapp's doctrine of money factually stands and falls with that proposition and that point of view, and to explain why it was that the factual failure not only did not correspond with external failure but rather with success, the likes of which has not been encountered by many books on scientific economics.

He who derives his position from Knapp or only wishes to honor his great name, tends today, in utmost good faith, to shift the battleground to more harmless areas and no longer to the fundamental errors, but elsewhere: to the monetary-historical accomplishments that the work includes, to, e.g., its spirit

---

[67]From this Knapp concludes that money must be treated *in terms of legal history*. That would not even necessarily be correct if money were the creature of law. Incidentally it follows from the above core proposition that Knapp's key aspects are not accurately determined when one employs them, as is usually done, in opposition to "metallism." Admittedly this opposition gave them alleged or actual practical significance and in any case their once so great popular interest. But this contrast is common and by no means a new perspective, as we can see. The feature that distinguishes Knapp's doctrine from all other antimetallism is *just* the epithet "state" and the fundamental rejection of entering into the monetary value problem. Certainly Knapp himself believed that his position was the only possible alternative to metallism.

[68]The utter worthlessness of this pseudo-legal approach precisely from the standpoint of the jurist is rightly emphasized by Martin Wolff, *loc. cit.,* p. 165.

[69]The reader may consult the view of the author regarding the problem of the fundamental relationship between money and the legal system in "Das Sozialprodukt und die Rechenpfennige" [The Social Product and the Unit of Account], in: *Archiv f. Sozialwissenschaft und Sozialpolitik* [Archive for Social Science and Social Policy], vol. 44, 1917-18, pp. 627-715.

or method, to the doctrine that the essence of money is not exhausted in material of intrinsic value, etc. These claims are not all unfounded. To surround the ancient patrimony of science with new splendor is also an achievement, even when it manifests itself alongside unfounded claims and mixes with - in part, ancient - errors. Nevertheless, the fact remains that the supporting beams have been broken out of the building once those two points are removed.

Knapp's success had originally to do with the force of his presentation and the highly subjective originality of his thought. It is not a scribe that speaks from the book, but a spirit with power. That had to be fascinating. Strongly-worded phrases impressed, and some of the many new conceptual characterizations were useful and were liked, while other good keywords were supplied. To then-prevailing orientations of literary taste, the presentation itself seemed to be a work of art of high rank. This performance appeared to a public for the most part lacking in professional judgment. Competent critics were not lacking, but the public did not listen to them. Error remained unnoticed, the content of each page was held to be a new finding. At the time, the public longed for conceptual construction, having been theoretically famished after the long period of mostly economic-historical interest. Here now was a work that accommodated this need, without setting unrealistic conditions for the average reader and without breaking with historical principles. The irritability of competent theorists, that sometimes could not do enough in the way of sharp condemnations and denunciations of the ignorance of the author, only benefitted the success of the book - as in scientific life generally, the effect of sharp attacks is a dubious affair.

To this is added the economic environment at that time: gold currencies began to settle into many countries, accompanied by many difficulties. Many old gold currencies, and especially the German, under the influence of political pressure, began to move in the direction of lower interest rates and abundant credit to politically powerful but economically unproductive groups, and under the influence of the economic policies of neo-mercantilism presented those problems that the much overrated policy of a *gold-exchange standard* were to solve. What was believed to be the practical message of the book - it is without doubt that this did great disservice to Knapp himself - in these circumstances had to find approval in the widest circles. And finally, it need hardly be mentioned that during the war there were naive minds that believed that, regarding inflation policy, they could take comfort in the shade of Knapp. But today, with that amateur enthusiasm having abated along with ill-tempered indignation, it is permissible to refer to all the suggestions that so many minds received from

Knapp, and to the fact that there is no greater proof of personal power than to lead a bad thing, albeit only temporarily, to success.

We find this metabasis to other thought processes especially with F. Bendixen,[70] who entirely independently – and scarcely having been aware of his predecessor – came to a *claim theory* [Anweisungstheorie] of money and then, with the best intentions and amiable modesty, recognized Knapp not only as his ally, but as his master. But, as Von Bortkiewicz (in Braun's *Annalen* [Annals], 1918) aptly pointed out, if this is called *nominalism*, one ought not be of the opinion that one is "extending" Knapp's nominalism or *chartalism* on the economic side,[71] but rather that one is maintaining a doctrine that objectively owes *everything* to other sources and *nothing* to Knapp.

---

[70]*Währungspolitik und Geldtheorie im Lichte des Weltkriegs* [Monetary Policy and Monetary Theory in the Light of the World War], Munich-Leipzig, 1916, but most of all *Das Wesen des Geldes* [The Nature of Money], 2nd ed., Leipzig, 1918, and *Geld und Kapital* [Money and Capital], 2nd ed., Jena, 1920. [Two things deserve mention:] In addition to imperfect mastery of the scientific craft, it was precisely the connection with Knapp that brought to this excellent author the recognition that would have been his anyway.

[71]Knapp himself, however, was of the opinion that Bendixen attempted "to provide an economic analysis alongside the state analysis" (p. 446 of the 2nd edition of the *Staatlichen Theorie*). But if this were true, then far and away the most money theorists of every era likewise made the same "attempt" by which everything economically relevant to the money issue would be resolved. See Melchior Palyi, *Der Streit um die staatliche Theorie des Geldes* [The Dispute over the State Theory of Money], Munich 1922.

Chapter IV
The Economic Account in
the Socialist Commonwealth

Following the old saw that socialism complicates the practice of economics but facilitates the theory thereof, we wish to make clear the essence of the matter with which we are dealing, namely the nature of the social economic account [sozialen Wirtschaftsrechnung], initially by considering the case of a socialist commonwealth.[1] Indeed, the meaning of economic action as well as the social economic plan, that in the economic form of private property must be arduously pieced together out of the results of the interaction of individual income interests, here confronts us immediately and directly. Especially if we restrict ourselves, as we wish to do, to the sub-case of centralized socialism, i.e., a socialism in which all means of production stand under the disposition of a single central office, and all economic considerations and decisions, especially regarding the what and how of production, proceed from this central office - then one has before oneself locally and physically, that which otherwise is revealed only through scientific analysis.

Of all the differences that the economic process of such a community has over against the economic process of private property, we are interested now in only one. In the private property economy, there is no separate allocation process. Although we often speak as if the production and distribution of that which is produced are two different things, this is only an abstraction that is practical for some purposes. In fact, production and distribution constitute a single operation: that which is economic - not technical - in production takes place and is exhausted by the fact that the entrepreneur buys certain amounts of certain types of means of production. And at the same time income formation, i.e., *distribution*, likewise takes place, precisely through the sale of productive services to him. This is not so in a socialist community. Its production

---

[1] For our purposes we must limit ourselves to that which is essential to our purposes. Regarding the problem area as a whole, see Cläre Tisch, *Wirtschaftsrechnung und Verteilung in zentralistisch organisierten sozialistischen Gemeinwesen* [The Economic Account and Distribution in the Centrally Organized Socialist Community], Wuppertal, 1932.

process is a *mere* process of production and does not decide the question as to what of that which is produced should be assigned to each of the comrades. In other words, *income formation* is not tied to the pricing of productive services, and because this connection is what gives the economy of private property its quantitative determination, the income formation in a socialist community is indeterminate. So here the distribution of consumer goods to the comrades is a special process for which the commonwealth not only *can* but *must* establish a specific arrangement. Such arrangements are of course infinitely many. One such example would be that distribution should occur according to the value of the service that each person provides to the community. This would result in a distribution relatively similar to the result of today's income formation, only it should be noted that not only would today's income from holdings disappear, but that as a result of such disappearance, the assessment of individual performance would lead to different results. Or one could distribute according to the principle, to each according to his needs. Or by the number of hours worked, etc. For simplicity's sake, we wish merely to establish the rule that every adult comrade should receive "equally as much."

If there were only one consumer good and only one kind of that good, if, for instance, in the community under consideration there were no other wish of an economic nature than the desire for bread of a certain quality, thus no other possible use of the means of production, then the task of the central office would obviously be extremely easy. In fact, one might say that in this case that there is no *economic* problem at all, but only a *technical* one. It would in fact only be a matter of manufacturing, according to the state of technical knowledge using the existing means of production, as much as possible of this one consumption good and distributing it equally. The best technical solution would *ipso facto* be the economically correct one, i.e., it would realize the maximum of welfare that is consistent with the principle of equal distribution of income per capita. It would still require keeping an eye on technical sub-processes. But an *economic account* that would mirror economic considerations would not need to be administered.

If, by contrast, there were indeed many need-categories for which the production of many different types of consumer goods was to provide, but for which only a single means of production of a single quality was needed, things would not be so easy. In order to attain some clarity, we make an appropriately given supply of labor power – thus strictly equal in partial quantities – into this single means of production by assuming that the other "original" means of production, i.e., the "natural" soil, water power, minerals, etc., are available in virtually unlimited amounts. We eliminate an additional difficulty by making the assumption that all consumer goods have an equally long production period and that, because of legislation regarding working hours, the available supply of working hours is rigid. The task of the central office now, is for this stock to be distributed to the various branches of production such that maximum satisfaction of needs or economic welfare is achieved for the community. Even if the central office goes at its task without any experience and statistical data – as we must accept, if we wish to work from the essence of the thing and do not wish to run in circles – it will have available to it the knowledge, for example, of the life-necessity or relative urgency of the various types of production, so that it is not dependent merely upon experimentation. But according to its discretion in terms of this knowledge, it produces the quantities of each consumer good and distributes them equally to the comrades, so that the *distribution arrangement* set by the community will appear to be met in a very obvious sense.

In such a way the layman may think of the process in a socialist economy in general, and thus did he obviously imagine the original program of Bolshevism. But if this presents no difficulty to the question as to what is to be considered "equal" distribution, then another question arises in its place. Namely, we lack a criterion whereby the central office disposes "rightly"[2] over the social supply of labor power, meaning that quantities of individual consumer goods are generated such that the maximum possible satisfaction of demand of the comrades is actually attained, whereby they would not be better served by any other quantity combination, such as more skirts and fewer shoes. There are situations in which this difficulty recedes and some vague expressions of popular discontent are sufficient to make evident the grossest errors of arrangement. These would be situations of enormous destitution of goods, where that which is most important is what matters and not the fine weighing of particulars, as is the case in Russia today, or in primitive conditions in which types and amounts of the required consumer products, the *consumer combination*, are fixed traditionally.

---

[2]The following contains the reasons why I think that the term *natural account* [Naturalrechnung] in the sense of Otto Neurath (see in particular his study, "Das Begriffsgebäude der Wirtschaftslehre und seine Grundlagen" [The Conceptual Edifice of Economics and its Fundamentals], in *Zeitschrift für die gesamte Staatswissenschaft* [Journal of Joint State Science], Vol. 73, Tübingen 1917/18, p. 484) seems to imply a contradiction in terms, and the idea that the doctrines of costs, of assignment [Zurechnungslehre], and the like, are "offshoots of the money account," seems in need of a correction that robs them of the acuteness of their attack directed against the "customary" theory.

But otherwise – and, in principle, even in the cases just mentioned – there can be no rational economic management without such a criterion. Obviously a new aspect enters into the considerations of the central office, namely, the consideration of the amount of demand satisfaction of the comrades, the need to *choose* between different production possibilities in terms of that amount, in short, the *actual economic element in the economic plan,* which through numeric specification makes up the *economic account.* This new variable is not amenable to ascertainment with physical [technischen] units of measure. Neither piece numbers nor weights nor lengths, in which consumer goods may be technically measured, say anything directly about it. Whether one thousand skirts or ten thousand kilograms of bread are "more" in the economic sense cannot be deduced from the number of skirts or kilograms of bread alone. Obviously it would actually take a measurement of the variable of social satisfaction. We do not now wish to trace this possibility, but rather in the following make use of the fact that the central office, for the purposes of deciding on what is to be produced, need not know the different possible magnitudes of satisfaction states, but only whether it has achieved the maximum possible condition of satisfaction under the given circumstances and in terms of the given wishes of the comrades. But this can be inferred from the behavior of the comrades,[3] if one

---

[3]It should be pointed out here that, because it here has to do with outwardly (one of the many meanings of the word "objective") perceptible behavior, no "psychological" major premises are needed, and in particular, the fundamental concept of marginal utility can be defined "objectively." The reader is free to *interpret* this concept and the concepts of demand variables and satisfaction conditions psychologically. Hereafter, for the sake of convenience, a "psychological" expression will often be chosen, but, of necessity, assumptions about psychological variables will be made only in some special cases, while essentially even those readers can accept our argument who refuse to work with psychological variables or the acceptance of their "measurability." Regarding this state of affairs, see Bowley's assumptions in *The Mathematical Groundwork of Economics*, Oxford, 1924, pp. 1 and 2.

The fundamental concepts of marginal utility, total utility, utility function, utility value (= marginal utility times quantity) are assumed to be known. The reader should not consider this condition to be self-evidently fulfilled. Because it also includes familiarity with, apart from the concept of marginal *utility*, the essential thought-form of *marginal analysis* (the infinitesimal method) and the logical nature of "relatively extremely small" magnitudes. The lack of this familiarity is the source of most of the controversies that have arisen in particular with the concept of *marginal productivity*. This term and

gives them the opportunity to express themselves in a way that can be condensed into a numerically ascertainable index. We will see that this yields a *unit of account* useful for most practical purposes of the economic account, and also why it does so.

A Simple Model

2. It is possible to construct a case that is far removed from reality, in which the mere agreement of the comrades over a number of alternative proposals from the central office is sufficient, so that the area of the *natural economy* need not be vacated, when by natural economy one understands an economy that applies no specific economic units of measure. To this end, we make the further assumptions that our community has only two consumer goods, that the consumption desires of all comrades, insofar as they are recognizable, are of exactly the same type and intensity, so that agreement is necessarily unanimous. Then the central office can approach the comrades with the following questions: "Our community disposes of more than 400 million working hours per year. With them, we have this time around produced ten million skirts and twenty million pairs of shoes. The production of a skirt requires twenty working hours while a pair of boots requires ten. Are you satisfied, or, taking into account the fact that every skirt entails the eschewal of two pairs of boots, while each pair of boots means eschewing a half of a skirt, would you like more skirts and fewer boots or fewer skirts and more boots than we produced this time?" This question generally allows for a numerically precise and unambiguous answer, and if one wishes to follow this line, it is clear that under equal and stationary conditions, the *maximum economic welfare* is thereby achieved even though we know nothing about the absolute magnitude of this welfare.

We wish to make use of this case to put before our eyes some phrases and expressions of general theory in its simplest form that are of importance to our topic. Above all, we see that the quantities of skirts and boots that are produced or can be produced are not independent of each other, because they draw upon a common stock of means of production, in this case mere labor power.

---

its relationship to the concept of marginal utility is also assumed to be known, as is the distinction between "physical productivity" and "value productivity."

Here we have before us one of the fundamental relations[4] that make a meaningful whole out of the various parts of the economic world, or as the phrase goes,
a *system of related, interdependent elements.* We therefore speak of a general
economic constellation [Zusammenhang], of a *general interdependence* of economic variables.[5] In our case, one can more easily see what otherwise is not so
easy to see, and in some important cases is not even true, that the dependencies
existing between our two goods are sufficient to determine unambiguously the
amounts that will satisfy the comrades. The condition in which they are unambiguously determined can obviously be characterized by the statement that the
transfer of a small subset of work from skirt production to shoe production or
vice versa would reduce the economic welfare of the comrades. Therefore the
marginal utility of a smaller subset of skirts in this condition must just balance
the marginal utility of a smaller subset of shoes, which is why we call it the *state
of equilibrium.* Its existence is the necessary and sufficient condition for the
maximum satisfaction possible under the circumstances to be reached. These
statements apply and these expressions fit for any type of economic system. But
phenomena that we are accustomed to look for only in the private property
economy already occur in our case.

Initially we find the phenomenon of *costs* expressed in a unit of account,
in the same sense and with the same function as in the profit economy. What
the production of a skirt "costs" the community is the satisfaction value of the
shoes that one could produce with the same amount of work. Skirts and shoes
are put in relation in terms of the only means of production common to them,
the labor power ratio, by which the unit of the labor power ratio obtains a utility

---

[4]The case under consideration presents the archetype and the greatest simplification of that system of economic variables that received its first scientifically satisfactory presentation from Léon Walras.

[5]Of course, not the only one. Here the relations of *complementarity* and *rivalry*
should be pointed out. These relationships exist initially between individual goods, e.g.,
a cigar and matchstick on the one hand and a matchstick and lighter on the other. But in
a broader sense, *all* elements of a consumption or production combination form a coherent whole from this point of view, for which reason, strictly speaking, marginal utility
and total utility should never be considered merely as a function of a single good, but
only as a function of all goods within the circle of the economic subject. And accordingly
there is a broad sense of rivalry, in which the relationship goes far beyond the circle of
substitute goods in the technical sense. It is obvious that such cases do not, as one might
infer from their treatment in the older theory, form exceptions, but on the contrary the
virtually invariable rule.

significance, thus a significance that extends beyond its role as a technical economic measure, for which significance, doubtless in our case, it has to thank its fitness as a unit of account.[6]

It is important for the reader to be aware that in the profit economy this state of affairs is obscured by intermediate links, but in essence is no different.[7] Note also that we can express the equilibrium condition by the proposition that the marginal utility of working hours must be the same in both uses. Since this condition must be established for each comrade, each must estimate a skirt to be the equivalent of a pair of shoes "at the margin of his consumption combination," if one may consider a skirt and a pair of shoes to be a small part of his total consumption; thus both goods must be proportionate to the quantity of labor they contain. Since this obviously includes the principle of the decision of the comrades, we encounter here in the socialist community the phenomenon of the *exchange ratio:* the comrades exchange that for which they choose against that which they otherwise could have produced with the same amount of work.[8]

---

[6]Strictly speaking, even this very simplified case cannot do without an "economic unit." "Working hours," in themselves and without utility connotation, which makes them something else, would say nothing either to the central office or to the comrades. If we nevertheless in this case admit the possibility of a natural economy, we do so because, where only two goods are extant, the utility comparison itself requires no extra unit, and the comrades do not need knowledge of that unit for their economic considerations. Nor is it needed by the central office for this purpose, but only for scientific analysis.

[7]This alone justifies a warning against overestimating the purely economic difference between the profit and the subsistence economy. With the latter we certainly have an emotional aversion to speaking of exchange ratios or - even though we will be doing it soon enough - of prices. But although the principle that one should not project the concepts of one economic system onto another is valid, it is invalid for theoretical analysis that does not impute its concepts to individual cultures when it detects essential similarities among their manifestations and makes use of the ways of speaking of that culture in which the phenomena in question stand out most clearly.

[8]This is particularly useful if we assume, what to that extent would be the same thing, that the community factually produced those other goods, and exchanged them for what it desired with a foreign country. Conversely, one can see in every exchange ratio of the transaction economy the quantitative expression of a choice act [eines Wahlakts], which is essentially the same as the decision of the comrades regarding the quantities to be produced of the individual goods. The concept of choice act (Pareto) brings the basic element of economic activity common to all economic systems, which

And this exchange ratio is subject here to the law of *labor value* [Arbeitswert-gesetz], which thereby reveals itself as a special case of the law of marginal utility. The law of labor value in the sense of Ricardo and Marx is proved here not because we are dealing with a socialist community, but because we introduced certain restrictive conditions that we could, with the same justification, introduce in the consideration of a profit economy.

Adding Consumer Goods to the Mix

3. Imagine what would change in all this if we were to drop the recently introduced additional requirements while holding onto the remainder: if the community therefore meets not only with two, but tens of thousands of consumption goods, and if the nature and intensity of consumer desires is not the same, but differs from comrade to comrade. In that case, the central office no longer can come before the comrades with such a simple question, for when dealing with ten thousand consumer products it is no longer sufficient to establish the – as we can now say without further ado – exchange ratios of different pairings. Rather, a yardstick applicable to all exchange ratios must now be found that makes them all comparable to one another at the same time. The agreement also could now at most lead to a majority decision, and it is easy to see that its implementation would result in an outcome that would lag quite unnecessarily behind the attainable maximum of welfare. Rather, if indeed the achievement of this maximum is the objective of economic management, each comrade must be given the opportunity to take an individual position. The expression of desires is insufficient, because these desires *may* be unsatisfiable and generally *are* incompatible with the condition of equal distribution. Because everyone wants something else, the question now arises: What does "equally as much" mean? Or what is "more," an increase of ten cigars or an increase of a bottle of wine? Hence a criterion is necessary for both the comrades and the central office, to ascertain at what point the share of each comrade subject to his decision becomes exhausted, since physically equal distribution of all consumer goods no longer solves the problem.

In fact, when we consider this state of affairs, we see, *firstly*, that the only way out of these difficulties lies in the creation of a special economic unit of account. *Secondly*, that under our conditions, the unit of labor would readily

---

in the exchange economy expresses itself in exchange or price in the idiomatic sense, to its purest expression and therefore has meaning beyond the ambit of the tendency from which it emerged, namely the tendency to avoid working with psychological variables.

provide the expected service of such a unit of account. The central office itself could calculate and keep accounts in labor units because there is indeed no other means of production it has to worry about, for which reason the total account tallies when the work statement tallies. The quantities of consumer goods could easily be equated to the sum of working hours put in during the same period. Neither the presence of produced means of production nor the need for continuous work on its maintenance, repair, and replacement would require otherwise. Likewise, every comrade could specify his freedom of choice quantitatively and numerically and give sufficient expression to his claim limits when he is told how many of the working hours embodied in the consumption articles over the accounting period are allotted to him and how many working hours are put into a unit of each consumption good: for him as well as for the central office, the problem of "equally as much" is solved in a sense that probably would be obvious to most people.

Let us now consider the process as follows: the central office, based on antecedent knowledge of the wishes of the comrades, in turn will have certain quantities of consumer goods produced, thereby applying the entire statutorily fixed quantity of labor, in its books crediting the working hours of all the comrades that result from dividing the total number of hours worked over the accounting period by the number of eligible comrades. This quantity of consumer goods, disregarding the fact of continuous production, will now be laid out in the warehouses of the community to be handed over to the comrades, whereby each exemplar of commodity is marked by the number of the quantity of labor embodied in it. The comrades may have been issued certificates in the amount of their credit, thus *labor notes*, such as those Robert Owen had in view for his socialist society. With these labor notes, the comrades now show up at the warehouses to draw objects of their needs, at which point their withdrawal is charged in the books of the central office, their account is netted, their labor notes are destroyed. If everything has gone as the central office thought it would, then naturally the claims certified in the labor notes extend far enough to empty the warehouses.

It is just as natural, of course, that somewhere else, for example in the boot warehouse, more labor notes are presented than there are boots expressed in working hours available, whereupon elsewhere, e.g., in the skirt warehouse, the reverse situation must transpire. Of the measures that the central office may take in this situation, an obvious one is proportionately to divide both the extant boots and the extant skirts among the actually presented labor notes. We can picture the matter as the central office expressing its willingness to do this by appropriately changing the labor numbers attached to the exemplars of the relevant commodities. In that case, the labor unit presented in the boot warehouse has less, while that presented in the skirt warehouse has more working hours than are embodied in one pair of boots or one skirt, i.e., the labor note has a discount vis-a-vis the boots, or the labor embodied therein, while compared to the working hours embodied in the skirt it has a premium. This will induce many people subsequently to prefer skirts to boots, but the matter can only be mitigated in this way, not cured. The central office in any case sees that it has scheduled wrongly and will henceforth produce more boots and fewer skirts. Such disparities will always resurface and be eliminated, and their appearance and disappearance is the sufficient and automatically functioning sign by which the central office can orient itself. Parity between working hours presented and working hours embodied in goods is powerfully valid evidence that the quantity relation between the produced goods corresponding to existing interdependencies has attained an appropriate balance, reached equilibrium, and attained maximum satisfaction consistent with the conditions – again, without measuring the condition of satisfaction itself.

Building on our previous observations of a generally theoretical nature, we now go one step further. We saw earlier the phenomenon of the exchange ratio in the image of a socialist community; likewise, we now meet with an exchange ratio directly comparable to all other exchange ratios, because expressed in a unit of account common to them all: *price*. The messages pinned to the commodities in the social warehouses, regarding the quantity of labor embodied in them, are also statements about the possible real content of the claims of the comrades, "asking prices" as it were, and both for the comrades and for the central office, in every respect fulfill the regulatory functions that price has in the profit economy of private property. We also continue to encounter a phenomenon that, to the untrained eye, in even greater degree only seems to have meaning within the profit economy. In the warehouse into which more comrades crowded than the central office had foreseen, more labor notes came to hand than were embodied in the working hours of the commodities, i.e., there was a *surplus* of the former over the latter; while in the warehouse in which less of a reception followed, there transpired something that required the surrender of a greater number of working hours embodied in commodities than were contained in labor notes submitted, hence, a *deficit compared to the effort*, the costs, hence a *loss*. If we now note that the size of the surplus and the deficit is the index by which the central office establishes its behavior, and that this behavior simply consists in increased production of the goods that showed a surplus, and reduced production of the goods that showed a loss, we immediately note the essential equality between this index and the index according to which the competitive economy is directed, as well as the essential equality of the behavior of the central office and the process that takes place in the competitive economy in the analogous case.

Even as the entrepreneur positively appraises his surplus, his "profit," while the central office perceives an incorrect[9] disposition as much in the surplus as in the loss, yet in *both* economic forms both surplus and loss are symptoms of an imbalance, that in both triggers the tendency to eliminate it.[10] Without risking a misunderstanding, we can formulate this by the statement that the *index of profitability* is crucial for the economy of the socialist community as well. But in this statement one must think of the mechanism of profitability in competitive capitalism and not the mechanism of profitability in the case of a monopoly – such an error lies close at hand perhaps while the central office has no competitors – in the latter case, the "profit motive" leads not to the elimination of the surplus but rather to its maximization. Here the observation of a socialist commonwealth sheds light on the social meaning of the competitive economy, obscured by the play of individual profit interests.

Also regarding a further aspect of the same matter: assuming the constancy of all basic facts of the economic process and the absence of all random disturbances, the economy of perfect competition would function quite as profitlessly as our socialist central office, since in both cases, as long as profitlessness is not established, efficient economics and economics in the direction of greatest profitability are synonymous. If the economy operates without profit and loss, this means that the "*law of costs*" is realized, and because the perfect socialist economy under the same conditions would operate just as much without surplus and deficit *in every individual* line of production, this means that for it as well the law of costs must be realized, and this in turn means that each of the consumption goods in itself must pass from the warehouses to the comrades precisely at cost-covering prices and no more, and thereby all inventories must precisely be depleted, if maximum satisfaction is to be achieved. Note: on its own, the law of costs presents only a necessary, not a sufficient condition. Marketability of the whole product at these prices must be added, and it is easy

---

[9]Original text: "fallender" [descending].

[10]The socialist central office is therefore the ideal "entrepreneur faisant ni bénéfice ni perte" [entrepreneur making neither profit nor loss] of Walrasian theory.

to verify that this amounts to the so-called *law of supply and demand*,[11] that here shows its deeper meaning, beyond what it has in the profit economy.[12]

Adding Cost Factors to the Mix

4. The assumptions of a single factor of production and equally long periods of production meant that the special economic problem of production, the problem of the rational combination of the means of production, did not yet emerge. Under these assumptions, the "what" of production was a question of economics, while the "how" of production was a mere technical question: technically the best solution was *ipso facto* also the economically rational one. Things are different if we now drop the first of these two assumptions. To this end it would be enough to recognize that human labor has qualitative differences that cannot be broken down into working hours spent in the acquisition of skills. But we wish straightaway to introduce yet other factors of production, land, mineral resources, water power, etc., that were previously regarded as free goods. With our discussion we expediently proceed from the standpoint of the layman, for whom it is suggestive to believe that it [i.e., taking these other factors of production into account] can make no difference, because even in a socialist community only working comrades are entitled to consumption and because the other factors of production are not private property and therefore would "cost nothing" – even labor of a higher natural quality cannot be used for private gain. Indeed, the consumer demands of the comrades can still be expressed in terms of any kind of work. But the achievement of parity between the units of this form of labor embodied in the individual exemplars of merchandise and the

---

[11]Both the law of costs and the law of supply and demand, as is also apparent from our brief hints and as must again be stressed, are not however dependent determinants of equilibrium, but derivatives of the more fundamental rule of the *marginal utility level*, from which initially the law of costs follows in its value-theoretical meaning and then, using this, in its just-indicated superficial meaning.

[12]The marginal utilities and the collective satisfactions realized by the individual comrades were still different. One may speak of *social marginal utility* or marginal utility level in a socialist state only by making a number of other assumptions. However, these differences are smaller than in capitalist society, in which the differences in "capacity for enjoyment" are added to the differences in consumer demands. Of course, in a socialist community of the type under consideration, "pricing" would be "democratic." But that is of as little interest to our subject as the other differences between the two economies, the existence of which, of course, is not to be denied.

thus-defined units of consumption claims, the delivery of the goods to the comrades under the stipulation of this parity, which under our previous set of assumptions was a condition of "correct" disposition, i.e., that which brought about maximum satisfaction, is now reconcilable with the achievement of maximum satisfaction only in the very special and trivial case in which the relation between this kind of work and the quantity of all other means of production is equal across *all* produced goods taken as a whole.[13]

Otherwise – and for implementation by the central office, even in this case – rational economics is only possible if the economic account does not pass over the fact that the production result also is dependent upon the relation of, in terms of demand, "scarce" material means of production, which consequently must be economized or accounted for just as was done with labor power, and likewise must be rationally distributed among the possible lines of production [Produktionen], and, when deciding "whether" and "how much," must be "valued," each individually. That the community disposes over them and does not need to pay for them does not change the fact that its application of those means signifies "effort," i.e., eschewal of other possible production in another direction, thus eschewal of the satisfaction of needs, and in this sense constitutes a cost item just as much as labor effort does. In a rationally directed economy that beyond manpower has even one non-free means of production, the labor law for this reason cannot apply to the internal accounts of the central office, nor to *settling-through* [Durchrechnung] *within the economic process,* nor to *settling-up* [Abrechnung][+] with the comrades, i.e., to the ratio by which the products are delivered in exchange for the units of consumption demand of the comrades,

---

[13]To prove this theorem it is best to proceed from the case that the central office insists on the delivery of commodities according to the working rule, in order to recognize that in many warehouses this must lead to the preferred satisfaction of some and the rejection of other comrades, who then could only be directed to undrawn-upon quantities of commodities in other warehouses. The second step is to prove that the increased production of the former commodities and the reduced production of the latter now is no longer able to mend the situation satisfactorily. The last is that this mending is not possible by varying the combination of the means of production.

[+] The terms *Durchrechnung* and *Abrechnung* are closely related. *Durchrechnung* refers to a provisional settlement or payment, *Abrechnung* to a final settlement. The point is that, in Schumpeter's framework, in the production process settlements are provisional, so that what occurs there is *Durchrechnung*; final payments – *Abrechnung* – are made at the level of consumption. To maintain this distinction, I will use the terms settling-through (provisional payment) and settling-up (final payment) throughout.

the "labor notes." Note that the principle of the equal distribution of the total product would no longer be compatible with distribution on the basis of the quantity of labor embodied in the products. The reason is that the equality of the shares in this latter sense would no longer be synonymous with the equality of the shares in the total inventory of the means of production and the yield thereof.

This applies already if the combinations of the means of production in the units of the individual products were given differently, but constantly, i.e., fixed by technical necessity. As a rule they nevertheless result from an *economic* decision which is new to our horizon, namely a choice between in principle infinitely many possibilities, each of which is characterized by the quantity of all means of production that are to be put into the unit of each product, the "*production coefficients.*" The choice obviously depends on the relative significance of the alternative possibilities of application that are open to each of the means of production. If the central office initially produced experimentally, then to the question, whether in future they should produce more or less of the individual products, comes the further question as to whether they will maintain the past production coefficients or change them, for example, whether they will more extensively work the soil, i.e., per unit of soil add less labor to the product unit, or the reverse, more intensively work it, i.e., to compose the product unit of more labor and less soil. And this question is not only reversibly connected with the product quantity in prospect, but also with the similar question for all other goods still produced otherwise. Expressed in another way: what now is at stake is to distribute the other means of production over the production orientations as much in accordance with a law of equal marginal yield as in former times only labor of uniform quality was to be distributed according to this principle. However, to this pertains the knowledge of the production coefficients that give us the relation between the quantity of each product and the quantity of each of the means of production. And this relation is now no longer a constant and a given, but a variable and an unknown quantity.

Of course that is also the case in the profit economy. But the price formation process gives the individual entrepreneur the relevant data [Bedeutungsziffern] for its means of production just as well in hand as it does the prices for its products, so that, as can be strictly demonstrated, he may clearly calculate and choose between the options open to him. We saw that in our scheme of the process of the socialist economy, the relevant data of consumption goods, with the cooperation of the comrades, are set in a manner very similar to prices in the profit economy. Here, on the consumption side of the problem, the comrades make the same contribution for economic management to the central office that customers provide to the entrepreneurs in capitalism: if the central office does not insist on "parity prices" in the previously expressed sense, but rather follows the lead of the comrades, it will unambiguously be able to determine "prices" adjusted to the quantities of goods produced in that case. But the quantities produced and even the "appropriate" production coefficients are not fixed either. And here, on the "production" side of the problem, the analogy to the market mechanism seems to be lacking, because the means of production are not "sourced" [bezogen] from anyone and because there are neither owners of natural means of production nor can comrades be conceived as being workers in the sense of sellers of labor power. So where is the necessary clue the central office needs to conduct rational economic activity? What replaces the missing "prices"?

The Problem of Capital Accounting

To these questions, one sometimes[14] answers "no one" and "nothing" and then declares that, quite apart from practical difficulties, rational economic management in a socialist community would be impossible in principle. This assertion is now to be considered.

First, it is clear that the central office just as well, and in the same sense in which it equated the number of available (however many) units (e.g., working hours) of work of a certain quality taken together for all consumption goods, can equate precisely this number for all the available productive services - labor services, land services, etc. - for the production of an accounting period. Just as such a labor unit in the hand of a comrade does not now signify a claim to a quantity of goods, in which a unit of such labor is embodied, nor a claim to an

---

[14]Cf. in particular Ludwig von Mises, *Die Gemeinwirtschaft* [The Socialist Economy], Jena 1922 [English translation of the second edition of 1932: *Socialism: An Economic and Sociological Analysis*, New Haven, Yale University Press, 1951]; "Die Wirtschaftsrechnung im sozialistischen Gemeinwesen" [The Economic Account in the Socialist Community], in *Archiv für Sozialwissenschaft und Sozialpolitik* [Archive for Social Science and Social Policy], vol. 47, Tübingen 1920/21, pp. 86 ff.; "Neue Beiträge zum Problem der sozialistischen Wirtschaftsrechnung" [New Contributions to the Problem of the Socialist Economic Account], *ibid.*, vol. 51, Tübingen 1924, pp. 488 ff. Max Weber appears to have had the same point of view; even so, this viewpoint did not become the general one. Cf. Enrico Barone, "Il ministro della produzione nello Stato collettivista" [The Ministry of Production in the Collectivist State], in *Giornale degli Economisti* [Journal of Economists], vol. 37, 1908, pp. 267 ff. Other literature in Cläre Tisch, *loc. cit.*

aliquot portion of all individual goods, but rather a claim to an aliquot part of a mass of consumption goods made homogeneous by a particular procedure, so now the same number is not now simply set over against the "inventory" of labor services of this kind, but against all personal and material - yet "original" - productive services that initially are expressed, each kind for itself, in terms of its technical length, weight, and whatever other dimensions. It therefore has to do here with a similar "special procedure," which also makes this heterogeneous mixture into a homogeneous mass for the purposes of calculation, by generating a ratio, clear in each case, between our unit of account and the technical units of individual productive services, and so gives meaning to the total number.

This method presents us with two findings: 1. Let us remember what we said about the nature of prices as a numeric expression of choice acts. Such choice acts are made by the central office. Any decision to apply a technical unit of a means of production to produce a small additional amount of a good at the cost of a previously (experimentally) produced quantity of another good, is such a choice act and signifies a swap of the former against a portion of the latter. 2. But the comrades value this growth in units of their consumer demands entirely in the way they hitherto valued the small quantity of the goods now lacking, at which cost the increase in production took place. They do this by presenting units of entitlement in the relevant warehouse which then has delivered from the central office the additional amount in proportion to the presented claim units. But these claim units are also the units of account of the central office, which uses the recovered claim units as an index of the economic success of their action, "crediting," so to speak, the branch of industry that produced more, while also "charging" it with the number of claim units that previously the other branch of industry, the production of which is being restricted, "released" for the now discontinued product amount, i.e., booking the number of these claim units last drawn for the dropped product element as "costs" of this economic result. Since the action only consisted in the diversion of an element of a single factor of production - e.g., re-ordering a few workers - while changing nothing else, the comrades, with their valuations of the discontinued and increased amounts of product, at the same time supplied significant numbers for the relevant small amounts of the means of production for both applications, the numbers for marginal productivity of these means of production in these two industries, thus answering our first question.

Now, if there are several means of production, the maximum condition of equal marginal productivities must obviously apply for each of these as it applies for one, when there is only one. Only then are things properly arranged, is equilibrium attained. In that case, though, the amounts which, in the case of extremely small rearrangements of the kind described, the industries concerned are to "credit" and to "charge," are equal to each other across the entire economy,[15] so that the central office only presents itself a relevant datum for the unit of each kind of means of production and quality, thus, that which we need to answer our second question. It is easy to see that the central office must deliver its products to the comrades - leaving aside non-economic viewpoints - in terms of the rule of costs, in that the *labor* cost of each commodity cannot any longer be equal or proportional, and that the "law of costs" must be valid for every single industry and every single business; that in equilibrium, therefore, every production must have "marginal net proceeds" equal to zero; that, excluding cases of technical impossibility, all non-free means of production must find application; that in the same act [uno actu] with the determination of the equilibrium relevant datum of each means of production, that condition of all production coefficients is realized which, in accordance with the understanding of the central office, is the most rational of all possible conditions.

That under these circumstances it is mere coincidence that just such, and so many, goods accrue to the individual comrades from the total return of the economy of consumer goods over the accounting period (*social product*), that the quantity of labor contained therein is precisely equal to the number of labor units with which their consumption claims are set in the society's books, at bottom is self-evident. But also in the internal accounts of the central office, no parity between working hours as unit of account and actual working hours could exist - which indeed seems to be a paradox, but is not further disruptive. The remaining non-free means of production indeed also have to be charged in the chosen unit of account, thus in working hours, and the sum of all the variables - the relevant datum of each factor of production times its amount per accounting period - must be equal to the sum of consumer claims. This would be the fundamental accounting equation of socialist accounting, the fulfillment of which would be an essential criterion of proper economic management. That the socialist track record ideally would not show a profit balance, while such obviously is the ideal of the profit-making businessman, is only due to the difference of standpoint: from the standpoint of the economy as a whole, that would be a symptom of the highest perfection of economic management in capitalism as well, *under given and stable data*.

---

[15]This applies strictly to the equilibrium *point*. Should this already be achieved (and whether such is the case can only be determined experimentally), then any small redisposition made for this purpose would result in a small "loss."

The importance of the magnitude just mentioned would however be lesser in the socialist economic constitution than in the profit-making one, because in the former it is not the basis of the distribution of income from production. To the degree, however, that in the latter wages and rent, the prices of the original means of production labor and forces of nature, are indices of the respective marginal significance of these means of production, they play entirely the same role there as here: only in socialism, the sociological content of the terms wages and rent is lost completely, which is not the case with economic content. Incidentally, it is also indifferent to socialist economic management, even if it distributes the product as always, to know what part of the economic result depends on the cooperation of a comrade, and how that relates to the share accruing to him.[16] In this sense, but especially in the sense of the significance-index of the units of the various means of production, the manifestations that we call wages and fixed income in a capitalist economy make their appearance also in the socialist. With these, however, there is also a cost concept that is more similar to that of the profit economy than that based on the essence of costs, which we discussed earlier: namely, a notion of cost completely analogous to the money-cost concept of the entrepreneur, a variable expressed in the unit of account for an effort of social productive power needed for production in general, regardless of what specific means of production it may comprise in the individual case. We have chosen our assumptions so that we could disregard the interest rate and the extent to which a similar phenomenon would occur in the socialist economy. This question is connected with the theory of interest to which one subscribes, and is answered "yes" from the standpoint of nearly all theories of interest. But for our purpose it is meaningless.

The reader can now easily imagine how socialist accounting, the calculation of the economic process, and the settling of accounts with the comrades, would proceed. We have before us a system of mathematical equivalences that would numerically reflect the entire economic life of the community, each element of which would correspond to an element of the economic circular flow. We can assume that everything happens in bookkeeping acts in the books of the central office, thus every comrade is credited for his *consumption claim* and charged for his withdrawals, and every industry is treated similarly. But we can conceive of the labor notes as being physically created from the central office

---

[16]In other words, what part of the consumption claim of the comrades, who also are pro-rata "landlords," is covered by their economic wage and what is of a different economic character. The phrase that in a socialist community "the entire product is wages" is wrong in every sense.

and issued to the comrades, whereupon they hand these over in the warehouses in exchange for consumption goods, at which point the industries obtain them from the central office against allocation of new means of production. Thinking through this last case, which differs from the others by only a minor technical feature, is particularly instructive because it thereby reveals itself as a method of performing that procedure of *clearing* operands, which is the essence of any economic account. (What is the deeper reason for the fact that economic life – and not merely in the formal sense of accounting technique – is always represented as a system of mutually compensating variables?)

The Common Denominator of Capitalism and Socialism

5. So we see that the rational economic *account*, the first prerequisite of rational economic *management*, is quite possible, at least logically, even in a socialist community, and in fact there clearly manifests itself in essence.[17] The unit of labor in particular proves itself in its function as a unit of account for the central office. But we also see that it has completely lost any relationship to the labor value of the goods and thereby to its original meaning.[18] The meaning that it retains is only that *its choice gives a clearly determined number for the total sum of the consumption claims of the comrades, the total amount of consumption goods (social product), and the total amount of non-free productive services.* But because obviously any other number can serve this goal just as well, and would arise from the determination of any viable unit of account, so it is preferable to designate the selected unit in a meaningless, or at least generally colorless, way, especially when the name could evoke misleading associations. *In this method of obtaining a - basically random - unit of account as well as of entitlement, lies, as we shall see, the core of the institution of money of the profit economy,* that we therefore also discover in the economy of socialism. That this

---

[17]It still remains true that the rational economic account historically developed in the capitalist firm and that this set of circumstances [Verumständung] compels this rational economic accounting by motives of particular strength, perhaps not given in socialism. Nevertheless, our argument implies that it is wrong to link "calculability" *logically* to capitalism, and dangerous to conceive of the connection between capitalism and "calculability" or between the profit economy and the money economy too narrowly: the richer yield in insight lies with the opposite point of view.

[18]One would retain a certain but completely different meaning when the consumption claims of the comrades were graded according to the labor units performed by them, a case that, however, has no special features to interest us.

number, when set equal to the labor units performed in the period under review, would vary with that number, would not decrease but increase the similarity, because in the profit economy the combination with the quantity of a good is historically given.

This insight, the derivation of which was the purpose of this chapter, we round out when we consider that the computational mechanism of the central office initially only makes it possible to determine whether under the given circumstances it has planned "rightly" or not. And that is indeed what matters above all. But obviously the possible purposes of the economic account are not yet thereby exhausted. If, for example, the decision regarding a new production method for an already produced good, or the start of production of a new good, is in question, the described calculation process can also provide this answer; while the central leadership very well may have the desire to determine by *how much* numerically the community will have progressed through the new method or the production of new goods.

The described means of account says nothing about this. Rather, if the total number, once chosen, is maintained, the appearance must be as if the total amount of consumer goods had remained the same. The reason is that our "measurement method"[19] works in a way as a length measure would work, according to which all men would be equally tall, while the unit by which they were measured would vary from person to person in an uncontrollable manner. If the total number is not maintained, but might vary according to a rule which is given by a possible association with the units of a commodity, the matter might be even worse if such were possible, because then, among other things, it could even vary inversely to the measured object. In the case of the labor unit, it would occur, for example, if as a result of fruitful technical progress the community decided henceforth to work less, since regardless the social product would be larger than before. One should now try to correct this measurement method so that it does what it should do. If, for example, a new production *method* is concerned, its superiority can only lie in its producing the same amount of product that was already produced, while requiring fewer resources. Through its application, the society will be richer by the amount of production expressed by the unit of account. The central office could now bring this fact to

---

[19]That is why there is a reluctance among many theorists to describe the unit of account as a unit of measure. But the unit of account arises from the assignment of a number to the social product and as such is quite like any other unit of measure. "Measure" and such assignment are synonymous.

expression in the manner such that they add this amount to the calculation expression of the actually existing means of production, and also increase the sum of the consumption claims of the comrades by that amount. Nevertheless, this issue arises here in no different sense than in the profit economy, the money of which in the simplest case exhibits the same defect.

Furthermore, among the comrades a phenomenon would set in that would be entirely analogous to the *consciousness of monetary value* of the economic agent in the profit economy: for each comrade, the unit in which consumption claims are measured would have a marginal utility, and this marginal utility would be used as a unit of utility similar to what was mentioned earlier. This now means that, because of an increase in the social product together with a constant calculated expression of consumption claims, the unit of the last increased good, thus the unit of utility or welfare defined by it, gains another significance. But there also arises from this situation a problem no different than one that might arise in the profit economy, namely the problem of *transposing the operands of management into computational expressions of variables of utility that are temporally, locationally, and inter-individually comparable.* Here it is sufficient to note that this problem is different from that mentioned in the preceding paragraph and calls for a special solution – considered by many economists to be fundamentally impossible: economic doctrine thus requires, apart from the physical dimensions of quantities of goods, which it uses, not just one but two specific economic measures, one for detecting changes in the quantities of goods which consist of disparate elements, and another for detecting changes in the condition of economic satisfaction. Only the former problem is essential for monetary theory. It will occupy us in connection with the measurement of the "purchasing power" of money. The treatment of both, however, assumes the unit of account of economic practice and presents itself as an attempt cognitively to reshape its functions such that it achieves what is desired. It is obvious that precisely the solution to the second problem[20] is of crucial importance for the theory and practice of a socialist community.

---

[20]Compare the author's treatment regarding "Wohlfahrtsökonomie" [Welfare Economics] in *Zeitschrift für Nationalökonomie* [Journal of Economics], 1931.

Chapter V
The Capitalist Economic Process

In the organization of the profit economy as well, *the* social whole engages in economic activity *for* the social whole, but this no longer happens as it does in the socialist economy, *by* the social whole, but by the interlocking of individual or "sub-group" motives and initiatives. Therefore, although we expect that the equality of the social meaning of the economy in both cases will generally lead to the same basic categories, many phenomena, such as monopoly profits, will occur only in the one case.

We start from the notion of the *social product*, by which we mean the totality of all consumer goods which enter into the realm of consumers in the period under review, including immediately consumed services of the original factors of production "labor and land" - in the manner of the services of singers, doctors, civil servants.[1] This social product is not given as a reality for individual

---

[1]The concept of the social product (a fundamental instrument of theory since Adam Smith took it, under the name of *annual produce,* from the physiocratic doctrine), can be variously defined. Marshall, who used the term national dividend, and following him A.C. Pigou (*Economics of Welfare*, 3rd ed., p. 34), define it as the flow of goods and services produced in the period under review, thus including newly produced means of production (but taking into account the wear and tear of the old and any wear of this new, even during the period in which it appears). Irving Fisher (*The Nature of Capital and Income*, New York-London, 1906, reprint 1930, p. 104) is closer to our version, but does not include the physical goods themselves, only their uses during the period. Pigou rightly remarked that there is little purpose in arguing about the "rightness or wrongness" of these versions. Our version seems to us to be appropriate to the theory of money and, by the way, beyond. But nothing prevents us from making use of the Marshallian conception on occasion. With this determination, however, not all problems are resolved, especially the statistical. See also Pigou, *loc. cit.*

Our term excludes the goods of *reproductive* consumption, namely those used in the train of a production process. In this context, a concept of *consumptive usage* would be useful, which alone is what is intended here. Apparently, it depends on the totality of goods definable by this term. It is the central "variable" of the economy, and all others,

economic agents as it is in the socialist economy for its only economic agent, the central office. It reveals itself as such only to the scientific perspective, as it were from the bird's eye view, and from the point of view of the social whole. As highlighted earlier, this *distribution* now is even less a special real process. Rather, it is a fiction of theory, presentationally appropriate, which is why we likewise make use of it, and therefore assume that the elements of the social product, continuously produced, flow together somewhere and from there are sent to those "containers" that we call *places of consumption* or *households*.

The social product is not simply an absolute quantity like a stock, but a *flow of consumer goods* or, what amounts to the same thing, a stock that gains its meaning only through its relation to time. We can always choose the "period under review" freely, but three types of such periods lend themselves to this role. First the *production period*, which we define for each enterprise as the time which runs between the instant that a partial quantity of a raw material enters into it and the instant that the partial quantity of its product, that contains that individual partial quantity, exits from it. From this we distinguish the *economic period* [Wirtschaftsperiode] as that period of time to which the *behavior* of each economic agent is geared.[2] And from this again we distinguish the *accounting period*, which is given by the practice of accounting and which is imposed upon us by the nature of our statistical material, as a rule the calendar year. Of course in important cases we have to do with an instantaneous observation, in which the concept of *social product per time element* arises.

The Circular Flow

2. The next step leads us to the concept of the *circular flow* of economic life under stationary conditions. No sane person, whatever subject it might be that he wishes to examine, will pick a point in time in which this subject is exposed to fierce random disturbances or changes, as for example a human body torn by a jacketed bullet. Instead, everyone as far as possible will choose for his observation a "normal" case, and have in mind the intellectual penetration of its

---

even the produced means of production, only gain significance to the degree that they determine the future amount of this - complex - "variable." Note that the formulation is geared to the goods prepared for consumers, not goods actually purchased or consumed.

[2]Practically, this is the time span for each firm within which its most durable elements are fully depreciated. The *horizon* of the economic entity may of course extend further than that.

subject matter. If we wish to do this as well, then there is revealed in the seemingly utter randomness of our material, e.g., the existing economic *time series*,[3] above all the fact that in economic life essential things repeat themselves year after year. And it is obviously always the fundamental economic process of production and consumption, or in monetary terms, production expenses, income formation, consumption spending, which, without beginning or end, is always flowing out and back into itself. Now in order to make the phenomena of this logically closed process clear before our eyes, we, in the sense of the just-sketched reasonable practice, disengage disturbances, statistically if we can, but above all intellectually. But it is subject not only to disturbances from outside intervention but also from internal changes. And these we also initially expediently ignore when it is the essential traits of its course with which we are concerned. With the proviso, therefore, that we may reintroduce missing elements into this picture, we make the assumptions of constant population size, natural set of circumstances, social structure, taste, technical insight or production method, so that we gain a picture of an essentially stationary economic process, which we describe as a circular flow because each of its phases leads back again to itself, the image of a *purely self-replicating* economic process (Marx).

That the basic economic process repeats itself year after year is, of course, in itself no fiction. What at most is fiction is the process, the manner of production and its results, and product quantities and prices *remaining constant*. But even this is not *just* fiction: namely because a large part of the practical behavior of people is oriented to the condition of substantially constant data from year to year, and, incidentally, factually also consists in the essentially uniform execution of the routine management of existing and routine-bound businesses, the theory of the stationary circular flow also directly covers an enormous mass of

---

[3]By time series we understand sequences of statistical figures, all of which relate to different points in time and which are lined up according to their position over time as successive annual, quarterly, monthly or weekly data on goods prices, sales volumes, interest rates, stock prices, bank reserves, loan volumes, deposits, clearing totals, sales totals, import and export figures, unemployment, wages, freight transport, and the like. Most of these series were initiated first in the post-war period, while a minority extend to the beginning of the century; only a few extend back into the mid-19th century, and these are only price series, which for some countries continue uninterruptedly back into the 18th century. However, our holdings increase each year. An overview for America is best gained from the *Review of Economic Statistics*, for Germany from the publications of the Berlin Economic Institute, and internationally from the London and Cambridge Economic Service.

economic processes of reality – it is, while being the unrealistic escalation of a thought experiment, a *self-sufficient* theory of a part of what actually happens. It is also an instrument of essential significance for monetary theory.

As is well known, this circular flow does not run uniformly but rather is exposed to *seasonal fluctuations*[4] that provide monetary theory with the special problem of explaining seasonally varied sets of conditions. For some purposes this problem can be neglected, thus leaving aside the difficulties arising from the seasonal unevenness for the task to be resolved by money, especially in the theoretical base case, which one should highlight as simply as possible. In general, one has to get used to the idea that, depending on the research purpose, i.e., depending on the point that in each case is to be worked out, the circular process needs to be defined differently, sometimes enriched with facts, sometimes freed from – momentarily insignificant – facts. It is not a rigid category, nor is its construction an end in itself, but it is a flexible instrument for intellectual mastery of the material – and only those can take offense for whom the meaning and purpose of such an instrument are foreign. When my only purpose is purely to represent the basic monetary flow from the market of productive services to the market for consumer goods and from there back, then I would add to the above general assumptions still further restrictive ones. If I wish to depict other phenomena or even these basic flows with incidental but less important ones, I will try to mitigate the strictness of those general assumptions. This apparently complicates our view, the more so because it would be unbearable at each point to treat all the resulting special cases in detail next to each other; but this alone leads those who put in the required effort to real clarity, which clarity is missing in our field, as it is in the field of the theory of international trade, above all because the *distinct* special cases, separated by different – but equally justified – systems of preconditions, run together *in*distinctly in the discussion.

The other important restrictions that we add to the circular flow concept in appropriate cases are:

---

[4]About the statistical treatment of the problem see *inter alia* Otto Donner, "Saisonschwankungen als Problem der Konjunkturforschung" [Seasonal Fluctuations as a Problem of Economic Research], Sonderheft 6 of the *Vierteljahrshefte zur Konjunkturforschung* [Quarterly Journal of Economic Research] (1928). For some purposes, one can avoid the problem by using annual figures. Of course, seasonal variations include not only rhythms more or less forced by nature, such as in the cases of agriculture, construction, etc., but also irregularities that are based on social custom, as the phenomena of Christmas shopping, travel times, tax maturity dates, etc.

Where the fact of seasonal fluctuations does not interest us, fluctuations in stockpiling do not usually interest us either – although this is not always the case, as *in principle* these two have nothing to do with each other. These fluctuations are of the utmost importance to understanding the monetary process. In material respects, the behavior of our material, the rows of data on prices, credit volume, etc., are completely incomprehensible if we do not take them into account. Important non-economic impacts, as well as important changes in the economic condition, and significant changes in economic agents are expressed in them, each of which has its complement in the monetary management of economic agents, not to mention that they also issue in initiative changes in the practice of inventories, cash, and reserve holdings. But all of this is no logically necessary element of the basic process, but rather an added complication, the treatment of which functionally forms a special step of the analysis.[5]

The matter is similar with the processes in the *markets of income sources*, property rights, debt securities, otherwise known as land, house, stock, bond, etc. markets. Apart from the special problems that arise there, the question of the back-and-forth flow of funds between these and the markets for consumer and producer goods makes it doubtful whether a theory of money and credit transactions on the former without a theory of money and credit transactions[6] on the latter is at all possible. It is *not*, in the sense that all phenomena on the consumer and producer goods markets can be satisfied apart from the connection with the land market, stock exchange, etc.; it is, in the sense of a preliminary theoretical orientation regarding the basic process, especially while those markets – certainly those that actually do play a role – would hardly play a role in a merely reproducing economy.

The Production Process in the Circular Flow

3. Sometimes it is also recommended that those phenomena be excluded from the theory of the stationary circular flow that are linked to the presence and reproduction – not the *initial emergence* – of those produced consumption and production goods that outlast the accounting period, without, however, being practically as "eternal" as a canal or embankment. This latter can – again, where this does not deal with the problem of their *origin*, but only with the role

---

[5]It is similar in price theory, as soon as we try to use statistical data in it. Nevertheless, it is developed initially without such complications – and rightly so.

[6]Original text [des Geld- und Kreditverkehrs]; Mann substitutes "money and credit markets."

they play *once they are present*[7] – be summarized with the inherent factors, since they, as the general theory teaches, do not behave differently than these. Those others, the *durable goods,* not only give occasion to the phenomena that arise monetarily from the need to provide for large payments separated by long periods of time, but also to the value-theoretical difficulties with which the general theory of value has had to deal with since Ricardo's day, which is why the best thing is firstly to picture the matter as if there were no consumer goods, production goods, and services than those that continuously would be bought and consumed during the accounting period. But we shall see directly that the consideration of the *presence* of durable production goods does not signify any special complication.[8]

The process of the circular flow of the stationary economy therefore takes on this appearance: at any one time, the community lives from the preparation of the particular immediate past, and in each case it provides for the fulfillment of demand for the near future, so that the same economic condition is attained at the end of each suitably chosen time element as where it was at the end of each previous time element – which for many purposes we can identify with the accounting period. This economic provision consists in the repeated equal productive application of the "original" productive services of labor power and "nature," accruing during the time element. The exchange or price mechanism works only for those services and their products, consumer goods, because repositories of natural services – land etc. – do not go from hand to hand. There is also no "having to wait" on future production results and no "discounting" their values, because in the economic process conceived as a steady course of events, its results are continuously presented – the uniform social product – and continuously used, while new production methods, commercial combinations, consumption goods, make no appearance.[9] The economic process is, as we are

---

[7]This eminently practical distinction, taken directly from the thinking of business life, provides good evidence that the construction of the "circular flow" is not as unrealistic as it seems.

[8]The matter stands otherwise from the viewpoint of Böhm-Bawerk's and Gustav Akerman's construction (*Realkapital und Kapitalzins* [Real Capital and Interest], Diss. jur. Lund, 2 vols., Stockholm: Centraltryckeriet, 1923, 1924). For us, a problem requiring special treatment never arises from the presence of a supply of produced means of production, but only from its initial creation or "introduction" into the production process.

[9]See the previous footnote. It is essential to be very clear on this point: the labor on a production process that is newly to be orchestrated, of course does not live by antecedent results of the same process, but must provide its livelihood at the expense of

in the habit of saying since J.B. Clark, *synchronized:* there are no temporal discrepancies that could be the source of particular phenomena. Labor services and natural services *immediately* receive their product in the sense of the marginal productivity theory, just as if *that* product that they create is available immediately, and not at a future date. There is no particular act of *advancing* consumption goods – production is, to introduce a term that we will often use, "financed from current income."

The situation is not changed if we make room for produced durable means of production. The difference in the length of the production or even utilization periods of the individual goods creates no problem under our conditions and leads to no new phenomena. In particular, this circumstance does not signify any profitability difference between firms. If one firm works with a one-year production or business period, another with a two-year period, once both are underway, this will not have the consequence assumed by Ricardo, that in the second case a surplus arises that compensates for the greater length of the production period – either the result and its application flow equally continuously in both cases, or when this is not the case, nevertheless in both cases the necessary funds of equipment or products are present from previous production, so that it does not matter whether – without its size changing per unit of time – the product accrual takes place every year or every two years.

This *makes it easier*[10] to see that under our current assumptions no *productive interest* would arise. For the base case, it is also expedient to dispense with the occurrence of *consumption interest*, and also the occurrence of *saving*, although both can be found in a completely stationary reproductive economy. But they can better be introduced separately. Where they are excluded, it may be made more bearable by the consideration that interest on loans, intended to tide over disturbances, in the absence of such disturbances obviously would be absent, while interest for another kind of consumption loans would find its explanation in emerging or anticipated changes in individual and social situations

---

results of other previous production processes. And that in fact leads to new problems, regarding which, by the way, the traditional teaching, with its concepts of "having to wait" and "making advances," likewise does not do justice.

[10]The evidence for this statement, still regarded as paradoxical, cannot be provided here. See also my *Theorie der wirtschaftlichen Entwicklung* [Theory of Economic Development], chapters I and V (Berlin 1911). The statement is to be formulated exactly like this: in a merely self-reproducing economic process, interest is not a necessary element of the market-economic production process and that part of the distribution process dominated by the production process.

and is to be dealt with only in connection with these and not with the stationary economic process as such. Even saving, that, as far as rationally understood, is to realize or improve individual economic situations, on analogous grounds may initially be set aside for some purposes of investigation, even if this entails disregarding the changes of individual stages of life. We lead all of these aspects, even a possible tendency to "perspectival undervaluation of future needs," back to their place.[11] Likewise there is no place here for – right or wrong – anticipation of changes in the entire economic condition, which plays such a huge role in the actual money process.[12]

The social product, which thus only consists of consumption goods (including services ready for direct enjoyment), is broken down in the distribution process into *wages, fixed income,* and *quasi-rents,* the definitions of which follow later. But there is no reason to exclude *monopoly profits,* as has been often claimed, unjustly. Since, however, the function of implementing new combinations of means of production,[13] which is constitutive for the concept of an enterprise, is lacking, there is here no *entrepreneurial profit*. The entrepreneur, if we wish to use this word at all here, is an *entrepreneur faisant ni bénéfice ni perte* [entrepreneur making neither profit nor loss] in the meaning of Léon Walras, in that at the most, wages, fixed income, quasi-rents, monopoly profits could accrue – an admixture that removes much of the paradoxical character from this concept of a profit- and loss-less entrepreneur, to which many, including Edgeworth, have taken such offense.

In this model, the so-called *law of costs* does not entirely obtain. There is, however, an economy that corresponds to it, at all times in a state of clearly defined, stable *equilibrium*, i.e., all of its elements, goods quantities and exchange

---

[11]As is well known, this perspectival undervaluation of future needs was introduced into theory by Jevons and Böhm-Bawerk and made the basis of the explanation of interest. Irving Fisher made it into the sole ground of explanation of this phenomenon.

If the reader thinks that our requirements tautologically exclude interest, that indeed would not be true, but in the context of this book only hoped for. If the reader cannot free himself from the idea of "static interest," it is sufficient for our purposes if he in each case fits it into our argument at the position that corresponds to the theory of interest he holds to.

[12]*This* finding is in fact – in contrast to our claim about interest – a finding *ex hypothesi*, in this sense thus truly tautological.

[13]Cf. my *Theorie der wirtschaftlichen Entwicklung* [Theory of Economic Development], *loc. cit.,* chs. II and IV.

ratios being lined up with each other, adapted to each other, so that they mutually, sufficiently determine each other. In other words, all the elements of such an economy form an equilibrium *system* that has as many equations as changeable magnitudes,[14] thus a logically coherent whole. If the law of costs is to apply, we must make the additional assumption that there is complete freedom of competition. In that case, wages and fixed income – the only cost items that can be found here – necessarily equal the values of consumption goods that are generated, directly or by produced means of production or *intermediate products,* by the services of labor and nature paid by these wages and fixed income, the values of which likewise are equal to the values of the services of labor and nature "embodied in them": consumption goods "buy" or "pay" for the "original" means of production, labor and "land," and their services reciprocally, in necessary correspondence. We say with regard to the purpose of this presentation: consumption goods and labor and land services constitute for each other, in our case, the single but at the same time always sufficient and necessary "fund of purchasing power." Their exchange against each other is that which money has to accomplish in such an economy, and money accomplishes this exchange without changing anything essential to the process, thus moreover making it possible for the most primitive monetary theory to answer to the phenomena thereby indicated.

Another terminological remark: In the process of the circular flow that here constitutes economic life, three categories of goods emerge, as we saw: consumption goods (the social product), original means of production (labor and natural or land services), and produced means of production or intermediate goods, which we divide into *raw materials,* supplies, and semi-finished products, in short, material on the one hand and *industrial equipment* on the other. The latter we break down, where there are grounds to do so, into "buildings" (residential buildings are among consumption goods) and "machines." Here at least there is as yet no reason to abuse the word "capital," that at best should entirely disappear from our vocabulary and which for us is only a monetary and, in particular if not exclusively, an accounting term.

Stretching the Boundaries of the Model

----

[14]This equilibrium system, the core of pure theory, although it is more or less completely implied in any economic argument, was consciously and fully grasped first by Léon Walras. Later advances only signify improvements in detail to his accomplishment. For an initial orientation, the simplified presentation by G. Cassel in *Theoretischen Sozialökonomie* [Theoretical Social Economy], *loc. cit.,* is sufficient.

4. As in the case of special purposes, in which we often simplify the image of the stationary circular flow still further by deleting from it processes that occur in any normal cycle, we stretch its scope to other purposes beyond the limits that, to us, its nature seems to set. The perspectives that we gain from its analysis acquit themselves also in the treatment of the effects of - *not in favor of* - disturbances in its uniformly streaming flow, e.g., of changes in the cost of production of a commodity due to the imposition of a not overly burdensome tax, moderate random fluctuations in crops, etc. It turns out that not only can we capture the undisturbed process, but also its adaptation to changing factual situations. Here lies nothing less than a principal value of the analytical instrument with which we have just become acquainted.[15]

Two cases of this type are of interest to us now. One of the most important *impetuses* for earth-shaking innovations, that we can*not* deal with in the context of circular-flow analysis, is population increase. But this is not what we are concerned about, but something else. From year to year the number of new laborers and consumers entering the economy is small enough to permit the assumption that the basic outlines of the economy will not be affected. We can then ask the question, what would be the effect of each relatively small increase in the labor supply, if nothing else changed. But we can go further. These effects occur from year to year even if innovations also happen *apart from them,* that overshadow them, so that one does not *see* them in the material: if those gradual increases in the labor supply, imperceptible at any point in time, did not exist, the overall result of these changes would be different. Though not in the old circular flow, which no longer exists, they make themselves felt in the formation of the new circular flow, which emerges after adaptation to the innovations that have taken place. Thus when we pose our question, we again gather an element of actual occurrence, even if it is not true that in the meantime "nothing else" changes.

---

[15]Previously I have called this procedure the "variational method," which because of the word association with the calculus of variations perhaps was not felicitous. However, no special expression is required for a process which is particular to every exact science, and the logic of small magnitudes absolutely. The analysis by means of the equilibrium system is a method for gathering the same facts that the circular flow analysis targets. But they do not simply correspond, and only equilibrium analysis has a formal similarity with "statics" in the scientific sense. We cannot here enter into a discussion of the relationship between equilibrium and circular flow.

The matter is entirely the same when the economic subjects[+]do not fully use consumer claims to purchase consumption goods, but feed a part thereof, either directly [selbst] or via the banking system, straight to the market for means of production - by *saving*.[16] This process, which is also of interest to us in terms of monetary theory, will occupy us further on. Here, we only consider that this *can* lead to an - incrementally barely perceptible - increase of produced means of production (though it does not *have* to), whereupon for this process the same is true word for word as in the case of population growth. We summarize both cases with the word *growth*, that here does not have the usual less specific and broader meaning, but only this special sense.

Hereby we depart the precincts of circular flow analysis, the strictly stationary as well as the "growing" economy, to enter another area. That the former cannot contain everything that is purely economic in the social world, we see from the fact that the circular-flow theory, especially the theory of the strictly stationary circular flow, that with its portrayal always presupposes the process of just those previous cycles, for that reason can never explain the emergence thereof. The matter is not quite the same with changes in cycles once they are up and running, because "external influences" and growth are available as explanations. But it is clear that this is not sufficient. In both respects - in terms of emergence as well as internal change - our circular-flow theory is in a similar situation as any theory of the functioning of an organism, such as the circulatory system.

First, it is easy to see that both problems flow together in one and both are solved when one reaches the explanation of those changes that cannot be explained by external factors or growth. It is as easy to determine in what those changes consist: if neither outside intervention nor growth, then the fact that the cycle does not unchangingly repeat itself in time, but apparently only comes from the emergence of novel sorts or qualities of consumption goods or of the old being produced with new methods of production - and therefore usually also in other quantities. Both, new consumer products and new production methods, signify that the existing, already previously used means of production are now being *used differently,* under which formula we can also understand both processes. We also speak of new commercial and industrial *combinations* of the means of production and of the *implementation of new combinations* as

---

[+] The original text has "economic objects" [Wirtschaftsobjekte], which seems to be a mistake.

[16]This is - please remember - not meant as a definition of saving; it only targets a special case.

the content of *economic development,* so that this last word should not have the usual meanings here, but *only this technical meaning.* If we have precisely the problems before us that are connected to *that,* then we can reasonably set the rate of "growth" at zero, and can thus assume a constant population and stock of produced means of production, just as in the analysis of the circular flow or growth we disregard development, although with regard to the individual practical case we usually must arm ourselves with the tools of all these theories at the same time. *It can be shown[17] that the phenomena that we encounter in the analysis of development in our sense are precisely those - and indeed all of those - purely economic phenomena that we miss in the circular flow,* so that the elaboration of the theory of the implementation of new combinations brings our theoretical construct to completion.

Development as the Driving Force of Business Cycles

5. Since monetary quantities and monetary processes in the economy receive their meaning from goods quantities and processes in the world of goods, to which they correspond, for which reason the understanding of monetary operations requires understanding of what happens in the world of goods and cannot be taught independently thereof, we have, with the considerations just made and the conceptual constructions that have arisen thereby, already gained an initial approach to an analysis of the credit and monetary sphere. Reference must be made to an especially important practical point and at the same time to a difficulty adhering to it: the implementation of those new combinations is the key feature of the *prosperity phases of economic cycles,* while their integration into the organism of the economy is the key feature of *depression phases* of those cycles. A number of secondary processes are adjoined in both phases, but the core of the phenomenon of alternating boom and depression periods lies on the one hand in those new systems or modifications and extensions of firms, in which is embodied the "other use" of the means of production, and on the other in overcoming those disturbances that the new inflicts on the existing economic

---

[17]It belongs among the not entirely surmountable difficulties of the presentation of this book that the theoretical foundations upon which it rests cannot be developed. Here I can only provisionally refer to chapter 6 of my *Theorie der wirtschaftlichen Entwicklung* [Theory of Economic Development], *loc. cit.*

body and price system, the struggle for a new equilibrium condition corresponding to the now altered production data.[18]

The characteristic processes that take place within the sphere of money and credit in the alternation of trade cycles first becomes understandable from this standpoint, which also makes possible the theoretical insight into the functioning of those markets that do not manifest themselves in the theory of the circular flow, especially the real estate and securities markets. The difficulty of which we spoke is not merely the immediately to be mentioned external disturbance, which only in particularly favorable cases can be excluded satisfactorily from our material,[19] thus in all others tarnishes the picture of our time series in an uncontrollable manner, but especially a situation that more recent research has brought to light and we at present cannot completely overcome.

Thirty years ago, the laborers in the field of economic theory were of the opinion that with alternating booms and depressions we had to do with *wave motion*, namely those which had been statistically determined by Clément Juglar,[20] which incidentally were already known of, as by Marx. Later investigations have shown, or at least rendered highly likely, that in addition to this wave, the existence of which nevertheless predominantly was maintained, and rightly so, others also were under way, longer as well as shorter, and that economic development therefore throws up not one kind of wave but several. Quite apart from the new theoretical problems that arise with it, in particular the question of whether all these waves are uniformly to be explained or whether each of them owes its existence to entirely different circumstances, the statistical problem now manifests itself as extremely thorny: because our series seem to reflect

---

[18]This equilibrium condition would be reached and permanently preserved if the same kind of disturbances did not keep occurring. Only this circumstance also explains those discrepancies, overproductions, etc., that can be observed in economic cycles [Konjunkturwechsel] and which would have to cancel each other for there to be no new problems. In the depression period, a quest for a new equilibrium is under way, finally being *approached* though not attained. To find the *point of closest approach* in the curve of our data is a special, very difficult problem.

[19]The support of the French franc by the United States in the World War is such a favorable case. Where we do not see an influence so clearly, and with all *small* effects, there only remains the - often unjustified - hope that they neutralize each other to a certain degree.

[20]Clément Juglar, *Les Crises commerciales et leur retour périodique en France, en Angleterre et aux États unis* [Commercial Crises and Their Periodic Return in France, England and the United States], first published in 1860.

the interference of the individual waves and, without special treatment, to say nothing about the course of each individual one. To analyze a single sort and try out a monetary theory and its consequences on it, it would have to be possible to isolate it from (external disturbances and) the others, a problem the solution to which, at first glance, not only looks difficult, but impossible. Under these circumstances, the view that underlies this book can only be stated, although in this immature state of affairs each new working day could change it, as follows.

The new combinations tear up the paths of each cycle in very different ways and need very different amounts of time to manifest their effects. Obviously a railway line through uncharted territory signifies a complete revolution of all economic and living conditions in that area, while the emergence of an industry that produces razor blades brings much less interference with it. Especially in the case of the railway line, it is also clear that some of its effects need decades or more - it takes at least that long for prairies to be transformed into urban areas and for the whole social existence in the area to change - while others - the collection of grain production along the railway line, for example - emerge in a few years, and yet others immediately after commissioning. A boom that consists in a dozen innovations of the rank of those razor blades will, of course, quickly play out. And all those kinds of innovations, and the various effects of each individual innovation, concurrently go side by side, albeit in manifold entanglement, and produce each for itself their special booms and their special depressions. It is therefore no wonder that, on the contrary, it was to be expected from the outset - although it was not what we in fact expected - that there are not one but many concurrent "waves of progress." And it may be added, without further explanation, that basically they all can be explained in the same way.

Four of these wave motions appear to me to be proven: first, the 7- to 11-year wave, the first we had in mind and which we will call the Juglar wave. Second, the "long wave" of about 50 years, which Spiethoff first pointed out and has been most thoroughly analyzed thus far by Kondratieff. Third, at least one wave the span of which lies between these two spans, that in America lasts 15-22 years. This was first investigated by Kuznets. Fourth, a wave of 3-4 years that Kitchin discovered and the existence of which, outside the results of many other investigations, appears to speak to the experience of business life. The above-mentioned difficulty and the imperfection of our technical apparatus make the dating and characterization of all these movements a very uncertain affair. At present we can speak only of an impression we gain from the consideration of our material and which easily can be deceptive, especially in individual cases, the more so since the interference of the waves renders the high points and low points on our charts unreliable. The main outlines nevertheless should be established. For us it is only these, and the monetary-theoretical understanding of the process that is thereby concerned, that come into consideration.

External Disturbances

6. Finally, monetary theory, as well as theory in general, has to come to terms with *external disturbance*.[21] This is not merely a matter of excluding such disturbance in theoretical thought experiments or diminishing them in our material. Rather, the main practical achievement of our theory is to depict those effects, so that one can define our theoretical apparatus precisely as a means of thought for this purpose, especially with regard to the theory of free competition, as a means of thought to capture the deviations of reality from it. The first step the analysis makes to solve a practical problem always comprises the reshaping of the presented question such that the event to be examined appears from the perspective of a given outside influence acting on a theoretically clarified economic course of events. Having succeeded in that, the theoretical and statistical logic runs automatically when the influence or disturbance is "relatively small." In the case of disturbances of such magnitude that adaptation to them by relatively small price and volume changes is not possible, but rather the basic outlines of the existing cycle change, our apparatus, strictly speaking, does not work, and there is basically nothing left but descriptively to determine what happens and how the new cycle looks. However, while adjustment by means of a gradual change in the price and volume system nevertheless practically never is entirely absent – not even in Soviet Russia – and while some theorems remain approximately correct even with great changes to the system, while lastly we can still say a few things about economic matters even where the ground is unprepared for our precision skill-set, so we are left with our scheme upright, albeit with diminished worth, the circular flow and disturbance standing opposite to each other.

---

[21]The misunderstandings that technical terms in our field encounter because our public has the naive habit of clinging to the usual meanings of words, make it desirable to emphasize that the word "disturbance" [Störung] here does not imply a value judgment. It only describes influences other than those that are constitutive of the processes that we consider in each case. Even a *stimulating* influence would, from this point of view, be a "disturbance." And interventions that fall under this term should not thereby be characterized as unusual, illogical, etc.

We will group the disorders as follows: the type of the first group is given by the example of a sufficiently significant earthquake. This has the advantage that everyone realizes that it is an event acting "outside the economy," that cannot be ascribed to the economy, especially not to a particular economic system. In cases of wars, revolutions, etc., various viewpoints are possible. But regardless of which of them one adheres to, from the standpoint of the interconnections that here alone interest us, those events are included in this group. Likewise weather influences, insofar as they cause deviations of crops, construction activity, etc., from what is perceived to be a normal extent, discoveries of stocks of raw materials as far as *purely coincidental*, and the like. The second group, which might be called *interventions,* is exemplified by *changes* in public[22] commercial, social, or fiscal policy: of course, every economic course proceeds under the influence of a particular design of legislation and administrative practice. One adapts to it, and it pertains to the data. *New* problems only arise when it varies, although we make the comprehension of the effects precisely of those given by our indicated method accessible in such a way that we compare the case to be examined with an economic course that does *not* contain the relevant statutory provision or administrative practice.

The money-theoretical and monetary-political relevance of all of these disturbances is clear. Of special importance to us are those that not only compel reactions in the money and credit sphere, but - directly at least - develop within that sphere. Discoveries of new gold stocks belong to our first group, changes in mint legislation such as the transition from one coinage metal to another, bank legislation such as a change in the legal reserve requirement, inflationary or deflationary policy and the like, pertain to our second. The latter *must* have motives, and these need not be rooted in monetary policy. Devaluation of the coinage metal would be an example of a purely monetary-political motivation of a coinage reform, but the cases are much more frequent in which the nexus of complete explanation as a rule cannot be derived from currency disturbance. Here it is only to be stressed that there are also purely monetary causes of disturbance. Even if the causal relation spills out beyond the monetary sphere, for the purposes of theory it is often sufficient to halt at its borders - regarding which, what is needful was stated in the first pages of this book.

The circular flow, seasonal variations, growth, waves (development), and external disturbances are thus the chapter headings of the system of teaching

---

[22]It is not essential that intervention proceed from the public power. A change in the payment habits of businessmen would also belong here, even if not decreed by a public or other agency.

and the program of research of modern economics. Any investigation that applies an economic question might, as the reader might convince himself by checking, be classified under one of these chapters or pertaining to economic sociology or economic philosophy. Only the problem of the *trend* still seems to be lacking.

Chapter VI
The Vehicles of the Social[1] Accounting Process:
The Household and the Firm

The Economy-Wide Ledger

1. As the central office of a socialist community must settle *up* [abrechnen] with the comrades and settle *through* [durchrechnen] within the production process, and all these operations yield the organic whole of the social economic account [Wirtschaftsrechnung], just so must the economic agents of a market economy-oriented community settle up with each other and settle through in their individual production processes: except that now all these operations do not seem to merge into a social economy, and a social central bookkeeping observable with the senses nowhere manifests itself.

Only the case is no different with the economic processes themselves, the often distorted reflection of which yields the economic account. Nor does the production process of the market economy proceed with a conscious plan. Nevertheless, a certain order prevails there, and not anarchy. Economic understanding begins with the insight that the market economy is a *planned economy* as well, and the capriciousness of legally sovereign entrepreneurs and merchants is effectively limited by the social realities of the economy, presenting themselves to the actors under the viewpoints of beckoning earnings and impending losses, such that an outside observer would have to believe that these industrialists and merchants acted according to specific instructions. Similarly – and precisely in consequence – all this individual settling-up and settling-through, all payments and income, merge into the *organic whole of a social economic account,* which is not any the less real because it is not elaborated in a physically existing central bookkeeping. It is readily apparent that any credit or debit made by a single economic entity corresponds to a debit or credit at some other single economic entity, and that this intertwining must yield the accounting-mediated image of the social economic constellation [Wirtschaftszusammenhangs].

---

[1]Original manuscript: "socialistic."

We can even go one step further, to where the production process itself provides no complete analogy: the central organ for settling-up and social bookkeeping not only exists in the same sense in which a social economic plan exists in the market economy, but, although incomplete, also as a directly observable fact. The settlings-up of the individual economic entities between each other – and, insofar as these settlings-up are at the same time a reflection of settlings-through, these latter also – take place in part by transfers to accounts which they maintain with their banks, and these banks in turn settle up directly with each other or with the *central bank*. Of course, compensations are made every step of the way, so that the books of the central bank apparently only reflect a part of the economic process. But this excerpt is the final distillate of all transactions passing through the banking system, and would be no different if they were to appear in full detail in a giant ledger. Even if we imagine the capitalist economic account in this way, pieced together from all the particular transactions on bank accounts, it would still be incomplete, because a greater or lesser part of all goings-on does not have to do with banking transactions. But even with this limitation, the social central bookkeeping in the capitalist economy is given as a fact and not merely as a theoretical construction.

To understand this social economic account and the phenomena linked to it, to recognize theoretically its meaning and functioning, and to provide the intellectual tools for the treatment of their practical questions, is our goal. In order, first, to recognize its features in the facts of the practice of monetary and credit transactions, we wish to work up a scheme that, while it will fit no single country particularly *closely*, will fit *roughly* for all countries of the Euro-American cultural sphere and make familiar the essential features of the case as far as is necessary for our purposes. As some criminal anthropologists have attempted to make us acquainted with the criminal type by successively photographing a number of specimens of this type onto the same plate, so that the similarities are emphasized and the particularities are toned down, so we wish to focus our attention on an average image gained from practice, where it does not concern the discussion of a special case. Initially, we continue to use most terms according to their meanings in daily life, which are either known offhand or can be found in any textbook of bank management – just as generally, the beginner again is reminded that the knowledge of accounting and the basic concepts of management science and legal science are assumed.

The Current Account as the Basic Concept of Monetary Doctrine

2. Even so, we refer in particular to that the contract figure that puts before our eyes the meaning of money better than any other, and is much more suitable than the act of handing over coins to explain to us what is at stake with the institution of money, to wit, the current account contract. This contract[2] creates the *current account relation* within which each monetary quantity that corresponds to an economic action is added sequentially into a single account and thereby loses its individuality. This is legally expressed in the fact that claims regarding the individual transactions cannot be independently invoked (sued). In place of these particular claims appears the abstract unilateral claim to the *deposit balance* that arises at the end of the accounting period or at the time of a cancellation that can be made without notice. Admittedly, the consideration of, e.g., legal practice and legal doctrine regarding securities provided for individual claims prevents this construction from being taken entirely seriously.[3] All the same, the assets and liabilities springing from economic life as well as the effectuated monetary services are thus stamped as what they are, mere accounting items, with the balance of which nothing else usually happens than that it is carried forward to new account, while practically speaking a "payment" comes into consideration only in cases of the interruption of the normal course of things.

The generalized concept of this current account relation, i.e., the idea that everyone's economic act is recorded on a real or imaginary current account, is extremely revealing, and so useful in capturing the social relationships and processes that make up the monetary and credit system, that it could be called the basic concept of monetary doctrine. Accordingly, each "service," whether it consists in money, money claims, or goods and services charged in money, is to be *credited* to each person's current account, while every receipt of money, money claims, goods, services is to be *charged* to it: should someone render ten working hours, he is credited in the sum of ten times the hourly wage and, when he receives this wage, he is charged by the same amount; should he then buy a skirt, he is charged for the amount of money corresponding to this skirt; when

---

[2]Older legal theory, on the other hand, was reluctant to accept a "contract," and often only spoke of a "relation" [Verhältnis]. Although this position is not legally tenable, it expresses a real feeling for the much more comprehensive nature of this relationship [Beziehung], which is not exhausted merely in legal defense [Einrede des Kontokorrents].

[3]The reluctance to accept a *novation* of claims arising in the current account rests on this, which has much to recommend it *logically*. The consequence of payment for securities is explicitly ruled out in §. 356 of the German Commercial Code.

he pays it, he will have the amount credited. Without further ado, one sees that the supply of labor services and the acquisition of the skirt are what matters, while the charging of the wage and crediting the price of the skirt are only technical accessories. Secondly, in the example of labor service-skirt acquisition, we encounter the basic process of economic life, which above all is the thing that must be worked out. Thirdly, in an equilibrium state, the long-term normal balance quantity for each complete cycle would be equal to zero. In this case, the settling-up for each household and each company would be recognized not only in the formal accounting sense consisting in the balance being set to the "smaller" side of it, but also *materially*. The former fact we call *accounting equivalence*, the latter *economic equivalence*.[4]

We first consider an area of investigation which is characterized by uniformity of currency and banking organization without commerce with other such areas. In this *currency area* we group the *primary vehicles* of the monetary phenomena of interest to us into four classes, which we would like to call, in short: *households, firms, banks, and central bank*. Next to and between these primary vehicles of the monetary process, there are also *secondary* ones, the function of which is merely payment-technical in nature and which we will call *auxiliary classes*. As an example, the case of a state that raises taxes, the income of which it passes to the local communities in its territory: the real beneficiaries here are the communities, but the tax revenue first comes into the treasury of the state, which in the relevant transaction slides in as an auxiliary fund.[5] The same example shows that primary vehicles can also act as secondary ones.[6]

---

[4]We need yet a third term, that we would like to call *financial equivalence*. If a debit balance is offset by a loan, the account obviously is not settled in terms of economic equivalence. But neither is it there only in a mere accounting sense.

[5]Neither is this process indifferent in terms of monetary policy. We will be coming back to it. But it has no place in this basic scheme. That accordingly we consider the case of "out-door relief" otherwise than as support provided within an institution, forms no difficulty: in each case, the sum in question appears once and only once.

[6]Without prejudice to its other "cultural content," we summarize the civil service contract, including the right to the enjoyment of rest, as a purchase agreement regarding labor. Note further that the public budget *consumes* these services and does not use them as "production of government services" to be taken into account as a special case: these services of state officials and soldiers, as well as the goods "consumed" by public authorities, such as office furnishings or weapons, pertain to the social product, and are not to be conceived as goods issuing from their use, such as national security, internal order, and the like. It cannot be stressed enough that this procedure has nothing to do with the

The Household as Alpha and Omega of the Economic Process

3. We conceive of households on the one hand as places of consumption, on the other as suppliers of productive services. In them, therefore, the objective

---

valuation of the results of government activity. Of course, it is not merely terminological either. It brings the fact to expression that there is no private demand for military services; that from the standpoint of the private household budget, it is an uncompensated liability; and that it makes no sense to construe tax rates as prices for state services. Only the recognition of these facts leads the way to a useful definition of the sums of income (*national income*) in the economy and to a meaningful definition of the social product. At the same time, it is necessary to separate expenditure on civil service labor from expenditure on support payments, that economically have a different effect – the buying activity of the state, from the income transfers mediated by the state. If the state produces services or goods that it sells to households, then it enters the ranks of those vehicles of payment processes that we call firms. If it raises the means needed to that end by taxes, then initially the taxes are to be treated as taxes and thereafter their application to this goal is to be treated just as when another household applies income to build a factory. A road built from state funds, the use of which is permitted on a fee basis with price character determined according to market principles, would pertain here, while on the other hand the construction and maintenance of a public road the use of which is free of charge would pertain to state expenditure of the military-expenditure type. That according to our determination it is not the people who actually use the roads, but the state that is to be characterized as the "consumer," is only paradoxical if one overlooks the meaning of this determination, which should take account of the difficulties arising from the juxtaposition of a market economy and an *organic economy* [Organwirtschaft] (Gerhard Colm, *Volkswirtschaftliche Theorie der Staatsausgaben* [Economic Theory of Public Expenditure], Tübingen, 1927). Our principle can cope with the complications just mentioned, that for the rest are left to the reader: the case in which the fee is not calculated according to market principles, in particular cost-covering, or surpluses not being desired, and the case in which consumers do not have the "act of consumption" at their discretion.

The monetary-theoretical relevance of the matter, especially for all propositions that assume the formation of economic value aggregates, for many propositions that appear under the title "velocity of circulation," finally for the treatment of the topic of taxes and currency, was first recognized in its full significance by Hans Neisser, *Der Tauschwert des Geldes* [The Exchange Value of Money], Jena, 1928.

meaning[7] of economic activity is fulfilled. In line with statistical practice, we distinguish between individual, family, and institutional households. *Public budgetary units* [Haushalte: "households"], for Germany in particular the budgetary units of the empire, the territorial states, and the municipalities, pertain to the last-mentioned category and are generally regarded here as "places of consumption" of the services of officials, soldiers, as well as of office furnishing, items of army equipment, and the like. Insofar as, in money-theoretical as in other relationships, these budgetary units are households of a special kind, we wish to use the word household without prefix firstly for private households, mainly [a potiori] family households.

In modern industrial society, the places of consumption are factually largely separated from the places of production in the broadest sense, our "firms." But if, conceptually, we wish strictly to carry out this separation, as we have to do for the purposes of the clear ascertainment of the contours of things, then we encounter difficulties that have discomfited economists and statisticians many times in another connection. That households and firms often – in modern society, especially with the economic activity of farmers and artisans – are *one*, conceptually – and even statistically – they can be brought under our scheme if we set the farmer over against his "firm," his activity, e.g. labor power and land services, and have this activity supply returns to the farmer in money and in kind. In the end, every farmer connected to an accounting office learns to understand the practical meaning of such an arrangement. Also, it is not bad if we speak, as is the practice of some countries, e.g., of legal or medical firms, especially since many services consumed directly, such as labor provided by a doctor in a private hospital, by an artist in a theater, a teacher in a private school – factually reach the consumer through the mediation of entities that unconstrainedly can be conceived as "firms."

Nevertheless, we must allow exceptions to this manner of seeing things, which is so practical because it could be easily said then that all services ensue from households to firms and all counter-values of firms are "paid out."[8] Households of public officials sell their services to the consuming public-institutional

---

[7]The objective sense of economics, to the degree that the observer formulates it for his purpose – the word "objective" does not mean anything more here – is of course satisfaction of demand. But the desire for that can by no means be the only possible motive or the only possible subjective meaning of economic activity.

[8]For the sake of simplification, we might disregard the less important things, such as the granting of loans between households. In general we shall do this as well, which will not prevent us from considering such things when it seems desirable.

budgetary units directly. This item is too large to be neglected, and in terms of monetary theory shows peculiarities too important to be constrained into our scheme. Also, it is statistically impossible to neglect those domestic services that not always (tutor), but usually (wages of domestic help) lead to payments within the household. Although we cannot here speak of services and payments from household to household, we summarize these services by analogy to the services of public officials, i.e., as if they were made from household to household. Finally, the introduction into our scheme goes against the great and, what's more, variable mass of those directly consumed services that a household makes to itself, particularly the work of housewives. For our purpose – not for others – it is recommended to refer these services to the sphere of that degree of activity that ultimately is inseparable from any act of consumption. That makes this the only item that we exclude from our economic current accounts always and at all levels of abstraction and generalization.

Yet note: durable goods also enter into the consumption sphere of our households, while it is not actually them but their use that is consumed per accounting period. For our purposes, what is important is their entry into the consumption sphere and not the process of their utilization. We treat them according to the analogy of those consumer goods that tend to be purchased in large quantities – for us, a car is a stock of driving performances, a residential home is a supply of living services and is booked as such, although not in step [pari passu] with consumption acts.[9]

Household income

4. We now wish to split the "statements of account" of households, which we initially think of as extending over the entirety of economic life and therefore, apart from the services the household provides itself, reflect everything economically that happens there, again into the individual items for which they are the crucible. We do not now do this from the standpoint of the central office or bank in charge of the account, but from the standpoint of the household's own bookkeeping. That households keep ordered books on the principles of double-entry bookkeeping, is of course as unrealistic an assumption in itself as that they maintain "complete" current account statements. But as this latter assumption only brings into full light the facts that every bank statement in actual practice express, so does the former only formulate clearly that which

---

[9]This view, of course, is not useful for all purposes. See for the opposite – and a very elegant arrangement of the goods sphere – Irving Fisher, *The Nature of Capital and Income*, New York, 1906.

actually happens. Many households actually maintain books, although imperfectly, and even those that do not, still have a vague or even subconscious idea of their *budget configuration*. Otherwise they could not "conduct" themselves. It would be quite wrong to object here, where we are dealing with the logic of the matter, that our assumption is contrary to the facts and in particular that their application to real or alleged "uncapitalistically" thinking people – whatever that might mean – especially historical or sociological pre-capitalist types, signifies a non-historical projection of the mind-set of the bourgeois world of today into a different sort of environment. Our assumption is only an artifice that permits an expedient description of real behavior, not a statement about the socio-psychological factual situation.

The items in these budget books are of course only a replica of the items in the current accounts. We wish to make an outline of the most important of these items, thus of the *income* and *expenditure* of households. However, we now omit precisely that which has just been described as essential, namely, the items of the type of the expense of productive services and the income of consumer goods, and book only, e.g., the income of wages and the expense of purchase prices of consumption goods. However, we still construct the monetary quantities to be added where they are lacking in practice, e.g., in the case of the farmer who himself consumes the products of his "firm" and "supplies" his labor force to this firm. The first operation is classified as the expense of a monetary quantity, the last as the receipt of a monetary quantity, if his work in his own enterprise is paid at the same rate and at the same time as an agricultural worker of equal rank, and when he pays for his consumption at the same prices and in the same manner as when he purchases the goods in question from another firm.[10] Keeping these arrangements in mind, we initially book the following income of households, that we thus sharply separate from firms where firm and household form a life-unit.

a) *Wages*, including "salaries" and "royalties," furthermore proceeds from the sale of labor services in the exercise of free professions, etc., finally the elements of income in money or in kind to be booked for labor services to the worker's own firm, which last indeed correctly represent labor income quite like

---

[10]Here we can only refer to the statistical difficulties that hinder the implementation of this nevertheless essential idea. They can be overcome in part by admittedly crude estimates. For another part, they lie not merely in the people's habits of reckoning but in those of acting, especially in the agricultural sector of the economy, in which it is often not possible, e.g., to book to the farmer's account that wage that he would actually be paid for the same kind of service.

contract [ausbedungene] or remunerated work - thereby we only correct for a nonsensical usage of accounting practice, that usually conceives of such income in the case of the single firm as "profit."[11]

b) *Fixed income* [Renten] - stipulated or assigned income from services of natural factors of production, which also are only correctly captured by accounting practice when they occur in an independent legal entity.

c) *Quasi-rents* - income from services of produced factors of production, the supply of which so slowly adjusts to changing situations that they behave temporarily as if they were naturally given in a certain amount.

d) *Monopoly profits* - including monopoloid profits that arise in cases of limited competition. Salaries of business owners, fixed income, annuities, quasi-rents, and these monopoly and monopoloid profits, in quiet times make up the foundation of what businessmen and bookkeepers understand by commercial profit.

e) *Speculative and windfall profits.* The distinction between the two is based on a difference in the behavior of the economic actor in both cases. The cases of pure speculation, that is, speculation not tied to a productive or commercial operation, that primarily pursues other purposes, are, outside of the securities and commodities exchanges, of course relatively rare, while speculation as part of such business operations is, practically speaking, hardly separable from those operations.

f) *Entrepreneurial profit* - in our special sense, the premiums that in the capitalist economy are set for the successful implementation of an innovation in the economic process. Example: he who knows practically how to apply a new production method successfully by which, say, the unit of product can be made cheaper, will, as long as his firm can purchase its means of production at the prices corresponding to the old method of production, and sell their products at the corresponding prices of the old method of production, make an essential temporary gain - as is readily apparent - which is what we mean. The cumulative appearance of these entrepreneurial profits is a characteristic of a boom period, their disappearance an essential trait of a depression period.

g) *Interest remuneration* - including dividends, in view of the fact that the shareholder as such, economically speaking, is nothing other than a creditor who, for the sake of hoped-for benefits, enters into a position devoid of legal protection for creditors. Interest on loans applied to productive ends, is, as was

---

[11]It is not superfluous to point out that this also has practical significance. For example, he who does not think to make this correction when buying property, can easily come to feel that significance.

already said, a phenomenon of "development" in our sense, and basically arises with the implementation of innovations in the economic process, although it extends from there throughout the entire economy. It is a derivative of entrepreneurial profit, which it reduces. For loans that serve other, basically consumptive purposes, this is not the case, but here again interest has no independent source, but rather derives from wages, fixed income, etc., especially from tax revenue.

All this income we will, for want of a better term, call *economic income* of households. They [the various forms] have in common that they accrue to households as stipulated or assigned remuneration for any services in the economic process.[12] However, they do not flow to them exclusively from firms, although that is the fundamental flow, and, in terms of both general and monetary theory, it is such an important relationship that one prudentially simulates it as the only one that matters, in order to gain an initial impression of the essence of the matter. In fact, though, some of these receipts to receiving households come from other households, sometimes public but in particular, as was already said, other private households.

We book then a second set of income that we, again for lack of a better expression, would like to call *auxiliary income:* these are income from consumption loans, proceeds from the sale of household articles (houses and stocks included) or asset securities (stocks, bonds, mortgages, etc.), insurance income if not with the character of interest, and assignments. Among the latter we understand generosity-oriented [liberale] benefits (including public poor relief), alimony, etc., and *political income* [politische Renten], which express such things as the pensions of the French court nobility of the "ancien régime" and social pensions, provided they are not meant as components of wage contracts or insurance benefits on the basis of consideration assessed in terms of actuarial principles. Although part of the allocations comes from firms, it cannot be said that this source has a fundamental priority here. On the contrary, these receipts can just as well come from the sphere of other households, and indeed they do for the most part. But interest payments on government debt do not pertain here.[13] Taxes are political income of the public bodies to which they accrue. Since our

---

[12]Although not merely for what we call technically productive services. Even the monopolized service is a valuably done - albeit possibly "artificial" - service.

[13]This question has been discussed in the literature in connection with the problem of determining the size of the tax burden. It also has significance for monetary theory: an interest payment is payment of a purchase price, while a disability pension is a benefit that lacks a market-based complement, unless it is based on an insurance contract.

list is geared to accounting facts, these taxes, if they, for example, are transferred from one public body to another, from e.g. the kingdom to the states, and from these to municipalities, are now to be booked as often as this happens. Therefore, even those ongoing items are to be taken up in the list that are of the type of the transfer of a sum via mediation, e.g., of a mutual friend, hence the sum appears among these receipts. However, capital gains from property [Sachen] or titles held by households have no place on the list, as little as do transfers of estates [Vermögensmassen] (inheritance).

A word is still needed about the item, loan proceeds [Darlehnsvaluten]. First, a purchase on credit can be split into a fictitious "income" of the purchase price as a loan and its simultaneous "expense." If our accounting scheme is to reflect all relevant economic occurrences, then this must occur here as with withdrawals in kind of goods from one's own firm. But not every purchase of goods or services without simultaneous payment is a purchase on credit in this, *for our purposes relevant, sense*. If someone, e.g., pays his club bills once a month, that in itself simply signifies a convenient way of completing ongoing payments, but no increase in the purchasing capacity of the club member, although this aspect can easily creep into the picture; in particular, the initial introduction of this payment habit can signify actual credit provision. By the way, the accumulation of bills, even where nothing else than a mode of payment is concerned, is by no means inconsequential in terms of monetary theory.[14] But *to the degree that it is only a mode of payment*, it makes no sense to book each individual commodity procurement as a "loan proceeds" income item.

Household expenses

5. We now set this income against the expenses of the households, which may be greater or lesser than these, although every time someone spends more than he has, we feign the receipt of a loan sum.[15]

a) Fundamentally the most important, and indeed largest item among the expenses is formed by *consumer spending*, that, together with economic revenue, makes up the base case of the economic processes of the household. Here we must point out an arrangement that might seem strange at first glance. We consider, as already said, public bodies, states, communities, etc., to be locations

---

[14]Cf. Irving Fisher, *The Purchasing Power of Money,* 2nd ed., New York, 1922, pp. 81 and 89.

[15]What we feign there is the *income* of the loan amount but not the granting of a loan, which must indeed actually take place in such cases. The only exception is formed in cases of error, fraud, and unbalanced bankruptcy, which are set aside here.

of consumption of goods, military equipment, office supplies, buildings, and services of public officials. As we said, we are not talking of a *production* of such "goods" as public safety, etc., by the state. For us, the state will be a producer – and then a "firm" – only when it *sells* goods or services, even if this does not take place according to the viewpoint of profitability. Furthermore, it is merely an auxiliary fund if it passes tax income to other public bodies, or *even as support or political income,* while the economically and monetary-theoretically relevant disposition over them proceeds from the households receiving them. Should the tax revenues or operating income of the state be applied e.g. to pay salaries of employees of the general tax administration, then on the one hand account must be taken of the fact that here, in contrast to the case of using the same amount on support, there is a purchase of services, whatever else the public officials' relation might be from another point of view. The paycheck in any event corresponds to a market-valued good, a market-valued service of officials, that is drawn from the state without ceasing to be an element of the social product. On the other hand, the broader factual situation must be accounted for that, whatever these officials may provide for the welfare and even the economic welfare of households, nevertheless – in contrast to the performance of an "official" of a state railway – this service has no corresponding market-based complement. This also applies to the service of a public road or other services or goods if provided free of charge, even if people are quite willing to pay prices, and actually do so for similar services and goods offered on market principles. There is no sense in characterizing taxes, even regulatory taxes, as prices for services of the state, or to equate the missing price with the costs that these services bring to the state.

Our view takes both facts into account, according to which the state itself or, if you will, the "collective," is the consumer of state services not offered on the market and not subject to the market-oriented choices of households.[16] If one objects that this would eliminate from consideration things very important for prosperity, it may be replied that we are not dealing with prosperity but with the calculation mechanism, and that nothing paradoxical lies in the

---

[16]Of course, our conceptual arrangement implies no value judgment of economic policy. Rather, the conception is unrealistic that makes these state services into elements of the social product, identifies political with market-economic valuation, and overlooks the fact that a tax payment, even if used in each case for something for which the taxpayer certainly was ready to pay as much in price, is something else, and has a different effect than the payment of a price.

twist that such state services enrich not the social product but the social environment. Incidentally, the concept of *national income* only gains in clarity when the view here presented is supposed. It is no argument that in that case it would not be a faithful expression of the economic condition of a nation, because otherwise it would not be either. Naturally, shifts in the boundaries between market economy and organic economy must always be considered in monetary-theoretical argument.[17]

b) We further book the expenditure items of *investments* by households, which of course may be offset [gegenüberstehen] by *divestments* of other households or firms. Loans, stock and bond purchases, as well as profit of business (firms) as such, come primarily into consideration. We book the acquisition of durable consumer goods to consumer spending. Investing in one's own company pertains to loans, which corresponds to accounting practice.

Although investment can also be financed by the use of credit, in the case of investment by *households* – in partial contrast to investment by *firms* – economic income is actually and basically the most important source. Could we also disregard the granting of consumer loans, then the base case of household investment would be defined as: provision of economic income in favor of firms in exchange for the guarantee of a share in production yield or, in short, although not entirely correctly, purchase of claims on revenue. Note that, contrary to typical consumer spending, this does *not* mean the purchase of goods or services. The investing *household,* when it invests, neither buys consumption goods to use directly as consumption goods, nor means of production in order to pass it on as a productive loan, or immediately to apply it. Rather, that is what its – in the economic sense – debtors do. Of course *this* provision is basically the important thing and what exercises the essential effect on the economic process. But the process of the older theory, that sees the matter as if the investing household already had gained or used consumption or production goods – if possible, in the latter case, even those consumption goods that the people who supply the production goods, in particular laborers, eventually consume – is not always admissible even for general theoretical purposes; for monetary theory it means skipping intermediate links, to which very substantial matters may be connected.

Therefore, it should be emphasized that in the case of firms, investment typically, albeit not always, means the purchase of means of production. *Household investment* often stands several steps removed from this act, as is shown in

---

[17]Cf. G. Colm, *loc. cit.,* and H. Neisser, *loc. cit.,* p. 8, 35 and others. Cf. above, p. 134, n6.

the following chain: a household buys shares in an *investment* trust, which, for
the sum in question, buys shares in an industrial *holding company*, which in turn
buys shares in one of its group companies; and this may have a subsidiary, to
which it directs the sum; the subsidiary does not need the sum but lends it on
the money market, where the amount – again, not necessarily directly – is taken
up by a company that spends it on the market for means of production. All
these hands through which the amount passes are accorded the limited but still
great monetary-theoretical significance of auxiliary funds. Even the investing
household, with reference to this amount, which in its hand is not offset by any
goods, is to be approached as an auxiliary fund.

   Note further that within the household's *budget figure*, investment com-
petes with other spending, especially consumer spending; but in terms of the
broader economy, it is not that it is incompatible with the expenditure of the
same amount on consumption, but that *in the normal course of things* it in fact
implies such expenditure, so that the amount invested – only a period or a few
periods later – *normally* is effective in the same place that such an amount spent
on consumption by the investing household would have been, to wit, on the
market for consumption goods. If we disregard all intermediate links, the
amount invested either flows directly – in the case of a consumer loan – to the
consumption goods market, or it first encounters – in the case of a production
loan – means of production in order then to be paid out, likewise on the consumption goods market, by the households that provide these means of production – possibly as quickly and for the same consumption goods – just as if the
investing household did not invest it, but spent it on consumption. *Basically*,
the difference between an investment and a process triggered by consumption
expenditure lies not in the fact that in the one case, a consumption good is purchased, while in the other a production good is purchased, but in the direction
of production to which the relevant portion of the economy's productive forces
are made subservient – an insight the practical significance of which, although
restricted by various circumstances, is not voided by them; we will yet encounter
it.[18]

   c) Expenditure items are, finally, debt repayment and interest payments
and transfers to other households. These we divide into gratuitous [liberale] donations and tax payments, including compulsory contributions that do not run
through a state budget, such as contributions to social security. Whatever the
values, even economic in nature, that offset all these expenditures, in our sense

---

[18]Similarly, we will encounter the question as to whether savings accounts pertain
to investment.

they are made free of charge, and pertain among the *transitory items.*[19] The tax payments here include all factually outgoing compulsory contributions to public bodies, as well as fees and excise, income, and property taxes, but not the taxes that households *bear* without *paying* them – for the purposes of monetary theory, the only possible arrangement.

When Income Does Not Match Expenditure

Households

6. As stated above, these expenditures can be greater or lesser than the sum of all revenues, even if defined as we have done. The main cases of this are here briefly mentioned. It is true for all of them that they have a different effect in an area with an organized banking system than in an area in which transactions are conducted only with metallic currency, as we will see in what follows.

The first case can only happen at all in banking. For all or many accounts, banks insist that a *minimum balance* be kept, which the discrepancy between income and expenditure of households or firms, of course, not always in each period under review, but non-recurring and possibly with changes of the amount of the average balance or of turnover, brings to the account. This minimum balance is to be separated from what might be called, from the standpoint of the customer, the amount below which he does not wish his disposable income to sink. We make no attempt to classify this hardly important aspect in our framework, and let it go with this mention.

To be judged analogously is the case when someone finds that the amount of his *cash on hand* for his *normal* business is too small, and gets to work supplementing it, a process that likewise is not very important if one distinguishes it from similar-looking but differently motivated processes.

Hoarding, thirdly, can also be defined as an "expenditure" – from the household budget to the hoard – but is a *sui generis* phenomenon that can be set aside here, with the understanding that it be taken into account when it gains actual monetary significance. *Untoward* [uneigentliche] *hoarding*, which can occur in times of distrust of banks or currency, *in itself* is only a conversion of

---

[19]A warning against possible misunderstandings is inserted here: we are talking about *transitory items* firstly in the sense of the practice given by the example of the state, which collects taxes to pass the amount on to sub-associations. But we speak of transitory items also in a broad sense in which, for example, household income used to buy a share represents a transitory item. The feature of such, then, is that it "passes through" the household budget without buying goods.

cash balances from one form into another, and in its effect is to be separated from the often, but not necessarily, associated fact that these holdings are then withheld. In the general argument, we do not consider this further.

Fourth, not all expenditures need to take place in any accounting period that we arbitrarily select. If the means required for the purchase of goods or supplies that are not purchased in each accounting period are continuously collected, but these goods or stocks are paid for when purchased, then in the periods in which the payment falls, revenue will lag behind expenditures, while in other periods there will be an excess. We call this pooling of means *saving* when it happens for the purpose of new investment, i.e., of investment that does not take the place of other investment. The reader should be aware that this saving has played a major role in the scientific as well as in the economic policy debate of all times. It has been said of it, that it is the most important lever of the increase of wealth and prosperity; already in the 18th century it was identified as the source of crises and misery. Currently a discussion on the question of its "absurdity" has been dreamed up. These contrasts are not all objectively to be explained; in part because this word means very different things, it is strongly recommended that every time it is used, one makes clear what one really means by it. Here we already depart from general usage insofar as it indicates the sometime provision of funds for the purchase of consumption goods – one of the meanings of the term, *special-purpose saving*. As little do we depart from usage when we use the term for the rational distribution of consumption acts in time – going easy on provisions during a mountain-climbing expedition, rationalizing the use of a good, economizing on coal and money by improving the heating system.

Fifth, it happens that some people, even whole groups of people, out of sheer indolence do not have control over the total amount of their income. This hardly important case, that we wish to ignore, although it has eased life at many a bank with a clientele of wealthy retirees, and that we do not regard as a kind of investment, nevertheless leads us to a much more important phenomenon. It always happens in individual cases, and en masse in certain economic conditions, that households simply refrain from those expenditures, both consumption and investment expenditures, that they normally make – actually intend eventually to carry out – and to which the economic process is adapted. The seemingly trivial insight that the monetary unit is not swept along its path by any force of nature, and that, for it really to come to a normal or even intended expenditure, it yet requires the presence of many motives and the absence of others – e.g., the absence of the belief that what one wishes to buy today, one

will not get cheaper tomorrow – is of the greatest importance for the understanding of the monetary process and particularly its disturbances. We will return to this. Think only of a "buyers' strike." What people do there is not saving,
which we thus, as we did with investment, now have to distinguish from merely
non-spending, although the objective factual situation, before the investment is
actually made, is not different from what we now mean. But neither is it
different from the objective factual situation of the collection of funds for a
consumer expenditure, for example, buying a car. And saving is analogous to the
latter process, not to not-spending; whoever has gained that insight has freed
himself from many popular prejudices about saving.[20]

Now to the question : What is a *savings account?* The inability to give a
satisfactory answer statistically or theoretically is suitable to make us familiar
with a class of difficulties encountered by monetary research at every turn. The
most obvious answer is this: a deposit to a savings account is an investment,
basically just like buying a government bond – which one can also sell at any
time, and which therefore is considered a very liquid investment – and no
different an investment than if the thrift or bank in question were to issue a
bond and sell it to the depositor. And very often it is that way, although we shall
have cause to make a large distinction between the "purchase" of such a bank
"bond" and the purchase of the bond of another economic agent. At any rate,
the deposit to a savings account is an expense that the depositing household or
firm must charge to its cash on hand if it pays, e.g., coins, which otherwise *gets*
charged to the checking account, if a transfer to the savings account takes place.
Since we may assume that one does not often accumulate on his checking account with the idea that investment consists only in that, we might, one would
think, be happy about maintaining a sharp antithesis between checking account
and savings account, which in that case would be completely different things.
That the statistics are not entirely satisfactory, and American *demand deposits*
are not only checking balances but also contain short-term – up to thirty days –
tied-up funds, does no essential harm to our happiness. But we observe – in fact,
in all countries of which the author has some knowledge – that the turnover on
many so-called savings accounts is suspiciously large, and the difference between
them and the less active checking balances is less than between these and the
more active checking balances. That is probably nothing more [than] that very
many people, especially farmers and artisanal types, but others as well, add

---

[20]This threefold interpretive possibility of a seemingly clear and simple factual
situation has many parallels in the economy. It is senseless to reject it as pedantry, because quite special consequences are attached to each of the three possible cases.

amounts to their savings accounts that other people hold on checking accounts, especially if no value is placed on the capability of disposal by check or bank transfer [Girozettel]. But then deposits to such accounts signify no expenditure but rather only a special technique of cash management, and the deposited amounts relate to the goods world in the same way as if they had remained as cash reserves or checking deposits.

When things are like this with savings accounts, then it must be so in even greater degree with those balances that cannot be disposed of by check, although they are not characterized as savings deposits – better: *investment deposits*. First, some of them are suited to the nature of such investment funds. But how much of American "time deposits," English "deposits," German *Depositen* – to which also belong checking deposits – can be so characterized is very difficult to estimate.[21] The remainder forms the middle, waiting on larger discontinuous expenditures, and *cash reserves* – which can occur the more easily, while a check that is not covered by a checkbook balance but by the tied-up balance of the customer is usually honored if the bank does not want to lose customers. Therefore, one cannot draw very far-reaching conclusions from the figures available for America and recently also for England for the two categories (checking balances are called *current accounts* in England, which does not quite match up with the German current account balances, that do not include all checking balances),[22] although we surely ought not disdain them.

Firms

7. Much of what has been said can be applied directly to firms. We concentrate all business activities in them and visualize them best as joint stock companies, as unusual as that may seem when one considers that we refer to everything as "firms," e.g., farmsteads. We expediently distinguish retail, wholesale, and production, including transport, firms. We however insert many intermediate elements – agents, etc. – as well as financial companies – among which

---

[21] Even the banker can be easily fooled. He will often be inclined to speak of small deposits or deposits of "little people" as savings. This is acceptable only in part because the "deposit account" is used by such clients precisely as a cash reserve or reservoir of funds for major expenses. The rapid growth of the deposits of "little people" in Germany after stabilization therefore does not signify all that much.

[22] A more favorable view of the value of these statistics can be found in J.M. Keynes, *A Treatise on Money*, London, 1930, chapter 23. Note that his distinction between cash deposits and savings deposits is not entirely covered by our distinction between checking balances and investment balances.

we do not include banks but insurance companies, investment trusts, etc. - where this is desirable. In general, we think of those three types.

While households stand side by side, so to speak, with other households, the three types of firms, and even many of the firms in each type, are arranged one behind the other. With exceptions, the statistically most important cases of which are salaries of public officials and wages of domestic help - loan transactions between households can be neglected for most purposes - there are no pecuniary transactions among households that need worry us in terms of monetary theory. Typically the business transactions of households take place with firms that supply original means of production, and those from which consumer goods are drawn. The beginning and end of the economic nexus lies in the world of the household, which basically is only one link of its chain. Within the world of firms, this chain winds from retailer through the wholesaler to various finished goods producers, from these through other wholesalers or retailers, to intermediate-goods and machine producers, etc. through possibly very many such stations, all of which give rise to income and expenditure, to converge again in the world of the household. The *single* act of buying a loaf of bread by a household is equivalent to very many acts in the sphere of production, that are not simultaneous in terms of monetary theory and which conceal obviously existing relations of size between the items of the households and the items of firms.

These relations are therefore not discerned immediately, when one sums the typical revenues and expenditures of firms and sets the sum over against the sum of the fundamental income and expenditure of households, opposing business revenue and consumer spending. The typical revenues of each firm, that is the revenues that reflect their economic life process, consist in the proceeds of products sold (services included), while typical expenditures consist in the payments for purchased means of production. These values obviously may equal each other only under very special sets of circumstances - which, however, are of great theoretical interest - and, what in turn is of course something else, when business income equals consumption spending.

To the fundamental revenue of production income are added, as auxiliary revenues to firms, gratuitous donations and political income (*subsidies*, for example), income from sale of elements of the apparatus (outdated machinery) and of purchased materials (which can happen not only in emergencies but also in appropriate price constellations, with speculative intent), and income from loans by firms other than banks and households, to which, since the legal form does not matter to us, "capital contributions," especially proceeds from share issues, are to be considered equivalent. Since we consider investing in one's own firm to be an expenditure of the relevant household, it is also a revenue of the firm. In order not to be deprived unnecessarily of an important element of economic life, we do not extend this approach to firms that we not only feign to be joint stock companies, but that actually *are* joint stock companies or similar entities. Those net income elements actually realized but not actually remitted, *retained earnings* and the disclosed and hidden reserves [Reserven] of accounting, will therefore not depict expenditures with simultaneous revenues, but under the title *reserves* [Rücklagen], will be separated from the savings amounts of households, to which they otherwise are equivalent. In this context we expressly warn about the word *reserves* [Reserven] that favors erroneous associations and the significance of which in monetary and banking theory has nothing to do with the sense in which one speaks of retained earnings and the like. Even the word "reserve" [Rücklage] is not free of misleading associations, particularly *non-spending, accumulation* [Thesaurierens], and the like, but at least in our presentation it appears with no other meaning.

The fundamental expenditure items of firms, *production expenses*, are payments for purchased means of production and are broken down into the cost of maintenance and operation of the installation, and the cost of expansion or modification thereof, to which the possible necessary increase in operating equipment [Betriebsmittel] of the new installation is to be added. Only the former are *necessary* elements of the completion of the economic process, and only they *have* to repeat periodically, while the latter are unique in the sense that any such repetition basically does not signify replacement, but increase. The former we call current *production costs,* the latter investment – and precisely *production investment* if it involves distinguishing it from investment of the type involving share purchases, which of course also occurs with firms.[23] *Depreciation* is the bookkeeping provision for renewals, that are not, as repairs are, made continuously, and are not investment. In itself it signifies no expenditure and, in terms of our terminology, is also not a reserve unless there is a "hidden reserve" contained in it.[24] This type of depreciation, the only one we call such, is strictly to

---

[23]Note: if a firm buys a machine that not only is to replace existing production power but is to add more to the operation, then that is investment. If a household, that for example previously had no automobile, purchases such, then that is consumption expenditure and not investment. It is recommended that one make the theoretical basis of this differential treatment of similar transactions clear to oneself.

[24]The creation of hidden reserves may, among other things, also have the motive of making provision for obsolescence other than wear and tear. This brings us to a difficulty that we treat by restricting depreciation to provision for renewal of a building

be separated from those write-downs that are mere corrections of some asset category (e.g., accounts receivable).

The - thus, third - group of expenditures of firms, which we will call *handovers* [Ablieferungen], are the counterparts of the economic revenues d, e, and f (4).[25] Whether category "g" revenue belongs here depends on the theory of interest to which one adheres. These items are not payments related to means of production - and would be lacking in an equilibrium state with complete freedom of competition - but for the purposes of monetary theory, they behave quite similarly to these.

Fourth, here as before we have to book debt payments, gratuitous donations, and tax payments of households.

Finally it should be emphasized that non-spending at certain times and in certain situations, as discussed with households, plays an even greater role with firms, particularly in the category of wholesale trade. But if one disregards this, and the reserves with which they are not to be confused, it turns out that for the rest, firms - *and in contrast to households* - are mere way stations of goods and money of account [Rechenpfennige]. Economically, nothing - no good or money quantity or money sum - stops here during a suitably chosen period of review (although, of course, it often does physically, as in the case of consumed auxiliary materials). Nothing originates or ends here, although everything is transformed here. Therefore, the revenues and expenditures of firms not only must *balance* in the same sense as the income and expenditure of households, but must also *cancel* if there is a stationarily reproducing economic process. This is made clearest when one pierces through the monetary sphere to the underlying economic process - which in the realm of consumer satisfaction creates an uncompensated asset item, whereas elsewhere it everywhere creates asset items only in the same act [uno actu] with liability items.[26]

---

or a machine and we book the provision for devaluation due to obsolescence to reserves. When the practice of the German tax administration is to "pass" 5-10 percent depreciation on ordinary operating machinery, it apparently is taking the same viewpoint.

[25]Compare above, subsection 4, pp. 137 ff.

[26]The fact that we leave a revenue element, the reserve, with the firms, entails a deviation in this presentation, which incidentally does not affect the essence of the matter, from that of Irving Fisher in *The Nature of Capital and Income*, New York, 1912, to which fundamental work we once again refer. See also John B. Canning, *The Economics of Accountancy: a Critical Analysis of Accounting Theory*, New York, 1929, regarding which I. Fisher, *American Economic Review*, vol. XX, 1930, p 603; regarding German

From our income and expenditure we could construct, for households as well as for firms, both of those accounting forms, of which one, the *profit and loss* or *income statement*, describes the process of the economy that transpires in the time interval to which it refers, while the other, the *balance sheet*, presents the cross-section of stocks at the moment of balancing accounts, and which is the integral, as it were, of the former.[27] The latter reflects for firms, in assets: fixed assets (buildings and equipment), inventories (securities), receivables, cash and bank balances, and in liabilities: "capital and reserves" and other long-term debt, bank loans, merchandise accounts receivable. But let us leave the execution of these things, which incidentally are fundamental to monetary theory, to the reader.

---

literature, see in particular the books of Johann Friedrich Schär and Eugen Schmalenbach. Additionally, one may refer with benefit to any of the textbooks on financial statement analysis.

[27]The values of the balance sheet preceding in each case, form, as it were, the constant of integration.

Note: even the income statement includes mere [subjective] valuations; even the balance sheet includes actual incoming money quantities, e.g., "incoming payments" made at some time or another. But while the backbone of the income statement consists of the results of business events that actually occurred and that actually gave rise to "money movements," the balance sheet is in the nature of a computationally created entity, the monetary quantities of which are not, or were not, present in the same physical sense as the monetary quantities of the income statement, and therefore are not a part of the nexus of the money process in the same sense as those others are.

Chapter VII
The Vehicles of the Social[1] Accounting Process: The Banks and the Central Bank

1. *Banks* are firms as well, but firms of a special kind that, as we initially, entirely tentatively suggest, attend to a portion of the money and credit transactions of households and firms. We also include institutions that language does not call banks, if they fulfill the function of banks – thus the American trust companies and German giro institutions, thrifts and account-managing, possibly also credit-issuing, post offices, and all the satellites of the banks that are hive-offs of individual functions, such as *discount houses* on the London *money market*, *stock exchange brokers* when they also finance the transactions that they provide, etc. In addition, finally, even "bank branches" of other firms, such as department stores, travel agencies when they perform real banking activities, structures of the type of the General Motors Acceptance Corporation that provide retailers of a large production firm with easier and cheaper credit than they could procure themselves, etc. Of course, we have no statistical figures that include all of that. The *banking statistics* that are most advanced, those of the United States, firstly provide the data of the Federal Reserve System member banks and trust companies [Trustgesellschaften],[2] thus also the figures for "all banks" including thrifts and private banking firms under state supervision. That is not everything, but for the main purposes of theory it is enough. The banking statistics of other countries give only, albeit steadily increasing,[3] excerpts, those

---

[1]Original manuscript: "socialistic."

[2]Which are simply banks, and are not so called only for reasons involved in banking legislation, and have nothing to do with, first, the also so-called trusts [Treuhandgesellschaften], and secondly the sometimes so-called large industrial corporations. But the most valuable part of these statistics covers the "weekly reporting member banks," which, measured by balances, make up only a quarter of all banks. For the period prior to the Owen-Glass bank reform (1914), we have mainly the material of national banks, i.e., banks under federal legislation, although others as well. Very important series go back to 1867, some to about 1820.

[3]This fact, and furthermore the advancing concentration of banks and the advancing implementation of banking in the economy, entails that bank data lacks full

for England, Holland, and the northern states provide us with our statistical subsistence minimum, less so for France and Italy. In Germany we are very well provided for since the introduction of the publication of bimonthly balances of all major banks.

For some purposes, we will assume the existence of only a single bank, which of course coincides with the central bank; otherwise, a very large number of competing banks, as there are, for example, in the United States. In England and Germany, as well as in other countries, a few banks are so preponderant that there can be no question of *competition* in the theoretical sense; and even when there is no question of collusion, each of these big banks in their behavior take into account what the others are doing. This *joint action*, or action in lock-step, changes the very essence of our phenomena and must always be considered in the application of our theorems. Furthermore, one must never – theoretically and statistically – lose sight of the influence on the data and practice of banking stemming from the movement toward concentration in the banking industry.

Banks also do other things than those that one thinks of with the words money and credit transactions. Some conduct e.g. *merchandise departments*, the business of which grew out of the credit relationship to certain branches of production. We intend to disregard these as well as ancillary businesses such as *safe deposit box rental*,[4] but currency metal trading, *investments* and *divestments* – here of the same kind as with households, but the objects of which in many countries are limited by legislation or practice[5] – and securities issues (not securities trading on behalf of others) are partly so common and partly, in some countries, so important for understanding the functioning of the monetary mechanism and so inseparable from the lending business, that we cannot (or can only in a specific case), exclude them from our depiction. We cannot even exclude them where the banks do not "go public" and where they do not, as they do in Germany, play a direct role in industry, which is contrary to their nature and restrictive to their functioning.

The basic outline of the matter is only clear when we imagine that the entire payment and credit system of transactions centers in the banks. This is

---

comparability over a longer period and that one must be very careful about drawing conclusions therefrom. Different accounting methods and business forms render direct international comparisons completely impossible.

[4]The fact that objects kept in a strong box do not occupy the same place in banking as do safe custody accounts, is the most important economic motive to construe the strong box contract as a rental and not a bailment contract.

[5]But such restrictions are frequently evaded by way of affiliated companies.

the theoretical base case that shows the social account-settling system in its purity, especially if we include those revenues and expenditures of households and companies that we have merely feigned. For this reason we will always be falling back on it. Here, however, we must take into account the fact that a part of economic life makes use of *commercial credit*, and that also even in the countries that have become most organized in terms of banking, England and the United States, at least 10-20 percent of sales occur outside of the banking system. Commercial credit is the deferral of claims on sold commodities. For one thing, it is of interest that this business form can lead to the emergence of a negotiable document, e.g., a bill of exchange,[6] *without a bank intervening;* for another, that the penetration of bank credit vis-a-vis commercial credit allows intermediate forms to arise, of which the most important is the bank *discounting of bills of exchange:* if a firm sells a product to another firm, e.g., "on three months credit," then in and of itself this must be interpreted as a loan. But without prejudice to the legal situation, the money-theoretical aspect of the process is extinguished when the firm that has provided the term receives a bill of exchange and endorses this over to another firm, thus proceeds with it *as it would proceed with a cash payment.* If, however, it sells the bill to a bank, the commercial credit is eliminated and economically a similar situation is produced as if the business had been financed from the beginning through a loan by the bank to the buyer of the goods, even though his books look different. Here, commercial credit is only a technical accessory.[7]

Something similar also holds for non-interbank payments in an economic territory organized in terms of a banking system. Certainly there can be closed circuits in which, e.g., metallic money circulates without ever touching the banking sphere. But one must travel to the Balkans or Morocco to observe this. Otherwise, each such sector communicates with the banking world at least in the way of savings deposits, but usually much more directly. In many cases it can be assumed that, e.g., a worker, even though he gets a *paycheck*, cashes it immediately, but that the retailer who receives coins or notes from the worker, transfers them to his account. In this way - and similarly if it happens quickly, even if not through a single change of hands - to use a nifty expression of Irving Fisher's, the bank becomes the coin's "home" from whence it is never far off,

---

[6] The "negotiability" of bills of exchange gained acceptance in the 16th century.

[7] The discount of open accounts receivable differs only technically from bank discount, namely in reduced negotiability entailing that the former much more clearly "immobilizes means" than the latter.

and in which it leads its actual life. Its payment function is reduced to the humble servant role vis-a-vis bank-mediated payments – certainly less modest than statistics would indicate at first glance, which also include exchanges and purely financial transactions that ought not be put on a line with goods transactions – similar to the role of barges that take over the steamer's cargo, where the latter cannot moor. And as the steamer's cargo compartment also includes those parts of the cargo that are landed by means of the barge, so also does the volume of bank-mediated payments also include the greatest part of those payments that ultimately are effectuated by handing over coins. The amount of wages paid in the case mentioned previously is listed on the account of the wage-paying company. The coins received by the worker come in place of a part of that account balance, allowing one to imagine that balances and coins "circulate" through economic life independently of each other.

Not only *that* portion of the money process, thus, that takes place entirely between bank accounts, but also that which still makes use of coins, belongs to the mechanism of bank-mediated settlement, where bank-mediated payments predominate. Coins in this case serve a different purpose than in non-banking money transactions, if they do not always remain in the bank but occasionally or regularly depart from it to complete payment acts that at any one time are inaccessible to banking instrumentality [Banktechnik] – if the draft of the bank steamer, so to speak, is too deep. The existence of such payments, particularly when they make use of full-value coins, is, as we shall see, of the greatest significance to monetary theory and currency policy.

Bank Income and Expenditure

2. It is impossible with the necessary brevity to provide a satisfactory interpretation of the banking business. This is all the more worrying because in fact it is essential to understand the economic settling-up and settling-through processes, while precisely at present many outlandish judgments of a monetary-policy nature – as well as many reform proposals – have their source in an imperfect understanding of these things, or a lack of perception of them. We emphasize again that at the very least, the study of a book on banking instrumentality and banking policy (such as the excellent book *Bankpolitik* [Banking Policy] by Felix Somary) is a prerequisite for the following, if it is to convey to the reader what it wishes to say. With our remarks we wish to establish an overview of the main items of the income statement and the balance sheet of a bank – omitting all fundamentally insignificant items and as much as possible typifying by analogy the aforementioned forensic anthropological method. Because the

logic of the matter is interspersed throughout,[8] this can very well be done in connection with German conditions.

The main liability items of the profit and loss statement are - apart from profit - operating costs (especially salaries), taxes, depreciation, and interest payable. The main asset items are *interest, commissions,* and gains from securities and issues of securities. The latter, which with German banks play or have played such an outstanding role, one which for obvious reasons has been entirely inadequately highlighted [bevorstehende][9] by accounting practice, interest us only in part. What one calls a *consortial* or *syndical* or *participatory,* collectively usually *financial,* operation, is not material to banking operations and is not included in our framework of financial firms, even where these activities, as in Germany, are conducted by the banks themselves, which however also fulfill the functions of *investment trusts* and *holding companies.* The difference then practically is not very great, as in America when "pure" banks simply acquire a formally independent investment trust.

But, as already mentioned, *banks' investments* - which we view as non-speculative purchases of government and industrial bonds - form an essential cog in the mechanism that we wish to comprehend. When, namely, banks buy such securities from other firms or households, they make them quite as liquid as if they were to give them loans - in both cases, new credit is created for the clientele.[10] However, when a non-banking firm buys securities from another non-banking firm, for which they pay out of already existing balances, then the firms taken together are not more liquid, and the total of their balances is not increased. One need only consider that it is the sum of these firms' balances that buys means of production and generates income, to see already how important

---

[8]Laymen and practitioners often accuse theorists of taking too little account of the peculiarities of individual cases. In fact, our subject matter is so "institutionally" determined that we cannot carefully enough do justice to the historical relativity of these things. But the facts themselves have a much greater uniformity than the practitioner believes.

[9]Mann substitutes "comprehended" (erfaßte) here.

[10]One can also clarify the matter with the consideration that in this respect something analogous is on hand with the discount of bills of exchange, which in fact is a legal purchase of a claim. If we do not follow this analogy, this happens not because of the non-essential aspect for us of the liability of the drawer or of the endorser or payee, but because the discount of the bill usually is associated with a particular economic transaction, which justifies a different classification.

this difference must be for us. We at once add in anticipation, that it is something else again when a *central bank* "invests," because then it is the other banks as such that become more liquid. Therefore, we henceforth wish to keep strictly separate *central bank investment, bank investment*, and investments by households and (other) firms – under which, one should not forget, are included gross investment [Investitionen ohne Zusatz] and production investment.

Commissions are partly actually that which the name suggests, namely remuneration, but also partly interest, and thus represent the typical earnings of the banking business. This interest is obviously received for granted "credit" – although the legal form need not be that of a loan – that puts firms or households in a position to make any payments. And because bank investment also has no other economic *effect* than this, we can define *for our purpose* and *in our view the only essential function* of banks to be the *making available of balances to firms and households*. Lending to other banks or the purchase of the securities of other banks constitute a particular case, which does not merit the same importance, although it does have another.

This definition also covers the case of the establishment of a credit balance by the payment of coins or paper money, but only if the payment makes it possible for the payer to make bank-mediated payments,[11] not when it takes place with the intent to invest. When we say that banks make balances available to firms and households, usually this is also technically correct if the customer withdraws coins or notes: the withdrawal is made *from* the balance, or this part of the balance is made available *in the form*, e.g., of coins – the purchase of, for instance, government bonds that someone brings to the bank, in exchange for coins or notes so that no bank balance arises, we may safely neglect. But bank-technically our language is *not* correct when a bank "grants credit" to its customers without crediting them the money in their checking accounts. This does happen in America, in England, and in those countries – particularly overseas – that follow Anglo-American practice. But even here one can simply enter into an agreement whereby the customer can overdraw his account (overdraft), in place of this legal and accounting figure. Now statistically this is very inconvenient. Because the customer behaves in this case just as if the loan were credited to him, it is not permissible to say that this credit, which has only been prom-

---

[11]Cf. for the following, L. Albert Hahn, *Volkswirtschaftliche Theorie des Bankkredits* [Economic Theory of Bank Credit], 3rd ed., Tübingen 1930.

ised, has not yet materialized, is not yet offset by the goods, and therefore exercises no effect.[12] Rather, the businessman views his unused credit as his cash reserve.

An important element of the monetary system in this manner eludes statistical measurement, although of course the utilized parts of "overdrafts" appear in other people's accounts. In England, this practice is historically explained by the penetration of Scottish cash credit, that in the beginnings of the banking industry financed current operations and was secured by guarantors, usually also periodically dropped to zero, and only paid interest on the amount upon which the customer drew. Luckily for us, it never became native to America. Rather, it was, and is, viewed as an abuse, and is officially opposed (regulation of the Comptroller of the Currency to national banks, 1915). It is limited essentially to cases of error, arrears in value received, and exceptional situations.[13] But in Germany it is not general practice for a bank loan to be credited to the beneficiary on the checking account and treated on the books as a payment (deposit). In the law on checks, however, the legislator proved to have a truer sense of the meaning of the matter by on the one hand making the existence of a balance one of the requirements of the check (deposit clause §. 1, further §. 3), and on the other hand permitting the issue of checks on the basis of a loan commitment, thus viewing "credit extension" as the establishment of a balance to the borrower. We only take the essence of the matter into account if we determine henceforth to envision each credit extension of a bank to a customer as being immediately reflected in the balance of this customer – of course, with the caveat that the effect on statistics of the deviating practice in Germany (and most continental countries), and in England regarding "overdrafts," must be kept in mind in the study of these countries' deposit data.[14]

---

[12]That would be entirely the same as if, in the case of a currency system in which we make payments only by transfer of coins, not the entire available quantity of money, but only that part of the same that is spent each time, would be taken into account. Leading authorities are of a different opinion. But we can appeal to J.M. Keynes.

[13]For America, one can therefore *in principle* (not only, as one must, statistically) exclude unutilized "overdrafts" from the total amount of "bank money" and take the position that the "overdraft" understanding is not "credit" but only gives rise to a claim for such, and that [a] "credit" only arises, and only in that amount, when there actually is an overdraft.

[14]Attention must always be paid to the effects of various business practices and payment instrumentalities on the statistical figures. Thus, it also makes a difference, e.g.,

With our definition of the function of those vehicles of the money process that we call banks, we come again to our fundamental conception of the social account-settling system. The provision of funds takes place in the course of account management by the banks and is an element of the instrumentality thereof, the management of that part of social bookkeeping that is located within the compass of each bank, an auxiliary of social account-settling, that reviews in summary the income and expenditure of households and firms.[15]

The Bank Balance Sheet

3. The role of the banks in the economy-wide account-settling process can be read even more clearly from their *balance sheets*. As with other firms, on the liability side is listed "bank means of operation," information about the "application" of which is provided on the asset side. They [the former] break down, again as with other firms, into *own funds,* share capital, accumulations – here as well, we must issue a warning about the word *reserves* – and *borrowed* funds [fremden Gelder]. The amount of liabilities and their ratio to the amount of assets is of course important for the balance sheet picture and the bank's reputation, and also for many practical purposes, especially in the case of bankruptcy. But for understanding the function of banks in the economy, own funds are of secondary importance, since by contrast to households and firms, banks typically – disregarding bank buildings, office equipment, etc. – do not buy goods. The only liability items that interest us are borrowed funds, which alone we wish to set against the essential asset items.

Borrowed funds initially include the check and cash management balances of households and firms (and of other banks), whereby we again encounter the constitutive feature of the banking business and its characteristic position in relation to all households and other firms. While the payables of household and business balance sheets signify received goods deliveries or advances, the payables of banks simply depict the sum of cash means of payment made available to customers and the main part of their liquid asset items. We will shortly have occasion to note that in its application to these items, the term "borrowed funds" is misleading. In the meantime, we note that it also includes balances

---

whether the bank payments are made by check or giro transfers. In our presentation we always have the first method in mind.

[15]Of course, that only happens completely in our mental simulation, in practice only as far as banking transactions extend. We will assume that *all* firms maintain bank accounts, but only a portion of households.

arising from loans by banks to their customers, thus all sums that customers have at their disposal whether they correspond to "deposits" [Erläge] or not, which only expresses a state of affairs in itself indisputable and uncontroversial. With the previously mentioned exhortations of caution, we set, alongside these checking balances, investment balances (savings accounts), to which this does not apply and which do not signify "bank means of payment at the disposal of customers." Both together we also call *accounts payable*. The third fundamental liability item accrues to *acceptances*, partly financing international trade (e.g., respecting raw materials), partly to present the banks a method to take up short-term debt in the domestic money market, which as a rule is: to borrow from other banks and, in a similar manner to e.g. the state administration, to issue short-term debt. For the banks that buy such paper, this forms part of their investment.[16] If, as also happens, the bank acceptance goes from hand to hand completing payments, it is analogous to the banknote.

On the asset side, we have in the first place the item *cash*. Firstly, this is the amount of legal tender money (domestic and foreign: *notes and coins* [Sorten]) that at the point in time to which the balance sheet refers, stand ready to be converted from balances into non-bank means of payment. The cashier of a bank is the bridge between the sphere of bank-mediated and non-bank-mediated payments, payments by transfer and payments by handover. Or, to use another image, the sally port from which the coins based in the bank take their excursions, and also the gateway through which they enter or reenter the banking sphere. Inasmuch as the money corresponding to this item is actually physically held at the ready to serve the ongoing needs of customers, it has more right to the name *reserves* than any of the items that we have come across under this label. But for the sake of greater clarity we wish to avoid that word here and will speak simply of *cash money* or *bank cash* (till money). The reason for this is that, to the degree that this item only fulfills this function, it is not a "reserve" against all obligations for the services of legal tender money that can arise from the total amount of borrowed funds, but is simply the expectation-oriented part of it that tends to be converted by customers into non-bank money.

However, cash on hand may have other functions. Above all, it can be a real reserve with respect to borrowed funds in the sense of being kept ready to form a first line of defense against an onslaught of "depositors" when they make withdrawals, not as part of ongoing activity but with the intention temporarily or permanently to retire from bank transactions, as is wont to happen in panics.

---

[16]See regarding bank acceptance, Felix Somary, *Bankpolitik* [Bank Policy], *loc. cit.*, pp. 24 and 32.

Because of this contingency, bank practice and sometimes banking legislation sets a *reserve proportion*, a percentage of all borrowed funds or a percentage of the "accounts due daily" or different percentages for these and for time-bound borrowed funds, below which cash items must not decline, so that in addition to the above so-called cash money there arises a *panic reserve*,[17] which is also listed under cash items. But we do not wish to insert this practice into our picture; rather we assume that in such cases, thus always when withdrawals are to be met that are not part of ongoing business, such as e.g. wage payments, the banks procure the necessary funds from other banks, and ultimately and fundamentally from the central bank, and that this happens not just in the case of panic but even with extra-normal or also seasonal or cyclical demands. For this reason we stick with the actual practice of countries with advanced banking systems, all of which have adopted the *principle of gold centralization*. In the United States, the *banking reform* of 1917 also drew the consequences legally by establishing that banks are no longer allowed to include their holdings of legal tender money in their deposit reserve, so that these exist only in their balances at the central bank, in this case one of the Federal Reserve Banks. A similar condition, although less pronounced, has slowly emerged by way of practice [via facti] in England , where a "metallist"-oriented criticism, in partial misunderstanding of the meaning of this development, precipitated concerned complaints about the inadequacy of the gold foundation for the immense credit edifice.[18]

Finally, a bank's cash could have still a third function: if its customers have higher check amounts tendered to customers of other banks than they have received from them, the bank will have to pay the balance to the other banks. This can be – and in the past often was – done by handing over legal tender money, in which case the banks' cash items must also include provisions for these occasions. However, we will assume the existence of *interbank clearing* as it currently exists everywhere in various forms, and in a way that the liability balance resulting from the implementation of the clearing be paid by check to the credit of the banks at the central bank.

---

[17]Since this proportion must be *maintained* also in the course of those abnormal withdrawals for which such a reserve is provided, this practice means not only an unnecessary sharp credit crunch in the panic, but basically also that in addition to this minimum panic reserve, another, free panic reserve is to be kept.

[18]In his famous book *Lombard Street* (London, 1873), Walter Bagehot gave this criticism wide popularity, so that in banking literature up until the World War, it pertained to good manners repeatedly to refer to this point in admonitory fashion.

The items, deposits with other banks and the central bank, therefore contain the true *cash reserve* of banks, which is to be set in relation to their checking balances or to the total of their borrowed funds. From this ratio - taking into account each bank's debt to the central bank - one can recognize the *degree of fluidity* or *tension* of the banking situation, while the proportion between cash holdings and checking balances in principle is only[19] a symptom of payment practices in the relevant area of study and in itself says nothing about the momentary state of the credit system. As regards balances with other banks, however, this applies only to balances of the smaller banks and banking houses at major banks. Every major bank fulfills the functions of a central bank towards a number of smaller banks, and the London, Berlin, Paris or New York banks do this to a certain degree for provincial and local banks generally. But the balances of large banks with smaller or foreign banks do not have this reserve character. In many cases they represent loans to subsidiary institutions or to those banks that conduct their market transactions through the major bank in question. As far as balances with foreign banks are concerned, they serve ongoing commerce, especially since it is in contradiction to etiquette in big banking circles to owe another bank directly,[20] even if it is only a letter of credit. After all, interbank lending relationships signify a substantial easing of the principles according to which banks otherwise must be directed, and a substantial gain - *assuming* it is a gain - in elasticity for the banking system. We must always keep their aim in mind, even where it is not possible to point it out every time, and even when for purposes of presentation we must refrain from doing so.

The balances of banks with the central bank - and the undrawn-on credit each bank has at the central bank - largely are actual reserves, thus the only thing we wish to characterize as such on the balance sheet of each bank. Where its amount, i.e., its minimum ratio generally to the overnight funds, or to the two types of borrowed funds, is normalized by law, only the excess reserves are freely available to the banks. But this statement loses much of its importance in the fact that the banks can keep their reserves normally at the statutory minimum by availing themselves of credit at the central bank when these reserves threaten to fall below it, so that the matter in the case of legal standardization of reserve proportions in reality is not so much different than in the case of the

---

[19]However, the variation of this proportion in the cycle, and also in seasonal change, is of symptomatic significance.

[20]We nonetheless see already that this likewise happens via the roundabout way of acceptance credit, in international commerce especially by the practice of *advances on bills of exchange* [Wechselpensionen].

absence of such standards. The logic of the matter asserts itself in about the same way everywhere, and is embodied in practice; and the "this is not done," so important in banking, basically is just as effective as laws are - *but only just as effective:* the reader must never forget how lax, and *variously so at various times*, all of this is, and how much leeway this whole living organism has in all its manifestations, to which in our presentation we often lend an unrealistically mechanical rigor.

Of the remaining items on the asset side, since we exclude consortial activities, long-term participations, etc., we are interested in *contangos* [Reports] and *advances against securities* [Lombards], advances on commodities (and commodity shipments), rediscounts, other *accounts receivable*, and own securities. In the latter we see our investments, i.e., temporary assets in readily liquid, partly self-liquidating securities - treasury bills, for example, belong here and not to the category of rediscounts - which in practice, because of this characteristic, are sometimes referred to as *secondary reserves*. We also include *acceptances of other banks* here, even though in terms of monetary theory they are accorded a special place. Obviously, a firm that obtains acceptance credit from a bank, when the acceptance is acquired by another bank in the money market, actually gets a bank loan from the second bank guaranteed by the first.

The remainder of these items we summarize under the term "credits" (*loans of all kinds plus rediscounts*).[21] They break down into business with industrial and commercial customers, and loans "in the money market" and "the stock market" (*call money, money for monthly clearance* [Ultimogeld], and *contangos*, which latter, despite the legal form, belong here and not to investment; the difference between contangos and advances against securities is only of a technical nature). The loans to the stock market or for stock market purposes take place partly between the bank and its securities-purchasing clientele, partly between banks and *exchange agents* (broker's loans in the United States) and other intermediaries, in turn including banks (and their affiliated entities), so that possibly the same "money" is shuffled back and forth in a way that complicates and veils the operations of the financial sphere.[22] For us, the key is the

---

[21]In some places, especially in the United States, the term *bank credit* denotes those credits plus investments. We here allow the term *accounts receivable* to have the same meaning as "credit," although wider and narrower meanings are also common in practice.

[22]In itself, the *intent* to disguise is not needed for this. But such an intent often tags along, as in general there is much to remark in the business and accounting practice of wide circles of the banking sphere in all countries. Here only the ensuing difficulties

credit of industrial and commercial customers, and for the practice of banking, this credit is the main thing in all cases where the interest in issues and the like does not entail aberrations. Stock market loans and bank investments normally and supplementarily stand alongside the main line of business, and from the standpoint of banks' profitability [Erwerbsinteresses] supplement an absent or inadequate scope of opportunity there, as important as that role is in the mechanism of the monetary process. It is essential to understand this branch of operations as composed of elements of an organic unity oriented to credit for trade and industry, and not to believe that these elements stand disconnectedly or on an equal footing side by side, or that their connection is exhausted in the current relation of their rates of return.

Bank Association and the Central Bank

4. Rarely do banks work in disconnected fashion. From the very beginning of the banking system and by the time of the Provençal fair bankers, it was the *interbank exchange of claims* or particularly organized interbank *clearing* that was the heart of the banking system and the main girder of the edifice of bank means of payment. Proliferation of the clearing function was also an important motive behind the monopoly aspirations of the early city banks, as with, e.g., that of Barcelona.[23] The *clearinghouse* enters the scene wherever there is a multiplicity of banks, and once it is there, it shows a tendency to be a *super-bank* and to provide help to individual banks in difficult situations, such as through the issuance of *clearinghouse certificates*. In our picture, we let it be subsumed in the central bank, to which indeed clearinghouses usually connect in terms of organization.

Furthermore, as we have already indicated, in each banking system a tendency manifests itself for individual banks to finance or otherwise patronize other banks and so become "banks of higher order." From an easy-to-understand practical need, banking systems develop in which banks settle with each other and make reserves available to each other, and their many members keep

---

of a statistical nature should be pointed out. In this context we yet wish to mention the practical impossibility of a reliable evaluation of banks' bill portfolios. Even if it were statistically feasible, nothing would be done with the distinction between *commercial* and *financial bills* (regarding which every book on banking technique provides information).

[23]Cf. the seminal works of A.P. Usher [mainly *The Early History of Deposit Banking in Mediterranean Europe*, Cambridge MA, 1943].

reserve balances with and take loans from each other. We see how closely this approaches the constituting of a bank as central bank, and how little the various legislative acts founding central banks have done violence to things or have brought an essentially alien element into an arrangement in which, as some representatives of *free banking* assume, central entities otherwise never would have been born. Actually, albeit often only in rudimentary fashion, these organs manifest themselves even in countries that do not or did not have a central bank, as with the United States before 1914, Argentina, India, and others.

In our picture we wish generally, and where we do not explicitly state the opposite, to allow no other banks of higher order than the central banks, and to allow only one in each currency area. The first provision is not unproblematic, because in practice the figures of the large banks of the most important financial centers cannot be interpreted without taking into consideration their position as banks of higher order; in particular, the flows of money and balances between the parts of an economic region cannot be understood apart from this aspect. The second provision is much less of a concern. Because if in some countries a plurality of institutions are extant that have a claim to being central banks, still, as in Germany and Italy,[24] either one so much outweighs the others that they pale beside it, or a central organ of central banks forms. In this regard, the course of events in the United States is instructive. The law of 23 December 1913 is explained by the will of the legislature to create a multiplicity of central banks. Although more than a mere supervisor, the Federal Reserve Board initially by no means was intended to be the soul of the system of reserve banks and a vehicle of its own bank policy. But this body grew inexorably into that role. And not only that – a second central organ arose entirely on its own, filling a generally perceived gap: the Federal Open Market Committee, that gives uniform shape to the investment policy of the Reserve Banks, so that by way of practice [via facti] the "system" came to be something that functions very much like a European central bank. It takes a metaphysical belief in free competition and a complete misunderstanding of the nature of the banking business to evade this testimony of facts.

No matter what the central banks otherwise are or have been in the course of their eventful history – credit or inflation instruments of states, etc. – for us they are simply *banks' banks*, everything else is secondary. However, at

---

[24]Of course, one ought not make note issue into a feature of a central bank. We say that there were several central banks in Germany only because the southern note-issuing banks originally were actual central banks, and retained remnants of this position even after 1909.

the same time we wish in every region to allow them to be the government's bank, into which taxes are deposited and which make the state administration's disbursements, and which thus conduct the public accounts, which in England is the case at its purest. We do this because in this case, tax payments and government spending, beyond their usual meaning for the money process, are accorded yet another special theoretical interest that they would otherwise lack and which deserves to be highlighted. That is to say, government expenditure which is effected by a check drawn on funds of the state administration at the central bank, increases the reserve funds of the bank of the recipient of the payment, and thus facilitates credit expansion just like a gold inflow.[25] Tax collection has the opposite effect, so that in this case a tightening or loosening effect on the money market proceeds from the financial management of the state,[26] which comes on top of the influence that financial management already exerts in all cases.

Furthermore, our central bank will not only keep accounts of all banks – which by the way is likewise not universally the case – but also corporate customers, although it will not count households among its clientele, so that for many though not all firms it maintains accounts, immediately discounts their bills, etc. This is not universally the case. The U.S. Reserve Banks have, e.g., no corporate customers, and few central banks maintain the smaller business customers to the degree that the Banque de France does. However, the full realization of the function of a bank of banks, even though it is not first made possible by having customers other than banks, is made very much easier if it does, which is why we want to include this characteristic in our picture. Precisely the example of the [12] U.S. Federal Reserve Banks illustrates the reason that we place value on the characteristic. Namely that during the world crisis, they repeatedly expressed the threat that they would procure the legal powers to conduct private banking operations if the member banks did not become more willing to follow their lead. It is also evident that the possibility of customers' migrating to the central bank can be an essential cog in the machine of any active central bank

---

[25]The importance of this aspect for the mechanism of English war inflation is obvious. If the state pays war supplier A with a check drawn on a non-central bank, then A is credited with the amount, the state debited for it, and that is all. If the check is however drawn on the central bank, then A is still credited by its bank, but in addition this bank now has a larger reserve than before, so that it can issue more credit.

[26]Therefore, the influence of tax maturity dates is particularly pronounced in England and makes itself felt hardly or not at all in countries in which the taxing power does not work with the central bank.

policy and, where it is missing, it is just this activity that, so to speak, is deprived of its spurs. That partly banking operations, partly political aspects have the effect of keeping the best paper from flowing in this manner to the central bank, while the paper of smaller players in particular does arrive there, is not of further interest to us here.

So we envision the central bank, apart from its basic function and its - accessory - function as banker to the state, as a deposit bank like any other, conducting all regular banking business - albeit sometimes more, e.g., foreign exchange business than others - thus in particular, bill discounting, providing open credit facilities and the like, and regularly making investments and divestments. Because in terms of monetary theory, banks are its major customers, credit provision to these customers and *rediscount* of their paper will occupy the foreground. Also, the central bank's investments and divestments should be primarily thought of as purchases from and sales to banks. The "means" of the central bank are basically no different than those of any bank. In particular, its right to issue banknotes, or even the exclusive enjoyment of this right, is not essential. Rather, in many countries note issue pertained to the normal transactions of all banks especially before the *modern* phase of deposit banking, thus before roughly the middle of the 19th century. And even today it is not everywhere limited to the central banks. When in our picture we nevertheless furnish the central bank with an - exclusive - right of note issue and furnish our picture with these notes having the power of legal tender, this is only for illustrative purposes to show in this special case certain relations, possible also in other guises, and not because we wished to concede special theoretical or practical priority or even any inner necessity to this institutional arrangement.

The *banknote* is nothing but a ticket [Zettel] embodying balances, the handover of which takes the place of the transfer of those balances. Also the *relation to the discount of commercial bills*, to which, in pursuance of an old view of business life and literature, nearly all central bank legislation has been geared,[27] and which has often been hailed as the focus of all sound banking wisdom, has nothing to do with the essence *precisely of the banknote*. In contrast,

---

[27]It is characteristic of the strength of this tradition that the issue of Federal Reserve notes, although in many ways peculiarly arranged, is nevertheless based primarily on the rediscounting of commercial bills, although such bill material does not exist in the United States to the extent necessary, so that the system of 1913, geared, as it were, to a bank-policy lie, from the beginning functioned differently than the professional advisers had assumed: an illustration on the theme of the "theories" of practitioners. The

two other well-known features interest us. First, the unbacked or incompletely backed banknote is the prototype and most obvious example of the fact that, and the means by which, the banking system creates *money*, or, more neutrally [*unverbindlicher*], *means of payment*, or more clearly, the means by which it *creates* credit, a phenomenon to which we will immediately turn. Second, it is the vehicle by means of which bank credit penetrates beyond itself and the circle of bank customers to the mere "monetarily" functioning circles. It circulates, often simply replacing coins of higher denomination, typically for all intents and purposes alongside these coins and all those means of payment that exist independently of the banking system, and fulfills, without thereby ceasing to be a part of bank credit, all their functions, including those serving as means of backing and discharge for other sorts of bank money or bank means of payment. Hence, it is quite conceivable, for example, for a central bank to consider its holdings of its own notes to be backing for its balances. In this way the central bank note has gained a peculiar, basically completely illogical double character.

We envision the central bank, according to the standard case, as a corporation, although there are examples to the contrary – the Australian central bank is, and the pre-revolutionary Russian central bank was, a state institution. Practically it makes no difference. Even a public institution of this kind is wont to enjoy considerable departmental autonomy; even a central bank corporation comes under political pressure, usually in the direction of *cheap money* and "economic development" (= "inflation"), which as a rule constitutes a major obstacle to rational behavior, and a crisis-intensifying element. The strength of this pressure is very different in different countries. The Bank of England has always had the most freedom of movement, and it also provides the only major example of a purely private organization of management, although the Treasury gained a factual dominant influence during the war and postwar period. This arrangement of administrations of the central banks, with the manifold attempts, for good reasons and bad, to ensure the felt need for representation in them of the state authority and all possible interest groups while still preserving their independence, otherwise provides a pattern card of shapes and viewpoints which is of great sociological interest. We have a picture before us which, with the advancement of trends toward the planned economy, perhaps may serve as an example of how real or supposed "public" interests can be looked out for in other spheres of the economy, without – immediately and completely – delivering these over to the politicians or the bureaucracy.

---

notes of all national banks, on the other hand, were a – hardly tempting – example of an entirely different basing of the banknote, namely on government bonds.

More important to us are the legal rules to which the operations of central banks are subject in all countries. Disregarding their justifications and the objectives expressed therein, there remain commands, prohibitions, and powers, all of which amount to restrictions, the most interesting of which in terms of monetary theory we will divide into four groups.

A *first* group has the purpose of protecting the central bank in different directions. This is the meaning of frequently prescribed restrictions – which are simply prohibitions in individual cases – on credit granted to the public authorities: a paper wall, but which in quiet times do what they should. So too is to be understood the oft-encountered stipulation that in certain cases an expansion of the granting of credit is permissible only at a specific minimum interest rate, which, often "appropriate"[28] in terms of bank policy, without such sanction would expose bank management to public indignation regarding usury and the like.

Second, all legislation is in agreement that at least the central bank has to be a real bank and not a Crédit Mobilier, which explains the prohibition on industrial operations, particularly participations, speculation in shares, etc. The importance, in terms of banking policy, of banks engaging in investment activity does not generally receive adequate attention; what attention it does receive comes mainly from the United States.[29] Even so, the purchase – in the case of the Swiss National Bank, with the very appropriate addition: to temporary deposit – and the pledging of bonds, including those of public-legal domestic borrowers, is often explicitly allowed. In this vein, the discounting of bills jumps out as the key form of lending in all cases known to the author, although the rediscounting at least of fixed-income securities is allowed (their purchase using money-market technique [i.e., open-market operations] partly replaces this), as well as, usually, the pledging of bills, of foreign currency, of gold (also gold in shipment), sometimes also warrant discount, in some cases even granting mortgage loans (e.g., in Denmark, formerly in Austria-Hungary), etc., also usually under certain restrictions. In accordance with the character of the central bank

---

[28]Anyone who takes offense at this word may replace it in all cases with "according to the objective of the system."

[29]However, that was – another example of the logic of things – not at first the outcome of money-theoretical recognition or money-policy intention. The Federal Reserve Banks were simply opening up another revenue opportunity, because given their assets it was not very clear what they were to live from. And only from this viewpoint did management turn to this line of business. Only gradually (about 1922) was the credit policy aspect of the matter discovered.

as a *super-bank*, and its credit as a layer of credit underlying ordinary bank credit, in the United States above all it is concerned exclusively with rediscounting. In accordance with the *commercial theory of bank credit,*[30] it is primarily the discount of *bona fide* commercial bills that is intended – whereby the attempt is made to exclude *accommodation bills* as much as possible. Almost without exception, acceptance of bills of exchange is prohibited.

A *third* set of limitations arises from the intention not to allow the central bank to compete with other banks but to lift itself from their circle. In the United States, this went so far as to deny the Federal Reserve banks the direct discount of commercial bills and acceptance of deposits from non-bank firms. In most countries, the assumption of interest-bearing deposits is not allowed; and so forth.

Of most interest to us here, *fourthly,* are those provisions that are intended to regulate the quantity of means of payment that a central bank can put into circulation. The universal emergence of such rules today, expresses the recognition that a central bank subject to no external restrictions would be technically capable of pumping arbitrarily large quantities of means of payment, such as via investment, into the economic process – which will be formulated and proven in more detail.[31] Disagreement can exist only on the question as to whether it is not sufficient to limit the central bank to such transactions, especially the discount of commercial bills, in which, whether real or imagined, the initiative does not lie with it but with the other side, that is with trade and industry, which must have a "demand for credit" in order, directly or through others, to "access central bank credit." Certainly, a construction of the central

---

[30]This expression is particularly common in American literature and corresponds approximately to our notion of *classical money creation*. It refers to the view that "bank money" "should" arise in connection with transactions in commodities, while the "financial theory" proceeds from bank investment, whereby it assigns to "bank-mediated money creation" much greater freedom of movement than accords with currently popular ideas of active and, in particular, therapeutic bank policy.

[31]For the time being this much is clear, that an institution that issues an arbitrary amount of unsecured notes with which it can purchase interest-bearing securities would face no other barriers than its own ethical inhibitions, or those based on political considerations. It should be equally clear, one would think, when such purchases would be paid for not with notes but with balances, the amounts of which the seller could access via check or giro transfer. We emphasize here the case of investment in order to take into account the objection that could be raised from the standpoint of the "Banking Theory" against an analogous assertion for the case of credit provision.

bank's business circle and business practices, by which every expansion of its credit provision plus its investment beyond any particular desired limit, e.g., beyond the amount of investment funds coming in, would be rendered impossible, is *conceivable* without having to add further braking devices. Just as surely, as we will see in more detail, this brake is inherent to all cases of lending activity, albeit in inadequate manner from the standpoint of most monetary policy objectives, so that, as we always emphasize, an element of wisdom lies in the view that, for example, the backing of notes with commercial paper signifies actual backing in the monetary-policy sense.

Even the duty to exchange banknotes – and obviously that also indirectly means balances – on demand at any time against something that the bank cannot create whenever it likes, e.g., against other legal tender money or, in the case of a gold currency, against full-fledged gold coins or currency metal, or claims for money on foreign countries (*foreign exchange, gold exchange standard*), proves to be a *second* step in this direction: the *conversion obligation,* coupled with the duty conversely to buy something, gold for example, at fixed prices, is just another brake that normally holds the note or the deposit of the central bank at exact or approximate parity with the selected standard and that reinforces the first brake inherent to the operating mechanism.

The circumstance that the behavior of the bank could easily make the fulfillment of this duty impossible, explains why all legislation in turn fortifies this second brake by a third, which again is to ensure convertibility. Since the central bank, if it is subject to the obligation to convert, must in all cases maintain a reserve of the object with which conversion is to take place, e.g., gold or foreign currency – this is another meaning in which the word "reserve" is not out of place – then it makes sense to dress this further precautionary measure in the form of a rule regarding the minimum amount, a *backing rule,* which then is done in various ways, first with respect to the banknotes, then more and more with respect to balances. Such a determination may be replaced or supplemented by the promulgation of a maximum note issue or a maximum amount in excess of full metallic backing or a *banknote tax* on the surplus over a certain amount (direct and indirect curtailment). Hence,[32] at the Reichsbank the marks are to be backed to 40 percent in gold and foreign exchange, at the Bank of France notes and balances to 35 percent in gold, at the Bank of Italy notes and balances to 40 percent in gold and foreign exchange, at the Federal Reserve Banks notes to 40 percent and balances (nearly exclusively the reserve balances

---

[32]These provisions in many countries were swept away by the storms of the world crisis.

of banks) to 35 percent in gold, at the Swiss National Bank notes to 40 percent also in gold. Austria has basically one-third backing for notes and balances in gold and foreign exchange. Note issue in Sweden hitherto was allowed for the double amount of the gold stock plus 125 million kroner; in England, the portion of notes metallically unbacked is maximized. The majority of the laws contains a banknote tax in various forms.

The Central Bank and Monetary Policy

5. We do not care about everything central banks "should" do, but only about what they actually do, or can do, and what effects this has. The range of tasks attributed and prescribed to them from the various points of view extend from the relatively modest formulation of the German Banking Act of 14 March 1875, "to regulate the circulation of money in the entire Reich, to facilitate payment settlements, and to provide for the utilization of available capital," to the popular ideal of keeping interest rates as low and stable as possible – which to some extent is like having an ideal of an "as stable as possible" barometer – and stable exchange rates – also such things as "protection of the currency," securing the credit edifice, etc. – all the way to the stabilization of the price level, to the control or even prevention of booms and depressions, to general economic theory, finally to the credit-policy realization of a planned economy. What central banks actually do and can do will of itself become clear to us in the course of our investigations. Here a preliminary overview will be given of the means available to a typical central bank to conduct an *active money market policy*, i.e. a set of actions that, extending beyond commercial adaptation to given situations, seeks to achieve some other goal. All of these actions are now based on a central bank's capacity to be a bank of banks, although in times and areas in which the central bank is the only major bank or at least the largest one generally, the matter is different.

a) Apart from side issues, the position of the central bank is entirely analogous to the position of other banks vis-a-vis their business clients: as these do for their customers, so do central banks make available funds or means of payment generally to other banks. In individual cases this need not signify much: just as there are bank customers who never run a deficit, using the bank only for convenient cash management while not being able entirely to do without it, and who are thus free from bank influence in their individual business practices, so are there also banks to which approximately the same applies. But the central bank is always for the banks what the banks are for their customers, the ultimate source of credit, the entity that always can procure it – although, if need be, in violation, winked at by government, of applicable laws. The power of the central bank over the reserve balances of banks (bankers' balances) is yet greater than the power of banks over customers' balances: to be specific, while banks namely can cut credit to their customers but cannot easily force funds onto customers who do not desire them, when the central bank buys securities, bank reserves are increased whether the banks want this increase or not. How much or how little this signifies will become clear to us later. At any rate, it means *additional liquidity* in the money market and elimination of the *restraints* that can arise in business activity due to a shortage thereof. Conversely, the sale of securities by the central bank signifies a contraction of reserve balances, a "tightening" of credit offered by the banks and therefore, depending on circumstances, a more or less palpable curb to business ardor.

This relationship between the position of the central bank as a bank for banks and their - greater or lesser - power over their reserves, thus over their activity in extending credit, first appears in its true light through the realization that these central-bank investments or divestments, these open-market operations, proceed on another level than analogous operations of other banks - that it is these banks themselves that are made more or less liquid, for which reason, as we shall see, the effectiveness of central bank operations is measured not by the amount of these operations but by their amount times a factor. The importance of this means of power therefore must not be despised just because it does not achieve everything that is sometimes asked of it, and because there are situations in which it fails. But it seems as if all the monetary theorists and monetary policymakers of today either overestimate or underestimate it.

b) The same is true of the classical tool of monetary policy, the *discount rate* [Diskontschraube], although even less than investment can it be regarded as a panacea for all manner of ill, and it is even less effective in times of severe economic fluctuations, and, in particular, of political disturbances. Although in part this is because the influence of the state and of public opinion often hinders its proper administration, and both the business world and the parliament are up in arms if there is talk of a drastic increase in the discount rate, yet by its nature the effectiveness of *discount policy* is restricted to moderate seas.

Where the central banks were the chief discount places for trade and industry in their locations, and the bank rate directly indicated the rate at which a large part of bill material was discounted, they at least appropriated all the influence that accrues to the discount rate generally. Since central banks have ceased to be the determining factors in the bills market - a process that took place in the third quarter of the 19th century in both England, the country of the theory and practice of discount policy that has become "classic," as well as else-where – the discount rate has typically become the rediscount rate,[33] although the central bank's own discount business has remained a sufficiently important cog in the money market mechanism to justify inserting it in our picture.[34] The bank rate, as rediscount rate, then acts as the *price of credit for lenders* – for forms of credit other than the discount of course as well – and upon bank re-serves. Subsequently, through its effect on these reserves, it has an effect on the liquidity of the money market generally, just as investment does, although the effect of the bank rate is weaker, because the readiness of banks to rediscount, and the presence of corresponding bill material, are a necessary precondition for any influence that may be exercised in this way. If one wishes to revive the pulse of industrial activity by providing liquidity to the money market, one usually encounters this difficulty, because when business is down, people do not wish to discount anything. If, on the other hand, one wishes to slow industrial activity down, *refusal to rediscount* in particular will often exert a strong effect.

---

[33]As long as the Bank of England felt in possession of the main part of the Lon-don discount business, it looked at the emerging deposit banks as intruders, and it was not always inclined to ease competition by means of rediscount. In this way it raised itself to independence and contributed to the emergence of a tradition that makes resort to the rediscount rate more difficult for a bank of lesser rank, a tradition that was also received in Germany and almost everywhere. However, this must not be taken too seri-ously, as one can see in English practice as it developed in the 19th century. The big banks do not submit paper for rediscount, but rather conduct their bill business largely through the mediation of *discount houses* and bill brokers. They finance them through their own loans, mainly in the form of call money. When it suits them, they call these in. And this has exactly the same effect as if they themselves discounted the paper and submitted it in the corresponding case for rediscount. For now the "bill broker" just goes to the Bank of England to acquire the means to repay his loan and offers his "bill material" – basically, the bank's that financed it – for loan or discount. And he is welcome there. No other financial arrangement works quite like that. But analogous *modi vivendi* have everywhere been formed; in prewar Germany without very happy result for the Reichsbank, when in times of even seasonal strain, short-term paper was offered for rediscount, while oth-erwise the central institution was quite disconnected from the bill business, putting it in danger of feeling itself a mere collection agent.

[34]For obvious reasons, many central banks, especially the Bank of England, since 1878 have calculated a preferential rate for direct discount of the bills of their own busi-ness clients, which of course is detrimental to the official bank rate as a symptom of the price of credit, but was only a logical consequence of its functional change.

What the relation of the rediscount rate would be to the market discount rate if this relation were left to the mechanism of the money market, depends on the structure of the banking system. If, for example, the rediscount is a normal element of the life history of a commercial bill, the bank rate as rediscount rate would as a rule be lower than the rate at which the member banks discount bill material.[35] However, where the rediscount is an emergency exit, so to speak, used only at a moment of ultimate tension and the like, the opposite would be expected. But the rediscount is not simply left to the market mechanism; rather, as just noted, it is a means for the regulation thereof. It follows that a general rule for this relation cannot be given. Admittedly, it is a fact that the classical models of European discount policy predominantly exhibit a higher bank rate. Thus, for example, between 1845 and 1900 the British bank rate was lower than the market rate only ten times; for the remainder it was always higher, sometimes considerably so. But this circumstance is only due to the fact that a responsible central bank management much more often sees reason to slow than to stimulate; the fact brings no general principle to expression. Of course, this bank rate in excess of the market discount rate is effective on its own only in situations of tension in which, for the time being, the central bank again has become the key – sometimes the only – functioning source of credit. But should the central bank exceed the market rate in a liquid market, it at first only has the significance of a demonstration that might be taken as a warning signal. If in such a situation the bank rate is to be effective immediately, it must "be made effective" by the central bank by its taking up the credit offer itself, the pressure from which otherwise would thwart its policy. The Bank of England, for example, already in the seventies and eighties in such cases spot-sold consols and forward repurchased them, and thus took up contango credit, which apparently has the same effect as a divestment. Here discounting and investment policies run together – and here open-market policy was implemented in practice long before it was hailed as a newfound safe haven.[36]

---

[35]This concerns the usual bank-mediated commercial paper. Everything that goes directly to the open market and that there, whatever the situation might be, can be accommodated at a particularly low rate (because it is free of all risk premium), never reaches the central bank unless by way of "investment." In Germany pertain here, in particular, the so-called *private discounts*, the acceptances of a small number of banks and banking houses of the first rank, which, as already indicated, play a role on the money market similar to government treasury bills.

[36]Incidentally, elsewhere as well. Thus, at about the same time, the Austrian government, in agreement with the Austro-Hungarian Bank, alternately issued and retracted

Sometimes the central bank - or the business or political world - desires that, whatever the braking effect of the bank rate might be, it be exercised not generally but in certain directions. Nevertheless, attempts, e.g., through *punitive rates* on speculative loans, so far have technically failed to achieve anything in the desired direction without raising the price of credit for other purposes, which of course does not mean that they must continue to be fruitless in future, particularly with the progress in the knowledge of the facts at the disposal of the central bank.

c) Both the investment policy and the discount policy of the central bank act fundamentally on bank reserves. But the bankers' bank may also exert direct influence on what happens with these reserves and the "means" of banks generally, similarly to the way that an able banker is not without influence on the use of credit that he grants to a firm. This kind of leading, braking, encouraging influence is so often exercised that it has become a notable element of the functioning of the banking organism. In the United States the expression "moral suasion" [English in original] is used for this, which is most faithfully translated [into German] as "gütlichem Zureden" [amicable persuasion], although the "persuasion" is not always amicable. Finally, the goodwill of the central bank is not a matter of indifference even for the largest bank, and therefore an energetic desire from that quarter is always a serious motive to do what is desired, especially since the threat of legislative intervention often looms behind it. This influence not only makes many increases in the discount rate effective that otherwise would not be so, but sometimes as well implements differentiated treatment of individual categories of credit applications according to intended use and other aspects. This practice has very different meanings in different countries, and has been employed mostly in Germany and - recently - in the United States, while - not at the present, but before the war - the Banks of England and France enjoined greater restraint. But also apart from this, the psychological effect of a change in the bank rate on the banking and the business world in general is a factor in its own right that quite often achieves more than would be intelligible from the merely mechanical effect of the bank rate.[37]

---

their treasury bills (on the Gmundener Saline *partially mortgaged mortgage payment orders*) to regulate the money market. During periods of liquidity undesired by the Reichsbank, it sold imperial treasury bills.

[37]Recall for example the sudden reduction in contango credit by German banks in May 1927, which took place at the "wish" of Reichsbank management and brought about a collapse in stock market speculation. The case is instructive because it took place

Points of Controversy

6. Finally, the old points of controversy will be mentioned. To what extent is the policy of the central banks more than behavior that would correspond to their mere *business interests?* Is the bank rate – generally, the totality of the conditions under which the central banks grant credit – *declaratory* or *constitutive?* To what degree does the monetary and banking system determine the bank interest rate of a country? Although the reader will gain definitive answers to these questions only when the analysis of this book is fully assimilated, preliminary ones are possible right now.

Regarding the first question: it is readily apparent that any active central bank policy in the service of any goals, even those most generally desired, such as concern for the "health" of the credit system, stability of exchange rates, etc., not only often entails waiving possible profits, but also makes financial sacrifices necessary. But precisely today, as extensive demands are made on the central bank and wide swaths in both professional circles and the public uncritically accept as an axiom the contrast between the duties of public monetary policy and the profit interests of the central bank, it is important to draw the reader's attention to the fact that what already has been said is sufficient to suggest the old truth that the profit interest of the central bank dovetails for a large part with the public interest in the performance of those monetary duties. It depends, of course, on what is meant by "business interests." But such a large company as a central bank always is, and one that feels as much as it does the backlash of any carelessness, would, even if it has only its own pecuniary interest in mind, have to make such far-sighted policy that "business" and "public service" from the standpoint of many goals (and all "classical" goals) would largely coincide. To be convinced of this, one need only consider when a high bank interest rate is possible and desirable in terms of the benefit of business, and when it is possible and desirable, for example, for the sake of maintaining relatively stable price levels. They do not always coincide – but they do usually.[38] And the reader

---

in a situation in which the "mechanical" means of the central bank had failed because of the plentiful and cheap short-term foreign credit available to banks.

Regarding American practice, see in particular Seymour Harris, *Twenty Years of Federal Reserve Policy*, Cambridge MA, 1933, a work that can be recommended generally as an introduction to the questions of modern central bank policy.

[38]From the mid-19th century until the War, the Bank of England, as far as the unrestricted gold standard permitted, *actually* served this goal by being guided in the determination of its rate *primarily* by the ratio of its reserves (coins plus notes in the

sees immediately why such questions can never be dispatched with common phrases and how difficult it must be to make oneself understood about it to the economic policy dailies.

It is not very different with the second question. What jumps out especially is that the policy of the central bank in general and the bank rate in particular cannot arbitrarily distance itself from the state of affairs in the money market. But the leeway for commercial behavior of central bank policy is much greater in the short term than the doctrine of the merely *declaratory* character of the setting of the bank rate would have us believe. This is above all self-evident for those times and situations in which the central bank's own customer business dominates the discount market. Then it would be quite as absurd to say their rate is only declaratory as it would be absurd to call the price-fixing of an industrial firm declaratory when that firm has a leading position in its industry and incorporates a significant portion of the range of products of this industry – such as Ford or AEG, especially in a case in which the "cost of production" is as a doubtful a matter as is the "commodity," central bank credit. In the transitional stage, which with the Bank of England began after 1844[39] and in which *adjustment to the market* was necessary, it is still the case that, simply by abandoning its centuries-old policy of ignoring the competition – in the entire one hundred years prior to 1839, it had kept its rates within the limits of 4-5 percent – the bank experienced a second flowering of its business customers, adapted a rate, the formation of which found an essential element in the bank's own supply.

Beyond that, the position of the central bank and the distinctiveness of the credit market entails that the other banks are inclined generally to follow its lead, especially since in some countries, especially in England, they themselves are not uninvolved in this leadership. The latter was also the case in the epoch in which the bank rate essentially became the rediscount rate. For the rest, this has of course less of a merely declaratory meaning because as such it has an

---

Banking Department) to its liabilities (cf. R.H. Inglis Palgrave, *Bank Rate and the Money Market in England, France, Germany, Holland, and Belgium 1844-1900,* London, 1903), which *at the same time* meant prudent management in its own interest *and* economy-stabilizing bank policy.

[39]In that year the so-called new system of discounting was introduced, which was to set the bank rate with regard to the market rate. See the *Report from the Secret Committee of the House of Lords appointed to inquire into the causes of the distress which has for some time prevailed among the commercial classes, and how far it has been affected by the laws for regulating the issue of bank notes payable on demand,* Session 1847-48.

entirely monopolistic character. The error of the opponents of the *doctrine of the declaratory rate* therefore lies not so much in the fact that the elbow room they claim the central bank has is not present, but that they underestimate the objective restraints on this freedom and overestimate what can be wrought economically with this freedom. For, keep in mind that we spoke of the importance of a bank rate for other bank rates, not the importance of bank-mediated conditions for the pulse of the economy.

The third question is rooted in the popular prejudice untouched by any analytical insight, that the bank interest rate lacks an inherent ground of determination, and can be molded arbitrarily in the service of any goals whatsoever, and that the legal framework governing the banking and monetary system represents an appropriate, if not the appropriate, means to those goals. Thus formulated, this view is hardly worth a word. But things are very different if we positions ourselves so as to take the short- and shortest-term perspective that alone interests the businessman and the politician. What from a fundamental point of view is obvious nonsense here becomes truth. Not only can the suitable design of the [legal framework of the] central bank make possible – and unsuitable design make impossible – the alleviation, and sometimes the prevention, of functionless panic-inspired damage to the economic process, not only can such design iron out short-term fluctuations in the discount rate that otherwise might cause serious disturbance to such a sensitive money organism, but it can also make all the difference between *control* of the discount market and central-bank impotence. Especially in connection with exchange-rate policy, here mentioned in passing, the discount and investment policy of the central bank can leave its mark on the economy-wide account-settling process depending on the existing legal monetary and banking framework. To understand how much or how little that may mean, and how *institutional formation* and *economic logic* conduct themselves in this field, analytic mastery of the entirety of economic life is necessary. No amount of detailed knowledge of the "local" phenomena is sufficient to this end. Concerning the bank rate in particular, its long-term level certainly cannot be affected in this way, even though its statistical picture may be distorted by having its peaks legally lopped off. But that its short-term sensitivity particularly to political interference can be abated by provisions of the monetary and banking framework, is as sure as that all active central bank policy has statutory banking preconditions. No doubt reasons of this kind were behind the fact that during the relatively trouble-free period 1876-1907, the Bank of England changed its rate 187 times, the Reichsbank 116 times, and the Bank of France 29 times.[40]

---

[40]See Georg Schmidt, *Der Einfluß der Geld- und Bankverfassung auf die Diskont-politik* [The Influence of the Monetary and Banking Constitution on Discount Policy], Leipzig 1910. The book is otherwise a good example of the so-widespread overestimation of the institutional design of monetary objects.

Chapter VIII
Bank-Mediated Money Creation

1. It will provide some better understanding and in some respects also be a useful repetition when we first very briefly, and without trying theoretically to penetrate to the essence of the matter, attempt to depict the banking system described in the previous chapter. To this end, we wish first to choose one of our many banks, Bank A, and put all the other banks, symbolically combined in Bank B (not to be confused with the central bank) to the side. We start from a condition in which bank A's directors are satisfied with the balance sheet at that point in time - according to their business habits and views and in the given situation - which means that till money, reserve balances at the central bank, the amount and structure of borrowed funds on the one hand, and investment and loans plus discounts (= "credit") on the other, stand in such a relationship that the directors would not wish it otherwise. This does not mean, as a segment of British and American banking theorists assume, that the income-producing or *earning assets* (= loans plus investments) must be utilized to the maximum and all possibilities of investing or credit provision pushed to the utmost limit. We will rather have to stress later on that such a condition would certainly appear abnormal to a reasonable banker and would lie beyond the danger zone - which, by the way, differs depending on the business situation and nature of the environment, and thus is never sharply drawn.

Reactive Bank Policy

Now we wish to change one of those items. This can happen for various reasons. As an example, we choose a case that serves just as well as another, wherein customers of Bank A, whom Bank A does not wish to lose and to whom therefore it does not like to say no, approach it with new credit demands. Bank A grants these loans, the amount of which we book *both as a loan and under checking deposits*, because this accords with the logic of the transaction, albeit not, mind you, with the general practice of accounting,[1] so that both sides of the

---

[1] Where accounting practice fares differently, it hides the true face of the balance sheet, and brings the actual situation of the bank to imperfect expression.

balance sheet are increased by the same amount. Now the directors of the bank are no longer satisfied with their balance sheet, e.g., because their cash on hand is no longer – or not so abundantly – sufficient, should the same percentage of new checking balances be converted into legal tender money as were the old, which by the way, incidentally speaking, is an important distinction between *loans for stock exchange purposes* and loans for production purposes: *usually* only the latter are converted into small change. What can the directors do?

a) Above all, they can take up foreign credit or offload granted foreign credit – a very important cog in the machine. While this affects *both* sides of the balance sheet in the same way, *beyond that* it acts either on cash on hand or, should the credit, or the money that flows in for it, be passed on to the central bank, it acts on the reserve balance there, so that in this way the supplementation of deficit items will factually be effectuated *within* the asset side. But we now ignore this because we do not wish to complicate our depiction by introducing international credit relations.

b) Or they can themselves take up credit in the open market, which essentially and ultimately means borrowing from other banks. We also ignore this, but for a material reason: banking custom generally prohibits it, and a bank that did so would very quickly cease being an "insider," for which reason this does not occur in undisguised fashion, although in interbank transactions and via acceptance issues, as already mentioned, the granting of loans plays a significant role.

c) Or they can take up credit or *rediscount* commercial bills at the central bank. In the circle of large banks, this also is considered – apart from customarily allowed cases – to be *counter-prestigious,* and the characteristically differing sensitivity to a debit at the central bank among the individual classes of banks is an essential element in the analysis of each specific monetary system. Always and everywhere, the rediscount nexus is so important that we include it in our picture without pointing out the mentioned restrictions every time.

d) Or they may restrict their loans to other customers. Here the asset and liability side of the balance sheet are reduced simultaneously, thus relatively increasing liquid assets. Without much disruption to economic life, this can initially occur regarding *stock market loans (contango, call money).* If this is done in a timely and appropriate manner, it does not need to signify more than realizing a degree of pressure on client profits or adjusting or restricting speculation from day to day. Therefore, these loans are usually listed among *secondary reserves,* and their statistical movement, explicable by this characteristic, has much to do with the popular impression that the stock market draws credit away from *legitimate business.* Credit limitation with respect to production and trade is much more difficult, by the way, and precisely in times that banks wish to reduce their loan provisions, is hardly possible without causing significant disruptions in the economic process: a loan regularly granted over a longer period of time is often more *formally "short-term"* than not.

e) Or they can divest *investments,* to which, from the standpoint of the individual bank, pertain (as already mentioned) bills purchased on the money market – as opposed to bills from their own customers – especially *bankers' acceptances* (that is to say, *private discounts*). When banks have unutilized "means," they invest in appropriate securities and, when they are "strapped," turn around and alienate these securities. This the most important of those methods subject to the free initiative of individual banks, by which they regulate their status and, by their behavior, the economy-wide amount of credit and the condition of the money market. Credit expansion is only possible if there are credit takers; credit restriction is often difficult, and is almost never possible without loss, but such investment policy is much more feasible in an efficient money market. In our case, the shedding of investment along with the restriction of stock market loans is the easiest way to increase the liquidity of the bank. If bank B is the buyer, the liquidity ratios of the banking system will only be shifted, but not improved.[2] If, however, the "public" buys, then not only bank A but the entire system comprising A and B is more liquid at the public's expense.

This can best be made clear if one imagines that the customers of bank A are the buyers. Their balances are reduced by the amount in question, the liability side of the balance sheet of Bank A is shortened by it, and on the asset side the related investments are withdrawn; the remaining cash and *reserve balances* have again the same ratio to the items to be compared with them as they had before the credit expansion, from which we started. The thing is no different when it is bank B's customers that reduce Bank A's investments, except that then the latter retains its borrowed funds and increases its balances with the central bank. The sinking of the credit amount of business and household customers occurs in this case at bank B, while the credit amount of all banks with the central bank remains constant. That is basically also what underlies the share purchases and sales of German banks as far as what is relevant to monetary theory goes, regardless of whether they otherwise have a completely different meaning and are made with a different intention.

---

[2]After all, this also means relaxation through a more favorable distribution of bank reserves.

It should be emphasized again that this business form, the monetary-theoretical significance of which has been developed by American research in connection with American practice, is sometimes overestimated in its importance. It is correct that one needs loan applicants to be able to increase loans plus discounts, but it is also correct that one needs buyers in order to get rid of investments, namely buyers who offer lossless prices - which practically means nothing else than that increased investment *can* be a more effective means of increasing the economy-wide amount of balances than by the provision of credit, and that credit restriction can be a more effective means of limiting the economy-wide amount of balances than the attempt to divest investments. But that hardly justifies pushing these "capital transactions" into the foreground to the degree that they dominate the scientific picture, and to posit an "investment theory" of bank assets in the place of the old conception, now referred to as the "commercial" theory.

f) Finally, the directors of bank A, as ought not be forgotten, can also *do nothing at all* but rather accept the newly created situation in the confidence that they indeed can always top up their cash from their reserves, and the latter from rediscounts. And this behavior will especially recommend itself to them if their loans bring increasing interest payments and their clients do good business, so that the thought of unpleasant incidents does not obtrude itself. We indeed started from a state in which bank A had no abnormal tension and stressed that this assumption usually corresponds to the facts of banking practice. In times of business recovery, therefore, we expect credit expansion and increases in the sum of assets, corresponding neither to measures on the part of banks to compensate for them - *for the individual bank* or *the entire banking system* - nor to attempts to compensate for them.

Active Bank Policy

2. Conversely, changes can occur in the balance sheet picture of our bank that *make it possible* for its management to exercise *initiative* to expand its earning assets. Again it should be emphasized, as we will need to emphasize time and again, that this neither means that they will really opt for such an initiative - rather, they will only do so if they judge the business situation favorably, so that it is ever also, and mainly, factors of this business situation that explain an initiative that is actually undertaken, and never just the condition of the bank - nor that this initiative will be successful, because there are situations in which all of the banks' readiness to act is useless.

One circumstance that may produce such readiness to act is not reflected in the bank's balance sheet, and acts simultaneously on all banks, namely an inviting attitude thereto on the part of the central bank, which can subsist in lowering the rediscount rate, that is, the bank rate, but also simply in the willingness to rediscount beyond banks' hitherto standing requirement [Obligo]. The banks then feel that their backs are covered, and they are able to push forward even if their situation comes under pressure, which, however, is usually not the case in such situations.

The typical change in the balance sheet picture, allowing the expansion of loans or investments, is the shrinking of both sides of the balance sheet by virtue of debt repayments of clients, through which the relative position of cash and reserve balances on the balance sheet is strengthened in the manner already indicated. Since we must spare no effort to completely clarify these simple but fundamental things, this will be shown by an example. Bank A grants its client, the firm C, a loan in the amount of one million marks. This credit, according to our scheme, is at that moment entered on the asset side of the balance sheet of Bank A, and the resulting checking balance of firm C on the liabilities side. Now C pays out of its balance for, e.g., raw materials, so that the sum traverses to the account of raw material seller D, the bank of which, as we shall assume for simplicity's sake, is also bank A. Then C sells products to the value of one million marks to a firm E, which also has its account at Bank A. And finally C "deposits" into its account the check received from E, so that it once again has one million marks in it, with which the loan now is repaid. D has a million marks more, E a million marks less on its checking balance than before. C has nothing and owes nothing. Compared to the condition after the credit provision, the total sum of "deposits" not only of Bank A but also of all banks taken together has declined by one million, not only in step [pari passu], but also in the same act [uno actu] as the decrease of the credit amount. *The loan has eliminated itself.* Note that this is independent of the booking method by which we credit the checking account of the borrower with the granted loan amount: according to the prevailing practice in Germany, which does not credit the loan amount, the loaned sum is not placed in the checking account of C, but first in the checking account of D, thus – in terms of logic, unjustifiably – appearing a step [ein Tempo] later, *but nevertheless still* appearing for the first time. And by using the payment from E to C to repay the latter's debt to bank A, that contraction of both sides of the status of A, as well as a balance comprising A and B, came about. From here, then, the statement of *deposit logic* that has almost become a proverb: *every debt payment wipes out a deposit* – which of course only applies within a banking system comprising the entirety of social account-settling traffic.

Let us consider the case of an impending increase of cash on hand, which we can imagine originating in metallic currency flowing to a customer either from abroad or from domestic mines, or by coins returning from, e.g., one of his seasonal excursions, or finally by a customer newly entering the banking sphere, for example a household deciding in future to maintain a bank account, that hitherto conducted its income and expenditures with coins. In all these cases, a *cash deposit* takes place in a different and more palpable sense than by the delivery of a check, and the amount is initially credited on behalf of the payer to an account of the desired type, by which we mean a checking account. Borrowed funds on the one hand, and cash on the other hand now increase in equal amounts. But the new asset is partly – if we start from the condition in which the directors of A consider their cash position to be sufficient – bank-technically unnecessary and provides no further yield, except in the form of – *which is very often more important* – increased mobility and prestige.[3] If banks put in all the trouble and expense to attract more and more people into the circle of the bank-services-availing class, and are crazy about *cash-saving payment methods*, the only reason for this (apart from the contact with these people to which this leads, which is useful to further business) is that one can use the excess amount of the payment or of the reserve balance to increase profitable operations. This, however, as is evident from what has been said, implies as a necessary consequence *a further propagation of checking balances, i.e., an increase beyond that effected by the payment of coins or bills.* For a correlate of our first proverb of deposit logic, which is to be demonstrated, conceived, and qualified in the same way as the other, is: *every bank credit and every bank investment creates a deposit* (in the sense of a checking balance). Before we continue this line of thought, some other remarks are to be inserted.

The Unique Way Banks Go About Their Business

3. *If* – which thus can in no way be assumed as being certain or even "naturally necessary" – our bank management decides to make use of the option

---

[3]In particular, one can thus increase reserve balances at the central bank and so impress it. For technical reasons, this usually happens first, and then, based on the increased reserve balances, "expansion" occurs. *This will almost always happen, however, when bank A previously was in debit with the central bank*, which is of fundamental importance to the effect of money inflows and outflows.

opened to it by the increase undergone by its cash position, the question is how this is best done, and not merely according to viewpoints of instantaneous profitability. Depending on the business situation, less profitable albeit shorter-term or specially secured assets recommend themselves more than more profitable ones, or it may be the desire for - or aversion to - a connection [Beziehung] that stands in the way of selecting the currently most profitable option, which is of significant importance for monetary policy and for the analysis of the data of banking statistics.

But actually, on the whole these aspects do not act contrary to considerations of profitability: if demand for credit exists among the clientele, it must be provided them if one does not wish to lose customers, but this is also usually the most profitable business insofar as the relatively expensive *overdraft facility* [Kontokorrentkredit] comes into consideration. The bulk of this overdraft facility within the *customer line of credit*,[4] e.g., in the United States until the onset of the crisis, returned 6 percent, while investments of the kind we have in mind here only returned about half as much. Of course, customers do not need to choose this business form. In particular they might, as already mentioned, make use of acceptance credit, which already funds the raw material supply from abroad, for the financing of domestic production and trade of commodities as well, and even for industrial plants. In Germany this happened before the war, in the United States to a large extent during the postwar prosperity, while in England, "this is not done" stands in the way, even though acceptance credit is only about half as expensive as the bank overdraft, because it, directly and viewed from the standpoint of the granting bank, at least ties up no "means" - more precisely, no part of the reserves. But precisely because it does not, acceptance credit does nothing toward solving the issue in our case, as to how bank A can take advantage of the increase in cash holdings. If no industrial and commercial demand for bank overdrafts exists, what remains is lending to the stock market or investment, which, apart from exceptional cases (and these then have their own down sides; there are no cozy situations in which one receives exorbitant rates for call money) are less profitable, for which reason they only play a subsidiary role.

---

[4]The expression "customer line of credit" means firstly, the promise of a loan within the framework of a current account relation, and then the loan actually granted on the basis of this contract. The operation of the loan promise *consists in* the provision of funds. This is what the bank surrenders: something that becomes a liability to it. And therein lies the recognition of the peculiarity of the banking business and the correlation between bank-mediated assets and bank-mediated liabilities, as will be explained shortly.

Even without entering into the individual forms of bank credit and their individual technical relations to the various stages of the economic process, or the winding paths of the perversions that the individual business forms take – often in unlawful manner [per nefas] – to serve other purposes than those in accordance with their purported meaning,[5] we see the social meaning of the banking business and the basic shape of its technique before us: again, we recognize that it deals with the provision of checking and giro balances to households and firms, while on the one hand the check and giro balances of the banks themselves, on the other the remaining balances of households and firms (*time deposits, savings deposits*) play a subsidiary and subservient role. With regard to the latter, to the degree that they are genuine investment deposits, the banks in actuality fill merely a mediatorial function that only becomes something special because it is accompanied by the above-mentioned provision for checking or giro deposits. Prescinding from this mediatorial function, what is reflected on the asset side of bank balance sheets embodies nothing else than a method – or two: credit provision and bank investment – to produce the credit items that make up the "borrowed funds" on the liabilities side, except for the case in which money that hitherto circulated outside the banking sphere, or currency metal that comes from the mines or abroad, or newly issued state-oriented paper money, enters into this banking sphere in a historically one-off transition. The nature of these credit items is that they are "cash" for the households and companies concerned, available quite as easily and for the same purposes as when furnished with an equal amount of physically-held coins. Suppose for a moment that the banking system had already conquered the entire payment process of the area under study, and no fresh quantities of currency metal entered into the payment circle; then the balances taken together *could only* – but *must* also always – *rise through credit provision or bank investment, and fall only by contracting bank credit and investment.* The balances of individual firms and individual households can of course also increase without these, but only at the expense of an existing balance at the same or another bank. Therefore, then, a

---

[5]Simply as an example, the method of many firms, agents, and banks may be mentioned, to obtain short-term credit by issuing a bill as if it were born from a sale of goods – for example, to have it drawn up in a non-rounded amount, etc. – without this being the case. In this way, credit is also sometimes abused that the granting bank intends as *goods reimbursement credit.* This practice has given the concept of the *accommodation bill* a subsidiary meaning that does not pertain to its essence. By this we understand, in accordance with prevailing although not universal parlance, any bill not immediately representing a sale of goods, even though it may serve the financing of goods transactions.

third proverb of deposit logic: *saving does not increase total balances* (*savings do not create deposits*). This sounds strange, but is basically self-evident. "Saving" is here simply accumulation on a bank account. But if this accumulation does not happen through the deposit of coinage, that thereby enters the banking sphere in a one-off transition, then the amounts to be accumulated can obviously only have come from other deposits, and therefore it is meaningless to infer the intensity of saving activity in the area of study from the increase in "bank deposits."[6]

This special nexus between assets and liabilities is peculiar to the banking business and is found nowhere else. From this also follows a sense of liquidity claims, and the correlation of asset and liability transactions, that is peculiar to the banking business. In itself, of course, any other firm and every household must be liquid and must keep its claims from asset transactions in proper proportion to its obligations in liability transactions, if it is not to cut a sorry figure or possibly come into serious danger. But here something quite different is on offer, namely, the fact that *bank assets create bank liabilities*, liabilities of a special kind, that for other people are cash. Without insight into the deeper context, and despite a basically quite lopsided idea of it, business sense and, in formulation thereof, banking doctrine developed the theory of so-called *regular banking business*, that in many respects, especially due to its being based on the paradigm of the discount of commercial bills, is outdated but in practice very reasonable and useful, and which is a good example of the old adage that one can come to quite reasonable results even from very inadequate starting points.

The doctrine of regular banking business poses as a doctrine of the commercial utilization of "means" that are "short-term committed" to the banks apart from the banks' own credit provision, together with rules of short-term maturity, security, self-realization or realizability of the "assets" [Anlagen] that stem from this condition. The business character that such statements usually bear, excuses to a certain degree the lack of theoretical foundation of the matter. Also the fact that when one makes this conventional banking business into the

---

[6]It is different with the relationship between checking and investment balances. But neither can one get very far here, because, as we have seen, booking to time deposits or even savings accounts is not itself evidence of the existence of an intention to save. After all, an important symptom of the economic situation is to be seen in a strong movement from time deposits to checking accounts, but this is not to be interpreted as a divestment without further ado (cf. the aspect of *disposition*, which we will encounter later). In this case, *checking balances* rise without new loans being granted. But this means nothing more than that one must step back a few paces to see the factual situation rightly.

main affair, one does not derive a completely accurate picture of banking activity, we may allow to pass. But the doctrine is wrong at the point at which it begins to speak of borrowed funds committed to the banks. It evokes the notion that *borrowing by banks* is the actual and logical precondition for their lending – as if one might engage in lending only if he first obtains the money to lend (from himself or from others).

Because this idea is very plausible, but at the same time as erroneous as it is plausible, and because even today it is still advocated by distinguished men of science and practice,[7] we will therefore again enter into the evidence that, apart from the mentioned exception, bank credit and bank investment create the borrowed funds on the liabilities side, while also dealing with a few related issues. It must be noted that the following evidence does not depend on the accounting method used, since the suspicion is unfounded that the entire *deposit*

---

[7]J.M. Keynes, *A Treatise on Money, loc. cit.*, p. 25, directed his argument – in essence entirely similar to ours – against Walter Leaf. We especially think of Richard Reisch. See his treatise, *Die Deposit-Legende in der Banktheorie* [The Deposit Legend in Bank Theory], in *Zeitschrift für Nationalökonomie* [Journal of Political Economy], I, 1930, pp. 189 ff. F. Somary also makes concessions to that view, although he concedes the central bank the ability of credit creation and thus (with the twist that banks could then grant credit beyond the means entrusted to them if they also decide to reduce their reserve proportion) appears to admit everything here advocated. The phenomenon with which we are concerned here is very old. It developed into its present meaning through a slow process of growth. It is therefore not surprising that, from the standpoint of each point in time, credit provision seems possible only within very fixed limits – expressed in the respective customary reserve proportion – while "credit creation" beyond these limits seems impossible. But "creation of purchasing power" is always present within these limits, and these limits are steadily stretched, as one can see, e.g., from the sinking of the reserve proportions of the English banks. The banking literature describes, although not always accurately and adequately, but usually sufficiently, what we mean. So thus Henry Dunning Macleod, *Theory and Practice of Banking*, 1st ed., London 1855-56; Horace White, *Money and Banking,* Boston & London, 1936 (1st edition 1895, 4th edition 1914). A very brisk representation is provided by Hartley Withers, *The Meaning of Money*, London, 1909, a partially improved version by C.A. Phillips, whose book published in 1920 is used a great deal today, *Bank Credit: a Study of the Principles and Factors Underlying Advances Made by Banks to Borrowers,* New York, 1920 (reprinted 1924). A more detailed theoretical interpretation can be found in L. Albert Hahn (see n11 above, p. 158). The classic presentation of this aspect of the subject is that of Simon Newcomb in *Principles of Political Economy*, London, 1885.

legend is only a deception stemming from the Anglo-American custom of crediting loans to the credit beneficiary. Furthermore, that the issue of *credit fabrication, credit creation, creation of purchasing power, money creation,* will become clear to us in its deeper significance only in the course of later discussion, and that here we are only dealing with the technical surface of the matter. When here and there we already spoke of "bank money," we were only making use of a common expression. If he wishes it, and holds it to be an accurate description of the process, the reader may provisionally interpret the edifice of bank credit as a system of claims on gold, etc., that the banks set up against themselves.

How Banks "Multiply" Money

4. Resuming a previous train of thought (p. 188), we thus have someone paying coins into bank A that either have been circulating outside the banking sphere or have just been coined - or new paper money received from the hands of the state. The bank credits him the amount in a checking or giro balance, either an already existing account or one opened on the spot. Here apparently is a real *irregular deposit*, which *in these cases* we wish to call an *originary* deposit (deposita irregularia also appear in other cases that we do not so characterize). In the first case, that of the payment of coins that circulated in the area of study, this is also a compensated deposit or credit, because it appears in the place of these coins and is offset in its effect on the money process by the disappearance of the coins from circulation.[8]

Our client now disposes over his balance just as he would otherwise do over the coins. He makes payments, he always replenishes the balance through the income of items offsetting these payments - but no longer from the extrabanking sphere - and he probably also holds a partial amount permanently as a

---

[8]We avoid the expression *"real* deposits" common in Germany, which mainly includes all checking and investment balances that are not "created" by the bank in the books of which they appear; also the expression of Phillips (*loc. cit.,* p. 40): *primary deposits* (by contrast with "derivative deposits"), which are defined by the fact that they arise "from the actual lodgment [of money] in a bank or its readily convertible equivalent such as checks and drafts drawn on other banks," but not in regard to the repayment of a loan.

Our concept of compensated deposits also includes all cases of origination in the way of credit in which an equal amount is "taken out of service" in the same act, as well as all cases in which a balance arises through payment from another. Even the granting of a loan on the basis of time deposits creates compensated checking deposits.

reserve, so that the balance never drops to zero, which, however, is not essential. Assuming his behavior and the nature of his business transactions are exactly the average of all the other customers of the bank, then a part of his payments will lead to *cash withdrawals*, another part will be made for the benefit of customers of other banks, and a third part, finally, for the benefit of customers of the same bank. For the bank, this last only means a transfer in its books and does not affect - directly and at least in principle - its level of liquidity. In the first-mentioned case, an additional cash supply must be held in the same measure as for the average balance, while for transfers to accounts with other banks an additional balance must be kept with the central bank. But that is not all. Rather, in order to meet the statutory or customary obligation to always maintain a minimum deposit reserve of a certain percentage of its balances - according to our assumption, at the central bank - the bank must acquire yet a further additional reserve balance at the central bank, to which end, say, it hands a portion of the customer's cash payment over to the central bank. For this requirement indeed does not simply take its place alongside the others: resort to these reserve balances reduces borrowed funds and [so] lessens the legal reserves that must be held, but their provision also leaves the other exigencies not entirely provided for. If the customary minimum reserve is 10 percent and the customer disposes of 10 percent of his balance such that this 10 percent is deducted from the reserve balance [e.g., by transfer to another bank's account at the central bank], the remaining 90 percent of his balance is unbacked. For this not to occur, the maintenance of the proportion must be especially provided for.

But for all that, something remains of the original "cash deposit" in cash holdings or in the reserve balance of the bank, and this remainder can, as already pointed out, be lent or invested. Here we clearly see the optical illusion that leads many practitioners to deny deposit creation by bank credit. In this case, the bank obviously lends only what was "committed" to it. And yet our example proves our assertion. For the borrower to whom bank A lends that remaining balance, proceeds with it just as if coins were put into his cash holdings - that is, deposited originally - *while the original depositor in respect of his entire balance, hence including this remainder, behaves likewise.* It is just as if the amount that was borrowed had now been doubled, and it has the same effect on the account-settling process. Nothing more than that is intended when it is said that the bank, through the act of credit provision, "created" the additional balance. Whether this phrase does more or less justice to the factual situation than the other, e.g., the phrase that the available money is now better "utilized," we cannot yet judge. Thus interpreted, it cannot be wrong. However, it is *false* to stamp the original depositor as the true lender, unless he deposited the money into an investment account. For credit provision is exactly what he did *not* wish to do when he opened his checking account. Rather, he wished to have the sum available at all times; and whoever makes him a creditor against his will, disfigures quite needlessly a clear factual situation, just as those writers do, who claim that the holder of a banknote, with which quite the same can be done as with a coin, has granted credit to the note-issuing bank.[9]

Imagine in addition that bank A counts the loan out in the received coins, which in turn the borrower immediately deposits. This does not change the essence of the operation. But we see in this scheme, first, that a cash deposit does not demonstrate the presence of an originary deposit, and that credit provision through the banks (i.e., the production of liabilities through lending, credit expansion), would be possible even if each balance or deposit actually originated from literal deposits. This would even be possible if all people continued to conduct all of their payments through the handover of coins, and if, for example, they kept their cash at the bank only for reasons of security, whereby the sums needed daily, e.g., would be picked up each morning. The temporal unevenness of the financial conduct of firms and households in this case would produce a surplus stock of cash in the bank, which, at least in part, could be loaned or otherwise invested short-term. This technical possibility – which of course never occurs on its own, but which always plays a part – could, for the sake of better distinctions, be termed the *first banking principle*, to which is added as a *second* principle the one we already mentioned, the reflux of the loan (*Fullarton's principle*) and, as a *third*, the further technical possibility of credit expansion that results from the fact that many payments can be done by transfer in the books of the same bank and as setoffs between different banks.

To the objection that this depiction proceeds from the originary deposit of non-bank money, and the expansion of credit beyond this amount is always to be interpreted as the disposition over the available non-bank money, we only point out here that we could just as well have proceeded from a decision of our bank to be content with a slenderer reserve; and for the rest, it was our purpose to show that even given the institutional preconditions of commodity money, our phenomenon is possible – essentially inevitable.[10] That it basically reaches

---

[9]Certainly one has to have confidence both in the bank in which one deposits his cash, and the bank the note of which one accepts. But that obviously proves nothing regarding our topic. At the most, the proliferation of the *trust theory* of credit explains the tendency of many professional colleagues to run both things together.

[10]One can easily see, in particular, that even a legal ban on credit creation, out of consideration of the difficulty of discerning the process concealed behind acts of deposit,

much further and also covers all the ground beneath commodity money itself, will be made clear later.

The Limits to Banks' Expansion of Credit

5. The borrower – the case in which he gets his credit in coins which he immediately redeposits, shows this especially clearly – for his part now leaves a surplus, albeit slight, in the cash holdings or the reserve assets of the bank. This surplus, in turn, can be lent, etc., such that the question now arises as to the (technical) limitations of such expansion of credit or provision of funds. This has already often been dealt with, most successfully by Karl Schlesinger.[11] We content ourselves here with this reference and a summary of the most important aspects that come into consideration for an answer.

If Bank A were the only bank, all payments would be done by transfer in its books – there would be no "cash transactions" – and if it were not obliged to redeem balances in anything else than what it could create itself, or to maintain a minimum reserve proportion, there would, in this isolated area of investigation, appear to be no limit to money creation, if we allow both credit and investment. But with regard to the loans, it must not be forgotten that the individual borrowers, whose individual loans do not exert significant influence on rates, will economically, if they do not speculate on an inflation policy on the part of the bank, only take on as much credit as they can pay interest on at existing rates or rates expected independently of the bank (see above, p. 171). And that is always a finite, theoretically clearly specified amount. In this respect, even under these conditions the matter is not like the financing of consumption expenditure by a government issue of paper money, as useful as this analogy might be for understanding the technical side of the matter. Our case also shows

---

would not be effective of itself. To make it effective, a monitoring of the intended purposes of all bank loans would have to be implemented.

[11]See his treatment, "Felix Somarys Bankpolitik" [Felix Somary's Bank Policy], in: *Archiv für Sozialwissenschaft und Sozialpolitik* [Archives for Social Science and Social Policy] 66, 1931, p. l; also J.H. Rogers, "The Absorption of Bank Credit," in *Econometrica* I, 1933, p. 63, and J. S. Lawrence, "Borrowed Reserves and Bank Expansion," in *Quarterly Journal of Economics* 28, 1928, p. 593. Most American discussions proceed from Phillips. See also the latest work by James W. Angell and Karel Ficek, "The Expansion of Bank Credit," in *Journal of Political Economy,* February 1933, pp. 1 and 152. Finally see also Keynes, *Treatise,* Chapter 2, pp. 25, 32.

us already how independent "deposits" can be from "deposits," or even how the relationship between deposits and balances is an institutional accident.

If the bank is obliged to convert (redeem) its deposits on demand at any time and at a fixed rate into units of a commodity, then its credit *and* investment expansion are of course given a very effective limit, even if there is no cash circulation. Because every credit expansion that drives the price of that commodity above parity with the deposit unit [Guthabeneinheit] would generate a demand for redemption. Cash circulation with or without legal reserve proportion draws the limit more tightly but does not change the principle of the matter, which still lies in the condition of parity between the market valuation of the deposit unit and the market valuation of the quantity of the commodity to which it is equated. Foreign trade, on the other hand, brings - apart from all the disturbances the source of which are political and the like - a new element, if foreign price ratios and the behavior of foreign banks are now also to be taken into account.

From this alone it can be seen that it can only be misleading if one calculates, either for a single bank or for a system of many banks, a *maximum amount of possible credit creation* on the basis of an experience-derived reserve proportion. In the simplest case this maximum would be set at cash growth times the reciprocal value of the reserve proportion. For a disturbance of parity between the deposit unit and commodity money unit [Geldguteinheit] could also occur when the reserve proportion is maintained. And how much in the way of deposits can be created without parity being lost depends entirely on how large a goods complement offsets the activities of the borrower - and at what time it does - how quickly prices react to the expansion of credit, and people to these prices. The loss of cash to circulation in turn depends very much on how the loans are used. Stock market loans, as already mentioned, generate no such losses immediately, industrial loans more so. In addition, the reserve proportion is not simply a datum of the problem. The ratio between cash plus reserve balances to short-term liabilities, which we observe statistically, is obviously generally the result of the particular level of credit expansion, that in each case, for a ratio considered by the banking world of a given country to be commercially normal, is nothing more than an average arrived at in practice over an arbitrarily chosen period, during which its downward trend is disregarded. And the inference [Schluß] derived from the part of the originally deposited funds that remains permanently in the bank, thus from the payment habits of the public, only conduces to a clear result when one treats variables as if they were constants.

Should we be dealing with a multiplicity of banks that we alike arrange around a central bank and likewise wish to immerse [einsenken] into a commerce that also works with non-bank money – for simplicity's sake, we disregard foreign trade – then there confronts us *again* the already well-known aspect of the loss of balances, cash, and reserves to other banks, that every single bank suffers in the train of its credit expansion. This fact in itself alone would prevent the individual bank from expanding its loans and investments to the point that could be described as a *technical maximum point*.[12] The obvious consideration that balances and reserves of other banks will be strengthened precisely by that outflow, putting them into the position of being able to expand so that the banking system as a whole eventually brings about what no individual bank can, is always to be supplemented, if one wishes to accept the reserve proportion as a given, by taking into account the loss of cash to retail transactions that accompanied the process of credit expansion. The extent of the outflow depends mainly on two factors.

a) The size of the individual banks. If some or all of them are so large that even individual bank lending can affect commodity prices and parity of the deposit unit – and thus for *this* reason alone, free competition among banks is absent – then also there is here fundamentally the same restriction as in the case where there is only a single bank. And the presence of these big banks makes the mechanism into something quite different than when all banks are "relatively small" – even though "big banks" may yet be found among them – and therefore *this* consideration only plays a role for the observer of the whole system, not for individual bank management.

But the size of the banks is also relevant for the practical importance of the chance that dispositions by customers will be done in favor of customers of the same bank. Structures such as Lloyds Bank or Deutsche Bank und Diskontogesellschaft serve such a "significant" part of the entire banking clientele in their countries that they can expand with fewer worries than small ones experience. Still other aspects work in the direction of the superiority of the large banking operations. The larger a bank is, the proportionally smaller can be its cash holdings (*vault cash, till money*) because the "law of large numbers" asserts

---

[12]The credit provision immediately possible to the individual banks is, as Phillips, *loc. cit.*, has pointed out, only slightly larger than the increase experienced by its cash holdings. But even if it were less than this, "credit creation" or new deposit creation would still be present. One does well fully to understand this, since one still encounters the view that the individual bank, if it, e.g., maintains a reserve proportion of 10 percent as normal, can lend out nine times the amount of its cash holdings.

itself completely and reliably with regard to the daily cash requirements of the customers, when these customers are composed of thousands of households and firms of all types, distributed over the entire area – which latter aspect also makes the existence, or lack thereof, of a branch network significant in terms of monetary theory. Practically, one must also never forget that credit expansion in individual cases often simply depends on what one wishes to risk. And in this respect a large bank with an international name and national importance is in a much more secure position than a small institution, about which no one cares, and for whom, therefore, the capitalist principle of personal responsibility is a matter of deadly seriousness and not just limited to fair weather. Therefore, the tendency to credit inflation is inherent in every system of large banks.

b) The nature and rationale of banks' cooperation. Commensurate behavior in the matter of credit expansion and credit restriction is partly already given by saying that all banks in a region confront one and the same economic situation, including the same phase of the cycle, and the same social situation. This already reduces the stringency of the fetter that otherwise lies in the leakage of cash and reserve balances to other banks, because outflow now also corresponds with inflow. If this movement in step becomes accentuated by practice, or even by arrangement, individual banks may directly or through the operations of the free market get credit from each other and count on responsive handling of debit balances in interbank clearing transactions and may also rely on a discount-ready central bank. Lastly, there are systems in the system, i.e., smaller banks group themselves in order to attain a higher order, in which case leakage occurs much less readily, and only after a bank rushes ahead particularly stormily with its credit expansion. And then, *when* it does happen, as long as the transactions which this credit expansion serves proceed according to plan, it is not that dangerous, in any case much less so than when a very large number of banks act without coordination.

It is therefore not at all strange that the expansion opportunities that are open to bank credit cannot be formulated in general terms, and that they are so obviously different in different countries and economic situations.

Quantifying Credit Expansion

6. In essence, the entire theory of the technique and economics of banking lies in the discussion of the ratios between – or the quotients of – the variables cash, reserve balances, loans, investments, checking balances of customers, investment funds of customers, and combinations (such as cash plus reserve balances, loans plus investments, etc.) or subdivisions (such as business and stock

market loans) thereof. So we can characterize the implemented considerations regarding the limits of credit and checking balance expansion as considerations regarding determinants of the bank quotients cash ÷ checking balance, and cash plus reserve balance ÷ checking balance. But this does not mean that one or the other [determines] the extent and rate of change [of credit creation].[13]

The principle of the matter is, however, easy to point out. Suppose that there is no central bank and every bank goes to work focusing on itself, and furthermore that all balances are checking balances [as opposed to investment balances], thus cash for their holders. As long as bank A under such circumstances neither provides credit nor makes investment in our sense, the ratio between its cash items and these borrowed funds must always be 1:1, disregarding the bank's own means, and neither the one item nor the other can ever change other than by an equal amount the one with the other. This *can* only change, but then *must* also change, if the bank makes loans or invests. And such a process must depress the bank quotient cash ÷ balances below 1:1, so that its sinking below 1:1 always means the emergence of means of payment through the act of bank credit provision or investment. Sticking to our accounting method, bank A, which, for example, has received a million [marks] in original deposits, provides credit in the amount of half a million; in that case, cash on hand of one million (and half a million in granted loans or discounts) face checking balances in the amount of one and a half million, making our bank quotient equal to ⅔. If both original depositors and borrowers withdraw half of their checking balances, the item cash on hand will sink to 250,000, the item borrowed funds to 750,000, and the quotient to ⅓. And yet, there has been no further "increase" in the means of payment circulating in the area of study, such as this decline might suggest – for the means of payment "created" by the action of the bank are now in circulation.

Created Deposits Versus Circulating Deposits

In this respect our quotient does not satisfactorily express what is going on. On the other hand, one can easily satisfy oneself that the *difference* between deposits and cash in this case achieves what we want, providing a viable measure of the particular state of bank-mediated "purchasing power creation," thus of course also of the original deposits available at the time. Should any borrower pay by check to customers of bank A who are also borrowers, and should these latter apply this amount to cover their loans, then on the one hand the loan, on the other the balances, will be eliminated in this amount. One sees this even

---

[13]Added by the editor.

more clearly if we assume that there are no other such balances than those newly formed in the character of credit provision, and that disposals thereof are always only disposals in favor of other bank borrowers, and finally, that each income item of an owing customer is immediately and automatically compensated by the bank's receivable. Each element of "credit expansion" then disappears as soon as it accomplishes that for which it was set up. If in the economic process there were a periodically recurring point in time at which all transactions were settled, then under these preconditions, there would be absolutely no means of payment in existence at that time, and all balances would be zero.

I insist on this basically self-evident matter again and again because it is essential to the understanding of the bank-mediated settlement process and because it forms a crucial difference between such bank money, that thus does not "circulate through the economy," and coins or banknotes or originary deposits, which latter, when seen from this point of view, are much more akin to coins than to balances created through credit operations. Note still that if a checking account balance thus created is applied directly for the payment of a debt to someone who also owes the bank, instead of, for example, to finance a purchase, it disappears before it has touched the commodities sphere, and therefore does not increase the sum of checking account balances relevant to us at all, and belongs to the category of compensated balances. Statistically, this means that checking account balances generated for this purpose, but not yet used, must be eliminated from the calculation of our quotient or our difference, if we are not to depend on a turn of events whereby, because this use usually follows on the heels of the origin of the balance, the amount of such balances on the particular reporting date is negligible.

All of this also applies to the cases in which payments of account holders are made for the benefit of customers of other banks, except that a movement of cash from one bank to another is to be added, and it should be noted that any resulting balances of banks with banks must be eliminated from the calculation of our difference.

Checking Deposits Versus Investment Deposits

Things are different if the bank's customers take either original deposits or income received as payment and truly commit them to the bank, i.e., leave them over to another use such that they no longer function as cash for the depositing customers. Such investment deposits, if statistically put together with checking account balances, render it no longer true that, using the sum of total balances formed in this manner, our difference measures the quantity of means

of payment put into circulation by the act of banks beyond the otherwise existing amount. Although it still measures the amount of balances that the banks
create, this amount is compensated by the amount of investment deposits. Up
to that level, the banks only mediate between depositors and borrowers.

If we indeed have a viable number reflecting investment deposits, we may
deduct it from the total number and only consider checking account balances;
and then the first would impact our difference, as follows. Suppose again that
bank A receives a payment of one million [marks] in original deposits, which
this time are investment deposits, so that a cash balance of a million once again
is set against borrowed funds of a million. Our difference is this: total deposits,
one million, minus investment deposits, also one million, minus cash, again one
million, thus "purchasing power creation" of minus one million, which obviously correctly reflects the process. If half a million are lent out, we obtain as a
measure of "purchasing power creation" minus half a million, and so forth
through zero and into positive quantities. Should the depositors transfer their
monies to their checking accounts, then the removed investment deposits decline, thus increasing our difference by the same amount, so that it - quite correctly - displays "purchasing power creation."[14] But this "purchasing power creation" does not now come by way of credit, and leaves unaffected the item, loans
plus bank investment.

If bank borrowers pay customers who do not owe the bank, and the latter transfer the amount to an investment account, this amount is eliminated
from the sum of checking deposits quite as if the receivers had been bank borrowers, and had now paid off or reduced what they owed to the bank. "Purchasing power" will be "decommissioned" or wiped out. The reverse transfer quite
as well "creates purchasing power." Our difference registers this, and our idea
that the rationale of an investment deposit is to be understood as the purchase
of a bank bond, explains it. The customer who received check deposit units,
which represent one kind of obligation by the bank, relinquishes them to the
bank against another kind of obligation, so that unequal things cancel each other
[per confusionem untergehen]. We see from this that savings deposits, and those
time deposits that are really to be regarded as investment deposits, can be - we
add, for the most part they actually are - traced back to the banks' "purchasing
power creation," although the "creative" credit provision is not done in favor of

---

[14]It is immaterial whether or not the bank meanwhile provided credit in the full
amount of the investment deposit, or perhaps even beyond that amount. *Uncompensated*
purchasing power creation is only present in the first case. Only in this can the transfer
as such make our difference positive.

the depositor, who rather made a "payment," which [banking] practice views as such a real deposit.

Apart from the entry and exit of currency metal that comes fresh from mines [and] hoards of foreign countries, or flows into hoards or to foreign countries, the difference of checking balances minus cash is thus far a correct expression of the respective state of "purchasing power creation." The issue or redemption of paper money, however, is equivalent to money movements in this respect, and so is the note issue of the central bank. We now include in our treatment, and likewise make the assumption, that the central bank holds[15] not only bank reserves, but also bank cash holdings up to a partial amount, so that each increase not needed for current account is forwarded to the central bank, which – διά χάιρυβδος [through Charybdis] – sucks up all cash income and spews it back out. So not much changes per se. The reserve balances (plus the nevertheless necessary cash stock) would simply take the place of cash in our argument. But, our difference is no longer an expression of purchasing power creation by the banking system, even when we leave central bank notes out of consideration, which are elements of cash on hand and which can, like coins, circulate beyond the circle of bank customers.

Since the banks can fill their reserve holdings through credit, their purchasing power creation now shows itself to be superimposed upon another [power], that supports it and in turn can be multiplied by it.

The Effect of the Two-Tiered Banking System

To see how this works, we divide our central bank into two departments, the Issue Department and the Banking Department.[16] The Issue Department, taking into account a backing provision – for example, dictating forty per cent backing – issues notes to the Banking Department against money it receives for this purpose from the latter, which in turn the latter receives from the banks, which now no longer carry gold stocks, but forward the gold provided them by their clients to the Banking Department of the central bank. In exchange, the banks receive, in the first place, notes that serve them as cash insofar as they

---

[15]Mann substitutes "receives" (erhält). We retain the original (hält).

[16]This separation corresponds to well-known existing English practice. The *Macmillan Report* (Cmd. 3897, 1931) finds (p. 145) it to be misleading. But the principle of separate presentation of the note issue and balances has in itself nothing to do with the relationship between the former and the gold reserve, and recommends itself for many general reasons.

hold "ready money" and, secondly, balances in a checking account with the central bank, their current reserve balances. Furthermore, the central bank also discounts bills from any firms by means of notes, which these firms deposit to checking accounts at any bank.

The matter, then, initially looks like this: if the other banks – this time taken together – have received 0.7 million in original deposits in gold, and exchange 0.2 million of it for notes that they carry, while they create 0.5 million in reserve balances, then the entire amount of gold in the banking system is concentrated at the central bank. The central bank then keeps the half million corresponding to reserve balances in the Banking Department, and assigns the 0.2 million to the Issue Department, which in exchange returns 0.5 million in notes [allowable thanks to the 40% backing requirement]. The surplus of 0.3 million does not go into the banks' coffers; rather, the central bank applies it to credits, for example bill discounts, and the recipients of these notes deposit them into checking accounts at other banks, so their cash holdings increases to 0.5 million. Now these other banks have cash plus reserve balances of a million, and if they grant loans for a half a million, one and a half million in balances. Our difference is therefore half a million – this is the "purchasing power" that the other banks "create" – to which we still need to add the business loans of the central bank, to obtain the sum total of the purchasing power "created" by the system, 0.8 million, that here thus equals the balances of other banks minus the gold in the central bank.

If notes issued by the central bank in the character of business credit ("commercial loans" in the sense of loans not granted to banks) are not deposited (or not entirely or not immediately) with other banks, the expression: status of "purchasing power creation" = checking balances – cash – reserve balances + commercial credit by the note-issuing bank, nonetheless remains correct because in that case the notes are not included in the subtrahend [i.e., under bank cash holdings]. If the central bank does not give business credit but only bank credit, such that the banks, first with cash holdings of 0.2 million and balances of 1.5, bring their cash holdings to 0.5 by debiting their reserve balance, and the central bank, by granting them a loan of 0.3, in turn replenishes their reserves to 0.5, then the expression: checking balances – cash – reserve balances + central bank credit, as long as this does not lead the banks for their part to issue more credit,[17] yields the same value as in the first case and a value 0.3 less than in the

---

[17]That may very well happen, less so if the banks borrow from the central bank – because they usually only do so if they want to do something with it – but more so if the central bank (directly or indirectly) acquires investments from them, something

second, and thus reflects the fact that the banks have set aside the credit "created" by the central bank, or that an amount of 0.3 in central bank credit has taken the place of the – now "constricted" – credit of the other banks. Again the difference: balances – gold in the central bank (and possibly in other banks) not only indicates the amount of circulating medium attributable to the activity of the banking system, but also the changes in the total volume of circulating medium over time.

If, however, new gold flows in from mines, hoards, or from abroad, or paper money is issued but not through the mechanism of credit, then there is more that changes than appears at first glance. Suppose that the new gold is first deposited in banks onto checking balances, from there to be given to the central bank; in that case, balances and bank reserves change by the same amounts. Beyond that, the status of the central bank changes. The differences, gold – balances and balances – reserve balances, remain as they were, although they have increased the technical possibility for lending and investment. But the change in the volume of circulating medium is now no longer registered. This does not matter if it only has to do with the banking world's contribution thereto, but it matters very much if we are interested in all the new purchasing power that faces the world of goods. This is even more the case when this purchasing power "created" from gold production, etc., *does precisely that* which bank-mediated "purchasing power creation" would otherwise have done. If new checking balances, for example, are used to purchase shares, bank credit can thereby be rendered superfluous that otherwise would have manifested itself in a deposit-creating manner. It is precisely this that often happens, and the bank practitioner is not wrong when he, sometimes without success, preaches to the theorist that new gold attains effectiveness (and often only flows in for that very reason) when it "is needed" and is absorbed by the banking system when commerce does not need it. As an objection to obvious inferences from primitive formulations of the quantity theory, this view has much to recommend it. Only that, among other things, this ought not be exaggerated. It is readily apparent that up to the

---

which, as has already been said, it has more leeway to do on its own initiative (open-market operations). Such things are done in the hope of stimulating lending and business. If the banks are unwilling or unable to participate, the above stated sequence comes into play, making it good sense to say that the banks have constricted *their* credit (possibly they can do so into negative magnitudes), even though the sum of checking balances has remained constant.

This note was written in 1929. The current (early 1933) situation in the United States nicely illustrates what is meant.

amount of newly inflowing gold, balances must in fact arise in the usual way, and to that degree there can be no question of any "sterilization" of that gold.

To this degree, then, it would be easy to add new gold or paper money to our difference. But since we can never determine which portion of the balances arising from gold consignment flows onto the money or capital goods [Produktionsmittel] market as directly as in the case of bank-mediated purchasing power creation, and on the other hand we can be sure that government paper money never directly does so, and finally that there are exceptions to the rule that new money means new checking account balances - the central bank can, for example, get money from abroad on credit [whereby the corresponding liability item (checking account) lies outside the domestic banking system] - we are then faced with a non-general question of fact that also is not usually answerable in a satisfactory fashion, if we wish to capture the volume of circulating medium that is available to the business world and that represents the magnitudes that are actually at stake in the analysis of the business cycle and for the purpose of correlation with such symptoms of the business situation as unemployment, etc. If the banks were in debit to the central bank and used a gold inflow to cover this debit, this would change nothing. Central bank credit is eliminated, but is replaced by an equal amount of credit on the part of the other banks, since the increase in their reserve balance falls short of the figure for the gold inflow by this amount.

Thus we see how difficult can be the interpretation of the quotients: cash plus reserve ÷ borrowed funds or checking balances, or the difference: borrowed funds or checking balances - cash - reserve balances or, finally, the difference: borrowed funds or checking balances - gold in the central bank (and other banks), and how little we may expect that they will conform precisely to those theoretical expectations that we form for the purpose of research. This holds also for all other bank quotients or other combinations of bank figures and puts in the reader's hands the rules that come into consideration in order to critique them. The ratio or again the difference between loans plus investments of non-central banks and borrowed funds serves as an example. Of course, there is no relationship between loans and checking balances alone, or between investment balances and investment alone.

Can This Be Captured Statistically?

Now we have the understandable desire to form economic aggregates from the mass of these calculated amounts, in order to be able to undertake something along the lines of monetary theory. Obviously, not all income and expenditure is equally worthwhile. Some reflect fundamental operations, others merely technical operations of monetary transactions. In this respect, therefore, we set ourselves the task of separating the essential from the merely technical, of *adjusting* the numbers regarding income and expenditure that are important to us from what is insignificant, on the one hand, and arranging the adjusted numbers so that they reflect the economic process, on the other.

The nature of this task becomes clearest to us through examples. When the Reich collects taxes the revenue of which it itself does not use, but transfers it to territories and through their mediation to local communities, obviously what is essential to this process is that the communities receive and spend these tax revenues. It may be very important in terms of tax policy that they take receipt through the roundabout route of Reich and territories. But for the monetary conduct of the economic process, this is just a technical detail that is not a matter of entire indifference, because monetary means are tied to this roundabout route or because by passing through the imperial treasury they can still perform other functions – but which for the essence of the matter, revenue raising *for* and *by* the local communities, is irrelevant. If we wish to envision the outline of the essential process, we have to deduct the income of the respective sums by the Reich and the territories, and "adjust" the occurred money movement for the bookings of *transitory items*. If we still wish to register exactly what has really happened, we will indeed introduce the imperial treasury and the territorial treasuries, the path through which the tax amount went, but not place them next to the local community treasury, rather treating them as treasuries of a special kind, called *auxiliary funds*.

It is no more difficult, one would think, to appreciate that it is not a matter of indifference whether two thousand marks be spent on consumption goods, or one thousand marks on consumption goods and the other thousand marks, for example, on the wages of workers in a factory, or on shares. If I express both cases with the phrase, two thousand dollars were spent on purchases, I obviously blur a difference to which everything that is important, both theoretically and practically, can be connected. The means to bring out this difference and thus the picture of the actual money movement, and the relationships between the economic money value aggregates, is the construction of various markets in which and between which the computing process of the economy takes place. They have here the same character as in general theory, and they indeed are, of course, defined differently in connection with economic reality, but also according to the particular research purpose. Consumption goods markets, capital goods markets, and money and stock markets, are the three types formed for the general goal [of market exchange], although the latter two are very quickly split into special markets.

But now we have the no less understandable desire to register the social aggregates of the calculated amounts numerically, which, with advances in statistics, indeed is getting closer to the realm of possibility.[18] Because for well-known reasons we have less influence on the formation of our observational data than do natural scientists, the task usually is inverted, i.e., we have to proceed from the statistical variables and seek to interpret them theoretically. Often this means that we can only make the variables presented to us subservient to theoretical purposes by transforming our theoretical aggregates accordingly or, where that is not possible, by looking for relations between them and the statistical series that allow the values or at least the changes in the values of the latter to be considered as exact or at least approximate symptoms of the values or changes in values of the former.[19] Some examples will make the nature of the task clearer to us and at the same time bring home to us the most important of the adjustments that we have to make to our income and expenditures for money-theoretical purposes, and of course other purposes as well.

For the United States in the postwar period, the estimate is available of the annual total of all checks drawn on all banks. There was, for example, an estimate of $750 billion identified in 1927; the part of this amount registered by the official statistics of the Federal Reserve Board, which is published regularly,[20]

---

[18]It may be mentioned in passing that, depending on the existence and scope of this possibility, different theoretical models may be appropriate. One is never entirely fair to a theory as [such] when one condemns it absolutely, i.e., in this case, regardless of what the material research at any time has on offer, or without regard to the extent to which theoretical reconstruction must replace missing material. Where, for example, the amount of legal tender money is the only thing that can be registered or estimated, the most primitive form of the quantity theory looks quite different than where the stream of facts relevant to monetary theory flows abundantly.

[19]These types of tasks are not lacking in any science. But nowhere do they play a similar role as with us, nowhere do they make up so many of the difficulties to be overcome – from a different standpoint, in no other field do they make up as much of the charm of the intellectual adventure that we call "scientific labor."

[20]These are the "debits to individual account" that yield the ascertainable sum of definable liabilities ("debits") of the checking accounts of bank customers. In assessing this sum, not only must their incompleteness be taken into consideration, but also the fact that perhaps 80 percent of stock exchange transactions are settled through securities clearing of the exchanges and only the remaining 20 per cent give rise to check drawing.

amounted to $606 billion. For the preceding time in America and for England generally, we have the number for bank clearing, i.e., the sum of checks which are settled in transactions of banks between themselves, thus not including those that the customers of a bank draw in favor of other customers of the same bank. The movements of the two series in America during the period in which we have them both, match pretty well, as is indeed to be expected. According to the estimate of Irving Fisher, checks drawn in the United States since the last pre-war year made up about 90 percent of all money transactions (*Purchasing Power of Money*, p. 317). Payments made by repeated handover of the same check may safely be neglected. The analogous figures for the countries of the European continent have, of course, the less value the greater is the role of other payment methods and the more the concentration of banking has advanced, although they are of course not to be despised as an economic indicator in this context.

If we could register all debits that are made to any particular set of accounts during the period under review, and supplement them with all compensations that make check writing superfluous, furthermore with all transactions that are done by handover of coins and notes, and finally with satisfactory numbers for natural self-consumption of products and services, we would have a variable that one might call the *economic*, or, when omitting the last-mentioned item, the *payment volume*. The question is, what could we do with it? Would we have a variable that, compared with a quantity of means of payment defined somehow, would reveal the quantitative contours of the monetary process and could serve as a starting point for a monetary-theoretical analysis? Basically, the second question is to be negated and the first answered with: nothing. For it must be declared above all that the throwing together of all money transactions makes the number meaningless in itself. Neither its absolute level nor its change in time tells us anything about the relevant flows in monetary variables or the economy as such. This is especially to be made note of, and it is also to be presumed in every interpretation of an argument that works with this number or, as in the case of bank clearing, with a number that is to represent that number.

Fortunately, the matter does not stand in quite that regard practically, which, if it did, would have been particularly dire because we can see neither

---

Nevertheless, 40-50 percent of the sum redounds on New York, which, given the fact that New York is the financial center, the largest trading center, the largest industrial city in the country – and the world, is not surprising. The above cited figure of $750 billion comes from Carl Snyder, "The Measure of the General Price Level," in *Review of Economic Statistics*, February 1928, pp. 40-52.

coins nor deposits, nor the purposes they serve, and therefore encounter an analogous difficulty on their level. In order to gain a favorable conception, it is enough for us to keep in mind what we do not like about the number. The total value [Wertgesamtheit], which obviously means everything to us in terms of theory, the most important number in the theory of money, is the monetary expression of the social product. Similar importance accrues to the monetary expression of the corresponding original means of production, for reasons that will become clear, while the value totalities of securities markets are of less interest. For one thing, the debit sum contains elements that correspond to no process in any way of interest. Thus, two direct debits would arise if A transfers a thousand marks to B and B, as an example, refuses to execute an order from A to accomplish something with the thousand marks, and instead transfers the thousand marks back to A. Many processes of the technical side of payment transactions pertain to the category characterized by this example, which also includes the case of transfers on the books of checks to other accounts, the role of which as a possible source of error ought never be forgotten. But many of these debits are eliminated when one removes bookings in interbank clearing from the number. Above all, in many cases, and as long as we are not concerned about accepting rough outlines, it may be assumed that these items either do not materially change their relative importance over time, or that such changes can be rendered harmless by trend eliminations for the purposes of short-term analysis.

Secondly, we come back to our example of the transfer of tax revenues from one public budgetary entity to another. This process normally does not run parallel to anything in the sphere of goods, not even anything negative, because it will not reduce *that* demand of the taxpayer, to which the business process is attuned. In the first place it is economically meaningless because even in the sphere of money it has only, as mentioned, that secondary importance that may be linked to the insertion of an auxiliary fund. Now, the range of this type of operation is considerably greater than one might think. The imperial and territorial treasuries in our example do not only act to that degree as auxiliary funds, but they, and indeed all the treasuries of public entities, also act as auxiliary funds as long as they do not use funds - however raised - to purchase goods or discounts, but rather forward them to other households or even firms without economic reimbursement, e.g., as support and political income. For it is only in the latter's hands that something economically relevant happens with the sum. Of course, this also applies to other "institutions" that, for example, are mere conduits for charitable donations. But even a household paying taxes or gratuities - the same holds true of a firm - to that degree only acts as an auxiliary fund. Finally, the matter is no different for a saver whose investment is offset by debit items – in fact, often a number of them – when he commits the saved sums to other households or firms and thus does not himself make those dispositions that shape the economic process. Certainly, *something* can be done to eliminate many of the transitory items. Along these lines, we can of course register and deduct the transfers between public treasuries. The deduction of liabilities of public accounts works in the same direction.

But even if we also adjust the debit sums of all transitory items of this kind, "double counting" of another kind still attaches to it. It acts, for example, on vertical combinations in industry, if these lead to a new concern, such as a steel concern, that purchases the mines that supply iron ore and attends to this section of the production process without check drawings or with fewer than were previously necessary. It acts on the insertion or elimination of middlemen, etc. Also, this aspect goes further than one might think. We see this when we pass to the consideration of another total value, one which has bestowed upon us the introduction of VAT in many countries and especially in Germany. Where this is organized as a sales tax on goods and services and excludes monetary and credit transactions, it [seems to us] much more likely to provide what we need, despite its incompleteness, which is attributable to the numerous exemptions (in Germany especially, sales from import and export trade conducted via the state railways, as well as many non-profit firms, are exempt; but the exemptions of the middleman make the material more valuable) and for a goodly portion remediable through other data and estimates. But, where the taxable turnover in a year – in 1928, for example, it amounted to 134¼ billion reichsmarks – contains, say, identical amounts of raw materials or yields of working hours several times over, there is a case of double counting or more, with regard to the element in question, in the final product, and with the final sale to the consumer, with regard to the entire price minus the net profit of the retailer. This [chain] – and analogously all the other hands through which the developing good passes – acts in relation to everything except its net profit as an auxiliary fund, and if it were practically possible for the final consumer to distribute the sum that he pays directly to all those firms involved in the production, transport, and marketing of the commodities, it would, *apart from those manifestations associated with the insertion of auxiliary funds,* change nothing in the economic and also the monetary settlement process.

It would be quite mistaken to think that while the adjustment of this item for other purposes is necessary, for monetary theory it is superfluous or even inadmissible, because, although debit amount = payment volume does not depict what can be managed with the existing money, the sum of all sales of goods and services = volume of sales does depict this, the labor to be performed by it, as it were. This is not the case. Rather, the splitting of the economic path of a product is *in principle* a matter of indifference for the money process as well. Regardless of the - diametrically distinct - phenomena that are linked to the auxiliary fund, a particular dose of inflation, for example, affects the prices of commodities no differently regardless of whether the business process into which it is injected is divided into more or fewer dealings.

We possess a pair of almost flawless variables (although they do not come to us annually) in the industrial added value of American statistics, and the net product of English statistics. With other material and estimates, these can be extended to production volume without insurmountable difficulties. There are the variables that we later, when we have reached a verdict about the meaning and possibility of eliminating the influence of price changes on them, will identify as physical production in the garb given by this correction, although they of course also include intangible elements. Under stationary conditions, they are indistinguishable from the social product of each nation. For a simple argument shows that we can then say that the entire physical product consists in consumption goods, even though the means of production are also produced. In the case of growth or development, taking both terms in our technical sense, *more* goods are handed over to production in the following period than are taken over from the preceding period; therefore, this physical product exceeds the social product.

The figure for production volume has no necessary relation to the trade amount and even less to the debit amount. But it may be assumed of both that they change pretty much as it does, although especially in the business cycle, the deviations of the movement of the debit amount from the movement of production volume are of particular interest. In this capacity of at least not being a useless derivative of production volume lies the significance of "debits" for monetary theory, and for other areas as well. This significance lies in the appreciation of the fact that the deviations of the movements of the debits from those of production volume, in particular the difference in the cyclic rate of change of both - the ratio of their absolute magnitudes at any time does not tell us much - comes not so much from the influence of transitory items and double counting, which presumably do not change much in the short term, but from the influence of the numbers from the securities markets and speculative transactions generally. It cannot be stressed strongly enough that the lumping together of transactions of various theoretical markets never has meaning, and cannot be justified by the fact that one must comprehend the entirety of economic life and not just a portion if one wants to have an overall picture, or because one must take into account all prices and not just some, or because stocks as well as goods face willing money.

Chapter IX
The Essence of Money

1. We now return to our basic idea of social central bookkeeping, which registers all economic activities occurring in the area of study and thus provides a complete picture of economic life processes and also of economic accounting and payment processes. This idea is supposed, first, to explain to us the essence of the social institution of money. For the sake of presentational simplicity, we will consider in this chapter only the bookings and payments of the current economic process, furthermore usually only those of a stationarily reproducing economic process. In this latter case, it is readily apparent that the systems of accounting equivalences, as are depicted by the balance sheets and profit and loss statements of households, firms, and banks, are themselves, in turn, elements of an *economy-wide equivalence system* and are items of an economy-wide *clearing process,* which must result in an *economy-wide bottom line* of zero.

How Payment Really Works

To derive the full theoretical gain from this viewpoint, and to understand it as a tool of monetary-theoretical and monetary-political problem-solving, one must be clear about the fact that, as already indicated, all the accounts and all the transfers in the social ledger also reflect the meaning of the actual processes even in those cases where life makes use of other methods than bank-mediated transfer with its attendant clearing, so that here we actually have the base case of all types of payment before us, with all other types of payment being only technical special forms of it - which we encounter in practice as bank-mediated credits and debits. The difficulty that this basically very simple affair offers to our understanding only stems from our habit of considering the reverse, payment by handover of "coins," as the base case, and deriving all other methods from it, or constructing them upon it. In this chapter we will see that this is to turn things on their head. Right now, putting the question of the numerical determination of the computation and claim variables that emerge and disappear in the economic process temporarily to one side, we wish to undertake the tracing of other methods of the thus somehow-arising claims back to our base case, and see how our approach relates to the usual - and legal - concept of payment.

For example, a claim may be settled in such a way that the debtor transfers a different claim to the creditor. A case of this kind, which is of considerable practical importance, is the transfer of a *bill of exchange by means of endorsement "in lieu of payment."* In the first half of the nineteenth century, this method dominated the business transactions of the Lancashire cotton industry, appearing occasionally later and even today. So the bill of exchange proceeds from hand to hand like a banknote, and with the same economic success, although technically and legally the modes differ from each other. The same is achieved economically *and essentially* as if the bill were discounted and the discount amount credited first to the holder and then, on his behalf, to the bank account of the creditor. Thus far, two operations have been pushed together into one, the meaning of which becomes clear only when ones thinks of the implied transfers contained therein as being conducted on the, in this case, invisible accounts of the economy-wide books: the firm in whose favor the bill of exchange was originally issued, has, by a productive service, just acquired a "credit" in the economy-wide ledger, which is embodied in the equivalent of the bill of exchange, just as well as if it were embodied in a certified check.[1] If it then obtains e.g. raw materials from another firm valued at the same amount, it would be charged that amount on the economy-wide ledger, its credit would disappear from its account and reappear on the account of that other firm – which is actually what the assignment of the bill of exchange accomplishes; it is nothing but an element of the economy-wide clearing process.

Compensation fits immediately into our scheme, which, with more than two participants, transitions on its own into clearing. If shoemakers and tailors mutually supply each other, bill each other for their goods and, with the same invoice sums and payment dates, net the resulting receivables against each other, then obviously nothing other has happened than if the tailor had bought from a shoemaker and the shoemaker had bought from another tailor, and the relevant credits and debits had appeared in full detail and statistical ascertainability; and only a technical simplification distinguishes the first case from the second,

---

[1] The "certified check" is a check for which the responsible bank officials have confirmed the existence of the credit and the authenticity of the signature of the drawer (but not of an endorsement) so that the paper can be taken as a banknote. This institution owes its emergence in the United States to the low elasticity of the old national banking system in times of stress, during which these checks sometimes really circulated as banknotes. Their sum appearing in a "certified check book" forms a particular item on the liabilities side of banks' balance sheets. Details of this are contained in any book on bank technique.

which latter alone also explains what happens in the first. If more than two households or firms arrange to pay off their claims against each other through exchange, thus entering into a clearing agreement, we have before us a small picture of economy-wide collective clearing, or the ongoing, advancing compensation process between every single firm, or every single household, and the rest of the economy.

Two remarks are to be inserted here. Where, in a system fundamentally working with bank-mediated transfers, such *compensations* or *clearings* actually occur, as they do in the greatest degree with the "arrangements" of stock exchanges, not only does a significant statistical difficulty emerge, but something also of great importance for the functioning of the monetary system in question. We speak in such cases, making use of an English expression, of *obviation* (= avoidance of check drawings).

We then note that our construction, because it culminates in the picture of an economy-wide clearing, is suited to bring out the merely technical and intermediary character of each type of payment. Essential and definitive for the economic approach is simply productive capacity on the one hand, the receipt of goods or rather the act of consumption on the other: not the wage payment, for example, but rather the acquisition of wage goods by the wage earner closes the loop [schließt den Zusammenhang], which is only meaningful and understandable as a whole. For the law, that is not so. There the reverse is true: a legally valid payment in legally valid money, whether it takes place in fulfillment of a contract geared to payment in cash or subsidiarily for another payment that perhaps has become impossible, is always final. But that only means that the legal system does not bother with what happens next, because it is outside its system of purpose, and is of no importance for the knowledge of the essence of the matter. We return to our train of thought.

Even natural economic processes can be interpreted according to our scheme. Of course, we only have reason to do that if there are elements of natural economy in the midst of a developed money economy. One can readily envision such a naturally occurring exchange act, including cases of indirect exchange, in terms of balances arising and disappearing in the national accounts ledger that are summarily merged and thereby eliminated. If, furthermore, a farmer consumes his own product, he compensates himself, so to speak: first he provides a service through his production, for which he is credited in the general ledger; and then he draws upon it, for which he is charged for the amount in question, and his balance is crossed out.

Finally, payment by handover of coins or paper notes also proves itself to be a particular case of the economy-wide account-settling process, the attraction of which is expressed in bookings on bank accounts, their netting, and finally in general clearing. When the passenger in a tram hands over a ten-penny piece to the tram's representative, the conductor, this means that ten pennies are deducted from his account and that the tram's assets are increased by ten pennies, or a debit, if such exists, is reduced by ten pennies.

Hereby we have not merely presentationally simplified all kinds of implementation of income and expenditure, and gained a comprehensive picture that can be juxtaposed with the statistics of the monetary and credit transactions as a scheme of interpretation, but we have actually, as mentioned above, worked out that method that expresses the meaning of the matter even in cases in which practice utilizes other methods. For it might perhaps appear as if our chain of thought cannot be applied as well to another [method]: the economic meaning of the handover of little pieces of metal fashioned in a certain manner, for example, is that it reduces someone's economic credit and increases someone else's by the same amount, in the settlement of an economic transaction. But the meaning of a credit item and corresponding debit item does not lie in those little pieces of metal thereby exchanging masters. If such nevertheless is maintained from the standpoint of a *metallist* monetary theory, we would get stuck at an intermediate link in the explanation that in itself is meaningless. The handover of little pieces of metal rather receives its meaning only if one continues the explanation beyond them, leading back to our point of view.

Legal Tender and Real Payment

2. Regardless of the viewpoint one uses to delimit the concept of money, this money is always used as a *means of payment* for the, as we have seen, provisional adjustment of credit relations deriving from the non-simultaneity of the services and counter-services entering into the economic clearing process. The credit relations of the production and consumption process, or the balances in which they present themselves, are the essential and logical prerequisite [Prius], compared with which money, defined in any other way than these balances, fills a technical servant role, that only becomes understandable on the basis of this system of credits and debits. Certainly, common language understands by credits only those balances that are booked for the purpose of establishing claims, not those for the purpose of repaying claims. But for us, it is now more appropriate to follow the language of accounting practice and call each credit item

[Gutschrift] a credit [Kredit].[2] We then distinguish credits that correspond to an advance to the receiver - and which in this sense are *confirmations of an insertion in the social product*[3] - from those for which this is not the case, i.e., credits in the sense of ordinary language. But both represent deposits with which one can make purchases, thus - if the not-quite-correct term may be repeated - *claims* [Anweisungen] *on the social product.*[3] The part of the sum of both that, e.g., actually consists in coins, basically has no other status than the rest, as one can most clearly see from the hybrid case of the banknote.

To get to the bottom of the difference between this conception and the one embodied in the legal system, we start with the double meaning that clings to the term *cash payment* [Barzahlung].[4] By this is meant *payment* by handover of *legal tender money,* especially in contrast to bank transfer. But the businessman says he has paid in cash precisely when he has effected a deposit to the bank account of the authorized recipient. The law usually stands on the first viewpoint, and in the second case usually says that the businessman has done something that may not in the legal sense be payment,[5] but with the consent of the recipient has the releasing effect of a payment. We will follow the conception of the businessman - procurement of an (outstanding) balance is for us not only *also* payment, but the typical case of payment, the handover, e.g., of coins just being a technical special form thereof. And we will understand the dissenting opinion of the law in the context of the purpose of all legal determinations, oriented, as they are, precisely to the mechanics of individual cases, which are not critical to an analysis of the nature of matter - namely, the purpose of deciding practical bones of contention. For the law, it only comes to determining that with which a claim can be settled *legally,* i.e., with which a claimant must be satisfied. For the law, "fulfillment" is just the performance of what is due,

---

[2]Accounting practice of course limits this manner of expression to actual booking acts. We have to extend this way of speaking to those cases in which the "credit item" is effected by, e.g., the handover of coins. That sounds strange, and it is. But such an essential piece of monetary-theoretical understanding depends on this manner of expression, that the reader is asked to empathize rather than take offense.

[3]Original text: "play product" [Spielprodukt].

[4]The same is true, as the reader can easily note, for the expression "cash" [Kasse], which likewise sometimes means a stock of legal tender money, and sometimes (and particularly in the relevant accounting sense) includes checking balances.

[5]Indeed, if a deposit is construed as a claim for money, the debtor who supplies such a deposit to the creditor has not quite provided him with what was owed.

regardless of whether the fragment of life-context that is subject to judicial review depicts a meaningful whole or not. Payment is fulfillment by money performance, the legal effectiveness of which can only be determined by defining
what is to be regarded as such.

Here aspects come into consideration that we divide into private-legal
and currency-legal. As regards the former, what initially is concerned is the manner of effecting the performance, thus in practice, in the main, protection from
chicanery [and] failure to attain a goal, as occurs with the handover of a check
drawn on a bankrupt bank. Considerations of this kind are mainly what justify
the careful and relatively narrow definition of payment in the legal sense.[6] Second, the object of the performance must be clearly stated. Primarily the will of
the parties is normally decisive for this, the determination of which, given *currency changes, inflation, devaluations*, can cause considerable difficulties, to
which we will return in the second volume of this presentation.[‡] If the will of
the parties has become impracticable or is concerned above all with the determination of compensation in money, then the decision presumes one of the
sorts of money plainly recognized as money by the legal system, which will be
that which the legal order intends whenever it has reason to name monetary
amounts. This already defines *lawful money* or *legal tender*.

As one can see, *compulsory acceptance* (*forced* exchange) is not yet included in the concept. Rather, *non-declinability* is a property of legal tender
money only insofar as one is involved in default of acceptance, i.e., if one rejects
a properly offered amount of it as the fulfillment of a claim, which is not expressly denominated in a different kind of money, or for a debt amount, in itself
specified in legal tender money, for which a particular standard of value is set
(e.g., gold clause). It is not the nature of legal tender money that it be *definitive*
in the sense that a *conversion claim* in a different kind of money does not in
turn attach to it. Thus, for example the notes of the Bank of England since 1833,
and the notes of the Reichsbank since the Bank Act of 1909, have been *legal
tender* even while readily redeemed in gold coins. Finally, that which a state as
a rule accepts in its treasuries as means of fulfilling all of its claims, it also rec-
ognizes as legal money, normally at nominal value. But this *treasury paying
power* is not necessary. Rather, it may occur that the state demands many ser-

---

[6]Such considerations also make the legal difference between *performance in order
to effect payment* (*solvendi causa*) and *performance in lieu of payment* (*datio in solutum*)
both important and difficult.

[‡]See p. xii, n5 above.

vices in another form than its own lawful money. Thus, paper currency countries sometimes require payment of customs duties in gold. Conversely, treasury paying power can occur without legal paying power, whereby it then forms a mainstay of the market valuation of that money, the practical and theoretical importance of which ought not, however, be overestimated.

Currency-legal viewpoints can both supplement and override[7] private-legal ones, not only in the way of legislation but also adjudication. The "supplementation" begins with the Coinage Act, which constitutes the national currency by selecting the unit of legal tender money, which only so *can* be created, although it does not *have to. Exergue, fineness of stamping, minor coins, least current weight, free coinage* or exclusion thereof, etc., supplemented mainly by provisions of banking law regarding legal money or the material in which the reserves of the central bank must be held – in short, the entire body of *monetary legislation* is compelling law for commerce and lends each country's account-settling system its special character. With currency changes, the function of a kind of statutory interpretation is added to the will of the parties, which initially is only intended to facilitate conversion and does not *need* to include the intention to eliminate the private-legal aspects. But the generation that remembers the maintenance of the principle that "mark equals mark" does not need to be told that this usually turns out to be the case, and often happens in a way that can only be described as a perversion of justice by the courts.[8]

For all of this to act in a controlling fashion on the whole credit system and the whole account-settling process, the sufficient explanation is the priority that public opinion as well as science customarily grants to lawful money. But that should not blind us to the fact that this practical privileged position does not readily also correspond to a logical one, and that even though the legal *order* can undoubtedly determine what is *legal money*, legal *doctrine* still says nothing about what money *really* is.

Commodity Money as One Means of Payment Among Many

---

[7]Original text: "run over" [überreiten].

[8]Legal problems of the indicated type have arisen again during the currency breakdown of the world crisis. Therefore, it is not without interest to look up an old book, that treats the same questions with the mind of another time, the seventies of the 19th century: E.I. Bekker, *Über die Couponprocesse der österreichischen Eisenbahngesellschaften und über die internationalen Schuldverschreibungen* [Regarding the Coupon Litigation of the Austrian Railway Companies and Regarding International Bonds], Weimar, 1881.

3. Payment – the *provisional* settlement of *temporary* balances – by hand-over of specially fashioned metal pieces is thus in any case only one of many ways to perform an act of social account-settling. But one could admit this and be fully convinced that it is not part of the essence of money to be *made of* a precious material or to be *backed* by such, and furthermore that it would be wrong, for example, to *define* a twenty-mark piece as J.16845878 grams of fine gold, and still be of the opinion that the full metal monetary unit is owed a priority of a fundamental nature. This might mean, *firstly*, that a monetary unit consisting of a valuable substance, or backed by such, has certain practical advantages. This is in many cases indisputable, in others arguable, but right now it does not interest us. This, *secondly,* might mean that the system of credits and debits, which, in terms of our conception, brings the meaning of the institution of money to expression, must be based on "money" in the metallist or other meaning of the word and depicts claims to such. But the fundamental provision of these "claims" is not that they be satisfied in that which they are denominated – which is the purpose of all other types of claims – but rather that they be cancelled by other such-like, but oppositely directed, claims, and to vanish in economic clearing. The function of a last resort in the payment process, an assurance of its discharge, belongs to the chapter of practical advantages. Here the question comes into consideration as to whether, *thirdly*, the phenomenon of material money does not deserve logical priority in the sense that it is essential to lend significance to the unit with which the social account-settling system works and with which firms and households calculate, thus whether, in other words, this device to that degree must remain metallic or "material" generally, whether association with the market value of a quantity of metal – or of some other good – would be needed for households and firms to gain some idea of it. For this fairly general opinion, there speaks, among other things, the fact that the units of account of deposit banking in the fourteenth century were metallically defined. To clarify the nature of the matter, it is necessary to conduct an investigation that may seem abstract and difficult.

It is assumed not to be controversial, that *if and when* the combination of the deposit unit with the unit of a commodity at some point has done its job and, with its help, the operands of the economy have been identified, at that point the link can also be cut and the further development of these operands can follow its own laws, such as we see in the case of adjusting the mintage of a devaluating metal. A viable explanation follows from this insight or treatment, toward a unit of account *ultimately* free even of the mere association of ideas with a material value, which can then be introduced into the theoretical argument without historical links to a metallist initial state.[9] Nevertheless, there is a scientific interest in demonstrating the complete logical autonomy of the unit of account vis-a-vis the idea of something "having value." This demonstration likewise leads us to both the essence and the peculiarity of the institution of money.

The Economic Process Yields Only Relative Prices

4. We consider for this purpose the state of economic equilibrium in a closed area of investigation in which totally free competition prevails. The first question that comes up here is whether this equilibrium exists and is uniquely determined, i.e., whether and under what conditions the actions of households and firms produce a condition in which quantities of goods generated, sold, and bought by all households and firms, and the prices of all goods and services, depend on one another in such a way that we can understand, based on purely economic considerations, that each of these quantities and each of these prices is the way it is and not otherwise, and why this is so. Obviously this is the basic question of theoretical economics, just as an analogous question forms the fundamental problem of every other theoretical discipline. Because on its answer depends whether we have before us a logically autonomous system at all, or not. Where we must deny it absolutely, i.e., where our mental tools are *not* sufficient to make us understand why the variables of the system are this way and not some other way, it is of course bad for the cognitive value of the relevant discipline. It isn't nice when one must, with one and the same set of assumptions, allow *several* possibilities for things to take shape in the area being investigated, without being able to specify the circumstances under which the one occurs, and under which circumstances the other occurs. But it signifies a declaration of

---

[9]The derivation of a "material-value-free" market valuation of a monetary unit by means of a *historical* link to a material value was given by Wieser. The idea of a logical and from the outset material-value-free money (in the form of a money good that serves no other use), was however already fleshed out by Walras. Walras first selected an arbitrary commodity as a "numéraire," i.e., he expressed all exchange ratios in units of that commodity, in order to transfer the result into units of the money good. The same process can be found in Pigou. The logical autonomy of money vis-a-vis material value does not quite satisfactorily take place here, although the essence of the matter is correctly captured.

bankruptcy if infinitely many such opportunities exist, if, thus, as expressed in technical terms, the "system" has infinitely many solutions.

The method which in the first place presents itself as a means to answer our question, always comes to this – to comprehend in equations our knowledge of the relationships that exist between the variables in our system – in our case, between all the quantities and prices of all goods – and then to examine whether there is generally a system of values of these variables, any *at all,* that satisfies all these equations. Logically this means nothing other than to determine whether the facts that make up our experiential knowledge can be condensed into conditions or factors [Bestimmungsstücken] which, first, are compatible with each other, and second, which for each of our variables eliminate all values except one. In our case it was Léon Walras who first clearly recognized the task and solved it in an initial approximation. However, later work has heaped doubts and difficulties on his solution, and even today the problem cannot be regarded as solved completely satisfactorily. But for our present purpose it is sufficient to reference Walras and the short and simple presentation by Bowley.[10] Also, we do not need to examine a complete economic process. Rather, to bring out the point about which everything turns here, it is sufficient to take a market of finished goods that are simply given in determinate total quantities, and are distributed among the people in arbitrarily given initial quantities.

If on our market there are m such goods and n people who initially possess an arbitrary partial quantity thereof and now, in accordance with their tastes, sell something from their possession and buy something else with the proceeds, then we have the following variables that in the final state, i.e., when no one else is inclined to buy or sell at the then-prevailing prices, have to be determined: the m prices, and the quantities of all commodities that everyone parts with or acquires, by which we mean that whoever sells a commodity "acquires" a negative quantity of it, and whoever neither buys nor sells a commodity, acquires the quantity "zero." Since then everyone "acquires" each commodity, this yields $m \cdot n$ variables, so that in all we need $m + m \cdot n$ factors.

The quantity n of these are given by the consideration that, for each of our people, under our assumptions, the money sum of his purchases must be

---

[10]A.L. Bowley, *The Mathematical Groundwork of Economics*, Oxford, 1924. For utmost simplicity of illustration's sake, we also disregard those objections that are raised against Walras and his successors for mathematical reasons. Also, we cannot now go into questions of the stability of equilibrium, etc. Theorists in the field are asked to forgive the crudeness of the above. It is simply a matter of making intelligible a point that is fundamental to the theory of money, even if it means accepting much impropriety.

equal to the money sum of his sales. Such "balance equations" are obviously as many as there are people.

Then of course it is clear that for every commodity, the quantities of it purchased must be equal. That would then be a further m factors.

But this does not mean that as a whole we now have $m + n$ usable factors. This is because the two sets of equations are not independent of each other. If, that is to say, one multiplies the quantities purchased as well as the quantities sold of each commodity by the price, and then adds all these "commodities equations" together, one then obviously gets the same result that can also be obtained by adding the n balance equations: *both* additions simply give the trivial equation, reflected in[‡] our assumptions, between total expenditure and total income.[11] Therefore, we must ignore one of our factors; i.e., of the factors mentioned so far, only $m + n - 1$ is applicable for our purpose.

Finally, such prices must transpire, and such amounts of all goods must be bought and sold by all the people, that no one can improve his position by further purchases and sales at these prices. This means that a certain relationship must exist for everyone between the quantities of commodities making up his final "goods basket" or his final "consumption combination." The best way to make this clear is with the help of the concept of marginal utility. If I were to consume only two goods, for example, cigarettes and wine, then for me to "be in equilibrium," obviously the marginal utility of the amount of cigarettes that I can get for one mark must be equal to the marginal utility of the amount of wine that I can get for one mark. Otherwise it would be beneficial for me to spend my "last" mark differently, namely for that good which provides me with the "market quantity" yielding me the greatest marginal utility. Consequently, in this case we have another factor or equation. If there are m goods, we have $m - 1$ for them, for the entire system of n people, then, $n (m - 1)$.

To determine $m + m \cdot n$ quantities, we therefore have $m + n - 1 + n (m - 1) = m + m \cdot n - 1$ factors, thus one too few. The system has infinitely many solutions or, in other words, our quantities can assume infinitely many values. Our attempt to define them appears to have failed.

---

‡ The text has "wiedergehende," obviously a misprint for "wiedergebende," which is the word here translated.

[11]Of course this does not mean that the n-system and the m-system both say the same thing, that is, the factors formulated by both would be the same. What it means, rather is only this: that those additions both say the same thing, so that one might derive *one* of the factors - and indeed any - from the other. But this must be disregarded, because it is not independent.

But things are not as bad as all that. One can easily see, namely, that the number of variables to be determined can be brought down to the number of factors - thus, reduced by 1. Nothing can be done to change the number of quantities changing hands. But if in the place of m prices we put *the relations between these prices* of which there are only $m - 1$, we are rid of one of the variables to be determined, and indeed without losing its significance. For these price ratios are nothing more than the exchange ratios of commodities one to another.

Thereby we encounter the economic meaning of our formal argument. The economic process - in our simplified case, it is merely the exchange process - of its own accord determines the commodity quantities changing hands and their exchange ratios, but not *absolute prices*. This is also very obvious. The latter depend not only on the former but also on something else, that decides on the unit in which the prices are expressed. This other thing, or this unit, is obviously completely arbitrary and cannot be immanently created from the system of economic variables, but instead must be provided by an act of choice from the outside. Basically, just as we in principle could reckon in pennies as well as in marks, the economy can work with one system of numerical expressions for its economic variables as well as with another, if only they are all proportional to each other. There lies nothing in the logic of the economic process that would indicate one such system rather than another; rather, it basically and always, apart from transitional difficulties, comes down to price ratios.

Absolute Prices and the Critical Number

5. Under these circumstances, *theoretically*[12] we can only proceed from price ratios to absolute prices or, in other words, procure the missing factor or missing equation by *equating any monetary economic variable to an arbitrarily chosen number*. Since we are talking about a state of equilibrium, and in such the relation of any economic variable to any other is unambiguously set, this is sufficient to determine *all* monetary expressions of the system. And in fact we wish to reach an agreement that the sum of the products of amounts of consumption goods and their prices shall be equal to any arbitrary number, thus, denoting the quantities of m goods by $q_1, q_2 \cdots q_m$, designating the general term of this sequence with q_i, and the corresponding prices with $p_1, p_2 \cdots p_m$ and general term p_i, the expression $\sum p_i q_i = p_1 q_1 + p_2 q_2 + \cdots p_m q_m$. This agreement shall

---

[12]Practical possibilities and impossibilities will be treated later.

also hold for the consideration of the complete system, in particular including production.

This argument already also contains the proof of our assertion that the unit of account *in strict logic* is completely independent of association with a goods value. For the unit of account is available for all purposes in the moments in which absolute prices obtain. But this only comes to us through the introduction of a pure number that is meaningless in itself, and in particular has nothing to do with the idea of any commodity values. Of course, the unit of account thus obtained, once it is available and people have learned to deal with it, *then* would gain a goods-meaning for everyone. And if people are to wield it in commerce, this is in fact necessary. But for its *logical* deduction, prior goods-meaning is not necessary. The confusion of these two facts is responsible for the conceptual difficulties that confronted the foundational research in this field,[13] and for the various *circular reasonings* [Zirkel] one finds at the starting points of monetary theory and general economic theory as well, the unit of account being an element thereof.

Because our random number determines the values of all monetary quantities of the area of study, we call it the *critical number* of the system. About this important tool of our analysis, the following should be noted:

First, the critical number is arbitrary not only in terms of sum, but also in terms of the economic variable with which we equate it. We could just as well, for example, equate it to the quantities times prices of all goods used in the production process [Kostengüter] or the quantities times prices of the original means of production. Nevertheless, reasons of expediency speak for the choice made. As has been emphasized elsewhere, consumption goods are accorded a position of favor in consideration of their relationship to the meaning of economic activity, that from the standpoint of the firm corresponds to the preferential position of "profits."

Second, the critical number defined in this manner is only equal to the actual *consumption expenditure* of households in a state of balanced equilibrium of all individual households and all individual firms, but is different in all other states, thus for all practical purposes, *always.* Now we have equated it to the "equilibrium consumption expenditure." But it is crucial to note that the concept also finds application in states of imbalance, and in practice is used precisely for the analysis thereof. Unfortunately, our idea shares the difficulty with many others of monetary theory, in that it has to gauge what the equilibrium consumption expenditure would be in a given condition, and even whether we are

---

[13]E.g., with the problem of the subjective exchange value of money.

above or below it. Reserves, profits or losses, unemployment figures and the like, nevertheless offer clues that usually suffice towards a first approximation. It is also essential to be clear about the fact that even in equilibrium the critical number is only equal to, not logically identical with, actual consumption expenditure. The former is a given, the latter is made up of items that are variables of the problem. For those for whom this distinction is difficult, think for example of the difference between mass and weight.

Third, if we only had to consider equilibrium states, it would be a matter of complete indifference whether we a) so defined the critical number that natural economic processes, particularly withdrawals by farmers from their own economic activity, are also captured by it or not, and b) so defined it that only goods sold in the selected period of time, or rather all goods and services prepared for sale, enter into it. Outside of equilibrium, however, this makes a big difference. In the theoretical models in this volume, we can disregard the difficulties that in particular may arise in the shifting of the spheres of the natural and monetary-economic processes that might emerge from a), and in general consider a purely monetary-economic area of study. Regarding the second question, we said in the second point that the critical number is related not only to the goods and services that are actually sold, not only to those that are actually offered whether they find a buyer or not, but also to those that *would* be offered, and in particular *would* be produced, in an area of study in which complete equilibrium prevailed, also, among other things, to all the people that held cash amounts corresponding to this condition – which almost always would signify different prices as well.

The Paper Money Method

6. In order to obtain the missing equation, in practice it would take a particular social entity[14] that in each case would have to set a critical number. We can imagine this as being identical to our "central bank." The inherent uncertainty of our system is expressed in the need of such an entity, standing outside the circle of the actions of economic agents and dictating to them the critical number: this entity does not, as is usually the case, regulate something that through the interaction of economic agents has arisen independently of it, but it sets something that without its act would be entirely lacking.

---

[14]This entity can also be social practice. To that degree, it gradually arises "on its own." From the standpoint of the logic of the economic system, however, it is also something coming from the outside.

If all that was needed was to demonstrate certain basic truths, we could leave it at that. Likewise, if the system were unalterably to reproduce itself over time. In making our initial approximation, further, we would likewise not have need of any further considerations if the system reproduces itself essentially unchanged over time, as the older theory of money, unconsciously of course, postulated in developing its fundamental theorems. Finally, we would need to take into account no other factors if we could content ourselves with looking at the system at different but isolated points in time. We have at moment A an equilibrium system before us, and at moment B again an equilibrium system, but a different one, that exhibits different amounts and exchange ratios, and no connection exists between the two – not even a connection of memory – in which case our entity would fix the critical number completely independently for both moments in time, without in the future of both even knowing of the fixing in the past, and obviously no connection would have existed between the absolute values of the economic variables of both conditions. But this could satisfy neither us, the observers, nor economic life itself, because both we and it wish to capture not mere isolated situations in themselves, but the successive situations in their relationship to each other and because in reality one situation extends into another, and both in settling-through and in settling-up, variables in both the past and the future continually relate to each other in an economic world changing over time. Therefore, the further problem of a unit of account and settlement now raises itself *outside of time*, i.e., a unit that can be applied to the settling-up and settling-through of the respective past or future processes, and can be taken over from a situation in the past.

That does not mean that this unit must "mean the same thing" in each situation, so that value variables of different conditions expressed with its help are comparable without further ado and for all purposes. Rather, this desideratum places us before another, third problem. We are not yet able to solve it, i.e., to answer the question whether and in what sense such a time-invariant unit is possible. This much is already clear, that in order to create and maintain a unit that satisfies this condition, our central entity in any case would continuously have to adjust the critical number to the changing economic body. Otherwise, the economic valuation of the unit would have to vary or, in other words, the *absolute* price variables would have to change with the change in goods quantities, if the *price ratios* shall not have changed: a constant critical number *signifies* change in absolute prices.

But we are all in agreement that the setting and especially the continuous change of the critical number in the sense of the just-mentioned requirement would encounter difficulties that amount to practical impossibility. Following this path, practical life would never have come up with a unit of account, and only completely rationalized cultures could maintain such a "pure" account-settling system. Having said that, however, practical life does not have the problem of a unit preserving the same content over time, but rather in its own way *indirectly* solves the problem of determining the critical number and the linkage of the critical numbers of different economic conditions, *and the methods that have evolved to the end of solving these problems make up the essence of the social institution that we call money.* Everything now depends upon clearly recognizing its essence.

Of the – basically infinitely many – methods that more or less completely accomplish this, we are interested here in only two. First, we discuss the one that conceptually is closest to the pure account-settling system, although historically it only occurs in connection with the second, as its historical – not logical – derivative: the critical number can be determined so that *the number of units of account* is fixed that *may occur simultaneously with the settlement of clearing balances.* To this end, these units of account are embodied in physical tokens, and it is determined – this method also assumes a social entity that handles them – that the clearing balances cannot be settled otherwise than by handover of these tokens. This embodiment and the resultant regulation of the number of units applicable to the settlement of the clearing results, is the *leading technical idea of paper money,* that thus in terms of its essence has no intrinsic association with a material value, although, as it is easy to see, historically it could not otherwise have arisen than in connection with such.

Since the respective balances of claims in the equilibrium state of a constantly reproducing economic process are just as unequivocally determined, and stand in just as unequivocal relation to the other economic variables, as any other such variables, this method achieves the determination of the critical number and thereby all economic variables generally. And as long as the same equilibrium state continues, it also achieves the determination of the critical number over time, just as would be achieved by an "ideal" account-settling system. Perhaps this method achieves something else also – certainly it provides, e.g., some guarantee against abuse on the part of individual economic actors [Einzelwirtschaften] – but whatever else it may achieve is of secondary importance compared with this essential aspect. Regardless, as we allow the quantities of goods and exchange ratios to vary over time, we see immediately the strange, in fact aberrant manner by which this method fulfills the function of linking the critical numbers of disparate economic conditions. This becomes particularly evident if we imagine that in the meantime the payment habits of the people remain the same. Then the changing real balances always confront unchanged accounting tokens in each payment period, and the arithmetical expression of the balances must then remain permanently unchanged, whatever their "goods magnitudes" might be. This way of expressing the changing balances and thereby all economic magnitudes would be comparable to a measurement method according to which all people are characterized as equally tall, for example, two meters in height, while their actually different body lengths are accounted for merely by changing correspondingly the length of the sub-units, e.g., centimeters. We can characterize the base case of paper currency as always forcing the economy to adapt, naturally under considerable disturbances, to the same critical number. The matter would be different, but no better, if - e.g., under the pressure of financial needs of the central entity - the number would be changed arbitrarily over time. The logical proximity to our ideal account-settling system becomes clear if we imagine that the central entity could vary the number of accounting tokens in adjustment to changes in the body of goods.

This logical proximity becomes even more evident in the case in which the units of account are not "embodied" but, as checking balances, would lead a mere bookkeeping existence when the central entity would determine their total, and henceforth keep them constant. In this manner as well, a critical number and the absolute value of all economic magnitudes *in a state of equilibrium* are determined, and, given the stationary reproduction of the condition, the same situation is attained as in the ideal account-settling system. In this manner as well, the critical number is maintained at a numerical value determined by the sum of balances, although of course not identical to it. Here also, continuous difficulties of adjustment would have to be overcome as soon as anything in the economic process were to change.

The Commodity Money Method

7. The *second* method goes to work differently. Its main idea is for one of the goods prices arbitrarily to be equated to one, or any other number. In this way an initial, and indeed distinct, albeit indirect, fixing of the critical number is attained, at given equilibrium conditions in the area under study. This could then always be arbitrarily treated: maintained or changed according to whatever rule. But if it is determined at the same time that the price of a single commodity continually should remain equal to one over time, then changes in the critical number in time have also thereby been decided, and a single, albeit continuously changing, critical number is always provided to commerce, thus also resolving the second of the two problems distinguished above.

The units thus created can be used either in mere calculation or by physical handover of quantities of the selected good, accomplishing a larger or smaller portion of payment. The second approach utilizes quantities of this good and thus acts on its market value. It therefore produces a different but also clearly determined critical number than the first version. To hold this to be conceptually essential, and to construct all processes of the monetary and credit sphere from out of it, is the content and the error of that money theory that we have called the *commodity theory*. One should note that if the obtained unit is only used in calculation, without exemplars of the selected goods going from hand to hand in the normal payment process, one can proceed within each economic situation from accounting in units of one commodity to accounting in units of another if one divides the prices of the first system by the price of the new money-good in units of the old. By contrast, if the money function utilizes a significant amount of the money-good, so that the latter is removed from its goods function, this rule does not apply straightforwardly, because now the price of the new money-good, as expressed in units of the old, changes.

This, then, is the essence of every *commodity currency*, in particular of a *gold currency*. It delivers the critical number and thereby all economic variables over to the vagaries of production and demand relations of the *money-good*, and imposes adaptation processes that have no economic function. It lacks the obvious absurdity that lies in adherence to the critical number in the context of a changing flow of goods, but the way in which it changes the critical number is no less outlandish and strange. A method that retains the critical number at one and the same value is analogous to a measurement method that tries to capture different lengths by varying the unit of length while nevertheless always according the different lengths the same number; the method that we are now considering can be compared to a measurement procedure that does allow a different expression of number for different lengths, but not according to these lengths, but according to wholly arbitrary changes in the units.

Of course this is insufficient to take a practical position vis-a-vis the *gold standard*. In very many cases this is not only the only possibility, often even the historical origin, but it also endows the unit of account, when it embodies a precious material, with a guarantee of its market value, that is lacking in any other prevailing system. Although it delivers the account-settling system of a people over to the vagaries of the production of the money-good, it protects it from even worse arbitrariness. It is not entirely unreasonable that most people previously, and many today, attribute a moral dignity to it. And it is readily apparent why such money then is also suitable for other functions, e.g., the function of *hoarding*, which it shares with the amounts of the money-good not serving as money, and also why it is, where other types of means of payment make their appearance historically later, it often gains the function of a *backing medium* for them. Whatever one may think about these things, it simply comes down to recognizing that logically, albeit not necessarily historically, they are incidental, and that the essential thing is solely the determination of the critical number of the system. As imperfectly as this is achieved – the imperfections of this method are the main source of all purely monetary problems – our admiration for this ingenious trick of cultural history cannot be great enough.

The reader can easily see that *this indirect method of determining the critical number is characteristic of all historically given methods of social bookkeeping, as is the characteristic that they are encumbered with an element that is foreign to the meaning of the calculation process and that adjusts results correspondingly.* This characteristic is never absent, grounded as it is in the practical impossibility of continuously changing the critical number in such a way that the economic process does not have to make adjustments simply because of the logic of its system of calculation. The methods of practice, indeed, achieve both the initial and the continued determination of the critical number. But at the same time they furnish its changes with an *autonomy* that takes no account of changes in the body of commodities, and which is senseless when seen from the point of view of the latter.

The result of the investigation of this chapter can now be expressed as follows: *this indirect and essentially nonsensical method makes up the essence of the social institution that we call money.* We take the fixing of the critical number to be also a kind of autonomous change of that number, i.e., a kind of continuous determination that in principle does not take the relations of the world of commodities into consideration, and now offer this definition: *the money method is that method of social account-settlement, according to which the critical number of the economic system changes autonomously.* Every such method creates tokens of account [Rechenpfennige] that exist as such – physically or on the books. *These tokens of account we call money.* Any such method subjects the economic variables to a new condition, to which they must adapt. We call *this* condition the *money tie* [Geldligamen].

Commodity Money and the Inversion of Meaning

8. Thus we see that the meaning of the social account-settling process is not changed by the money method. This is just a special case of accounting technique that is characterized by a peculiar artifice, just as the individual kinds of

money in turn represent only special cases of the money method and differ from each other only in the way in which each of them determines the critical number. But the autonomy of the critical number, characteristic of all the historical, and all conceivable, varieties of the money method, brings an element to the affair that is foreign to the meaning of the social account-settling process, that becomes the source of all specific monetary phenomena. Here we refer to one of the strangest of these phenomena, namely the inversion that the conception of the social accounting process and its variables, thus the entire economic thinking of the businessman, the consumer, the monetary policymaker, and even the researcher, underwent, such that this account-settling process is, in practice, available to us only in the form lent to it by the money method.

So much of the history both of the monetary system and the science of money is explained by this inversion, that it is worthwhile to dwell for a moment on it. It manifests itself most clearly in the case of a full-fledged commodity money – let's say up front, a currency of unrestricted minting and melting, and with an effective gold circulation. If this form of money method is so settled that it has penetrated the consciousness of the people and is held to be the only normal one, then everything in the money and credit sphere that is derivative, and is a technical artifice, becomes original and essential; a special case becomes the base case, the logical consequence of things is turned on its head, and in a historically very understandable way, which, as is well-known, has not lacked theoretical justification: it was provided by the *commodity theory* of money, in particular by its characteristic starting point, the *most marketable commodity.*

The essential process, the final clearing of all performances and counter-performances of services and goods, then vanishes behind the handover of gold exemplars derived from the theory of goods exchange. The true meaning of the construction of money claims as claims for gold, which only plays a security role, and the essence of the *redemption* of credit instruments, is lost, in that this construction and this repayment promise are regarded as expressions of the essence of the thing and as its necessary consequences. In this way, the balance sheet results of each firm expressed in units of the money commodity gain a life of their own that at bottom is a fantasy, even if under normal conditions it may be a *useful* fantasy – such that it cannot be stressed enough that our argument does not imply a value judgment regarding the gold currency or any other.[15] And

---

[15]By the way, our argument does not even imply a final judgment on the commodity theory of money. For it would retain meaning, albeit not as a theory of money but as a theory of an important special case thereof, entirely apart from the fact that the best money-scientific labor has been achieved on its basis.

in this way, finally, the layman believes he has reason to be surprised at the enormous edifice of "credit" or "claims" that is erected upon the base of a relatively small gold supply, and therefore often enough is also referred to as superstructure.

The inversion of things and the error regarding the essence of convertibility and thereby of money comes better to expression in this amazement than in anything else. Just another side of the same error is the *deposition theory* of deposits, the – erroneous – basic idea of which is already contained in the word "deposit." We have seen that the idea that a deposit normally and essentially arises through deposition is hardly less naive than the idea that all deposits correspond to money amounts that, physically piled up in the full amount with the depositary, await the disposition of the depositor. But according to the view that we characterize as the inversion of the real factual situation, both actually have to be the case, and in fact this view also constructs – with the help of feigned *direct* [brevi-manu] *handovers* of gold pieces – the process of the emergence and functioning of the credit system from out of physical deposition, making that system appear, through misinterpretation of the historical primacy of deposition, to be derivative and a product of technical artifice, as a special technique of managing the gold supply. And the idea of "tokens for goods" is so remote from life that not only is it not considered realized, however imperfectly, in the institution of money, but is considered to be something new and foreign to the monetary system, possibly a reform idea. And the much-invoked "confidence" of the holder of a checking account – or a banknote – that, in terms of its meaning, is confidence that the owner of the deposit is placed in the same position economically as is the possessor of legal gold, thereby confidence in market value and thus on the rational restriction of the total amount of all balances, is inverted into confidence in constant convertibility, which only has meaning to the extent that in practice, at market value, it is available to the degree that it is not resorted to.[+]

The Money Tie and Credit Expansion

9. However, the above analysis only covers the basic idea of the money method. If we wish to understand its functioning in the real world, we must fill out our picture with an important fact. To wit: economic life resists the money

---

[+] The original has "often is both available and lacking at the same time [oft mit der Marktgeltung gleichzeitig vorliegt und fehlt]," the meaning of which seems to be as translated above.

tie, the bridle that the autonomous critical number straps onto its settling-up and settling-through process, and it is actually able to evade it to some extent. Of course, only in exceptional cases – in an economy with perfect competition, not at all – will this have to do with conscious resistance by individual households and firms, for whom both the insight and the opportunity to do this would be lacking. Rather, we must investigate types of behavior otherwise motivated that objectively produce this effect.

First, we have to clear from our path an obvious and actually frequent mistake. It is often said that economic life itself "creates" the "purchasing power" that it "requires." If this means that each production, if not technically or commercially unsuccessful, creates the real demand that it absorbs, i.e., each properly calculated supply calls up a counter-supply of other goods and services, then this is essentially and usually correct. But that only says something about the sphere of goods and nothing about the corresponding monetary operations, and nothing about the prices at which a surplus product can be sold. And in every other sense, this tag is so misleading that one is better off avoiding it. In particular, one cannot refer to the possibility of closed-loop clearing to substantiate the independence of absolute prices and the critical number from money ties. True, if – to adduce an oft-used example – a surgeon operates on a singer, and this singer sings for an equal fee to the evening party of a lawyer, and the lawyer, again for an equal fee, prosecutes a lawsuit for the surgeon, it appears as if the amount of the fee would be completely independent of the influence of the chosen method of money on the critical number of the system, even as if, in turn, it would determine that number. The case is also by no means practically meaningless and can crop up where price groups are changed by corporate action and the resulting increase or decrease in receivables confront each other directly.

But one should not conclude that, because an isolated area of study at the end of the day represents a closed clearing system, that commerce can evade this simple kind of money fetter. Because here it depends on the actual technique of payment transactions. Had all people the same inspiration at the same time henceforth both to require and to grant double prices, and were there some segment of economic life in which, e.g., payment was made by handover of gold pieces or paper notes, then in this segment commodity quantities would be unsalable at the new prices, which is precisely what comprises the yank on the bridle. By the way, maintaining parity between the units of money-good functioning as money and the units of the same material serving in a commodity capacity exercises a similar effect. In our time, in which the detailed organization of the economy is so far advanced that the idea of a systematic and simultaneous markup of all prices no longer seems adventurous, we observe as well that, as soon as the like is tried only partially, currency difficulties immediately make themselves evident.

Mere surplus production at whatever position in the economic body has no tendency in and of itself to change a critical number fixed by whatever version of monetary method. To see this, one only need consider that any money method sets the critical number only indirectly and through the mediation of actual commercial custom. The social standardization of legal money only means that respective differences between definitive performance and counterperformance, i.e., the respective balances of claims and counterclaims of each household and each firm falling due, in principle must be paid by the handover of such legal money. Such a system therefore already contains all the compensations both of in-house consumption and the vehicles [Träger] of mutual payment processes – all obviations, clearing figures, and balance-affecting payment credits – that actually exist in the relevant economic body. The critical number emerges taking into account all these circumstances. If now somewhere more is produced than before, it can be generally assumed that the sale of the surplus product will be distributed in the same proportion to each payment as the sales of the entire previous social product, from which, as is easily seen, the assertion that was to be proved immediately follows, although naturally only under the condition of a perfect equilibrium of all firms and households disturbed only by the surplus supply of a commodity.

Only in one case can the money fetter be relaxed by the behavior of surplus producers and their customers. This case, however, lies outside the assumption of perfect competition. If a very large firm, which can exert significant influence through its own behavior or at least by its example, sells its surplus product, e.g., on the installment plan, this can lead on the one hand to the expansion of the compass of compensation, and on the other to the effectuation of a reduction in the average cash holdings of customers. Then to that degree the critical number could rise, even if nothing else in the money tie is changed.

But while otherwise a change in payment customs that could have this effect is not simply induced by surplus production, so here, in the case of gold money, a not unimportant automatic response of the system should be brought to mind. If surplus production forces down absolute prices, gold production becomes more advantageous than hitherto. Of course, this mechanism assumes that prices are going down, but at least it causes the mesh of the money tie to widen and prices to fall by less than they would otherwise. In passing, the possibility of a similar mechanism in the case of state-issued paper money should be mentioned. It would indeed be a very dangerous, albeit in principle quite a rational, policy if the government authority were to back some of its expenditure by continuously issuing new paper money in line with the increase in social product.

But the big lever that steadily expands the scope of the operands of the economy is of course the fresh creation of deposits. The word "deposits" is to be understood here in the broadest sense, so as to include bills of exchange as long as they go payment-making from hand to hand. Of course, only the introduction of this custom has the contemplated effect; once the change has been completed, the money tie again becomes active in the new condition of the monetary sphere, albeit at a modified level. But as long as this practice gains ground, so long does the critical number change, the number of "existing" settlement units or the total amount of "deposits" in the area of study increase, and the economic process is freed from the bridle of the money method, so that it develops in the direction of a pure account-settling system.

The driving force of such a process is obviously "credit demand" in the popular sense of the word. If increased production leads to heightened demand for credit, which it often does, and if this borrowing requirement is satisfied by newly created *ad hoc* credit, then pressure from the money fetter is eased, at most to that amount, and usually in advance, i.e., before the increased product is offered to the consumer, so that one may assume that this amount is ready in time to accommodate the increased product. We will return to this in detail later, and thereby see that this is not quite the case, as well as that the problem is solved only for the moment, while everything beyond that depends on what the surplus producer does with the surplus profit. Here the object was only to emphasize the fact itself, that economic life in this manner can put up resistance to the bridle of money, and to emphasize the limited truth that lies in classical money creation's shibboleth – by which is understood, in the sense of the old banking theory, the crediting of the discounted amount of commercial bills, the practice of which, indeed, does not entirely answer to the oft-sketched ideal picture.

As pointed out earlier, the banking system is the typical, and for our theoretical scheme basically the only, source of these new balances. In the business interests of the banks we discover another, and indeed the main, driving force in the struggle against the money tie and the steady increase historically of the critical number of modern economic systems. The unbacked banknote, or checking balances not subject to any backing requirements, allow the essence of the matter to come most clearly to light. For the rest, we refer to what was said in the chapter on the banks, regarding which, from the point of view now gained, a deeper meaning can be learned. Beyond that, the complete replacement of commercial credit by bank credit and the penetration of commerce with "cash-saving payment methods" naturally extends the realm of clearing and therefore has a direct effect on the critical number, and not merely indirectly, through both of these changes, but especially through the latter, facilitating bank-mediated credit expansion, as discussed in the above-mentioned chapter.

But even that is still not the whole truth. As the economy defends itself with partial success against the money tie, the latter in turn defends itself against the aspirations of freedom of the monetary variables in the economy. The linking of the deposit unit with whatsoever legal tender money, the structure of balances as claims for legal money such as is characteristic of the money method, puts the banks under liquidity considerations of a special kind that tend to be reinforced by legal or commercial-customary coverage provisions, etc. What is at play here is primarily a deliberate defense on the part of public opinion, that has learned from abuse and disasters, and legislation following in its wake. The memorial to this mentality, that pays homage to a naive but in practice often very healthy metallism and that views bank-mediated money creation as a shameful thing [pudendum] to be opposed, is Peel's banking reform. Elsewhere, and particularly later, public monetary policy fluctuates between the goal of putting fetters on the settlement process and the goal of, on the one hand, rendering these fetters "elastic," and on the other, nothing less than a progressive expansion. In the direction of restriction, namely, lies the extension of coverage requirements to checking balances that are gradually becoming the norm, although the consequences deriving from the realization of the essential equality of banknotes and checking balances have never been completely drawn. But having said that, the opposite trend has quickly gained the upper hand. At present it must be regarded as dominant.

Only now do we have all of the fundamentally important aspects together that constitute the essence of money and define its role in the economy of today. The reader might possibly linger at the individual steps of the analysis of this chapter and visualize what an ingenious whole life has woven here from practical insight and theoretical mistake: neither short formulations nor quickly readied reform proposals can do it justice. It pertains to those things that are made harder to understand when one tries to depict them too simply.

Chapter X
Consequences

1. From the insight gained into the essence of the money method, certain conclusions emerge directly that are summarized here. They arise partly from the realization that money is nothing more than a technical tool of social clearing, partly from the further knowledge of the peculiar way in which money performs this function.

a) Money is not a good and not a commodity, but it is characteristically the opposite of goods or commodities. That the unit of account, with which in a pure account-settling system calculation takes place and commodities are paid for, is not itself a commodity and does not thereby become a commodity to which all balance-derived value estimates are linked, is self-evident. It should be equally clear that the link between the unit of account itself and the value of a commodity changes nothing in that regard, even when the money unit, e.g., becomes embodied in a piece of metal. For such a link obviously does not mean logical identity. If, however, one considers this link to be essentially necessary, it becomes difficult to figure out these basically very simple facts. This explains the unsatisfactory nature of the attempts to assert from the standpoint of the commodity theory the essential viewpoint, for example the attempt to construct the valuation of money by analogy with the valuation of means of production (Pareto and others) or to derive it from the valuation of the money-good as a historical starting point (von Wieser).

If money is not a good, then there can be *no demand for money* in the same sense in which there is a demand for bread or iron. This is the logical basis of the old saying that, in contrast to the absolute quantity of a good, the absolute quantity of money is basically indifferent to an economy, although of course one may speak in a very understandable sense of the need for a particular form of money, of the money requirement at given quantities of commodities, prices of commodities, and payment habits – cash requirements and the like. But more is gained in clarity than is lost in convenience if one abstains from building on the harmless formal analogy that can be constructed between demand for money and demand for goods.

Therefore, it would be advisable to refrain from applying the apparatus of supply and demand to the problem of the market value of money over against commodities, and to limit it to the operations of the money market. We also shall speak only in connection with the price of "money" that comes to expression in the rate of interest, but not in connection with that "price" of money that is identical to the reciprocal values of the prices of individual goods.[1] In the first case the term money is used in a figurative sense, as is the term price in the second case, and to mix the two seems to be tomfoolery even if one is safe from the popular confusion of cheap money = low interest rates and cheap money = high commodity prices. But, of course, one may speak without further ado of supply of and demand for the *money-good* for money purposes.

b) From the knowledge that money is not a good and satisfies no needs in the sense in which consumption goods do directly, and production goods indirectly, the peculiarity characteristic of *claims to legal money* also follows, as opposed to claims to any sort of commodity, and *explains* the previously described technical possibility of *"purchasing power creation through credit."* Obviously it cannot happen that claims to quantities of any good, such as claims to wheat, horses, or shoes, basically and normally accomplish the same thing that wheat, horses, and shoes themselves do, such that they might compete in the use thereof, and gain independent significance. Only with money is this possible, and with money not only *can* certain types of claims to money, such as banknotes, be accepted as money itself, but in fact *must* be so accepted - whatever the theory of money might be to which one pays homage.[2]

It follows, in turn, that the same economic nature and the same purpose cannot possibly befit such claims as befit claims on goods.[3] The normal purpose and economic sense of any claim to a good is contained in the performance of what is owed. But with checking balances or banknotes and the like, the purpose

---

[1] The Marshall School in particular does this. The practice is defended by Edwin Cannan, "The Application of the Theoretical Apparatus of Supply and Demand to Units of Currency," in *Economic Journal*, 1921, pp. 453 ff.

[2] This also disposes of the objection that the money supply can increased as little through the creation of claims on money as one can multiply coats in safekeeping by multiplying the number of tickets to safeguarded coats: one cannot wear the ticket, while one can make purchases with the claim to money. We see from this that, instead of purchasing power creation, it is expedient to speak of better "utilization" of existing purchasing power, or of increased velocity of circulation of legal money through the methods of banking transactions (Wicksell).

[3] But it does not follow that, from the circumstance that the bank customer with a checking balance is in the same position as if he had "deposited" it, he actually *did* deposit it.

is not for them to be converted into *that in which* they are denominated. Rather, the whole organism is set up for counterclaims to confront them that cancel them *without* payment being required. The legal construction here does not express the essence of the matter as it does with claims on goods, but merely has technical and, as we saw earlier, security importance. Therefore, the *abolition* of the *obligation to redeem* notes does not have the same economic consequences that a like abolition of an obligation to "redeem" claims against any goods would have, and is something other than a moratorium. From which it follows that it makes no sense to regard, as many older theorists did, the holder of a banknote or a check deposit as a creditor of the bank. He transfers nothing and abstains from nothing. On the contrary, he *obtains* liquid "purchasing power" with which he can undertake just the same things and, in particular, purchase just the same consumption goods, as with the money in which his "claim" is denominated - and in the typical case, economically speaking, he is only the *recipient* of credit.

c) The quantity of an object that can be increased by the creation of claims to that object, obviously is a rather dubious affair. But we are not now dealing with statistical difficulties, that by the way are not lacking even in the ascertainment of the quantity of legal money available in the area under investigation,[4] nor even with the question as to what in each particular case should be included in the money supply, but with a deeper aspect. The older theory of money viewed the money supply as a given that determined the remaining variables with which monetary theory has to do, without itself being determined by them. As we know, and was well known to those authors, this view cannot be considered to be entirely realistic, a fact discernable even in earlier times because of the reaction of gold production to the movements of the prices of commodities; but from the standpoint of the classical theory, the money supply could be considered an independent variable of the equation [Problem], at least as a first approximation. In this special case of the money supply - since otherwise the quantity of a product can never represent a given of economic analysis - a real feeling for the essence of the money problem comes to expression. But as soon as one begins to work with the concept of the money supply, in particular with the desire to make statements about relationships between the money supply and absolute prices, one bumps up against the fact that not all money confronts goods, but only a part thereof. This fact can be dealt with in various ways, among others by distinguishing between *"existing"* and *"circulating"* or

---

[4]The work of e.g. Y.S. Leong conveys an idea of this: "An Estimate of the Volume of Deposit Currency in the United States," in *The Journal of Political Economy*, 37, 1929.

"*effective*" quantities of money. From the latter, that amount of money or money commodity can be distinguished that serves other types of money as "backing" or is hoarded. But whatever the reason is that coins are not operative, they are almost never permanently withdrawn from circulation. And how many are inert and how long they do nothing obviously can *never*, not even in a rough approximation, be considered a given of the problem, but in all cases is one of the variables that has to be apprehended. The newer theory therefore has the tendency to push the concept of money supply into the background.[5]

From our standpoint it is especially clear that in a pure account-settling system the concept of money supply would correspond to *nothing* at all. To speak of a quantity of existing units of account would make as much sense as to say that a certain number of units of length exists with which everything that has length must be measured. In either case, it is instead sufficient to indicate the umpteenth part of an arbitrarily selected magnitude of the same category to which the unit is to correspond, in order to determine the unit. But rather than this, the money method creates the manifestation, and is responsible for the emergence of the problem, of money supply; and this is so both when the critical number is determined directly, through the fixing of a money supply (as in the case of paper money), and when the money supply is determined indirectly by something else (as in the case of commodity money). Our analysis also shows us how this quantitative determination continues with respect to balances, and further, that this never occurs exhaustively, for which reason the content of the money concept, particularly the concept of effective money, can never be delimited differently than according to the principle: what performs the service of money is money. Fundamentally there can never be a question of an objectively preexisting amount of money that could be applied as a given, which is one of the reasons why we introduced a special value as the factor of the equilibrium state, which we need no matter how we try to avoid it: that is, what we have called the critical number. Note still that the occurrence of the phenomenon of the quantity of money, and in particular the quantity of balances, explains how it is that "money" as such [is] traded, and why there can be such a thing as a "money market."

Statistically, the effective money supply [is] of course unambiguously ascertainable, at least in principle, at any particular time. As we know, in addition to the various forms of legal money, the following are to be included: full-value

---

[5]For this trend, which also comes to the fore in Keynes's *Treatise*, a treatment by Joan Robinson is especially characteristic: "The Theory of Money and the Analysis of Output," in *Review of Economic Studies*, Vol. 1, No. 1, 1933/34, p. 22.

coins, small change, paper bills, banknotes, and amounts of whatever commodities there are that perform actual money services, securities of any kind, as long as they actually go from hand to hand paying off debts – in such cases, besides bills of exchange, also coupons, titles to fixed income, etc. – but most of all bank balances, minus the subset that does not render a service vis-a-vis goods, be it because they serve other kinds of money as a backing, or be it for other reasons. The difficulty presented by time deposits will be referred to again later.

d) From the fact that the money is not a good, the explanation follows of the phenomenon that we are accustomed to call the *velocity of circulation*.[6] Because this requires extensive treatment, we will dedicate the remainder of the chapter to it.

The Velocity of Circulation of Money

2. As we have already seen in our historical overview, the science of money very early had forced upon it the observation that the sum of coins going from hand to hand in the area of study is not equal to the sum of the transactions expressed in money, say, in an economic year, but is much smaller than that. A first refinement of this observation is given by the insight that this would also be the case even if all these transactions were done only by handover of those coins and if there were no other transactions than purchases and sales of goods and services in the train of the processes of production and consumption, transactions that thus consisted only in purchases of means of production, including intermediate goods, by the producing firms – with the help of mediating, but not speculating dealer firms – and in purchases of consumption goods by consumer households. We wish in the first place to consider this case, because for now we are only dealing with an initial notion of the matter.

---

[6]The literature on this subject has recently been enriched by a lively discussion. But it will be enough to indicate the main achievement: M.W. Holtrop, *De Omloopssnelheid van het Geld* [The Velocity of the Circulation of Money] Amsterdam, 1928, and the treatment of the same: "Die Umlaufsgeschwindigkeit des Geldes" [The Velocity of the Circulation of Money], in *Beiträge zur Geldtheorie* [Contributions to Monetary Theory], ed. F.A. von Hayek, Vienna 1933, pp. 115 ff., and the critical work of Marget, especially the treatment in *Economica*, 1933, and in *Journal of Political Economy*, 1932. Arthur W. Marget, "The Relation between the Velocity of Circulation of Money and the 'Velocity of Circulation of Goods,'" I. II, in *The Journal of Political Economy*, Chicago, Ill. 1932, pp. 289 and 477; "Definition of the Concept of a 'Velocity of Circulation of Goods,'" II, in *Economica* 41, 1933, pp. 275-300.

If all these economic acts are accompanied by the physical handover of coins to the full amount of the money expression of each commodity value, and yet fewer coins are present than the sum of these amounts indicates, this obviously can only come from the same coin, in carrying out this economic act, rendering a service multiple times. This is the essence of what is *meant* by the term *velocity of circulation*, although so much else has stuck to this nucleus that the words now characterize a set of facts that analytically is not easy to handle, and has lost all precise meaning. In itself there is nothing more evident than that shoes and bread, *with* the means of production incorporated *in* them, not only physically perish – which, by the way, the means of production partially do a stage earlier – but also economically perish in the consumption acts of households, while the corresponding coins basically continue to *circulate endlessly* and complete an indeterminate number of cycles[7] through the economy, which is to say, they can never return to the place that we first saw them. The matter can be most clearly rendered if we imagine marking some individual coins so that we can establish their identity, and then track their way through the economy. It is easy to see that for a stationary economic process, we change nothing essential to the process if we assume that each coin travels the exact same way in each period of circulation.

Therein already lies the fact that there can be no analogue for the velocity of money in the world of goods. If we nevertheless encounter a concept of the *velocity of the circulation of goods* in the literature, then either a different phenomenon is meant[8] or there is a misunderstanding, the symptom of which sometimes is the claim that money does not retrace its steps but always moves parallel with whatever good, and thus that the velocity of the circulation of money is always equal to the velocity of the circulation of goods, hence cannot be a special kind of independent driving force in the money process. What is responsible for this, is clear: the velocity of the circulation of money is obviously linked to the *change of hands* that coins undergo, and is observed in this changing of hands.

---

[7]These cycles are time bound, and therefore there are not an indeterminate number of them per time period. But one might imagine a payment organization in which the number of cycles per time period would be *extremely large*, even though technically they cannot well be infinite. Even so, this borderline case is of logical interest.

[8]Namely, the ratio between the quantities of a commodity sold in the period to inventories maintained. As far as one can speak of a physical total amount of all commodities sold and held in inventory, the concept can also be applied to the ratio of these two quantities. In both forms, the concept has its place. Only it is not analogous to the velocity of the circulation of money.

But all goods undergo such a change of hands, as do all productive good-elements contained in the final product, and thus so to the final product itself, e.g., on the way from producer to wholesaler and retailer on to the household, where it is disposed of. A superficial treatment can easily make it seem that with money nothing else is involved, and that the fact of the change of hands as such contains the essence of the phenomenon.

It also follows directly that in a pure account-settling system there is no analogue for the velocity of the circulation of money. For in order to be able to "render a service" vis-a-vis goods in the period under review, the clearing unit obviously must have an individuality that outlasts the individual payment act and can be maintained as such. Therefore, it must be a unit of *money*, and somehow "embodied." Because in the account-settling system a deposit element disappears with each act of payment and a new item, just as large, is created, it makes no sense to speak of "the same" deposit element just "changing hands." This now leads to a difficulty in the treatment of bank balances. In terms of their essence, they do not embody individual units with an ongoing existence. Rather, through payment – expenditures as well as possible repayments of loans that created the deposit – each deposit is destroyed, although an equal amount can simultaneously appear with someone else. But by virtue of the bridle of money, the sum total of these balances cannot freely shift – and this bridle forces them to behave not quite as if they were made of coins, but similar to that. Therefore, it is indeed never strictly correct but practically allowable to speak by analogy with the velocity of the circulation of money, of the *velocity of the circulation of deposits*,[9] as long as one does not forget that he is using a metaphysical manner of expression. This conceptualization brings to expression the fact that by virtue of the admittedly stretchable boundary condition governing the fluctuation of deposits, the emergence of a deposit, when offset by the disappearance of a corresponding deposit, is another matter in the monetary system than the appearance of a deposit that does not correspond to the disappearance of another in the same act [uno actu].

Without committing the error mentioned above, one might choose the number of times in which a coin or, as we might add with our caveat, a deposit unit, turns over in the period of observation and calculation, thus passing in

---

[9]See H. Neisser, *Umlaufsgeschwindigkeit der Bankdepositen* [Velocity of Circulation of Bank Deposits], in *Handwörterbuch des Bankwesens* [Encyclopedia of Banking], ed. M. Palyi and P. Quittner, Berlin 1933, pp. 567-572.

payment from hand to hand, as a *measure* of the velocity of circulation.[10] The reciprocal value of this number, which of course is equal to the quotient of revenue and the money supply, obviously signifies a time variable, namely that fraction of the period under review during which the unit on average "rests" in any cash box. If one selects the observation period such that each unit of money changes hands an average of one time, then velocity of circulation disappears as an explicit factor, and turnover would be equal to the money supply or the sum of business and household cash holdings. The factor that the word velocity characterizes, then, bears on the length of that period or, with a differently selected period, on the size of the corresponding fraction of total turnover. Instead of the change of hands, one therefore can start from this fraction of turnover, the fraction, namely, the equivalent of which [is the amount] people "wish to hold as cash" [i.e., which is kept out of circulation during the course of the chosen period]. This starting point is found in Walras and Marshall and is peculiar to the entire Marshall School. It does not signify a substantive difference.[11]

Refining the Concept

3. The velocity of circulation in this sense is unfortunately the only sense that is relatively easily accessible to statistical ascertainment. In a country, for example, in which *all* transactions are done by transfer in the books, the velocity would in each case be given by the ratio of debits to the average amount of deposits.[12] But the apparent conceptual clarity of this velocity is deceptive. For

---

[10]Of course, this is then an average magnitude. In principle, nothing stands in the way of the balance of this average. Only that little is served by it, even when it is a question of variations internal to groups of vehicles of the payment process, or variations within the observation period.

[11]Cf. A.C. Pigou, "The Value of Legal Tender Money," in *Quarterly Journal of Economics* 32, 1918, p. 38, where the demonstration is also made that the *Cambridge Formula*, so called by Keynes, which exhibits just this peculiarity, is equivalent to Irving Fisher's formula, which applies in the case of hand-to-hand exchange. Cf. in this regard Keynes, *Treatise, loc. cit.*

[12]Since both variables, the debits Db and the credits Dp, are to be considered as functions of time, the rate of change in velocity would be given by the expression

$$\frac{D_p \dfrac{dD_b}{dt} - D_b \dfrac{dD_p}{dt}}{D_2^p}$$

reasons that will become only too clear to the reader, we wish to call it *tautological* velocity of *circulation,* and for the rest avoid the term velocity of circulation altogether in cases in which precision is key. The reason is that a multiplicity of factors, which, considered collectively, are completely amorphous and are therefore theoretically meaningless, are found together under this term. Basically – although statistical possibility may set limits on this in practice – the measure of the velocity must exclude changes of hands the monetary-theoretical irrelevance of which is evident, such as the mere exchange of money, handover of coins to a messenger and remittances through an intermediary, loan payments and repayments, interbank transactions. To gain a theoretically useful concept, we must go further in this direction. Within the framework of the tasks of this volume, we will not bother about the extent to which this can also take place statistically.

The point is, if we inquire into the need for such a term [i.e., the velocity of circulation of money], we see at once that it will continue to be quite unwieldy as long as sales in land, stocks, bonds, and the like, are found among transactions that our coins or deposits deal with, because their number and the variables of the accompanying sales numbers have nothing directly to do with the economic process and its variables, and from this viewpoint rather are completely indeterminate. One can easily convince himself of this if he envisions operations on a speculative market, in which the same objects, within the range of physical possibility, often can be shuffled back and forth so that, incidentally, figures for revenues and therefore, according to the conception above, for the velocity of circulation[13] arise that must completely distort the picture of money transactions in the commodities process.

If we separate out these transactions – we can then still consider them separately – we come to the concept of *trade volume,* containing the transactions that take place between the purchases of productive services by firms and the purchases of consumer goods by households, inclusive of these two. In particular, then, these are all purchases of produced means of production in the sphere of firms and all transactions between producers and retailers, and these between each other. But the phenomenon peculiar to money, which is what we are concerned with here, is not thereby ascertained, as one can already see by the fact that this figure even includes transactions in which the same exemplar of a good or the same element of a good changes hands in the same sense as the corresponding coin.

---

[13]They could easily constitute a multiple-hundredfold of the velocity of money in commodities transactions.

We must therefore exclude these transactions or at least put them to the side, in order potentially to afford them special treatment, first apart and then in their relations with the others. What remain are the transactions of the production process in the broadest sense, the transactions between the buyers of productive services through firms and the buyers of consumer goods through households, inclusive of both. But we have still not come close to ascertaining the phenomenon peculiar to money, with which we are here now dealing. Because every change of hands in the train of production processes of course contributes to the sum total of all these transactions. And one can see that this *trade volume* is not the number with which we build a bridge to the turnover-effectuating coins and balances, from the fact that it includes not only the change of hands of the same coins but also the change of hands of the same quantity of goods.

Let us imagine for a moment the viewpoint of the received theory, that the velocity of circulation is an effectual factor, namely an independent variable of the price formation process. Then in the case of the insertion of such a change of hands – for example, a combined textile company that divests a spinning mill and from that point purchases that mill's products for the weaving mill that it retains – alternatively two statements are presented: 1) the velocity of circulation is now increased, and so prices have to rise; 2) the velocity of circulation is now increased, but so is the volume of trade, so prices remain constant. But both claims are false. The first is contradicted by the fact demonstrated by the second, that, when we so define velocity of circulation, we actually must recognize that the same commodity more often faces the money, and not only that the money more often faces the commodity: thus, a possible "acceleration" of money in circulation is exactly compensated by a corresponding "acceleration" of commodity circulation. But for this reason the second claim is not correct. For, although the change of hands *as such* as little affects the market valuation of the monetary unit as does the intervention of a messenger, still, if the change of hands thereby splits the production process, it nevertheless brings with it the emergence of a new cash holding. This holding now, in order to stay in balance with everything else, must likewise itself be supplied with holdings in advance – that is, a step sooner than it itself pays out. These holdings must come in the form of coins or balances, which in the pure account-settling system would not be needed.

Our hived-off spinning mill may make exactly the same payment act that it undertook for the purposes of its spinning operation before being hived off from the combined company. We will even assume that the spinning mill holds no more cash and reserves than the combined company did *for* its spinning mill before, although usually the opposite will be the case. Nevertheless, we see that the cash and reserve requirement is now greater than before, when the independent weaving mill now has to keep extra cash and reserves for its payments to the spinning mill. We will return to this question in chapter 12 and here content ourselves with drawing out the consequence that the effect of this acceleration of the velocity of circulation in the imagined case could now be in the direction of a price reduction, the magnitude of which obviously must be a function of the significance of the split that occurred.

If we want to find a measure of the manifestation peculiar to money which is important to us, we must also omit these transactions. Then we find ourselves, on the one hand, at the turnover of the social product between households and firms, and on the other at the turnover of productive services between households and firms, and gain the concept that we should like to call the *efficiency of coins* or of the deposit unit. This efficiency is measured by the number of times in which a coin unit or deposit unit is spent by households for consumer goods during the observation period - that it renders a service *vis-a-vis the social product.*

One easily sees, *firstly*, that all of the elements foreign to our manifestation are indeed thereby isolated, the inclusion of which only led to confusion and fruitless controversies; *secondly*, that the effect of the emergence of new cash holdings - in particular, the effect of splitting the production process - is correctly reflected under our concept; *thirdly*, that, although we of course are free to construct an analogous term [viz., to efficiency of money] for goods, this term will not capture the same kind of phenomenon observable on the goods side, but something else entirely; *fourthly*, that efficiency does have a correlation with the velocity of circulation in the ordinary sense, but that this is neither given by a constant factor nor does it at all obey a simple and common law, because splits and mergers can affect the operations of the monetary sphere in the most disparate ways; and finally *fifthly*, that efficiency has that immediate relation to the far and away most important - at bottom the only important - value aggregate or goods agglomeration of the economy, the social product, a relation we must insist on because it links the market valuation of the unit of account with the objective meaning of economic activity, hence alone has deep meaning, and also does not commingle the processes of the various [separate] markets, the communications [between participants] of which are the haven of essential phenomena. Therefore, it makes no sense to counter that the application of the ordinary concept of velocity of circulation would have to lead to precisely the same results, because it evenly raises the figures for the velocity of circulation and its counterpart, the transaction volume.

The Components of the Concept

4. But now the question arises regarding this concept, as to whether we can accept the older theory that the variable corresponding to it is a given of the money process, in the sense that it does not change, or only slowly changes, and above all changes, if at all, independently of the economic situation, namely goods prices. We are not yet in a position – and will not come quite so far in this volume – to assess whether and when this assumption is practical, and allowable for specific research purposes. In strict theory the reply can only be in the negative.

This is immediately recognizable if one envisions the following case:[14] let all households increase the wages of domestic staff employed by them, without this leading to a reduction in demand for the services of domestic help, who then acquire exactly the same consumer goods with their wage growth that previously were bought by their employers, and indeed at the very same points in time. While all of this may be unlikely, it is not logically impossible. Then nothing has changed in the economic process of the area under investigation other than that some consumption goods are consumed by service personnel that previously were consumed by their employers. But the price of a consumption good, domestic service, has increased, and consequently total economic expenditure. A number of coins now appears vis-a-vis the social product, which indeed includes these services, once more than they did previously; their efficiency has increased. And that, directly as a result of a price increase. Of course, from the standpoint of those monetary theory conceptions that place value on efficiency as an independent variable, it can be said that the uncompensated price increase for the same "quantity of money" was only able to happen because efficiency increased, without which it would have been impossible. But this is no great consolation, for a determining factor for goods prices that can be changed on this basis, is obviously not an independent variable. Practically of more importance is that such cases are of limited significance. A wage increase of industrial workers, for example, as one can easily see, would not trigger this effect.

Frequency and Disposition

However, it would not be correct in general to assert that efficiency is merely a function of the economic situation and especially price movement, or that it is determined by total expenditure, which in turn would be independent of it. To satisfy the conditions here, we need to introduce a further distinction

---

[14]This case was discussed by B.M. Anderson, *The Value of Money*, 1917.

and, accordingly, two further concepts. When we hear that in some country the freight trains operate on average at a "velocity" of ten miles per hour, obviously it is not a matter of indifference for all purposes whether they really are moving slowly or they just stand around at the stations long enough to yield this result. Or, if in a country the black race represents ten percent of the population, it is not the same thing if ten percent of this population comprises pure-blooded black people or the entire population is ten percent mulatto. Similarly, it may not be difficult to see that, despite our efforts to cleanse it of all impurities, two factors are still mixed in consideration of the efficiency of coins that in theory need to be kept apart. One of these is how often those coins that are held by households and firms for the purpose of spending at the ready, thus *not hoarded nor used as "backing,"* can confront the social product if they nowhere remain any longer than required by the payment technique. The second factor is, how many of those coins are actually sent on their way and allowed to circulate. The one we call the *frequency*, the other the *disposition,* of the coin or of the deposit unit. We measure them in such a way that their product is equal to the *efficiency* of the coins. One sees that as an objectively given and independent variable in the money process, only frequency comes into consideration, and as directly dependent on the reaction of households and firms on the business situation, only disposition does, and that our distinction is meant to keep apart the elements of efficiency that are objectively given from the standpoint of individual firms and households, and those that are immediately amenable to the caprice of subjects of the payment process.

Determinants of Frequency

5. In an equilibrium state in which changes neither occur nor are expected, frequency would be equal to efficiency, while disposition would be equal to one. Cash and reserves of firms and households would, if such a condition lasted long enough, reach and pause at the level that is just sufficient to ensure the smooth execution of payments, possibly taking into consideration the exact time of the uncertainty still adhering to individual receipts, that could occur even in such a state. If we allow the conditions of this state to lapse and changes in economic conditions to occur or be expected, we would almost always observe that firms and households now spend more or less than before: that they either separate themselves from previously held cash and reserve holdings, or refrain from or restrict hitherto regularly made expenditures. Actually this is the most important lever in the mechanism of adjustment[15] of households and

---

[15]Original text: "tension" [Anspannung].

firms to changing data. But frequency, i.e., the efficiency of those coins that are spent and not withheld, does not change easily, because in the case of individual households and firms, frequency [in the equilibrium condition] is given - institutionally, i.e., as a social custom, and yet compellingly. Even "big spenders," whose payments are not "drops in the ocean" but in themselves already mean something, cannot easily change this situation. If for example a state administration goes from monthly to weekly paychecks and overcomes the technical difficulties attendant to a smooth transition, frequency would not thereby be altered. For this to happen it would rather be necessary for the recipient and those who receive payments from the recipient, to adjust their *payment schedule* accordingly.

The matter is immediately illuminated when one considers the frequency-determining aspects, such as the number of cash holdings, their relationship to each other in geographical space and in the economic process, the manner of effecting payments and thus the conditional tarrying of money in individual cash holdings, the agglomeration of payments at certain places and points in time, and the existence of fixed payment periods and their relative importance with respect to those payments that, in terms of the point in time or the amount, are not, or not accurately, predictable. All of these are givens for individual enterprises, the pressure of which they usually can escape by taking on credit - which, however, does not alter the basic situation of constraint; but which they cannot evade through measures that would change the frequency, especially those which are independent of the prevailing price trend and the quantity of available means of payment, proximately also of the volume of business. We will return to these things in chapter XII and only wish to add the following comments:

One might believe that frequency will compellingly be given shape by the rhythm of production in a unique manner. This is not so. Indeed, this rhythm is certainly one of the most important grounds of explanation for any particular existing order of markets and deadlines. But regardless of this, there exists no *necessary* relationship between this order and the production rhythm. The reasons is this: a harvest occurring once per year can be sold in daily rates, while the result of the production of strictly uniform daily quantities [of a good] can be sold once per year. And this alone [i.e., the sales pattern] is determinative.

Regarding the figure for frequency, neither the number of paydays alone nor the number of spending acts by the recipient of the paycheck alone are of importance, but they must always be considered together. If all income was paid to households once per year - as occurred with the income of the dignitaries of the Byzantine court: an "egregius" or "illustris" on New Year's Day received (besides festal garb) a sack of gold pieces from the hand of the Emperor – the frequency would remain equal to one, even if the income were spent in equal portions each weekday. The same would be the case if the income were to be paid on a daily basis but spent all at once at a single annual fair, assuming of course that the money has actually been put into the hands of the payees [i.e., the amount in circulation remains the same]. From this facts stems the rule that frequency is always equal to the lesser of the two numbers [i.e., paydays and spending acts].

6. Furthermore, it should not be overlooked that in spite of our efforts, frequency is still not uniform in the sense that we could characterize it by the evidence of *one* month. One immediately plausible ground of determining frequency passes before our eyes if we construct the simplest case as follows: a business process is exhausted in the purchase of productive services performed by firms in a market held every Saturday and the purchase of all products of those firms by households on a market held every following Monday. The process is to be thought of as strictly stationary, so that the same (and indeed the entire existing) amount of productive services is always turned over on Saturdays, and the quantity (and indeed the entire available quantity) of products (consumption goods) is always turned over on Mondays, each of them against all of the existing coins, the amount of which remains constant, and for which there is no other use. These coins, in this way, move back and forth in a strictly regular period between markets for means of production and for consumption goods. This model will later serve as a starting point. In the meantime, we note that here, frequency and its ground of determination are unproblematic, strictly uniform, and in particular independent of the other variables of the economic process. The model contains only two masses of parallel payment records, which in terms of monetary theory are mutually identical in every respect. We wish to name those masses of parallel payment records, such as, e.g., the payments of households to firms for purchased consumption goods, or those payments, not included in the model, of the producers of consumption goods to producers of intermediate goods coming earlier in the production process, etc., as payments at the same economic stage, or, in short, as *payment stages.*

We remain in principle within the circle of this aspect of market order, when we bring together the two weekly markets and allow the possibility of feeding money received in the same "markets" – in the case of our model – back again to households or firms, as the case may be. Of course, this temporal *and* spatial combination of different payment stages takes place in reverse sequence to the merging of markets of the same payment stage: while frequency is decreased by the latter – if the consumption goods market is held every two weeks, it is cut in half – it is obviously increased by the former, because the same coin can be spent on consumption goods more often, without an observer generally being able to say how often: this depends on the payment method, payment custom, business hours, and so on. At the same time, two other aspects announce themselves, which fall within the sphere of *cash management.*

If for example a firm can expect that the money that it will need to buy its weekly amount of productive services on the day of the combined market, will flow to it on the same day – in our [hypothetical] case entirely; in all real cases, partially – then it will keep ready a cash holding for the start of business, and maintain it in the course of business, such that it does not get into a state of embarrassment when spending precedes revenue. If the exact points in time are established for both, then this case is not fundamentally different from the earlier one, and in addition it only need be noted that frequency *can* now extend beyond the base case, and payment acts of both payment stages can be spread in ever smaller subquantities over the entire market day. However, if the sequence of the payment acts during the day is uncertain – which is fully compatible with stability and predictability of all economic acts – then the need arises for precaution not only for actual but also potential cash shortages, thus a cash reserve, which in the model from which we started is missing and which, when it is present, constitutes a peculiar determinant of frequency. It counteracts the frequency-increasing effect of market aggregation. It is easy to see, *first*, that it forces an increment of cash holding that, because of the actual sequence of payment acts and individual cash receipts, very often will not be used, and in the overall financial management of all cash holdings *never* will be, thus one and the same actual sequence will lead to a reduced frequency number if it is not, or not as precisely, foreseeable than when it is known from the outset by firms and households. We again encounter the fact, obviously very important to the "value of money," that that increment [in cash holdings] accompanied by constant amounts of goods and services to be sold, can be lesser the more numerous (smaller) the individual sales are, which is why it generally increases less than proportionately.

But one can see, *secondly*, that this aspect is not given as objectively as the market order and the like. The reason for this is that households and firms can respond variously to one and the same objective measure of uncertainty. It is up to individual temperament and free resolve whether to sleep peacefully or risk embarrassment. Also, the particular business situation, especially the prevailing interest rate, will have influence on the decision. However, we need to distinguish *this* kind of uncertainty, and the reaction to it of households and companies, from that insecurity and those other factors of individual resolution that result from changes in the business situation that are not, or are not exactly, predictable. Conceptually, it is also quite possible if, from all the factors determining cash management, we thus single out those uncertainties regarding the sequence of income and expenditure, and the measure of cash holding conditioned thereby, that would remain even in a strictly stationary economic process. The aspect thus singled out does indeed have special features, in particular the independence of prices, and ought in a broad sense to be accounted among the "objective" factors of efficiency, which we then also wish to do. The assessment of economic agents is simply one of the givens[16] and falls into line, like other such givens, with the error law, so that we can speak of a normal response to the range of probabilities of individual sequence possibilities in the social average.

A similar line of reasoning applies to the case in which many expenditures – of the character of pianos, cars, and so on – are only repeated over longer periods, hence for example, to keep to our scheme, not every week, but every year. Again, the form and manner of provision is initially a matter of personal habit – some make provision through equal installments, others by supranormal withholding in the weeks immediately preceding the purchase – and occurring or expected economic fluctuations will also play a role. But even here we can stress a normal provision, as would be found in a stationarily continuing economic process, as a special aspect. The existence of such an expenditure is frequency-reducing even if sales of these goods, taking all consumers into consideration, is continuous and uniform day by day. Moreover, the case is recommended as an example for practice, as is its combination with the aspect of uncertainty and often existing freedom of choice with respect to the timing of payment.

The spatial and temporal consolidation of payments of variously oriented payment stages finally inaugurates the field of possibilities of compensation and clearing. To the degree that a *clearing institution* eliminates the uncertainty of the sequence of income and expenditure within the clearing period, there is only a rate increase and nothing really new. But insofar as it comes to the amount at which income and expenditure for individual firms are equalized over the clearing period, without use being made of coins or checks at all, then

---

[16]The reader will find that all these distinctions are complicated and difficult. That they are. But the yet existing confusion within the ambit of the concept of velocity of circulation, which almost never is completely overcome, makes it often appear desirable to emphasize the object in full clarity, even at the risk of appearing to engage in unnecessary and cumbersome "overanalysis."

obviously no increase in efficiency in the strict sense exists, but only a settling of claims without coins or balances, which coins and balances in turn only confront the leftover balance. From the standpoint of the real value of this balance, one might rather speak of an increase in units of money, or, from the standpoint of the cleared amount, of the creation of units of means of payment. In any case, here our notion of the social account-settling system becomes immediate reality, and the role of money becomes restricted to its basic function, fixing the unit of account. But we nevertheless would also like to extend the concept of frequency to this process also, whenever it is convenient, by analogy, and with the help of the notion of an en masse direct handover [brevi manu traditio] taking place. We can point out that even this variety of frequency is a matter of market order and payment technique and in each case is "given." Moreover, we shall assume that, except in the case of the personal consumption of (especially rural) producers, this actual clearing – by contrast with our theoretical construct, in which clearing is the strict general case – has no considerable scope in goods traffic, so that we only have to take it into account in trading on the stock market (under the name "obviation"). Note that this applies only to the transactions of households and firms. Within individual banks and between banks, further clearing acts take place that in turn reduce the need for the *"higher order" money* of bank reserves, and these of course cannot be neglected. But that happens in another sphere and does not affect the financial management of households and firms themselves, but only the type and quantity of "money" that they use.

Disposition

7. As many reasons as an analyst, compelled by reason of monetary matters, might have to mistrust the aspect of the velocity of circulation – that venerable article of faith in the apparatus of monetary theory – and even its most dependable element, frequency – just as well, comparatively, does frequency fare in the fire of modern criticism, as we have seen. We wish to make use of it and in particular allow it (multiplied by the disposition of *one*) to co-determine the critical number: when, for example, a specific quantity of a commodity is furnished with the price of one – i.e., when a commodity is chosen to be commodity money – then we know the critical number, which is the consequence of this choice, only when we know the frequency, and we thus know the manner in which firms and households handle this money if they want to do nothing more than complete their payments under the given market order and payment technique, and foresee nothing but an infinite scrolling of the same processes always succeeding each other. In general, frequency may here also be regarded as an

independent variable, and for shorter periods as a constant, of the money problem. Where it ceases to be so, we speak of *degeneration of the currency*.

However, the *disposition* of the cash unit is a matter of the free choice of
each firm and each individual household, which *can* behave the same in this
respect – and often actually do behave the same way, which leads to peculiar
phenomena – but never *have* to. While the aspects that we summarize under the
name of market order, payment technique, etc., are given to households and
firms in each case, and while furthermore in each case it is also established how
much cash they must hold in an uncertain succession of income and expenditure
to avoid embarrassments of a certain probability value, it is not predetermined
how much they wish to spend of their money amounts not bound by commit-
ments, and depends only on them and their expectations regarding future decisions based on business conditions. The term "disposition *of* the cash unit" here
has a special meaning, not the ordinary meaning that the phrase "disposition
over cash units" expresses. Of course, the caprice of firms and households is not
absolute: existing obligations ensure this, but the requirements of the ongoing
production processes and the necessities of life do so as well, which especially
in the mass of small incomes sets narrow limits to deviations from a disposition
equal to one. Yet here we have a substantial field of choice before us, equally
important in terms of monetary theory and monetary policy, in which only individual economic deliberation prevails.

8. We return to our weekly markets. The frequency there is thus equal to
52. Note that for the magnitude of the monetary expression of demand for consumer goods in equilibrium, only this figure is important, and any – now excluded from our conditions – change of hands of gold pieces between firms will
have no effect on this monetary expression or, if you will, only have effect insofar as they can influence this frequency. Now an event takes place that makes
everyone wish to be "liquid." If, for example, this event occurs on a Sunday,
households on Monday will not spend the entire number of coins they received
on the previous Saturday from firms, as beforehand, but fewer. This has its limits because it means – with a restriction immediately to be mentioned – a disturbance of household operation, and for many households it may even be impossible. But as far as this change in disposition occurs, it will have the effect of
either a part of the weekly national product remaining unsold, or consumer
prices falling. In practice, both will usually occur. In any case, firms receive fewer
gold pieces than on previous Mondays, so that they have fewer gold pieces to
spend on means of production on the following Saturday than they had on preceding Saturdays. They also are under the influence of the mentioned event, and
in practice can satisfy their desire for "liquidity" usually much more fully than

households can – they can in the limiting case adjust their operations – so that now the quantities or prices of sold production services, or both, in turn decline, etc. This *process of shrinkage*, which will yet occupy us, otherwise has no other theoretical limit than the sales sum of zero. The reader is likewise cautioned that the approach to this limit does not *necessarily, in terms of thought*, need to disturb the economic process and that it is a good exercise to work out the conditions under which this would not occur.

Surely we describe this case – and mutatis mutandis, the same is true of the opposite case, the best example of which is a bout of inflation fears – in a manner more true to life when we say that progressively *fewer* gold pieces go on their way, as when we say that an unchanged number of gold pieces go ever "more slowly" on their way. Let us limit the observation period to two weeks. If households spend only half of their income from the previous Saturday on the Monday on which we begin then, firms on the next Saturday only half of what they received, i.e., only a quarter of the usual amount hitherto, and then households on the second Monday again withhold one-half of their cash balance, thus one-eighth of the amount that used regularly to be spent, to receive back only one-sixteenth on the second Saturday, then obviously half of the "circulating money supply" for these two weeks has an efficiency of zero, three-eighths has an efficiency of one, one-eighth has an efficiency of two. But although the entire quantity – which both before and after continues to be devoted to expenditure *and is not "hoarded"* – has a frequency of two over this fourteen-day period, one-eighth has the disposition of one, one-half the disposition zero, and three-eighths the disposition of one-half. Of the figures for the efficiencies of the coins, an average efficiency can be gained, while from the figures for their dispositions a mean disposition can be gained which is necessary for some purposes, useful for others. But already our figures are themselves average magnitudes: essentially it is not true, e.g., that those three-eighths in our observation period have the disposition of one-half: rather, in the first week they have a disposition equal to one, in the second a disposition equal to zero – all the cash held for specific outlays experience, at a constant frequency, a progressively decreasing disposition, or, as we also mean, an increasing *under-disposition*. With depictions and interpretation of average magnitudes, which can easily distort the true situation, one must be careful here as elsewhere.

In the opposite case we speak of *over-disposition*. In our model there is no room for it, which is very instructive because it warns us not to exaggerate the scope of the aspect of disposition. However, over-disposition can always ensue when cash on hand is held as a precaution against the uncertainty of payment or for future major or unforeseen payments. But one must not confuse this with the behavior that could be referred to also, and which is in fact referred to in customary usage, as "over-disposition," signifying namely the overdrawing of accounts, the taking up of credit, thus the increase in means of payment and not the increase in the disposition of existing units. It is also a requirement of conceptual clarity to distinguish under- and over-disposition from mere *displacement* and *diversion operations*, that is, the case in which an amount is spent in the same market in a manner different than originally intended – e.g., buying a car instead of a horse and carriage. We must also distinguish it from the case in which it feeds into a different market than the one for which it was earmarked and to which it was hitherto regularly directed – e.g., the purchase of shares instead of labor services – although such phenomena can occasionally become confused with under- and over-disposition. Finally it should be noted that a general tendency to over-disposition is an essential vehicle for the degeneration of a currency.

That disposition is independent vis-a-vis frequency, and that it is worth the effort to distinguish between the two, one can also see from the fact that disposition, as opposed to frequency, has an analogue in the world of goods. It is obvious that as soon as we take changes in business conditions and, in particular, expectations of these changes, into consideration, the phenomenon must occur that producers and distributors force sales of inventories or "withhold goods." This can coincide with the corresponding, but also the contrary tendency of buyers, but it is significant in each case in terms of monetary theory and monetary policy, which is why we also wish to speak of the *"disposition of goods."*

Chapter XI
The Theory of the Price Level

1. From our analysis of the essence of money, there also follows a theory of the price level and its measurement, which is set out in this chapter. In doing so, we conveniently tie in with the method of price index numbers, which, however, we do not propose to consider in all its aspects.[1] The point which alone concerns us here can be introduced as follows:

The Theory of the Price Index

When I survey the changes of the price of a commodity during the course of a historical period, I can facilitate the understanding of the series obtained [by such a survey] by expressing the successive price quotations in percentages of one of those prices, e.g., the first, or an average of several of them. I can attain the same purpose even better by using a chart [graphisch]. Should I wish to gain an overview of the historical changes in the prices of several commodities, it is natural to wonder whether I should not go even further to facilitate the understanding of the material, and somehow combine different series into a single one. This alone is initially what the method of price index numbers[2] is to accomplish. The *price index* to that degree is an average of the terms of the price series of individual commodities corresponding to each other over time. One can also

---

[1] In the text the attempt is made to state the minimum of what is necessary to help the reader to follow, who is unused to statistical methods in general or to the method of index numbers in particular. However, it is not possible to go as far as would be desirable. We therefore refer to the standard work on the subject: Irving Fisher, *The Making of Index Numbers,* 2nd ed., Boston and New York, 1923. The other authors important to us: Jevons, Edgeworth, Marshall, Lehr, Laspeyres, Mitchell, A.A. Young, Bowley, v. Bortkiewicz.

[2] See, e.g., the definition of Y.F. Edgeworth, "The Plurality of Index Numbers," in *The Economic Journal,* September 1925, pp. 379 f. and A.L. Bowley ("Notes on Index Numbers," *ibid,* June 1928, p. 216). The translation "Preismeßziffern" [price measuring numbers] is not good – after all, it includes a *petitio principia* [because price is already a measure].

leave this unchanged and undertake the operation of the transfer to percentage terms first from its average. In both cases, a decision regarding the type of average to be selected should be taken, hence whether to use the arithmetic mean, geometric mean, harmonic mean, the median or the most frequent value, and a second decision taken for each case in turn regarding whether all individual prices shall have the same influence on the index (unweighted average) or whether we shall have them participate in its formation with different weights (weighted average). But there is a third type of index number. Instead of combining individual prices, one can make value variables with a specific economic meaning, especially sums of products from prices and quantities of individual commodities, and the index can be expressed in terms of how these sums change under the influence of varying prices. In all three cases, finally, either the same basis can be maintained or the index of each point in time can be calculated from the respective preceding point in time as basis (*chain method*).

Of the infinite number of possible ways to form a price index, three are to be mentioned. The reasons for this preference will of themselves become clear later. If one multiplies all the terms of the series of individual prices with those of the amounts of the corresponding commodities that were sold in the base period, we obtain the index formula proposed by Laspeyres. This index in each case thus informs us of the amount of money that would be needed under prevailing prices to buy the goods combinations actually purchased in the base period. But if, by contrast, one compares the amount of money actually spent on the goods in question in any other than the base period with the sum of money that would have been required to buy the same quantity of these goods in the base period at the prices that actually prevailed, we get Paasche's formula. If, finally, one forms the geometric mean from the formulas of Laspeyres and Paasche, we have Irving Fisher's *ideal formula*.

Now the question arises as to what such an index actually means. From the standpoint of numerous special purposes, the answer appears to lie close enough to hand. If, for example, an industry manufactures numerous articles and qualities of articles, the prices of which vary in different ways, we would obviously gain something worth knowing from such an index number regarding changes experienced in this industry. Then if the movement of this index number is compared to one similarly constructed expressing the change in the prices of those goods that this industry procures, then we would have a measure of what in the case of agriculture is wont to be called the agricultural scissors [Agrarschere]. Similarly, one can construct index numbers of import or export prices - and since the war, everyone has become familiar with the essence and use of an index of workers' cost of living. In all such cases it is at least readily apparent which goods prices are to be included in the index and what weight they are to have. Of course, the meaning of such indices is also only immediately given if the significance of each commodity remains unchanged in the combination in question. To the degree that this is not the case, difficulties of no merely technical nature arise. But very often the quantity combinations remain almost unchanged over a considerable period of time, so that index numbers maintain an approximate value and the uncertainty of the theoretical basis is little felt. But indices of this type are not of any further interest to us here.

Problems Attaching to the Price Index

2. This general index finds extensive applications in the most varied fields, not only of monetary theory but also of general theory, macroeconomic doctrine [Konjunkturlehre], and practical applications. One observes its behavior in recovery and stagnation, with it one "corrects" all sorts of monetary variables, in particular sales totals, to unveil the "real" meaning of their changes, etc. Obviously an idea of its meaning must underlie all of this, but the entire mass of literature that has developed around the questions regarding its construction for the most part slur over this fundamental issue, with such expressions as, e.g., the general index should capture the "general slope" (Irving Fisher) of price movements, the common movement or what is common to the movement, to put us in a position to eliminate this element. That does not mean much. Of the authors who nevertheless rise above this uncritical attitude – Jevons is one such notable exception – several of the most important, especially Knut Wicksell, Mises, Haberler, have raised fundamental doubts about the meaning and value of the general index and operations with it.

Apart from these authors, who came to basically negative results, one might almost say that the various index formulas provide a measurement method without knowing what one wishes to measure. Of course, apart from allowances for computational convenience and considerations derived from the theory of the measurement of collective objects, other factors also play a role. Against the background of the mentioned notion of what the index is to provide, some results seem plausible, others absurd, and even from the start, individual laborers in the field have concocted criteria to be met by their formulas, at first quite unsystematically and mostly without any deeper grounds. The more the supply of formulas has grown and the discussion regarding their differences, advantages, and shortcomings has developed, the clearer has become the peculiar lack of persuasiveness of the arguments, in particular for those arguments and against the particular means and the individual rules for apportioning weightings. Precisely the clarity that gradually spread across many individual points implied[3] the fact that, regarding the basic question, one had not gotten any further.

For this reason, Von Bortkiewicz characterized as great progress the contemporary attempt "to arrange the individual criteria and to balance them against each other, in order to use them, in accordance with the measure of significance one attaches to them, to judge competing price index formulas," as Irving Fisher has done in the finest style. Even this method is the embodiment of theoretical indecision; and this is much more the case with the effort to combine or "cross" or "rectify," on the basis of gained criteria, different formulas in order to come to compromise formulas that meet as many, or as important, criteria as possible – a procedure that completely devalues those formulas that are based on approaches to clear problems, and only makes sense if the formulas to be merged can be considered as equal, or equally unequal, and their deviating results can be considered from the point of view of flaws. But at the same time, both signify the completion of a purely statistical treatment of the matter and thus also a bridge to economic theory. While we will be interested in the rectification procedure only at a later point, we need to enumerate the most important criteria here, because it will be of interest to determine to what extent the result of our own analysis corresponds to them, in particular whether the objections thereto do something to mend the fact that many of them do not correspond.

We follow Von Bortkiewicz, and in doing so wish to keep in mind, as decisive viewpoint, that the index is to measure the combined movement of consumer prices or what is common to the movement of prices of consumer goods. Bortkiewiecz puts

a) the identity criterion at the head, the requirement that the index remain constant at 1 or 100 if all prices taken into consideration remain the same. Even if this is met, it does not yet mean that

b) the proportionality criterion has been satisfied, the requirement that if all prices rise or fall at the same rate, the index rises or falls in the same proportion. Even more illuminating is

c) the criterion of the independence of the index from the units used in its calculation, including, for example, whether one calculates quantities of goods by the ton or the hundredweight. Likewise

d) the start and stop criterion, which says that the index should not change when a commodity is inserted into it or when a commodity is omitted

---

[3]Original text: "stated" [stellte].

from its matter, the ratio price of which shows the same change as itself. While the above-mentioned criteria are, in the practice of the construction of index numbers, often breached but in principle are not lightly disputed, this does not apply to

e) the sensitivity criterion, which requires that the index basically react to any change in a price ratio. But from the point of view indicated above, it is to be accepted: only from the movements of *all* prices can what is "common" to them be developed. It distorts the picture when one, as with the application of the median, deprives the extreme cases of their influence.

Isolating the Measurable Core Component

3. The task that we have to solve now is to investigate *whether* – let's say up front: to show *that* – the common element in the movements of individual prices has a more than mere statistical existence, is more than the average percentage change in individual prices, namely, is a conceptually distinguishable and factually effective factor. Only by theoretically conceptualizing this common element can one decide whether it involves a "measure" in the strict sense, or, as Edgeworth opined, whether it rather involves a number charged with displaying changes in the factor without being able to measure the factor itself. Finally, a measurement method in accordance with the factor can only be derived from the theory of the factor, which then is no longer one of many that would qualify simply because of their practical advantages or shortcomings, but has the claim to be called "right," entirely independently of the very important but logically subordinate question as to how it stands vis-a-vis the present state of our mastery of the facts with their practical application.

We have seen that the economic process of itself can only determine the ratios of prices to one another, not absolute prices. To determine *those,* it requires a factor that we have called the *critical number.* The money method, which makes use of practical life to create a critical number, subjects all monetary economic variables, initially prices, to a new condition, itself foreign to the logic of the economic process - the *money tie.* This money tie follows its own law appropriate to the chosen sort of money method, to which all prices constantly have to adapt by actual or potential changes, which would not happen without the pressure exerted by the money tie. So here we have a real factor before us, a logically separable element of the historical change of absolute - fundamentally, all absolute - prices. Therein lies the importance of the distinction between the embodiment of the ratios of prices to each other, which we will call the *price system,* and the embodiment of all absolute prices, which besides this also contains the *price level,* which in equilibrium can be read in any arbitrary individual price.

The price *system* of commodity 1 to n is obviously not given by a single digit, but only by an expression of the form $p_1: p_2: p_3 \ldots : p_n$. Whatever in the economic process occurs or acts upon it, changes it; and through its changes, the economy adapts to the needs of each new situation. To eliminate them, i.e., to wish to keep the price system constant, would be to paralyze the organ of adaptation, and would in principle[4] be senseless both as an ideal and as a practical undertaking – although under the ideal of *constant purchasing power* practical life sometimes understands and pursues precisely the constancy of individual prices or groups of prices. Just as senseless, and not merely impossible, is the general task of measuring changes in the price system.

By contrast, it follows directly from the essence of the price level, that its change *fundamentally* must be amenable to numerical expression. This can easily be seen if one imagines only the price level changing while the price system remains unchanged, so that all prices fall or rise proportionally. However, since this has to do with a special real "level-force" [Niveaukraft] that operates not only in this case, but always on all prices whatever else happens, and though in individual cases it may be completely overshadowed by other influences, it also holds when the price system changes at the same time [as the price level]; therefore, each absolute price is the result of several factors. Thus our task is reduced to the question as to whether in these cases the effect of the level-force, the pure change in the price level, can be *statistically* removed.

But this theory is exposed to so many misunderstandings and requires so much clarification that the remainder of this section will be dedicated to its explanation.

A. First, note that a general index, which is defined with respect to the showcased concept of the price level, and expresses this numerically, in its essence is not a statistical mean, even if it should be represented by such, approximately or exactly, or calculated by averaging. It is no average of some other variables that exist independently, but is the measure of a peculiar variable that has a separate existence of its own. Any theory of the index that makes averaging to be its essence is fundamentally misconceived. The general principles of col-

---

[4] It is of course something else when, in particular cases, the aim is to mitigate especially violent revolutions of the price system or especially violent fluctuations of individual prices.

lective measures [Kollektivmaßregel] and considerations of a probabilistic nature are not at all applicable to our problem. If one can characterize the length of the leaves of a tree by their arithmetic average and a measure of variation, it is only because the leaves have a normal length, and the actual deviations from that may be treated according to the scheme of observation errors. Obviously, neither the prices of different goods themselves nor their changes correspond to this scheme. They form a system, and any change in one of them affects the others, whereby it fails to meet the requirement of independence and randomness of "deviations" from the norm. The leaves of the tree form no system, and a deviation of one of them does not lead to the deviation of another. Certainly, this consideration does not completely invalidate the results of labors that contain probabilistic elements. Because in the absence of antecedent knowledge of the nature of a "universe," one can at least make the attempt "to see how far you get with it," especially if one uses very many individual series and treats the changes in the price system as random in relation to changes in the price level.

B. Obviously, the general index is not a price index. Whether it nevertheless might make sense to treat it similarly for some purposes will be discussed later. For the time being we only note that it makes no intuitive [unmittelbaren] sense to refer to it as the measure of the purchasing power of money or the value of money, as so often happens. This is only harmless if it does not say anything, i.e., when one defines the value of money by means of the general index, however constructed. Otherwise, such as when this expression purportedly says something about its essence or indicates a program for its application, it asserts something misleading if not downright false. In that case, the value of money can mean nothing else than exchange value of money, indeed, what the older theory characterized as "external" exchange value. Now from the standpoint of our analysis of the phenomenon of money, it is already incorrect to apply the concept of exchange value at all to money, because only a good can have exchange value, and money in terms of its essence is not a good. But apart from that, as much exchange value should accrue to money, and hence as much money value should exist, as there are purchases of commodities in the area under review. And any summation of this money value in a number would destroy its meaning, rather than convey that meaning to this numerical expression.

There is no "internal" exchange value ("intrinsic value") at all that the general index could measure. This concept originating in popular conceptions or, if you will, Aristotelian sources, is unsustainable even for commodities. But even if by this expression one understands, mitigating its inappropriate basic meaning, nothing more than the sum of those determinants of absolute prices that affect the "money side" as opposed to the "commodities side" of the price formation process, it cannot be said that the general index measures the effect of these determinants or the internal exchange value in this sense. Instead, changes that we first perceive in goods act on it just as do changes that initially are statistically visible in the monetary sphere. The proper motion of the monetary sphere is expressed, strictly speaking, only in the *changes of the critical number.* But this would only exercise a clearly determined influence on prices in a state of equilibrium. In any other case, we could only speak of a *potential* influence of the money tie, of which it would be quite uncertain how far it really makes its appearance. *If one counts among the determinants stemming from the money side the behavior of households, firms, and banks in relation to balances and legal money, and if we come to the same agreement as with the definition of the critical number, we can consider the actual consumption expenditure of the period under review to be a measure of the influence exercised from the money side.* Only monetary determinants in *this* sense can be the *immediate* causes of their change – they or any other value variables of a similar nature, as for example the income sum, are primarily monetary phenomena and gain "real" meaning only in conjunction with other facts. Of course, this does not mean, for instance, that these monetary determinants could not in turn be induced on their part by the "commodity side." On the contrary, this is the rule – which is why in our analysis of money we have set so much store on commerce being able to loosen the bridle of money strapped to it, as it brings more or less means of payment into circulation *within* the room for maneuver that this bridle allows. An expansion of bank credit is usually the immediate cause of an increase in consumer spending. But it can – and in practice it usually *will* – be occasioned by an expansion of production, either prior to it or financed by it.

    C. The reader sees clearly that the distinction between the "money side" and the "goods side" of economic variables has its difficulties that can be solved in part, but not completely, by incisive formulation. He will be inclined to believe that the situation is not much better for our distinction between price system and price level. That, however, would be a mistake. Price system and price level, as we saw, describe different *things,* and no ambiguity attaches to their conceptual separation. Nothing more is claimed for it. In particular, we do not claim that monetary aspects only affect the price level while goods aspects only affect the price system, and absolutely not that the price system and the price level change when, as factually independent processes, they [somehow] cross paths. Instead, changes in price level, price system, and product combination are so interwoven that in practice they almost never occur except in mutual interaction, and when we trace a change in one of them we almost always come across changes in the other two. A change in the quantity of one good or in the quantities of several goods, for example, in practice will almost always result in a change in absolute prices that at the same time signifies a change in the price level. In fact, a change in the price level is practically inconceivable other than as a result of changes in quantities of goods or in the price system, or both, apart from which it can only be portrayed by means of a thought experiment.

Even such a typical monetary phenomenon as an increase in government paper money does not directly affect the price system as a whole, but only certain groups of prices, and the price level only in that way - usually also via changes in the quantities of commodities. The issuing authority aims to procure goods, and deploys with the newly printed notes a demand for certain goods and services. Therefore it only intervenes in some prices, not in all prices evenly, and only serves its purpose by doing this, thus by shifting the price system, and virtually almost always the combination of goods as well. To push the changes of these two into the background as "transitional phenomena" on the way to a new price level, does not work because they are no less important and can be as permanent as the change in the price level. Usually the economic body emerges from such transitions in a different form, and this altered shape determines the new price level precisely as does the issue of paper money in itself. Not to have taken this into account is one of the charges that justly may be levied against the more primitive versions of the *quantity theory*. In reaction to this, many analysts' tendency is - and it is not an unjustified - to now, in turn, push the changes in the price level into the background and to consider as essential the changes in the *diffusion of prices*, especially the shift in the relationship between groups of prices - e.g., consumption prices and prices of means of production.[5]

However, all of this changes nothing regarding the possibility and the value of the distinction between the price level and price system. Too, a change in the goods combination without a change in the price system could only happen as a result of a very unlikely coincidence, and vice versa. This obviously does not prevent us from recognizing these two processes as being different, and conceptually to be distinguished. On the basis of our analysis, as soon as we have identified the price level as a special fact in the same sense, we can distinguish it from the price system, just as we can do with the goods combination. To that end we construct the following mental scheme: if, for example, the quantity of

---

[5]With some authors, this tendency converges with a skeptical attitude towards the concept of price level. Characteristic in this respect is the presentation of Friedrich August von Hayek, *Preise und Produktion* [Prices and Production], Vienna 1931. Quite naturally, it is much easier to follow that tendency if one has other reasons to doubt the meaning and value of the construction of a general index.

a commodity changes for any reason, then its absolute price always changes as well; and not only its price alone, but also, and likewise always, the absolute price of each good in the area of investigation under consideration. In temporal and factual combination with this, the monetary and credit sphere reacts somehow, yet *nothing guarantees that it responds such* that the price level remains constant. In general, i.e., apart from a very unlikely coincidence, this also changes in the same combination. That means that the actual change in all absolute prices at the same time is a change in the price system and the price level. This one and indivisible operation, that sets prices in a new relationship to one another and at the same time subjects all to the - new or unchanged - money tie, we now mentally split into two steps by imagining, *first,* the new price system implemented at an unchanged price level, and *second,* the new price level implemented through a proportional increase or decrease of these new absolute prices. This construction naturally only gains practical value when the two components into which we dissect the observed price changes can also be separated statistically, which obviously depends on whether and under what conditions it makes sense to speak of changes in the price system at a constant price level.

Indeed, *statistical* sense. Because *conceptually* the matter is exhausted with the knowledge that the money tie signifies a special condition to which monetary economic variables are subject and which compels sui generis ongoing adjustments. We would therefore view a cash method that necessitates no such adjustments in prices, thus that works in such a way that the price level remains constant, as a characteristic of *neutral money.*[6]

D. Finally, one need not ascribe to the general index any such direct relation to the analysis of economic *welfare,* as so often happens.[7] In principle, such a relationship suggests itself immediately enough, and it has much to do with the interest that many take in the index method. It was the desire for a scale by which to assess the relationship between creditor and debtor, or changes in the economic situation of the working class or some other class, that led up

---

[6]With this, nothing is said either regarding the possibility of such a money method nor regarding its possible advantages and disadvantages. By this term, which to my knowledge stems from Wicksell, something else can also be understood. See also Johan G. Koopmans, "Zum Problem des 'neutralen' Geldes" [On the Problem of "Neutral" Money], in *Beiträge zur Geldtheorie* [Contributions to Monetary Theory], ed. by F. A. Hayek, Vienna 1933, pp. 211 ff.

[7]Typical of this is the statement in Edgeworth's treatise, *The Plurality of Index Numbers, loc. cit.,* pp. 379 ff.

to it [i.e., the index method].[8] But if we formulate the problem of this starting point as the problem of establishing the changes in the relationship between "money income" and "real income,"[9] we have already taken the first step on a path that takes us entirely away from our goal, although it leads to another meaningful one. If one asks about real income, one steps initially onto the bridge to its welfare significance [for the] individual income recipient, which obviously does not depend on the price movement generally, but on the price movement of precisely those goods that he, precisely, bought. When one is considering this issue, changes in the price system are just as relevant as changes in the price level in our sense, in fact, the change of a single price can change *this "price level for somebody"* or the *"subjective price level."*

At the same time, the thought[10] presents itself of overcoming the difficulty for any index calculation – even ours – that lies in the change in the combination of goods, simply by the relationship of the goods combination of real income to the satisfaction of needs of the recipient. One then defines two real incomes as equal (of equal value), when the recipient, if he has the choice between them, prefers neither one of the two over the other. If such a real income costs more or less at time B than at time A, the subjective price level has increased or decreased. If *the same* – not the equivalent – goods combination that was actually purchased at time A, costs twice as much at time B than it cost at time A, then the subjective price level has *at most* risen by double, *"at most"* because an *equivalent* combination possibly can be had for less while, given unchanged tastes, every more expensive combination must be more than equivalent. Of course, nothing is said thereby about how much this price level has

---

[8]Bishop William Fleetwood, *Chronicon Preciosum or An Account of English Gold and Silver Money* ... London 1707 and 1745, deals with a question from the field of cost of living; see the just-quoted treatise by Edgeworth.

[9]This has been done by Wieser, but without specifying a measurement method for real income. But he hardly had any intention to head in the direction in which many of his followers have headed. Instead, from this conceptual pair, this term leads on a path to the objective price level.

[10]Its introduction and development is owed to Gottfried von Haberler. See his book *Der Sinn der Indexzahlen* [The Meaning of Index Numbers], Tübingen, 1927, as well as the discussion by Hans Neisser, "Der volkswirtschaftliche Geldwert und die Preisindexziffern" [The Economic Value of Money and Price Index Numbers], in *Weltwirtschaftliches Archiv* [World Economic Archive], 29, 1, 1929, and 30, 1, 1930, and with Carl Snyder, "The Index of a General Price Level," in *Quarterly Journal of Economics* 42, 1928, pp. 701 ff.

risen, but it may be assumed in general that, if the cost of the combination actually purchased at time B shows another relationship to the amount at which
this combination was available at time A, this relationship forms the lower limit
of the subjective price level. If the combinations are very different, for example,
if the individual inherited a million marks between time A and time B, it may
happen that "his" price level from the standpoint of time A has increased and
from the standpoint of time B has decreased, just as generally a plethora of remarks could be made regarding this ingenious construction.

But surely it follows that from this point of view and in this sense, a
national economic price level cannot exist at all, or can only exist as the average
of real individual, possibly aggregate, price levels. Only this has nothing whatsoever to do with our problem, and when the term price level should become
commonplace for both things, then we would have to register an increment in
the sources of misunderstandings in this category, which flow so abundantly in
our area. The question as to whether our concept could have a place in the area
of problems of "creditor and debtor" and the like, will be touched on later. In
the meantime, it should be noted that an index of the type just discussed is more
closely related to the *cost of living index* than what we have called the *general
index*

How to Measure this Core Component

4. In possession of the knowledge that the common characteristic in the
temporal changes of commodity prices, which every diagram shows, really corresponds to a specific element of the price formation process, to wit, the change
in the *economy-wide price level* that we defined, we now return to our task. It is
a matter of specifying a method by means of which we can also statistically
separately represent this element or, what is here the same thing, measure it.

To this end, we tie in with the statement: the level of prices of these
goods, if the goods combination is (statistically) given on which a certain
amount is actually spent, is then clearly determined, whatever the price system
may be. This statement follows directly from our theory of the critical number.
From this it follows that a change in the price system, given a constant combination of goods *and total expenditure on these goods*, would *not* change the price
level, and furthermore, that any change in total expenditure given a constant
goods combination would change the price level proportionally.

Regarding the first of these claims, which needs no proof, we only note
that it does not mean, of course, that a change in the price system has no
influence on the price level, but only that such an influence can be exerted only

over and through a change in total expenditure. The second assertion may be in need of proof: if new absolute prices arise with an unchanged goods combination but changed total expenditure and a changed price system, it is always possible to replace these new prices with others that relate to each other in the same ratio, thus that form the same (new) price system, but exhibit the old total expenditure, hence by virtue of the statement from which we started, the old price level. This can occur by proportional increase or decrease of all new prices, consequently by mere price level changes. Thus, the occurred change in total output has only affected the price level, and indeed has affected it proportionally to itself. Incidentally, the statistical meaning of a change in the price system without any change in the price level is also defined thereby.

This is no longer so when, besides total expenditure and the price system, the goods combination also changes, which is not only virtually unavoidable but also is the theoretical base case because, as we know, these three things are but different aspects of the same process of change. Any change in the combination of goods also exerts a direct influence on the price level. And this influence is even exercised if the amount of a single commodity is changed,[11] a fact which it is not superfluous to emphasize, since one might be inclined to think that what happens to a single commodity can only act on the price system. This influence on the price level appears to act in the opposite direction from that exerted by changes in total expenditure: each increase of a quantity of goods acts as down-

---

[11]If this assertion is not immediately apparent, one may convince himself of its accuracy by starting from the case of an increase or decrease of all commodities, whereby the result on *all* prices of the pressure stemming from this change is clear, and then proceed, by setting all changes but one to zero - which does not change the logic of the matter - from this case to the case of a change in the quantity of merely *one* commodity. Of course this is no rigorous proof. Such a proof can be adduced in the following manner. Even when expenditure, price system, *and* goods combination change, and accordingly form new absolute prices, these latter can, just as in the case of a constant goods combination, be adjusted to the old total expenditure by mere price *level* changes. Were our assertion incorrect, this reestablished total expenditure would correspond to the old price level, just as in that case. Now, if the increase in quantity did not influence the price level, it would mean that the old goods contained in the new goods combination in themselves alone also would show that same old price level, although with a smaller sum spent on it than originally was spent. Consequently, the opposite of our assertion leads to a contradiction with a statement already recognized to be true. Consequently, it cannot be true. Consequently, our claim is true.

ward pressure, each decrease as a lift on the price level. Of course, this has nothing whatsoever to do with the decrease or increase of any marginal utility or with the demand elasticity of the commodities in question – a point about which the beginner should be careful to be clear.

This effect of a change in the quantity of each individual commodity is completely independent of the behavior of other commodities – it may thus be overshadowed, amplified, compensated thereby, but in any case it is quite as real and as strong as it would be if it took place alone: the effect considered here is not like the effect of the change of a quantity of goods on utility variables or individual prices, where the effect of the individual change itself is fundamentally different depending on whether the quantities of other commodities also change or not. The effects exerted by the changes in quantity of individual commodities on the price level are instead *algebraic,* i.e., taking into account the sign, *additive* – if we can find a measure of each effect, the total effect is given by the algebraic addition of these metrics. Likewise with the ratio between the thus-defined net effect of the quantity changes on the price level and the effect of the change in expenditure. The two are independent of each other and indeed are independent in the same sense as the effects of the quantity changes of the individual commodities. They are therefore to be combined on the same principle, except that it now of course involves algebraic subtraction. We can still say, e.g., that a quantity increase "absorbs" a simultaneous increase in expenditure or "prevents" it in its effect, but we must never forget that strictly speaking this is incorrect.

The possibility statistically to peel out and measure the change in the price level depends on whether we are given the measures of change in expenditure and in the combination of goods, each on its own. Their difference is a measure of their resultant, the "effective level-force," one might say, that both determines and measures[12] the change in the price level.[13] Rather than speak of this difference, we can instead make the following equivalent formulation: the measure of the change in expenditure is equal to the *sum* of the (sought) measure

---

[12]Usually a "force" is measured by its effect, not vice versa. But if one gains a measure of a force from the numerical values of its components (which, as we see, are measured by their effect, namely the effect they would have if they worked alone), then the reverse process is also possible.

[13]Again it should be emphasized that this formula does not recognize the deeper objective determinants of the price level, but only certain arithmetic surface relationships, below which play the economic relationships, which are far more complicated and cannot be represented by simple causal facts.

of the change in the price level and the measure of the change in the goods combination. In this form, an aspect of our task takes on greater clarity. We can also say that it has to do with dividing the statistically fundamental, although practically not immediately given, positive or negative growth in expenditure into a part that is absorbed by the change in the goods combination and a second part that affects the *actual* change in the price level.

We will build on this formulation. The difficulty to be overcome, out of which the application of the infinitesimal method will help, is that the measure of the effect of the change in goods combination on the price level is not as readily available as is the measure of the effect of the change in expenditure. Although we know how we could gain it if we had the measures of the changes in individual goods, these first have to be obtained. Before we take up that point and thus set forth the complete solution of the problem, reference must be made to another point.

So far we have simply spoken of taking any goods into consideration whatsoever, and of expenditure on those goods. Formally, the argument also applies in this generality. If we select goods from any point of view, e.g., all foods or all commodities which have cotton as a component of their production, etc., then, if we apply our approach to a variable that we would like to call the *sectional price level* and which is coessential with the economic price level that here interests us, we get an extract that seems to signify the same thing. This is not so; instead, there is in each such extract, besides the sectional price level proper to it, also the economic price level which is fundamentally different from it, from the data of the extract of which as little can be deduced as could be deduced from the movement of the absolute price of a single commodity. The reason in both cases is the same: the movement of the sectional price level asserts nothing about the movement of the economic price level and absolutely nothing about the money process, because compensatory movements of prices and quantities in other extracts may offset it; while they, in other words, are subject to the influence of elasticities of, and shifts in, demand of the selected commodities, just as a single price is, and less than such only in degree. Our index cannot respond in this way and does not so respond, from which it follows that it is *essentially*, not merely technically, different from a sectional.

One might believe that because of this, one must essentially use prices and quantities of all goods and services, possibly even assets, shares, etc., in the formation of the economic price level.[14] However, this would not serve. For the

---

[14]Carl Snyder drew this consequence. His all-inclusive index therefore is not applicable to our purpose.

money process does not consist in a single homogeneous total expenditure standing over against a phalanx of objects uniformly lined up, but it proceeds, as we know, in most definitely ordered stages or phases that, if we restrict ourselves to the basic process,[15] can be characterized under the headings "consumption expenditure of households" and "production expenditure of firms," or by the two fundamental economic "markets" of consumption goods and production goods. Within each of these phases, the money tie does not enclose all goods and services as such, but only very specific forms thereof. In an equilibrium state, the economic money variables of both phases of course stand in a clearly defined relation to each other, so that one might even combine them. But outside of complete equilibrium, thus virtually always, the fact must be taken into account that *different* movements, and also *the same* movements in different time intervals, assert themselves in these markets. Throwing the markets together blurs these distinctions and results in a meaningless average. The *concept* of economic price level *refers* to a complete economic market in the sense just mentioned: that is, a complete phase of the money process; the *real* manifestation of the price level can only be *seen* in a complete phase.

Consequently there are, strictly speaking, two economic price levels, which in the chronic imbalance of reality can have different - specifically, opposite - movements. Nevertheless, we wish to make a choice between the two, in a similar manner to the way we did with the critical number, and for the same reasons. Our choice will be in favor of the market of consumer goods, the price level of which is called "economic," although of course we must not forget the essentially analogous position of the price level of the means of production. In addition to this, we note: *first*, that therefore the quantities and prices that come into consideration for the economic price level are the quantities actually purchased by households (including amounts of directly consumed services of servants, teachers, doctors, etc.) and prices actually paid (retail). Figures for these may be unobtainable, in particular for the pre-war period. But other kinds and quantities of commodities (e.g., textile raw materials instead of clothing) and other prices (e.g., wholesale prices) could be regarded, at best, as substitute data of approximate value. *Secondly*, it should be noted that such a general index, even if it were technically identical to a cost of living index, appears here in a special role different from the cost of living index, and therefore notionally

---

[15]This occurs here not merely for presentational simplicity. We shall see - as already hinted, by the way - that the other markets take a significantly different position to the money tie than the two fundamental ones.

should be kept distinct from this. But we have seen that the principle of construction of the cost of living index is different and would have to take budget combinations of income groups, which are foreign to our purpose, into consideration.

Modeling the Index

5. We have before us a process of change of all quantities of commodities, prices, and expenditures, which proceeds unevenly in time. Even the changes in the price level follow accordingly, incessantly and irregularly, sometimes strongly, sometimes weakly, like the velocity of a car on a winding road, under the influence of ever varying level-forces. If we wish to capture this action and not distort it, then it can only be a matter of determining its tendency at every single point in time - its prevailing *instantaneous law*. We do this[16] with the help of that method that owes its origin to an analogous situation in other fields, the infinitesimal, the basic idea of which helps eliminate the logical difficulties that hinder treatment of unevenly running processes. We divide the history of price levels into periods that are so small that we comprehend the course of our process as uniform without errors falling into the balance, and may neglect some variables which should not be ignored when considering longer periods of time.

During such a small period of time, between two closely spaced time points t and $t + dt$, the consumption expenditure E changes in the area under investigation by the positive or negative small variable dE, the prices $p_1, p_2, p_3,...,$ p_n of m consumer articles $1, 2, 3,..., N$, by small variables $dp_1, dp_2, dp_3,..., dp_n$, and their quantities $q_1, q_2, q_3,..., q_n$ by small variables $dq_1, dq_2, dq_3,..., dq_n$, which likewise can all be positive or negative. We then have $dE = \sum_1^n q_m dp_m + \sum_1^n p_m dq_m ...,(m = 1 ...,n)$, neglecting a term $\sum_1^n dp_m \cdot dq_m$, which is of a higher order. If the quantities of goods remain unchanged, the second term of the right-hand side would be equal to zero - the inverse, of course, is not true - and the price level could only remain constant if the total expenditure does not change, so that its growth dE is also equal to zero. In this case, the expenditure index becomes a price level index. Should, however, all prices remain constant, the first term of the right-hand side would also be equal to zero. This would

---

[16]The honor of precedence is due, however, to François Divisia, who in his work "L'Indice Monétaire et la Théorie de Monnaie" [The Monetary Index and the Theory of Money], *Revue d'Economie Politique* 39, 1925, pp. 842 ff., first applied the infinitesimal to our problem.

mean that the level-forces emanating from the change in total expenditure and from the changes in quantities compensate each other precisely.

Although both cases *can* have the quality of entirely raw approximations, only the general case merits real interest, in which none of the terms disappear, so basically all prices and all quantities, as well as total expenditure, undergo changes. Now it is clear that the second term on the right-hand side yields the *resultant* of those positive and negative level-forces that emanate from the changes in the quantities of goods. Precisely by its amount, total expenditure must rise or fall if no "effective" influence on the price level should emanate from the change in the quantities of goods. We can therefore call this variable (to eliminate the effect of the level-forces from changes in quantities of goods) *necessary growth* (of total expenditure). In the advancing economies with which we are primarily dealing, we will, excluding very rare coincidences, not expect that resultant to be zero, thus compensating positive and negative quantity accruals in their effect, but rather that there will be a positive necessary increase. With $dE = 0$ or even $dE < \sum p_m \, dq_m$, a reduction in the price level must then occur such as the world experienced in 1873-1895 and which, of course, had nothing to do with the decline of marginal utility, which entails a more plentiful supply of goods.

But the significance of $\sum_1^n q_m dp_m$ already follows from this. This term yields that part of dE which accounts for the transpired price changes, namely because the quantities fall within the points in time covered by this term, and the growth increases have no influence on that part of dE that corresponds to the price changes in the unchanged social product. Admittedly, it encompasses changes in the price system as well as changes in the price level. But remember the evidence that changes in the price system at constant quantities of goods leave the price level unchanged. Therefore, however the price changes included in this term take shape, we will always measure the occurred change in the price level, and only this, just as if the price system had not changed, thus, just as if all prices had risen or fallen in the same proportion.

There we have the desired index of the price level, or, more correctly, the measure of the instantaneous tendency of the price level. We proceed from the case that $\sum_1^n q_m \, dp_m = 0$, i.e., that the level of total expenditure and the goods quantities just cancel each other, and thus the "uncompensated level-force" is zero. Then as well, all prices fundamentally change *although none do so because discrepancies between the movements of total expenditure and goods quantities made a special process of adjustment necessary,* and the price level remained unchanged. Then

$$\frac{\sum_1^n q_m \, (p_m + dp_m)}{\sum_1^n q_m p_m} = 1$$

must be the case. Any deviation of this quotient from 1 measures the change in the price level proceeding at every moment and the "effective" level-force in operation at every moment.

Formally, this is nothing other than the price index of Laspeyres, at least when applied to the comparison of point in time to point in time, thus allowing its fixed basis to lapse - using a kind of chain method which however is not exposed to the concerns otherwise voiced against the chain method - and at least when one uses *only* consumer articles and *all* consumer articles, including personal services directly consumed, and when one reckons these using the quantities actually purchased by consumers and the actual retail prices paid by consumers. Otherwise, the purpose of our method is destroyed and the Laspeyres index ceases to meet the requirements that arise from our analysis.

Instead of the equation $\sum_1^n q_m\, dp_m = 0$, however, we could also proceed from the equivalent equation $dE = \sum_1^n p_m\, dq_m$, which, if we add $E = \sum_1^n p_m\, q_m$ to both sides, yields

$$\frac{\sum_1^n (p_m + dp_m)\,(q_m + dq_m)}{\sum_1^n p_m\,(q_m + dp_m)} = 1$$

for the case of the absence of uncompensated level forces, which, as is easily seen, leads to the Paasche formula, which therefore stands in the same formal relationship to our result as does that of Laspeyres, and for which the same remarks apply. Both formulas are distinguished under our terms just by variables of higher order - from our point of view they merge together: from this viewpoint, they are not only *on an equal footing* but are actually *equivalent*.

If, however, one adopts, as in practice one must, not infinitesimally small periods of time for consideration but only the smallest periods that are possible in reality, the two formulas must in principle cease to be equivalent, so that the question of their value and their relationship to each other resurfaces, but now under the viewpoint as to whether they are - or whether one of them more than the other is - suitable to fulfill the purpose of our method with tolerable approximation when we proceed according to our rule in the other points. This requires answering the question as to whether our method retains its meaning at all in this case.

It has already been pointed out that our analysis is only intended to serve as a fundamental clarification, and that the value of this clarification does not automatically stand and fall with the practical feasibility of the statistical procedure that follows from it. That would still apply even if this statement were inapplicable, not simply given the state of our statistical means, but because of

unalterable characteristics of our material, as the reader unfamiliar with the
logic of the infinitesimal method will always be inclined to assume, perhaps because infinitesimally small magnitudes "don't exist anyway," etc. Nevertheless,
it is advisable to point out that the situation regarding the practical possibilities
of our method is not as bad as it seems at first glance. First, it must be admitted
that, even if we could divide the occurrences to be comprehended in arbitrarily
small intervals of time, it would still sometimes occur that changes in total expenditure, quantity, and price turn out "large" in the sense that that which we
neglect as variables of higher order would be of tangible importance. However,
quantities, prices, and expenditures do not normally fluctuate in retail sales as
they do on the commodity futures exchange or even in actual wholesale. And
where a large jump occurs in a moment and continuity is interrupted, it is an
event that at this stage need not escape economic observation and in any case
could be considered of some significance.

One such case differs from our normal case in that the term $\sum_1^n dp_m \cdot dq_m$ – which might now be written $\sum_1^n \Delta p_m \Delta q_m$ – may no longer be neglected.
But now the two aspects mingle in this term which occur separately in the two
other terms. But if it involves just one commodity, the new term nonetheless is
placed entirely on the account of the term $\sum_1^n p_m \Delta p_m$, i.e., the case can be all
but settled satisfactorily by inserting $(p_m + \Delta p_m)^{\dagger}$ instead of p_m, precisely
the new price. Further cases of appearances of new goods could hardly occur
that could not be helped in the same way. The objection, finally, that many
important goods are not produced continuously and others, the production of
which is continuous, are purchased only once or a few times a year, and that
therefore fundamentally one cannot choose arbitrarily small increments of time,
would *here* be completely irrelevant: to the degree that the purchasing acts of
the *totality* of consumers manifest points of accumulation, they will effectuate
seasonal fluctuations in the price level, which have now been taken care of.

The opportunity to apply in practice the rules of our analysis is therefore just a matter of data collection and not anything of a fundamental nature.
And the possibility of choosing time intervals sufficiently small is also simply a
question of data collection. As is known, there is no general criterion for what
is "sufficiently small:" here as elsewhere, it depends on our purposes and our
claims. Sometimes 1/100 percent is "large," sometimes two or three percent is
"sufficiently small." In quiet times, that is, times in which the economic picture
is not under the influence of social changes or events such as the great earth-

---

$\dagger$ The text has $(p_m + \Delta_m)$, which does not seem correct.

quake of Tokyo, weekly reporting would be entirely satisfactory, monthly tolerable, even yearly data would be enough to get started. What's more, in many cases of disordered states, e.g., in advanced inflation, the crucial data emerge particularly keenly. Of course, one must not underestimate the task of data collection. It appears before us in its full magnitude when one considers that relatively accessible wholesale quantities and prices are almost worthless, not only in themselves but as indices of retail prices.[18]

But as soon as we deal with fairly extensive intervals of time, e.g., monthly, the two price level indices derived from our equation in reality as a rule, in principle always, yield different results. The gap between them is even a sign of how far we have removed ourselves from the strict requirements of our analysis, at least in the sense that their presence implies distance, although their absence does not prove that we have not deviated. They do not represent approximate values in the strict sense of the word, but rather attempts from different viewpoints to measure a real object now clarified. And going from here, there admittedly is no criterion for choosing between the two ways of deriving the index – the methods remain "equal" – although there is an argument for taking an average, a stronger argument for the arithmetic than for the geometric mean preferred by Fisher. This argument, however, does not hold for the average between the formula of Laspeyres and that of Paasche in their customary construction and meaning. Incidentally, these formulas also receive their theoretical meaning only under the viewpoint of admittedly completely inadequate attempts to capture precisely what we have called the price level. However, we attach no importance to these issues. Instead, we wish henceforth always, if not explicitly stated otherwise, to argue on the basis of our strict requirements.

Of some interest is, finally, the finding that our index of the price level corresponds to each of the eleven previously listed criteria.[+] This is immediately apparent for the third, fourth, fifth, sixth, seventh, and eleventh criteria. Regarding the others it is perhaps not as clear, since the Laspeyres formula does not meet the intercalation, inversion, and multiplication criterion. It is, in fact, when we return to previously used notation, neither

$$\frac{\sum p_k q_i}{\sum p_i q_i} \cdot \frac{\sum p_i q_k}{\sum p_k q_k} = 1,$$

nor even

---

[18]Footnote missing from original manuscript.

[+] Only five of which were actually previously listed.

$$\frac{\sum p_k q_i}{\sum p_i q_i} \cdot \frac{\sum q_k p_i}{\sum q_i p_i} = \frac{\sum p_k q_k}{\sum p_i q_i}$$

But if we set $p_k = p_i + dp_i$ and $q_k = q_j + dq_j$, and multiply through, we find both criteria met up to higher order terms. The same applies to the intercalation criterion, although with regard to our method it is pointless because we only compare adjacent points in time. But when we plug in a third between our two initial points in time, we find the criterion likewise fulfilled. In fact, if we consider the three points in time standing right beside each other, and denote the related cost and quantity with $p_i q_i$, $p_j q_j$, and $p_k q_k$, whereby $p_j = p_i + dp_i$, $q = q_i + dq_i$, and $p_k = p_j + dp_j$, $q_k = q_j + dq_j$, the requirement of the intercalation criterion, namely

$$\frac{\sum p_k q_i}{\sum p_i q_i} = \frac{\sum p_j q_i}{\sum p_i q_i} \cdot \frac{\sum p_k q_j}{\sum p_j q_j}$$

leads, as can easily be seen, to

$$\frac{\sum p_i dq_i}{\sum p_i q_i + \sum q_i dp_i + q_i dp_i} = \frac{\sum p_i dq_i}{\sum p_i q_i + \sum q_i dp_i}$$

If we multiply each denominator into the numerator of the other side and cross out the terms which contain products of differentials, i.e., variables of a higher order,[19] the identity $\sum p_i dq_i \cdot \sum p_i q_i = \sum p_i dq_i \cdot \sum p_i q_i$ follows.

However, this does not satisfy the practical significance of the criterion. The reason is that this criterion requires that the comparison of *arbitrary* periods of time yields the same result, regardless of whether they are compared with each other directly or by way of a third period of time. But with regard to our index, *this* requirement is wrongly raised, even if it is justified with regard to the usual meaning of a price index. For in contrast to this, our index represents an instantaneous law; to read from it something else than the particular instantaneous tendency of the price level would be to misunderstand it. Therefore, while otherwise it can plausibly be argued that the reason why the direct route should return a different result than the indirect cannot be perceived, and that in that case it points to a deficiency in the method, this viewpoint does not apply here, because direct comparisons do not come into consideration. But if we cannot

---

[19] Of course, one may not – which the layman must think strange – first multiply the numerators and then crosswise, since then $\sum q_i dp_j$ remain, thus an inequality would result.

jump from one point to another remote one, we can still *crawl* from one to the other if we piece together the time periods and their instantaneous laws. In this way we can even span arbitrarily large periods of time. Note that for our purposes - certainly not for different and more important ones - we are independent of changes in the consumption combinations, so that in principle we can move from price levels that relate to halberd and pack animal gradually to price levels that include prices of machine guns and dirigibles. This is due to the purely objective, let's say, market-technical character of the proportionality factor, which has no time- or value-oriented meaning.

The identity and the proportionality criteria should dispense with their basic requirement for formulas which, like Drobisch's, can indicate movements in the price level between adjacent points in time, even if not a single price has changed, or which, as for example the case with Lehr's, can provide indicators that, when all prices change in the same proportion, can supply results that deviate from this relation. This basic requirement is satisfied by our index, just as it is with Laspeyres', even when the chain method is applied to it. If, however, with Von Bortkiewicz one extends the criterion to the requirement that the battery of price indices should always produce the same value when the same prices prevail regardless of any variations that may have occurred between the times of these equal prices, then the Laspeyres index as amended by the chain method does not meet this criterion. Our index is sufficient for it in the same sense in which it also satisfies the intercalation criterion. Again, it must be admitted that the practical goal is not met, which would serve the broader claim. But again we must refer to the meaning and essence of our index, which is alien to that purpose and entails that what happens in the interval between two significantly separate points in time is not a matter of indifference.

Further Criteria

6. The associative criterion could be combined with the independence criterion into the general requirement that materially apparently indifferent incidental circumstances should not lead to different numbers. Such an incidental circumstance is the combination of several goods into a position or the split-up of one position into several, such as for different qualities of one good. That the formula permits such an operation without necessarily providing a different price index, is a requirement of the associative criterion, but this is always violated when the influence of the price of a good depends on its independent stance.

7. Over and above the sphere of aspects on which the hitherto mentioned criteria [...], and into the sphere of economic interpretation of the index, penetrates the dual-form criterion [Zweiförmigkeitskriterium] formulated by Von Bortkiewicz, which first requires that each index number that represents a relation of ratio-prices can be converted into an index number which is a ratio of sums of sales, and vice versa. One can also base this criterion simply on both types of index numbers being equal, since a forced choice between the two must be avoided. But the criterion needs to draw its powers of persuasion from the knowledge that an average as such, i.e., an average that is not economically substantiated, can have meaning only under shaky [riskierten] assumptions, and that sales sums play a role in every attempt at economic substantiation. That this is what is meant is especially evident from the fact that von Bortkiewicz further requires that with the conversion of sales ratio formulas into averaging formulas, weightings emerge that have economic meaning, i.e., that obviously are not induced "merely computationally," and with the reverse operation into sales ratio formulas, factors of price emerge that yield meaningful sales magnitudes. So while the earlier criteria approach our to-be-derived result from the outside, so to speak, and can be met or not, compliance with this criterion is ipso facto ensured, since we assume an economic analysis.

8. The intercalation criterion requires that the price index P_{ik}, which is to characterize the change in the price situation between time points i and k, be equal to the product of a price index P_{ij}, that likewise issues from time point i in order to compare the change in the price situation at a third time point j with the state of things in i, and a price index P_{jk}, which goes from time point j to time point k.

9. A formula that does not meet the intercalation criterion can still fulfill the inversion criterion. And one may certainly attribute a high value to that criterion, in fact, as with Irving Fisher, a very high value, even if one wishes to deny it any significance. It requires that the relation that the price index expresses be reversible in the sense that it be equal to the reciprocal value of the index that is obtained if one first exchanges the data of the comparison period and the observation period: if the index with basis a doubled in time period b, the index expressing the same change must, with basis b, show a decline of one-half for time period a. A different measurement result, depending on whether one measures forward or backward, is so obviously suspicious, that I can hardly think of an excuse for the failure of this criterion.

10. The matter is different with Irving Fisher's multiplication criterion ("factor reversal test"), according to which the product of a price index and a quantity index formed by the same rule should be equal to the ratio between

the total revenues or expenditures of all considered goods in the observation and the comparison period. At first glance, this appears to be a hardly permissible extension to the index of a condition valid for individual price ratios, and the resultant tendency to regard this as a kind of price ratio.

Chapter XII
The Theory of the Money Process and of the Functions of the Money Market[1]

1. Now we have again to work through the processes sketched in the simplest outline in Chapter V, this time in the forms of the money and credit spheres. All problems of a monetary-theoretical or monetary-policy nature, however difficult or interesting, are linked to changes in money and goods flows. A stationary, hence constantly reproducing economic process exposed to no external disturbances is a very simple thing in terms of monetary theory, so that it would not be worth the effort to get into all of its details. To the degree that we nonetheless need it as a basis for the presentation of some elementary principles, we will therefore restrict ourselves to the roughest outlines and a few points that at any rate deserve special mention.

The Equation of Exchange

All monetary theories work equally well in *explaining* the sorts of money method in the *practice* of the stationary monetary process, and can be viewed from this standpoint as equivalent. For the moment, we can think of any theory, e.g., a commodity theory, and any money method, e.g., the method of equating a price of an arbitrary amount of a commodity with the unit. However the settling-up process may be organized, all the money expressions are unambiguously determined, therefore also all combinations of money variables and money expressions formed by whatever rule. Even the equation: money times velocity equals price level times quantity of goods, $MV = PT$, is then valid. This is formally the *Newcomb-Fisher equation*, but we must not forget that the individual symbols here signify other things than they do with Fisher: P is the price level of consumer goods, T is the "quantity" of consumer goods in the given time period, V is the frequency which, under our present assumptions, is to be multiplied by a disposition of *one*. The equation would of course also have been "right" with the meaning of the symbols given them by Fisher. The consideration of different kinds of money with different frequency numbers ($MV + M'V'$

---

[1]Added by the editor.

= PT), gold money and credit, for example, adds nothing to the theoretical thought process and is unnecessary in the course of a theoretical consideration.

Among the individual variables that go into this equation of exchange [Verkehrsgleichung], it may first be observed: M is obviously a *"mass,"* in this sense a "stock" (*stock* or *fund*), while PT is a "flow" of transactions expressed in money per selected period, and is precisely a flow of *goods* (T), expressed in ideal money units to be converted into the actual money unit by the multiplication by P, which has the character of a pure number. A stock and a flow have different dimensions and can never be equated with each other. This is precisely what the multiplication of M and V manages, making both sides of the equation homogeneous and also making the link to a flow that further illuminates the essence of V – in *this* connection the same is true for frequency as it would be in *any* interpretation of V. If we divide both sides by V, both are reduced to "stocks" in the above sense, and the right side $\frac{PT}{V}$ then means what can be called

a *"sales group,"* the transaction variable per frequency unit. In $\frac{M}{P} = \frac{T}{V}$, the left-hand expression is the *"real value of the means of circulation"* – in other words, because a mass divided by a pure number is a mass – the right-hand expression is the *"real value of transactions per frequency unit,"* hence likewise a mass. The meaning of these two very useful structures is self-explanatory. In $\frac{MV}{T}$ the "flow

dimension" is eliminated, so that the expression again can be equal to the pure number P. It is recommended that the reader linger by these conversions, the more so because, for elementary purposes, one often gets further with a properly understood equation of exchange than with the more correct conception here presented.

If we can imagine, which in dealing with our case can be done without substantial restriction of its generality, that money and goods flows (s) are strictly continuous and uniform in time (t), then the stationary economic process is characterized by the condition: $\frac{dt}{ds} = c = const.$ The interpretation

yields $s = ct + b$, where b is the interpretation constant [Interpretationskonstante], which we can set to zero for the start of the treatment. If we measure time in frequency units, then c identifies easily with our M and s with PT, which amounts to deriving the equation of exchange from the proposition: as long as the money-goods flow in an area under investigation flows continuously and uniformly, the circulating money supply is a constant magnitude. In general, however, it is more practical to derive the equation of exchange from a *Walras-*

ian system or simply from the scheme of social accounting of a stationary economy.

Despite the fact that the relation expressed in this "equation of exchange" is so easy to demonstrate that we refrain from executing the indicated proof, its existence has often been disputed. Under our conditions, it is meaningless when more is meant thereby than the rejection of incorrect formulations. It is correct, however, that this relationship gives no reliable Ariadne's thread with which one might walk through the maze of monetary interactions within the transformation process, and the correlation suggested by it, $P = T(M)$, M being the independent variable, is often downright wrong, and is misleading yet more often. This can be seen from the fact that an increment of M, which is never spent on all goods equally but always only on certain goods, can cause changes in the composition and size of T that are not necessarily temporary. Earlier observations have also taught us that an increase in T can exert an influence on V, because an increasing T does not necessarily need to correspond to increasing cash balances in the same proportion. A decrease in P can be the *cause* of a decrease in T and/or an increase in M. A money system that works with bank balances *can* show a dependence of variable M on variable T that is *direct*, i.e., that does not first pass through the price level, and such-like. Certainly one sometimes can neglect this dependence, which does require special proof each time. Certainly, in the way in which the equation of exchange is sustainable with sharp formulation but untenable with lax formulation, one can often with sharp formulations demonstrate the lack of justification of objections that seem convincing with lax formulations. But wherever these dependencies are essential (and they are, as a rule, essential; and the cases where they are essential are the sources of all truly interesting problems), it is, in light of the devaluation of the equation of exchange as a research tool that in these cases sets in, cold comfort to be able to characterize the equation as "correct," when one must drop the actual quantity theory as expressed by the formula $P = f(M)$.

One aspect of this situation can be expressed by the phrase, the quantity theory applies exactly when it is meant "alternately" [alternativ] and at best approximately when it is meant "successively" [sukzessiv].

Stripping the equation of exchange of its causal implications, the question arises as to whether it is not a *tautology*. When thereby more is meant than an incorrect term for "trivial" or "self-evident" – whether we hold it to be *that*, is a matter of taste – then the answer is obviously negative. The reason is that the equation is not a *mathematical identity,* because it is only true of an equilibrium state and is a conditional equation thereof. And it follows *a fortiori* that it cannot be a *logical* tautology. This is true for all interpretations of the variables contained in it, especially our own, but not just for them. The misunderstanding that has led to the opposite verdict comes from the fact that one apparently can set either of the two sides identically equal to the income sum E. Actually $E = PT$ if one *defines* income as consumption expenditure and only allows consumer goods prices and quantities into P and T. But then E would *not* be identical to MV, but a new, obviously not always valid assertion would lie in the equation, namely, that the disposition is equal to one. The same assertion lies in the equation of E with PT if one previously set $E = MV$, which of course is also possible and is only matter of terminology. E, however defined, can never be identically equated with MV and PT *at the same time*, which is also the case for all other versions of M, V, P, T, except for those that are intentionally based on a tautology. Read in our sense, the equation of exchange does *not* say: actual consumption expenditure in a period of observation is equal to the money supply times a factor that makes the money supply equal to consumption expenditure, *but:* in the equilibrium state, the quantity of money times *frequency* is equal to the *equilibrium quantity* of consumer goods times *that* price level that corresponds to the critical number.

Statistically, the matter stands thus: since at the moment it is not possible statistically to separate frequency and disposition,[2] the question arises as to whether there is a statistical tautology only for other interpretations of the equation of exchange and not for ours. M and P are always gathered independently, and he who gathers T independently, i.e., by means of data on physical quantities of production, has no fear of tautology even if he gains the V of bank balances from the sum of debit balances, since it is just this that depicts the required new given.[3] Only remember that in chapter VIII we found cause to *doubt* the meaning of *this* type of construction of an index for T. And if one calculates T by dividing a value-total by half of the same value-total, then the equation as such becomes a tautology, e.g., the sum of debit balances is equal to the sum of debit balances. But even then, what is expressed is a relationship between the two independently gathered variables M and P, which are not themselves tautological and are not always worthless either.

The Money Process in the Stationary Economy

---

[2]Footnote absent in original manuscript.
[3]Footnote absent in original manuscript.

2. Now let us first take a stationary cycle, the periods of which are interleaved in such a manner that all households live on the product of the respective preceding period, all firms work on the product that will supply the following period, and we exclude all consumption and production goods that extend beyond the individual periods. In this case, transactions are limited to the sale of original productive services by firms and to purchases of consumer goods by households, and no occasion is given for the emergence of other consumption and production goods markets than these – in particular, for the emergence of real estate and securities markets. Inventories exist only in the sense that things involved in the process of manufacture, of being sold, and of being consumed, must be stored somewhere, but not as a result of processes contrary to expectations or the expectation of economic changes, and analogously for cash holdings or balances. The system of variables for such an economy would be constantly at its critical number, which is set equal to consumption expenditure.

In a pure account-settling system, at the end of each financial year every household is charged an amount equal to fifty-two times its weekly consumptive purchases, and is credited with an equal amount, fifty-two times its weekly sales of performances, and vice versa for every firm. The social total amounts would be: debit = total credit = two times total income = two times consumption expenditure in the income period = critical number = fifty-two times the total amount of balances. Cash requirements and actual cash holdings would be identical – disposition would be equal to one. We can distinguish *corporate or business or financial assets* from *household or consumer or income assets.*[4] Alternately, the one is zero while the other is equal to the amount of balances, while successively they equal each other. Taking our observations regarding the velocity of circulation (chapter X[+]), the reader can easily deal with other cases of market order and payment technique, which are recommended as useful exercises. Regarding this, it is to be noted that the results only tell how those numbers would be if the market order and payment technique *were* otherwise, not as they would take shape if the market order and payment technique underwent *change* in the course of historical reality.

If this settlement is not conducted by a bank but by a banking system grouped around a central bank (clearinghouse), then the debits carried out at the central bank would dwindle *to* the amount of transactions between the banks, while the economic debit balance total would increase *by* that amount,

---

[4]Footnote absent in original manuscript.

[+] Original manuscript has "VII."

if the central bank has no other customers than banks and all *interbank trans-actions* lead to debits at the central bank. If the central bank has other customers too, as we generally assume, and if a portion of interbank transactions in the period eventually is deposited in offsetting nostro and loro balances of the banks amongst themselves, then a statement about the formation of economic mone-tary expressions is generally the less possible as it depends on how many of the transactions of individual firms and individual households lead to transfers within their banks. The elimination of interbank transactions from the total number is therefore a dictate of money-theoretical clarity – which in most coun-tries currently can be satisfied only with difficulty. The effects that an *association of banks* has on the total number is thus also made clear.

If we set opposite this settling-up traffic a different model, which works with the money method of physical handover, e.g., of fashioned metal pieces – with a specified scope for the barter economy sector and the opportunity for clearing – and we assume, for the sake of ease of comparison, the critical number to be the same as in the just-discussed model, we see that every week the – here entirely unproblematic – quantity of money flows back and forth between con-sumer goods markets and means of production markets, so that each coin ap-pears once in the income sphere and once in the capital sphere, hence *the same* money is alternately consumer and business money. The phenomena encoun-tered only here in the actual sense, velocity, efficiency, frequency ($V = 2E = 2F$), by all means find their analogue in pure settling-up traffic with the quotients, sales ÷ balances, or consumption goods sales/sales of means of production ÷ consumer balances/producer balances.

The Money Process in More Complex Situations

3. With a little practice in the handling of the presented theory, what has been said in previous chapters is entirely sufficient to treat the following cases, which arise first from complications of our scheme, and then from those small differences the consequences of which can best be made clear when one hews to the principles of the scheme, even though they gain their full meaning in the money process in another context. The treatment will largely be left to the reader.

Intermediate Goods

A. Let us allow for firms that sell, not to households, but to other firms, such as firms that produce means of production. It would obviously be possible that these sales – on our Saturdays, or sometime between the end of the Monday market of consumer goods and the beginning of the market of the original means of production on the following Saturday – proceed such that the consumer goods firms apply a portion of the balances or coins to the purchase of intermediate goods that otherwise would remain idle that week. Their producers can, if their maximum production period is a week, spend this partial amount on original means of production on the same Saturday, so that households receive the same amount and on the following Monday spend the same amount buying consumer goods as in the earlier case. Frequency, income, total balances, consumption expenditure, the critical number, and price levels remain as they would have been had we allowed no other transactions than household-firm purchases and no other goods than consumer goods and original productive services. The only change is that the debit (= credit) total – total sales – is now increased by the amount of purchases of intermediate products, and the transactions of the capital sphere are therefore no longer equal to the transactions in the income sphere, even though "business money" and "consumer money" are still equal to each other, or to be precise, the existing balances or coins alternate between the two.[5] *The amount of capital itself as well, that is, the sum of the amount expended in the course of the production process, has increased by the number of purchases of intermediate goods.*

A portion of actual economic processes in fact runs according to this scheme, but obviously only a portion. We account for another portion if we assume that the firms that produce intermediate goods make their payments, together with the consumer goods firms, just as before on Saturday, but only sell their intermediates to the latter on the following Monday, whereupon the consumer goods firms are *not* in the condition to apply the money that they take in on Monday to pay for the intermediate goods. *Firms in the sphere of production,* as we shall call the producers of the "produced means of production," therefore must now keep their capital in readiness ahead of time, which under our conditions is possible only when consumer goods firms in turn finance the sales of intermediate goods from proceeds of the previous economic period, thus separate the corresponding portion of *their* capital from the proceeds of the previous Monday, hold onto it on Saturday and do not let it become income. By this means, the *self-financing* of the stationary economic process is again realized, i.e., the principle of financing from current revenues is implemented. Again, each piece of gold and, if we apply the image of "circulation" to deposits, each deposit unit stands over against both consumer goods and original means of production. But not all of these units do this with *each* revolution

---

[5]Footnote absent in original manuscript.

of the wheel of the economy, as was the case before. Rather, an amount equal to the sum of purchases of produced means of production, even though made up of continuously different individual coins, is withdrawn from the immediate back and forth between markets of consumer goods and original services, as in an office, for example, comprising ten functionaries, of which, on an alternating basis, one is always on an inspection trip and nine are always present. If a million coins are paid out as income on Saturday, and are spent on consumer goods on Monday, and half a million in produced means of production is purchased on Monday, then one and one-half million coins must circulate if the Monday transactions are simultaneously to be possible.

Compared with the previous case, then either total income, price level, etc. must be correspondingly lower given the same amount of money, or, if these are to maintain the same level, there must correspondingly be more money available. Frequency is correspondingly lower. The coins – that is, the portion of them that must run through the produced means of production, a pure *"business sphere"* – *loses a step*, as it were; suffers a *phase delay*. There is still no coin that is business money in the sense that it only circulates in the business sphere, but there is now business money in the sense that a "fund" exists that is not poured directly into income but rather stands alongside the fund earmarked for that. The equation between income, consumption expenditure, and the critical number now still exists. But the money supply and the deposit amount is now no longer equal to $\frac{1}{52}$ of the annual sum of income, but is equal to $\frac{1}{52}(1 + \frac{1}{2})$ of the same. The debit total exceeds twice the annual income by the annual amount of payments to producers of intermediate products, and by the same amount the transactions of the capital sphere exceed those of the income sphere. The generalization of these relationships is easy, as is the application to the case that the producers of intermediate goods in turn buy intermediate products, as do their producers in their turn, and so forth.

It should be quite clear that at least in the cases discussed so far, no ground exists as to why a special net income should attach to the production or possession of intermediate goods.

Effect of Auxiliary Funds

B. Our models may seem cumbersome and unrealistic. At any rate, thinking through them promotes the understanding of the payment process and the essence and materialization of the national accounts [volkswirtschaftlichen Gesamtziffern], which is what matters. In particular, one realizes that this essence is not influenced by the disaggregation – nor, conversely, by the amalgamation – of the production process as such, but only by a payment-technical circumstance,[6] which is usually – but not always – linked to such disaggregation or amalgamation. We characterize this circumstance as the insertion of new funds, or the withdrawal of existing funds, which must now (or must have been) supplied *"in advance" with stocks*. This immediately gives a useful generalization. Because obviously the same thing holds true for the emergence or disappearance of trading and agent firms and also for public treasuries. Even if a public treasury does nothing else than disburse the money it receives, such as for support payments, and if the supported households buy exactly the same goods and services as those households from which the sum has been withdrawn would have bought, the "loss of a step" may still occur, which is the only essential thing. At the same time we also see, in this case even more clearly that in the disaggregation of production, that this is not necessary, and that *where* it occurs, it may occur in very different measure: obviously the treasury could also work in the way that it continuously makes expenditures as soon as revenues come in, and it is in no way unrealistic to assume that in many cases the market order allows enough space to, e.g., absorb the flow of items. The case of the public purse further clarifies the important question of the effect of tax rates on prices, frequency, and total number.

Durable Goods

    C. Let us introduce goods into our scheme[7] which serve either consumption or production for longer than a week. For this reason, these goods are not purchased by the individual household or the individual firm every Monday, although from the standpoint of their producer or seller, sales may still occur uniformly, i.e., in equal Monday quantities. As far as the individual households and firms are concerned, they must free up current amounts for these expenses that recur only over longer periods, so that cash items must be kept with them that are "staggered" from zero to the full amount of the outlay. Here we have a money pool from which as much continuously flows in as emanates out, but which always coexists as a separate pool along with the rest of circulation needs, just like the model described in subsection B above. To the degree that it can occur that firms (e.g., because they originally arise at approximately the same time) or households (e.g., because they originally take possession of the relevant durable good at the same time) undertake the replacement en masse on the same Monday, so that everything is sold to these, nothing to others, it would alter our

---

image such that we picture the pond being periodically "drained" and thereafter "dammed up" for a longer period of time. Both cases are easily expressed algebraically, and both only concern a decreased frequency of the relevant partial amounts and, because of this, a reduced average frequency. However, it is not always convenient to construct this average magnitude. Rather, it is often advisable to register the frequency differences as far as possible. This reveals to us what is wont to be called the opposition of "circulating" and "fixed capital" or such like. If we imagine a continuous scale between, say, wages on the one hand, and especially durable things like buildings on the other, then we have everything we need to understand the essence and value of this distinction, its role in the monetary process, and the difficulties one confronts if one wishes to draw [the boundary] sharply and in the sense of a contrary or contradictory opposition.

Here as well, the equations apply: income per period = consumption expenditure over the same period = the critical number derived over the same period = monetary expression of the social product = production expenditure = half the debits = coins times (reduced) frequency = amount of consumer credit times frequency = amount of business credit times frequency. The goods transfers, which now take place from period to period, have their monetary counterpart in the cash holdings accumulated for replacement purchases. These goods transfers plus these stocks - which correspond to depreciation for accounting purposes - are thus in each case the (relative) "fixed capital."

External Disturbances

4. "External disturbances," in particular the interventions of the political world in the economic organism, would exercise a much weaker and, above all, different - and more easily describable - effect if they impacted *an actually* stationary process that passively adapted to them according to the rules of statistical theory, and exhibited no impulse of its own. Then not only would the response of the financial conduct of households and firms to such disturbance be easy to predict, but so also would the effect of monetary and credit policy interventions as well, whether they be unintended side effects of otherwise political actions, or whether they be undertaken with the intention of giving economic-policy shape to the money and credit side. Now, if one points out this assumption of many monetary-theoretical attainments and monetary-policy proposals of our day, everyone realizes that things are not actually like that. But unconsciously and implicitly, the assumption nevertheless always is made - a *consequence* of the fact that a satisfactory theory of the self-motion of the economy is lacking, a *cause* of the fact that the results of current monetary theory and its

application are so obviously inadequate. Hence it is that effects are expected from the impulses which can be imparted to the economy by monetary- and credit-policy means, that experience belies, and hence it is that, with respect to the economic process, a freedom of movement is attributed to credit policy that turns it into virtually the sole determinant of the pace of economic life – a freedom of movement which it does not, in reality, have. In fact, the self-motion of the economy, which we delineate as "development," is the dominant basic phenomenon that above all first brings about the phenomena that we are accustomed to find in our mental image of the capitalist economy, and turns the monetary process into what we observe in reality.

Only with the understanding of the money and credit side of this basic phenomenon does the understanding of the capitalist money process even begin – among other elements of the process, the understanding of the monetary effects of growth and disturbances, monetary- and credit-policy interventions included, the results of which must appear to be completely random – "now this way, now that," a conclusion that the practitioner draws with great promptness – when we try to analyze these effects without relating them to the phases of the economic body's own life. Therefore, we now wish to work out the monetary contours of these phases under the assumption that there is neither what we would call growth nor disturbance in the area under observation.

From chapter V on, which the reader should now consult, we have become acquainted with the essence of this basic phenomenon, which accounts for the self-motion of the economy. As we did there, we here wish first, deviating from reality, to allow an economic body to grow from full static equilibrium, so that no elements of what is to be explained are included in the preconditions, which is another reason for the failures of important inherited theories. Furthermore, we also know that the phenomenon has an essentially wave-like character, and why it does, which fact is of particular importance to monetary theory and monetary policy. The *phases of these waves* are what we will refer to as *economic phases.* How many phases we distinguish is a matter of presentational convenience. Now we wish to define only two, which can be termed with the well-known words rise or prosperity, and fall (stagnation) or depression: we will often make use of the terms *positive and negative phase.* Finally, we know that there are always many such waves in progress at the same time – superimposing upon each other and interfering with each other. But for the sake of representational simplicity, we wish to express ourselves here generally as if there were only one wave, which comes down to speaking of a positive or negative phase, when the balance, so to speak, of all progressing waves is positive or negative. On the whole, the positive phases can be characterized by the implementation of innovations, the negative by the adaptation to the situation created by innovations, especially the price and cost situation.

The Effect of Development

We turn to the monetary-theoretical analysis of the positive phase. We represent the underlying process as the introduction of a better method of production – cheaper labor per unit of product – of an already available consumer good, which, however, requires intermediate goods – say machines – that do not yet exist. It is by no means a matter of indifference whether this is indeed so, or whether the innovation rather arises in the industry producing means of production, or whether it consists in the introduction of a new consumer good, etc. But our picture not only reflects a frequent process but also one that exhibits very many commonly occurring phenomena, from which transitions to other cases can easily be found. Entrepreneurs who go over to the production of consumer goods according to the new method might well obtain the required means of production through a low- or no-cost conversion of plant. Although this is not an insignificant case, we will assume, in order clearly to bring out the essence, that this is not the case, but rather that the entrepreneur does not "already have" any of the required means of production, and in general does not have other means, except possibly – but not necessarily – assets that can serve as collateral and facilitate borrowing.

Then the entrepreneurs who have not accumulated discretionary deposits – an aspect that actually is just as important, to be inserted in our picture later – obtain the amounts needed to purchase the means of production only by borrowing. Since there is no investment-seeking savings fund or such-like, they must obviously *either* induce people to give them cash which is used for the purposes of the stationary cycle and kept ready for it, *or* induce owners of means of production to lend them these means of production in kind or, for example, to provide work against a later promise of payment, *or* finally induce a bank to create new credit ad hoc for them to carry out their plans. The first way is not excluded and plays a role that cannot be neglected in an economy already in full development. However, under our assumptions, i.e., especially if we begin from a strictly stationary circular flow, such strict restrictions are set on this removal of coins or balances that we can disregard them for the time being. The second way is also undertaken in the real world. Many new hotels lend out their establishment, many shoe factories do so with their machinery, and it also happens that owners of, e.g., natural factors of production are won over by entrepreneurs for their plans, to provide the use of such factors or even to part with them in return for the promise of later quid pro quo. But this mode – which with the production factor labor mostly is quite impossible – is set such narrow limits, particularly under our conditions, that we do better to turn to the third way, the way of the typical financing of new things by the capitalist economy: *ad hoc creation of purchasing power,* and likewise restrict this to the creation of purchasing power by banks. We assume that banks add these credits to previously existing balances and do not, say, withdraw the corresponding amount or any part thereof from other customers. We also envision a multiplicity of competing banks grouped around a central bank, in accordance with the picture drafted in chapter VII.[+]

Credit Creation the Driver of Development

This model, seemingly so unrealistic, actually embodies the fundamental mechanism of the capitalist process. For the moment we will continue to disregard everything secondary that attaches to it, in particular the fact that firms and households not only are the leading objects of the action of entrepreneurs and banks but also act in anticipation of that action by changing their financial conduct, stockpiling, etc. Put this way, pared to its simplest form, and set in relation to our weekly scheme (with a financial *year*), things look like this: entrepreneurs during the first week of the year have the loan amounts booked to their accounts – we stipulate that the economic year shall begin with a Monday market, on which, as before, the equilibrium quantities of consumer goods are sold in entirety, and at the old prices. Through the grant of loans, the sum of balances increases during the course of this week by the amount of credit extended, and the critical number of the system increases correspondingly, but nothing else changes. In the market for productive services on the first Saturday of the year, that portion of the new funds which the entrepreneur immediately spends on original productive services, especially labor services, now comes forward. The social production expenditure, still equal to the sum of income, increases by the amount of that portion of new balances, and the prices of services (the same amount as previously offered) rise accordingly, including precisely the prices of the kinds of services demanded by the entrepreneurs that are naturally general for *all* firms, while the prices of the categories not demanded by the entrepreneurs rise according to existing "affinities," so that the prices of *all* services, while not rising equally, on balance rise by amounts corresponding to the increase in purchasing power. This increased total income on the second Monday buys the – not increased amount of – consumer goods, and so returns back

---

[+] The original manuscript refers to chapter VI.

to the firms – but not to the firms of the entrepreneurs; rather to the "old" firms, that thereby book a cost surplus on *this* weekly production. Under our assumptions – which in this context as in others, have to be changed the closer we approach reality – this partial amount of the newly created balances "circulates" for the time being at the same frequency as the old balances.

There are therefore, since the first period was omitted, fifty-one occasions on which consumption goods can be purchased in the first economic year. In addition, on the same Monday the entrepreneur purchases produced means of production. Insofar as only a part of the desired type of means is available, as is the case in the example that we treat, or insofar as they must first be (in part) themselves produced, as is the case with, for example, new machines, we will assume that the complete amounts of the desired materials, and the completed machines, are ordered and paid for on this Monday. As one may easily convince himself, this does not restrict the generalizability of our results. This part of the new balances thereby only gains effectuality vis-a-vis income on the second Saturday, and effectuality on the consumer goods market only on the third Monday.

This is all we need in order to understand the disturbances that occur in the previously stationary circular flow and the formation of total economic numbers. For, when we for example assume that the economic year under consideration is necessary and sufficient to establish the entrepreneurial firms and make them production-ready, so that their products begin to flow on the first Monday of the next economic year, and further that every week more loans are granted to them and credit is created in their favor in equal amounts, then these additional and successive "credit injections" into the economic body are not to be treated differently than the first. It is only important to note that as long as these injections are carried out regularly, each subsequent one partially compensates for the effects of the previous ones on the old firms.

While only *this* process is under way, i.e., before the new products reach the consumer market and the flow of consumption goods broadens, not only does the social product not increase, but [the consumption goods market] narrows such that the social product decreases. This is simply the consequence of the withdrawal of means of production incurred by the old firms [by their being shifted to new firms]. In reality, we do not observe this, or we observe it only rarely, because we are usually dealing with reservoirs of unemployed workers, supplies, etc., that firms have available to them. However, our scheme also develops an extremely important characteristic for the understanding of reality.

The Money Process in Cyclical Downturn

5. It would be to drag something accidental into our picture and distort its basic outline, should we *in principle* let this process be halted by the restriction that the banking constitution and currency legislation put on the increase of credit (deposit) volume. This may play a role often enough practically, even more often apparently, although a brake on *this* basis will not easily lead to a "crisis," but, because it obviously takes place by a gradual tightening of credit conditions, will only lead to a progressive throttling of prosperity. Even so, in principle it is a matter of complete indifference whether the upswing in demand for credit really approaches the legal or bank-technical limit or not. And when attempts at explanation that rely on this aspect imply that without any such limit there would be no reason for such a boom not to prevail without interruption or end, then they fall into error. For we have already gotten to know that aspect inherent in the goods process that is independent of the monetary and credit system, whereby every boom comes to an end and compels a period of depression: the emergence of new products, their penetration into the previous circular flow. Competition which, in both the consumer goods markets and the markets for means of production, new firms bring to old ones that, precisely through the emergence of the new, are *rendered obsolete* and undersold, is what that process of elimination and adjustment entails that is the essence of the period of depression – and the fundamental reason for the business losses that characterize it. We have now to introduce the money side of the matter into our model, and especially a very important aspect, which asserts itself in the depression and is peculiar to the money method.

To get an initial overview of the main contours of the money process in a depression, we wish to have the new products all appear at the same time beginning on the first Monday of the second year, although it would of course be more faithful to reality to assume that the buildup by the new firms begins not just at one point in time, and indeed in the first week of the first year, but rather continues during the course of the year. Obviously the flow of new goods begins only in a trickle but *soon* swings into line, so that the later stages of the boom are accompanied by a growing influence of the new products, which, until the culmination point, is overshadowed by the effects of the buildup of production capacity and the credit creation to finance it. This process affects the rate of change of boom symptoms, and bends, so to speak, the same graph *downward*, so that it continuously *flattens* up to the culmination point.[8] But if we

---

[8] Footnote absent in original manuscript.

make the mentioned assumption, it does no damage materially while being useful presentationally; so also the further assumption, that all entrepreneurs have calculated correctly, and sales of new products run as expected.[9]

Under these assumptions it is especially clear that the purchasing power newly created in the first year, the effect of which on socioeconomic numbers [sozialen Ziffern] was in part due the fact that it emerged without expanding the flow of consumer goods, whereby basically increasing money income purchased stable consumer goods quantities, now confronts increases in the flow of goods that in turn do not face any expansion of the money flow. If for example the new durable goods of the sphere of production are fully utilized in the second year, the Monday incomes of the new firms must be at least sufficient to cover not only the additional production costs of the second year, but also the original costs of the first year. And if everything has gone as expected, entrepreneurial profits and interest income must also pour in, in which case the deployment of the credit structure upon the production substructure, which resulted from the processes of the first year, is now more than made up for.

But that's not all. Recall our typical picture of the functioning of the credit mechanism in an area of study accustomed to the money method. We see that new firms not only bring new products *on* the market, but at the same time also take balances *off* the market, insofar as they repay loans from proceeds. We saw that this means the ipso facto extinction of balances. And that this happens quite automatically as a result of the crediting of the proceeds to their accounts. Let us imagine that those sums from Monday revenue that will be necessary on the following Saturday to buy original means of production, and on the following Monday to buy produced means of production, were initially reserved, whereby we can include in the latter amount the sum needed to cover the wear and tear on the equipment, which under our assumptions ought to be possible. Because if the plant produced in the first year is completely utilized in the second, it must be rebuilt in the second or otherwise there could not be production in the third. And this must obviously be financed through income, otherwise one would have a loss-making operation on his hands. In order to avoid unnecessary complications, we here merely add the assumption that rebuilding is actually paid for in regular weekly payments rather than the necessary sum being sporadically collected in order to be paid out all at once. The remainder, which under our assumptions is a positive magnitude and greater than the attributable

---

[9]Footnote absent in original manuscript.

share of interest debt, is likewise reserved up to the amount thereof until Saturday, and paid out at the same time with the other income. The rate of profit contained in Monday income reduces the debt.

In strict deposit logic, the settlement process of the negative phase runs like this: every Monday, the households (and those firms that purchase produced means of production) are charged an amount for goods purchased, which also includes the value of goods purchased from the new firms. This latter, partial amount reduces the balances of households (or firms), just like that part of the amount that is "remitted" to the old firm. And as was the old, so also the new firm will be credited accordingly. But while in the case of the old firm, this crediting leads to an expansion of balances corresponding to the diminished balances of its customers, thus leaving the social deposit sum unchanged, in the case of the new firm (possibly via a momentary increase of its balances) it leads to a debt reduction, hence to the extinction of balances and an equal reduction of the social deposit sum. The shrunken asset items are cancelled against a portion of the debt that sinks the "deposits" of the concerned banks. Of course, the entrepreneur must take up credit for the upcoming Saturday and, to the degree that he purchases produced means of production, for the upcoming Monday as well, so that the balances extinguished through receipts from consumer goods sales on the previous Monday are replaced again in part, but the further we come into the second year, the more this new deposit creation lags behind the antecedent deposit extinction, because income under our assumption - debt *on* January 1st, plus current production outlays *from* January 1st, plus interest on both - must be in excess of entrepreneurial profit. Meanwhile, however, the outlays - and the corresponding new loans granted - continue for the preparation of production to be carried on in the third year, i.e., for the recovery of the outlay.

But, for the sake of clarity we can imagine something that usually happens, at least in part: that entrepreneurial profits are applied to the reduction of the borrowing requirement to replace equipment, or more vividly: to cover the debits run up for this. Conceivably it would be so large that the new equipment would emerge in the third year debt-free *and* with a sufficient balance for current production expenses (*working capital*), in which case the newly created credit would be completely extinguished, the social deposit sum would be reduced to the level it had *before the onset of this wave of development*, and that while the social product has *increased*. If profit is even greater, the remaining balances are reduced by this additional amount, but the social sum is not touched. Even when things do not turn out quite so pleasingly for the entrepreneur, the newly created credit, always assuming that things develop according to expectation, *eventually* is extinguished even if only after a longer period of time, and a condition would be reached in which the firm finances its activities from current income.

The Money Process in Crisis Situations

6. If we recall the conceptual tools that our basic construction presents to us, it is not difficult to formulate the social meaning of this method of *implementation* and *adaptation* of the new into the pre-existing economic body. Money and credit do not play a merely subservient role therein, in the sense that they register only what would happen independently of them, although neither are they a first cause [primum movens] that would produce a wave motion – an alternation of positive and negative phases of the economic process, that without them would not exist. We are now in a position to recognize, precisely because of this fact, the truth and the falsehood in the so-called *monetary crisis theories,* which are not easily distinguishable. The account-settling system achieves something that in the economic system of private property could not otherwise be accomplished with the same effectiveness, and which becomes the vehicle of phenomena that are anchored in the money method and the credit system. It is the lever that lifts the existing means of production in capitalist society out of their previous courses and makes them subserve new uses. For this reason – through an ability, on the face of it not contained in the term "account-settling system," temporarily to commandeer transactions in existing goods – it really is the midwife of the new, but not more than that. It does not create the new, nor does it initiate it. It does for the capitalist economic process what would be done by the arrangement of the central office in the socialist process, in which certain means of production are made available for a new production direction or method. Such allocation of means of production would obviously only be incidental in the process of socialist economic change, not the essence or the "alpha and omega" of it. And nothing other than such commandeering of the means of production and their assignment to entrepreneurs (= to new purposes) is what, in the core of its essence, capitalist credit achieves. We can get an even clearer picture when we contemplate entrepreneurs and banks.

The allocation of the means of production is done by the allocation (credit) of *ad hoc* newly created purchasing power that appears in addition to existing balances. This purchasing power comes first on the market of means of production, then on the market of consumer goods, etc., always by turns brought to bear on income and revenue formation, on an equal footing with the previously existing purchasing power. But in contrast to the previously existing purchasing power, newly created purchasing power, in its first appearance, is nor derived from antecedent production revenues. To resort to a metaphor that we have already used but which is here helpful, we can express this with the phrase that newly created (credit) purchasing power in the hands of the one who first receives it, thus in our case the entrepreneur, but other (credit) purchasing power just as well, is a claim for goods, a ticket of access to the flow of (production) goods, but is not, like this latter, a certificate of accomplished production.

Deposit creation in the positive phases and *autodeflation* in the negative phases do not affect reality as simply as in our model. Nevertheless, it is obvious that a major characteristic of historical reality at this point becomes visible from our theoretical height, because factually the price level increases in times of prosperity and decreases in times of depression – not entirely without exception, nor entirely promptly, yet still with such regularity that superficial analysis not only sees therein the essential feature of economic waves, but even their cause. Let us now picture a historical sequence that for over a sufficiently long time, say over a century, is subject to no external disturbance, neither monetary nor political nor social, in particular nothing in terms of economic policy (tariff legislation, change of bank organization, etc.), and let us have a number of successive development-waves arise and subside during this period. Then we would conclude that the price level conducts its phased upward and downward movements about a declining axis: If in each positive phase the price level increases, and in each subsequent negative phase it decreases more than it had just risen, then obviously all the normal or equilibrium points lying between every two waves, given the same critical number and consumer spending, will show declining price levels. This important result, which we may call the *law of the falling price level*, is also confirmed by the history of the last hundred and fifty years. During this time, the price levels of all countries that can be called "capitalist" and have halfway decent price statistics have fallen steadily *whenever left to themselves,* i.e., in particular when increases in gold production, protectionism, capital inflows, etc. have not interrupted the process, and have done so *in spite of the likewise continuous expansion of bank-mediated elements in the account-settling system,* which naturally counteracts the fall in the price level. The objective effect or "social meaning" of the matter is easy to interpret: we are dealing with a method of channeling the fruits of economic development *to* households that do not directly, like the entrepreneur, make development profits, precisely thereby absorbing the growing surplus product.

Saving and Interest in the Money Process

7. To complete the argument of this section, it still remains to us to list some of the important phenomena that the described process, even in its simplest form, *of necessity* had to yield, and without which they would not exist or would function in a different manner than they do.

The Origin of Interest

A. The emerging entrepreneurial profit, and the circumstance that, in order to gain it, one especially needs coins or credit for the purchase of means of production, creates a premium for instantly available, "present" purchasing power units over future ones. In the stationary production process, present and future deposit units stand at par: during the course of a financially balanced production process, there is no reason to set the units currently passing through cash holdings in relation to those that, at the corresponding point in time in the next phase, will flow in equal numbers through cash holdings $\left(\frac{ds}{dt} = const\right)$; there is even less reason to value them as greater or lesser. *For in equilibrium each production outlay reproduces itself.*[10] But if, as in the case now under consideration, the production process on the one hand promises a surplus, but on the other hand cannot be financed out of current income – which is not yet to hand – so that the sum needed for production outlays must be procured [beschafft] by special act (in the hitherto considered model, likewise *created* [geschaffen] by special act), the procurement of which is the necessary precondition for everything else and eventually also for obtaining the surplus – the entrepreneurial profit – then the item set up in the expense calculations of the entrepreneur *stands for,* besides *that* item of proceeds that will refund it, precisely a "share" [Kopfanteil] of the entrepreneur's profit, which viewed from this angle is dependent upon the "principal" to be borrowed. In this sense, the equation holds for the entrepreneur: principal now to be borrowed K = *sum of future revenue S, S > K* [i.e., S must at least equal K plus a "share"].

---

[10]It is recommended that the reader concede the theory that the *interest rate, as a necessary element of capitalist production,* is a consequence of its development and would be absent in a stationarily reproducing economic process – consumption interest, and production interest as a result of consumption interest, could nevertheless exist, if not to the extent that it actually exists – at least as a representational hypothesis of the presented analysis. Should he however not be able to free himself from the prejudice of the omnipresence of interest, let him, as was already suggested in chapter 5, in the above representation replace the equilibrium rate of interest of zero by a positive magnitude (not necessarily a constant) and then allow what is said to apply to those fluctuations that indisputably are entailed by entrepreneurial demand.

B. If under pressure from the *demand for capital* by the entrepreneur, a premium on current deposit units has arisen, then this phenomenon, if indeed it is sufficiently marked and lasts long enough, will *spread* back over the entire economic body and be a part of all transactions that make up the economic process. It, then, penetrates actually into all calculations and into *all* economic actions of all firms and households so thoroughly that not only they, but even the scientific observer, apparently no longer can imagine the economic process without interest. In particular, the interest rate now becomes a general *cost element*, not only in those cases, which we will get to know, in which others than new firms are forced to pay interest, but also, and quite apart from any actual interest payment, because now everyone takes into consideration that if he lends his cash on hand to an entrepreneur instead of applying it to its intended purpose, he can capture a surplus, interest. The intended use is therefore henceforth charged with a cost element in the sense of "opportunity cost," and so the interest rate becomes a factor of production costing and financial conduct for *all* people.

Saving as Response to Interest

C. In these connections, the following two facts here interest us:

1) We have seen that even in our case we could allow *saving* in our stationarily reproducing economic process, although it nevertheless is recommended to refrain from this aspect because it fits better into a model based on an aspiration of people to *change* their economic situation, and because saving could play only a modest role in a fundamentally stationary economy. In all cases, however, saving becomes a different and much more significant phenomenon, both qualitatively and quantitatively, in a world inundated by waves of development. Above all, with the possibility of deriving interest income from investment in the production process, a new motive of saving emerges that must act on the magnitude of the portion of income that is saved – if we assume saving also in the stationary economic process – and which must create the phenomenon, if it did not otherwise exist. But for all that, the effect of the process in the sequence of the development waves must likewise be novel.

Saving is provision for capital expenditure. With firms, real investment can be made directly, while with households, investment initially only means transfer of balances to firms that then make the real investment – whether it be that the households directly leave their balances to firms (which we will disregard), or whether they buy securities (part of which ...[11]), or whether, finally,

---

[11]The remainder is lacking in the original manuscript.

savings deposits represent definitive investment for them. But making funds available already has an effect – because the bank can pass them on or create more as a result.

The operative point in the sphere of the problem of saving is that saving ensues in the process of waves of development and helps satisfy *its* credit needs. The paradox of the theory of the saving process, the unsatisfactory description of the effects of saving and investing, the difficulties, so to speak, of theoretically accommodating savings, all stem from the fact that one wishes to observe it in a state of equilibrium or in a uniform economy, i.e., an economy that above all progresses along constant cost curves. Since in that case it can only be a question of the expansion of production beyond equilibrium points, the problem emerges as to how that is possible without loss; and almost automatically, saving slides into the position of troublemaker. It is essential to recognize this problem as a pseudo-problem and classify saving within the overall process in which it is actually taking place.

2) We have also seen that, in the money process of the stationarily reproducing economy, the amount of cash holdings depends but little on the will of households and firms, and crucially on the market order and payment technique, which decide where and how long coins and balances must remain in cash holdings: the holdings are where they are, not because economic considerations of firms and households form this amount of holdings, but because the "existing" sums must be somewhere, and must be sluiced by the objective order of the payment system precisely to where we actually encounter them every day. For individuals, they are the single nearly intractable variable, independent of individual free choice. The situation in reality is otherwise: the cash on hand that every firm and every household has, does not simply turn up there, but is that which it wishes to have, according to situation, prospects, and intentions. The cash balance is tractable and determined by economic considerations in quite the same way as goods stocks, and is quite as "rationally" acquired and changed, and therefore is a variable in completely the same sense.

One source of this fact, whereby cash on hand is turned, if we can so express it, from a passive into an active element of the money process, originates in credit creation. We have already seen another when introducing the concept of *disposition*, which receives its full meaning, as we will see in greater detail shortly, in a business world evolving through the fluctuations of positive and negative phases. We here come up against a third source of this "active" role of cash, namely the interest rate. If one can receive a premium with a price character for the temporary transfer of a balance, one not only will offer deposits that one does not need, or the purpose of which one gives up for the sake of interest, but also those that one does need and still desires to direct to a purpose, if this "need" and the requirement of this provision lie in the future - though it be perhaps in the near future, perhaps even the very next day. Note that whoever so acts, has not saved, but rather invests; so that such *temporary investment* is a phenomenon in itself, that must be distinguished from investment in the sense outlined earlier, because it has a different effect on the monetary process. We speak of it, in directly understandable conciseness, as "diversion." Next we note that the possibility of temporarily disposing of cash on hand in a useful manner yet gains practical importance if it is customary at any time temporarily to acquire others' cash holdings at interest. Therefore one is not strictly bound to a time limit given by the purpose for which the deposit is held. One might even adopt the policy of lending income to the extent that it is not encumbered by simultaneous maturities, and borrowing for all ongoing expenditure to the extent that it is not covered by simultaneously received income. In that case it comes down merely to comparing rates of *interest receivable and payable*, and comparing the costs of these borrowing and lending operations.

Obviously what we have here is "purchasing power creation." We see that the process is not identical to the lending that entails renunciation of expenditure and hence does not increase the sum of goods transactions. Nor is there an increase in frequency; the market order and payment technique remain what they were. Also disposition, people's spending decisions, has not changed. Rather, something happens that works just as if more coins were made available. This increase in purchasing power would not be visible statistically in a monetary system that only knows of the circulation of coins, which explains in part why so many practitioners deny the phenomenon of purchasing power creation. If that happened without the intervention of banks - and to the degree that it does so actually happen - it would be a case of "purchasing power through commerce," a method by which the economy partially could free itself from the bridle of money. However, we wish to disregard this, and assume, following the way things usually happen, that all the diversion takes place through banks.

Forms of Saving

We wish to distinguish between three forms of saving. *First,* major corporations can lend cash on the money market that they do not currently need. *After that,* households and firms can invest such funds short-term - either in short-term assets, or by putting short-term funds into long-term investments that nevertheless can be cashed in at any time. We will get into these two modes later. *Finally,* they can just leave their currently surplus funds with the bank. By

virtue of this practice, the banking system realizes the tendency toward temporary use of cash on hand or, what is the same, toward limiting cash holdings to
the immediately required minimum, in almost perfect manner.

Insofar as the banks pay interest on checking balances to their customers
and these customers are satisfied with this interest, the tendency of balances
toward a minimum is overridden. The deposit amounts not currently required
by customers are not put to use elsewhere, but the fact that they are not otherwise turned to account amounts to nothing more than the effect that the banks,
which because of this need less cash and, where the reserve position stands at
their discretion, fewer reserves, correspondingly can extend more credit. For the
rest, this simply explains the practice (and the possibility) of interest payments
on checking balances. We also become acquainted with a new motive that moves
customers to give bank-mediated shape to their cash management. Finally, the
tension of the bank status at certain periods, during which those deposit
amounts are used by customers, becomes understandable. But that's it.

When customers turn their momentarily surplus deposit balances into
time deposits, this makes possible a credit that arises in the place of the cancelled
checking balance. At this stage, the former is thereby "compensated." And if the
customer then in turn wishes to have the time deposit revert back to the original
checking balance, the new borrower in our case pays back and by this act extinguishes the corresponding deposit amount, so that again there is compensation.
Therefore the deposit amount, apart from momentary fluctuations between the
points in time of credits and debits, has not changed, any more than it would
have if the holder of the original deposit amount had immediately lent out that
amount.

The Short-Term Character of Capitalist Finance

We can now better understand a major characteristic of the financial
management of the capitalist economy, which is just as important as it is
strange, and very much has to do with both the effectiveness and the sensitivity
to disturbance of the capitalist machine. We observe, namely, that a very large
part of the capitalist process is financed, as it were, overnight, which financing
solves its monetary and credit problems only for the moment, and that even the
most enduring and most regular things financially are taken care of day to day,
short-term for long-term. This fact will present itself more clearly to our minds
(and by the way, this aspect of things was touched on during our overview of
the credit technique), if we consider the fact that, even viewed superficially, lasting and long-term financing, such as a bond issue, in turn rests on a short-term

basis. There are of course many reasons for this, especially because momentarily changing situations and momentary external disturbance, and the expectations people harbor with respect to both these circumstances and their effects, compel provisional measures and interim solutions. But the fundamental cause of this situation lies in the just depicted aspect, that every household, every firm, every bank tries "otherwise to turn to account" momentarily excess cash holdings and ultimately become borrowers for their own needs.

This puts *business credit* and its role first in the proper light. Under the assumptions of the current thought process, *"circulating" capital* naturally must be put at the disposal of the new firm by the financing bank, in just the same way as must the layout for production equipment and its accoutrements, *fixed capital* – and this circulating capital must be "newly created," as far as the just-introduced aspect of saving[12] does not render that creation unnecessary. The old firm, i.e., the firm associated with the stationary circular flow, in principle requires none because it supports its production expenditure from income. Otherwise, only as much lending of this nature would be outstanding in the area under study as would be granted freshly to new firms for the first time or in the further course of things, until these liability items are paid off and the new firm – having become an "old" one - can cover current production expenditure from income. But in reality this is not only not the case, but almost the reverse of things. By virtue of the urge to temporary investment, the old firms expose their balances, so that they routinely become borrowers. And the new never penetrate to the point that they are funded by income. Rather, *all* firms now develop demand for business loans and for obvious reasons precisely this business tends to become the typical – "regular" – banking activity, whereby the bank in each case, for just as obvious reasons, prefers the loan application of the proven and settled firm to the loan application of the new firm.

To understand the nature and the role of working capital, it is nevertheless very important to understand that this appearance of reality does not represent the fundamental character of the matter but conceals it, in fact inverts it. Because, in [an economy undergoing development, business expenditure is financed through credit, this[13]] generates fluctuations that link to seasonal processes in the economic body but stem from the development wave, and gain their practical importance from the economic phase with which they coincide. In times in which payments pile up, for example each "last day of" and even on

---

[12]Footnote absent in original manuscript.

[13]The basis for the preceding statement and the transition to the following argument are lacking in the original manuscript.

the "payment date" of a week, we find *tension* in bank status. On dates or date sequences in which large payments of a certain kind are first prepared and then have to be completed, the same holds true. Hence, especially where *income tax* is to be paid at one time, the income tax deadline is noticeable in banking statistics. Thus also the *movement of crops,* particularly in countries with heavy capitalization. Thus generally the *campaigns* of industries that do not produce or sell evenly over the year. Thus also the travel time and the business of annual festivals, particularly *Christmas shopping.* Conversely, after these dates a relaxation occurs: bank loans sink, their cash and reserve holdings increase, and these times are particularly favorable to monetary policy interventions because the credit organism is then relatively insensitive and can be shaped, in particular curbed, without major disruption of economic activities. If, for example, the central bank wishes to put on the brakes, then at that moment, for example immediately after the settlement of Christmas shopping, it needs, through central bank investments, to absorb the excess reserves of member banks that otherwise would make them more inclined to easier lending; and the undesired credit expansion is relatively painlessly rendered impossible, while the same experiment undertaken *before* the holiday season could trigger a collapse.

The account-settling system of a stationarily reproducing economic process would not yield such fluctuations. Also, all large payments or payment accumulations, be they ever so discontinuous, would continuously be taken care of by households and firms, and the collected balance totals would just disappear from their accounts on the due dates to appear in the accounts of the receivers, so that the position of the banking organization as a whole on these dates would be different than usual only insofar as its cash holdings would be temporarily reduced, *but only for sums that at other times would be stored unused in its basements.*

An *income tax deadline,* for example, can have the effect that it actually has, therefore, only because the taxpayer *either* takes up credit *ad hoc* for the fulfillment of the payment, *or* temporary liquidates his investments. And this fact makes sense and becomes understandable only through the credit requirement of new combinations and the premium of the unit of account premised thereon. This also takes care of the fact that an approaching due date of this type tightens things up not only for the banks but also for business, which have removed from them precisely the temporarily available means earmarked for the purpose of tax payments. Also the necessary funds for the "movement of the harvest" would already have been made available to the participants in a stationary economic process from the proceeds of the previous harvest. When that is not the case, and a new financing problem arises every time (even if the harvest is just as great as the previous one, and prices and costs have not changed), which must be solved by creating additional balances and withdrawing balances from other courses, this has only to do with [... ¹⁴].

The tension of the bank status is eliminated and relaxation is precipitated by the fact that the recipients are credited with their income and do not use it immediately and completely, or, when the income extinguishes debits, do not borrow immediately and to the same extent. The tightening of money transactions that generally arises in those cases in which firms are not the recipients of the deadline payments (such as income tax) and in those cases in which sectors of commerce that are not involved in these cash receipts (such as with the movement of crops) receive those deadline payments, is eliminated by the recipient spending or beginning to borrow again. Both tension and relaxation are mitigated thereby.

The Money Market

E. Hereby (A-D) emerges a new market that we shall call the money market, which is of central importance to the remainder of our discussion. Of course, we could include this type of market in the image of the stationary circular flow of the economy, but nothing particularly interesting would happen there and no one would recognize it as the anchorage or epitome of unique phenomena in such an economy or, from the mere recording of events in the pan-economic accounts that would take place there, even connect it to the concept of a market at all. In this sense it owes not only its practical and theoretical importance, but also its existence, to development, although once present it also incorporates the monetary operations of the circular flow. It was development that first made immediately disposable sums of money into a "commodity" with a "price." We are so used to this amazing fact that we must immediately add that both expressions do not yet cease to be metaphorical and never should be used in entirely the same sense that they have in the world of goods. This already results from the relation to the payment system characteristic of this market, thus to that single activity of all other markets, which make its functions in the economic body understandable and which make it into the central organ thereof. This relationship between payment or settlement and credit is embodied in the banking organism and is equally fundamental to both the domestic money market of an area and the international market. The division of labor that creates special types such as bill brokers in many cases overshadows it, and

---

¹⁴The ending of this sentence is lacking in the original manuscript.

superficial or erroneous interpretations easily attach themselves to such – seemingly eminently "real" – component parts of the great machine.

Exchange of Present for Future Balances

1) Nevertheless, it is *here* – in contrast to the problem area of the value of money – that the scheme of supply and demand applies, as the reader has already seen in section A above. Here it is appropriate and faithful to reality[15] to characterize disposable balances as the commodity itself and not, as the language of practice partly does, the securitization given for it,[16] although for other purposes, particularly for the description of the various specialty markets (the bill market, etc.) another form of expression may recommend itself. We can, adopting a felicitous formula of Böhm-Bawerk's, define what happens on the money market as an exchange of present against future balances. Only this definition must be extended in two directions: *first,* the word "present," when we include inter-regional and international processes, can be understood not only in time but also in location, so that balances available *elsewhere* can then be set alongside future balances. *Second,* present balances can be exchanged against future balances in two basic forms, which one ought to distinguish: the "money lender" may in future receive back the principal plus a premium (interest), or he can, instead of the sum of these two items, receive a basically[17] permanent return.

This simplifies the picture in terms of a single viewpoint and eliminates apparent problems. But it distances us from customary terminology.

The Primacy of Created Deposits

2) Viewed from the standpoint of our model of economic development, the basic operation of the money market consists in the financing of new combinations of existing means of production by *ad hoc* newly created deposits. The strangeness that still adheres to this view disappears when we formulate it a little more cumbrously: the basic operation of the money market consists in the financing of production, trade, and speculation, the transactions of which ultimately require a special financing operation, since new combinations are being established with the help of "means," of which newly created *ad hoc* means have the logical priority.

---

[15]Footnote absent in original manuscript.

[16]Footnote absent in original manuscript.

[17]Footnote absent in original manuscript.

The Character of Demand

Demand on the money market thus is built upon the following components: demand from entrepreneurs in our sense; demand from firms that as a result of real income boosted by development, likewise in our sense, now can expand their production over that amount that corresponded to the previous equilibrium;[18] demand from firms that have occasion for production expansion due to population growth, progress in saving or changes in taste; demand from firms that temporarily wish to deal with stagnating sales, declining prices, or rising costs by taking on credit; demand from firms and households desirous of taking speculative advantage of opportunities or speculatively fending off threats; and finally, in the limiting case of fully developed credit traffic, demand from *all* firms in the full amount of their circular flow-oriented production costs, including interest payable and taxes, if we imagine that each item of income finds its way to the money market and each expenditure is taken out of the money market – that in this way each firm's cash holding is woven into the nexus of the money market. To this bulk are added demand for consumer credit, that we can divide conveniently into consumptive public credit in all its forms, from the bank-mediated current account credit line to "interest in perpetuity" ("rente perpetuelle"), to household consumer credit, the main form of which, installment credit ("installment selling"),[19] admittedly usually is subsumed in the credit demand of concerned firms, and for the quasi-consumptive credit of that business community that, like a large part of agriculture, is not in a situation to use the credit it takes up to generate a surplus return to cover interest and re-payment rates.

The Character of Supply

The "supply" of the credit market must be spoken of with even greater caution than demand. For here we have even less than with the latter to do with the supply of a phenomenon analogous to a commodity, especially even less with analogous objective determinants of supplied "quantities." As we know, this supply is composed of the deposit supply of banks, i.e., the deposit supply that the banks control, plus the deposit supply subject to the dispositions of others, such as for example when someone buys a share or acts directly on the "open market" at the expense of his bank account. Even the non-banking lenders – insurance companies, state funds, large corporations, households – make use of the mediation of banks (except when they lend coins or paper money, which

---

[18]Footnote absent in original manuscript.

[19]Footnote absent in original manuscript.

we wish to disregard here) at least to carry out their operations and usually also for further aid. But their supply is not subject to the dispositions of the banks and sometimes thwarts them.

Regarding the character of the supplied deposits, the sum that the banks are able and willing to create afresh is to be differentiated from incrementing amounts of savings and reserves, furthermore also differentiated from the sums that are released by transacted deals, and finally from the amount of deposits that, although earmarked for other purposes, are made available for temporary investment. As we also already know, these sums are not independent of each other. They influence each other and sometimes relieve each other. And for the individual bank and the banking system, the savings and reserve totals of customers, the freed and temporarily available balances, are among the factors that determine how much in new balances the bank or the system can create.

In the supply provided by banks, the difference between customer credit and interbank credit is especially to be noted. Balances that lenders mutually make available to each other of course are merely determinants of the sums corresponding to industrial, commercial, and consumptive demand, and must be separated out when this is the case. In particular, central bank credit granted to or allowable to member banks, and the credit such banks grant to other banks, making central banking functions accessible to them (see above, pp. 165 f.), is an affair in itself. But it cannot be stressed enough that this class of transactions cannot be separated from the economically relevant transactions with business clientele. Suppose, e.g., that a central bank, that also serves industrial clientele, in accordance with our basic scheme, discounts a bill from one such customer. This customer now has a deposit balance at the central bank. If it disposes of that balance in favor of a firm that has a different bank, the latter now acquires this deposit, which increases its reserve, just as if it had directly taken up central bank credit. And so there is one whole set of transactions that *at the same time* has both customer- and interbank-credit significance, and is attributable to both categories.

A similar phenomenon is based on the aspect of temporary investment. If a concern issues a bond, it signifies demand for *one* type of credit. But it also signifies supply of *another* type. Because the payments that it receives, or even a deposit that it receives with respect to expected payments, and which it does not need immediately, it can offer short-term, so that balances make their appearance that simultaneously or nearly simultaneously are both demanding and supplying, which then on the market leads to well-known, and at first sight astonishing movements, whereby the market "tightens" in one direction while it "loosens" in another.

The Interest Rate as Barometer?

3) The structure of the supply of and demand for deposits explains a curious contradiction in the factual picture of this market. The distribution and redistribution of the money of account of the economy-wide settlement process takes place on it in a manner geared to strengthening the false basic assumption that here something is being disposed of that has an independent separate existence. Because here, directly or indirectly, every economic act seeks possibilities of implementation and every actual or potential [vorhandene oder schaffbare] unit seeks to be turned to account: all processes of the region under investigation indeed flow together in this market. However incomparable they may be with each other, here they are all commensurable and communicating. The abstract balances of all households and firms are squared here, they all form a cumulative situation. Here present and future values, present and future possibilities find their common denominator. Although there is no tendency to form a single "rate" of profits in our sense and, e.g., a weighted average of business profits over a period of time only makes statistical sense, not theoretical sense, theoretically at any one time there should be a single interest rate as the price element of a homogeneous commodity[20] in a single market. This interest rate would give the most meaningful of all our time series and the best index for the pulse of the economy. It would indeed earn the name of a "gauge of the economy," which is so often attributed to it.

Note that the rate of interest naturally expresses the *current* overall situation of the funds market [Guthabenmarkt], which in turn is the *immediate* resultant of all current economic conditions and processes, whether temporary or permanent. It is the nature of the funds market, because all the different purposes of the economic world are to be capable of being compared, to make them comparable *from the standpoint of the current point in time,* temporally as well as materially, as would happen in an economic central office. If we bring this into connection with the knowledge previously gained to the effect that *temporary* provision is made for balances requiring financing, then the *totality* of the momentarily available "means" confronts the *totality* of currently existing demand variables, taking both as homogeneous masses. Of course there are funds, long-term assets and purposes, that seek satisfaction in a legally long-term form, such as bonds. But the mechanism of the market entails first, that they be made serviceable to short-term purposes, and second that, because of their fundamentally given marketability, they can be satisfied only with funds available short-

---

[20]Footnote absent in original manuscript.

term. It follows that there are no economic – as opposed to legal – long-term assets in fully developed capitalism at all,[21] and furthermore that the rate of interest by its very nature is always short-term. The long-term interest commitment, which a bond bears, is only of technical importance; the real interest comes to expression in the yield, that changes from day to day in the flow of financing-requirement balances and which conforms to the essentially short-term situation. When we speak of the long-term interest rate – the so-called "customary" [landesübliche] rate is a special form of it – we do not mean a particular phenomenon, but simply the average magnitude observed over a longer period of time, which may fluctuate around the actual interest rate, just as the long-term wheat price is not understood to be a particular kind of price that *exists* next to other wheat prices, but only a variable adjusted for seasonal or even cyclical and random fluctuations, which has the nature of a statistical norm.

But if we approach the material of interest rates observable in reality with this expectation, a disappointment awaits us. We find *many* interest rates and, worse yet, not one of them provides us with what we need; not one can be addressed as "the" theoretical interest rate. And even if we could catch sight of one of them in that above-mentioned gauge, then we would be dealing with an instrument that served a child as a toy before it came into our hands. Only[22] with this restriction can we offer the partial consolation that changes in the various interest rates provide more insight than their absolute values.

The metaphor of the toy is not in the first place here directed at the interest rate being subject to conscious influence of monetary policy considerations. Because after all, this could lie within the logic of the mechanism. Even an active discount policy, which does not simply express the market situation, can just correct aberrations and wish to ensure the systematic functioning of the machine, and in a deeper sense be merely "declaratory." When under a gold drain the central bank increases its bank rate and makes this increase effective by investments, this need not signify anything except that an existing imbalance should be corrected. We already know enough about the nature of the credit organism to understand that without such aids it can function systematically

---

[21]In particular it is not the case that long-term investment necessarily requires long-term funding. The individual borrower may be satisfied for the long term and protected against premature reclamation through the appropriate choice of legal form. But, economically speaking, things do not end with the pay-in of the loan amount – instead, the bond remains an element of the short-term market condition, as long as it lives: it is shuffled back and forth, its price is adjusted daily – it is, so to speak, refinanced every day.

[22]Footnote absent in original manuscript.

only under particularly favorable circumstances. Or, if the public is to be led back to normal cash management, and inflation is to be inhibited by "artificial" rate increases, the process by which this occurs does not ipso facto drop from the range of aspects of which the monetary life process is composed. But the rate of interest is also shaped from other points of view. Above all, there is always a politically very powerful desire for "cheap money" or – economically not much less senseless – as constant a rate of interest, or at least as constant a central-bank rate, as possible. The banking world and its central organ, which is especially exposed to political pressure, accedes to this wish, so that even the discount rate and current account rates of member banks are less flexible than accords with their organic role. This is the case to an even greater degree with regard to the central bank rate. Recently the idea that these kinds of adjustments are a cure for depression has led to manipulations of rates and in particular the money supply that rob interest rates of their meaning and, to the degree that they have an effect, are the fountainhead of bad investments.

But in reality, money interest is not just a spoiled gauge; it does not function satisfactorily even judged on its own terms. It is known to lag behind other symptoms in the change of phases. The reason is that there is unemployment of credit [Guthaben] as well as unemployment of workers. The statistical recognition of this phenomenon is complicated by the fact that while the unemployed worker is still present and can be counted, the unemployment of credit is expressed only in part in the inertia of the *"existing,"* [bestehenden] and in part by the fact that credit that no one wants cannot *"arise"* [entstehen] at all. If during previous periods a particular enterprise regularly conducted bill issues, bill discountings, and deposit creations, but in the current period has ceased to do so, and therefore presents no bill at the relevant bank, then the credit does not materialize and the potential presence of balances could at most be tapped from unused elements of the reserves of that bank. Every situation and every transaction of this market must be viewed in the light of these *two* types of [variations]. We will return to this point below.

More importantly, *thirdly,* we are not dealing with a perfect market of free competition. Such is known to exist if, first, none of the demanders or suppliers is strong enough to influence prices *by its individual* behavior, and second, every demander and every supplier is willing and able to transact *indiscriminately* with any supplier or demander. The first condition is not always met, the second never, which is why this market is divided into submarkets, where different prices and opposite price trends can prevail.

A large part of the non-bank supply of credit, particularly the actual savings supply, is supplied by "facilities" [Anlagen] determined by the public authorities. In Germany, for example, the rules on trustee security status [Mündelsicherheit], the area of operation of savings banks, insurance companies, social security agencies, and so on, work in this direction, which put these means almost entirely at the service of the borrowing requirement of the empire, the territorial states, the municipalities, agriculture, and the residential home. This removes these sums completely from direct consideration of other borrowers or of loans in other forms, and an interest rate differential arises that is not, or not fully, explanatory by risk differentials. Tax incentives and the like work in the same direction. Furthermore, many providers do not have access, or direct access, to many parts of the funds market. For example, private savers cannot just discount bills. Finally, the majority of remaining non-bank supply has its own habits or preferences that determine the path taken. Savers' hidebound and very pronounced inclinations (which by the way differ greatly in different countries – for example, their preference in some countries to invest in government bonds), belong to this category,[23] along with savers' habitual overvaluation of shares, sometimes also the overvaluation of "cheap," i.e., the most dubious, debt securities. That such external interventions, arational aspects, risk differentials, special advantages and disadvantages of eligible business representations and instruments embodying them (bills of exchange, bonds, stocks, and so on), or their characteristic sureties (guarantees, inventories, stock market securities, real estate, and so on), lead to various – stipulated as well as actually attained – returns, from which the element of pure interest that they may contain can hardly ever be satisfactorily separated out, is not further surprising.

Moreover, the fundamental marketability of each title in reality only imperfectly replaces the right to recover the amount surrendered, above all the right to recover it at short notice or at once. This aspect is particularly important for the part of the money supply that is seeking temporary investment while it is waiting to be used for other intended purposes in the future, and thus it is especially important for the part of the bank-mediated supply's "secondary reserve" and for the parts of the supply held by non-bank firms that wish to exploit their "cash in hand" temporarily. This aspect is particularly important for the part of supply that is seeking temporary investment while intended for other purposes, thus especially for part of bank-mediated supply's "secondary reserve" and for the supply of non-bank firms that wish to exploit their "cash in hand"

---

[23]Footnote absent in original manuscript.

temporarily. These sums are *needed* by the suppliers themselves. They are supplied because they are not *immediately*[24] needed. This means now not only that only particular, and not just any, demanders, intended purposes, and types of instruments come into consideration, but also that this part of the supply is inelastic, that is, interest-rate insensitive – it takes what it can get, regardless[25] of whether that is a lot or a little, and it is available independently of the interest rate offered.

It is much the same with demand. This also contains inelastic (although highly variable) elements, especially the credit demand from firms that, locked into running contracts, must continue to run even at a temporary loss, and credit demand for certain transactions, e.g., those of such a speculative nature as not to be calculated precisely to a few percent, or for situations in which one absolutely must have a certain amount to stave off bankruptcy or extreme developments. In itself, this would not matter – *every* demand has inelastic elements, for example, demand on the part of relatively wealthy segments for bread is inelastic. But while this demand for bread otherwise flows together indiscriminately with other, more elastic elements, the inelastic part of demand in the credit market – in turn in part – is thrown on to very specific sources of supply, and in particular certain categories of bank means, while other sources of supply are not accessible or are difficult to access, so that a semi-independent special market is created. And otherwise, for the most disparate reasons demand has a preference for many types of instruments or sources of supply, which are only in keeping with some and not all suppliers. In addition to the interest rate, the nature and timing of recovery claims always comes into consideration for demand, which often make the cheapest money unacceptable. But the latter is not thereby dispensed with. We again emphasize that, in order to understand the situation, it is essential to see that in this case the cheapest money helps to finance the actually selected contract figure. When an industrial company receives a "long-term" bond, other people, the signatories, as a rule take up "short-term" loans to make the payment. But here the basic principle of the *instantaneous financing possibilities of the single market* comes indirectly into its own, for which reason we assumed it. But it entails that a spread arises between the interest of such bonds and the interest of the credit drawn by the signatories, or that, as we might also put it, the interest burden borne by the bond debtor is split, or can be split, into various returns of diverse balances standing behind one another. The signatory, who himself takes on "credit" to make the pay-in,

[24]Footnote absent in original manuscript.
[25]Footnote absent in original manuscript.

fulfills the function of freeing the bond debtor from concern for ongoing funding, and for this receives, as it were, a kind of commission.

The motives that demand may have to prefer certain sources of supply are legion. Depending on the condition of the market, bank lending recommends itself sometimes more, sometimes less than bond issues, and these in turn more or less than share issues. Business policy may make "dependency" upon a bank desirable (because the "dependency" of a firm on a bank often in practice means that the bank is dependent on the debtor, and must keep re-borrowing to preserve what has already been lent) or policy may make desirable precisely independence from banks. It may be desirable to face a large number of small bondholders or shareholders, or else certain types of shareholders (as it is easier to live with some than with others), or to exclude speculation or, on the contrary, precisely to put it in the service of credit provision. All of which reinforces the tendency to the formation of special markets and differentiates the interest rate, especially in the form of price differences of instruments (shares and bonds), despite the same return and quality.

The Money Market as Heart of the Capitalist Economy

Therefore, our originally derived conception of a homogeneous credit market, that brings all demand for and supply of all credit to a common denominator and settles all balances at every moment *for* the moment, is valid only at a higher level of abstraction.[26] It should be seen in the light of the facts outlined above, and must be modified as soon as we turn to the reality of the presented material. But by no means does it lose its cognitive value with respect to this. Rather, this homogeneous market remains the basis for understanding the interactions of all of the submarkets that arise in practice, and from practice it can be divided into a variety of fine subdivisions and according to various aspects, in particular the types of instruments and business forms, as for example the private discount market, the overnight and time money markets [Taggelds und des fixen Geldes], the foreign exchange market, the bill market, the bond market (from now on, by the word "bonds" we mean all corporate bonds in the broadest sense), the market for government bonds (we mean "consols"), the stock market,[27] the market in mine share certificates [Kuxenmarkt], the mortgage market, and so on – all of which are nothing else than merely commercially and bank-technically hived-off parts of a whole that can be fully grasped only as

---

[26]Footnote absent in original manuscript.

[27]Footnote absent in original manuscript.

such. The contradiction between the uniform rate of interest postulated in theory, which [is] the expression of the instantaneous position of the entirety of economic life and which would in principle be applied to all economic activities envisaged at that moment, and the multiplicity of interest rates often manifesting opposing tendencies, is therefore only apparent and disappears when one penetrates through the surface of appearances.

This is also the reason why all previously proposed classifications of the funds market in wholes to which are attributed theoretical meaning, and which are more than the just mentioned submarkets of practice, have proven to be unsatisfactory. Practice itself distinguishes between the money and capital markets, and in general by the former – the language varies in different countries – comprehends that which the money market articles of the daily newspapers report on, the traffic in stock exchange money [Börsengeld], and thus also overnight, term [Ultimo], time money [Fixgeld], in private discounts, in foreign currency, mostly also in commercial bills, as well as central bank operations and the ongoing public financial requirement; by the latter, on the other hand, is understood the conditions and processes of the stock and bond markets. But this means nothing more than the stressing of those elements in the funds market that eminently characterize the current situation. Never can this money market report be kept free of elements that are anchored in the capital market in this sense.[28] From which one sees that it is only a short, and thereby incomplete, report on the "money and capital market" touching only on the most important factors.[29]

Science was and often still is inhibited in the task of unbiased recognition of the contours of reality in this area, and in the provision of clear terms, by the effort to put the phenomena of the monetary sphere into the straitjacket of a conception of "capital" that disregards money and its self-movements. On the money market or capital market, it is definitely real goods, machinery, or raw materials that are disposed of, or at least it is the "power of disposition" over such "in money form," which has led to quite unrealistic constructions of contexts and equally unrealistic ideas about what is to be viewed as normal, what abnormal, what is essential and what is nonessential. When finally [a] thorough analysis indeed has shown the existence of a multiplicity of sub-markets but also the inconsistency of drawing a fundamental distinction between money and capital markets, only the separation according to "maturity" is left, a consequence

---

[28]Footnote absent in original manuscript.

[29]Footnote absent in original manuscript.

drawn by Spiethoff in his prominent treatise.[30] It could here essentially be adopted if on the one hand it did not incline to overshadow the nature of inter-lacement of these two markets and evoke the idea that they are two different things, while on the other hand it does not do justice to the multiplicity of operations. This, then, is the value of our consistent view, that it brings to mind the coordination of all of the many sub-markets into which the funds market is divided, so that the analysis remains an analysis of the "capital and money market." Henceforth, we adopt the name "money market" for it.

It is always money, available or creatable funds, and not just goods, not goods "in the form of money" or "in the form of money-capital," which is trans-ferred on the "money" or "capital" or "money and capital markets." There is no point in disfiguring this completely straightforward factual situation with am-biguous words or hasty attempts at interpretation. The making of quite mislead-ing links between money and goods operations and the blurring of essential pro-cesses have been the result. In particular, the triad made up of saving – capital in money form – capital goods (by which is meant primarily industrial plants, buildings, and machinery), which was popular with the older theory, led to the erroneous conviction that capital in the capital market was withdrawn from the circulation of the income sphere, that purchasing power creation could not in-crease it, and that there is a necessary or even a clear relationship between those three things. Therefore a necessary correlation between savings and durable goods devoted to the generation of future production was constructed, between "money capital" and "real capital," which correlation was continuously fash-ioned on a special capital market; but this is an image of a case that, while cer-tainly intellectually possible, is very unique and becomes false when made into the theoretical base case.

But at bottom the older theory viewed the task that arises more cor-rectly than does much recent research. Just because the money market directly has to do only with money of account, and with "capital formation" only in the sense of providing credit, with "use of capital" only in the sense of allocating these assets to whatsoever demand, it can never be understood by itself, with e.g. the help of a mechanism of bank reserves, interest rates, and the like. This attempt leads to an overestimation of the causal role of monetary operations and thus become a source of errors regarding crisis management and so on.[31]

---

[30]Arthur Spiethoff, "Der Begriff des Kapital- und Geldmarktes" [The Concept of the Capital and Money Market], in *Schmollers Jahrbuch* [Schmoller's Yearbook], 44, 1920, pp. 981-1000.

[31]Footnote absent in original manuscript.

Rather, there is now only a particular problem, how the money market and goods markets working together produce those cash and goods flows that make up the economic process. Before we enter this set of problems again, we still need to add some other elements to our outline of principles of explanation. It should only be noted ....[32]

---

[32]End of manuscript.

Index

www.ingramcontent.com/pod-product-compliance
Lightning Source LLC
Chambersburg PA
CBHW061120220326
41599CB00024B/4106